MINORITIES
RACE AND ETHNICITY
IN AMERICA

ISSN 1532-1185

MINORITIES
RACE AND ETHNICITY IN AMERICA

Melissa J. Doak

INFORMATION PLUS® REFERENCE SERIES
Formerly Published by Information Plus, Wylie, Texas

GALE
CENGAGE Learning·

Detroit • New York • San Francisco • New Haven, Conn • Waterville, Maine • London

Minorities: Race and Ethnicity in America

Melissa J. Doak

Kepos Media, Inc.: Paula Kepos and Janice Jorgensen, Series Editors

Project Editors: Elizabeth Manar, Kathleen J. Edgar

Rights Acquisition and Management: Sara Crane, Kelly Quin

Composition: Evi Abou-El-Seoud, Mary Beth Trimper

Manufacturing: Cynde Lentz

For product information and technology assistance, contact us at **Gale Customer Support, 1-800-877-4253.** For permission to use material from this text or product, submit all requests online at **www.cengage.com/permissions.** Further permissions questions can be e-mailed to **permissionrequest@cengage.com**

Cover photograph: Image copyright disitalskillet, 2010. Used under license from Shutterstock.com.

While every effort has been made to ensure the reliability of the information presented in this publication, Gale, a part of Cengage Learning, does not guarantee the accuracy of the data contained herein. Gale accepts no payment for listing; and inclusion in the publication of any organization, agency, institution, publication, service, or individual does not imply endorsement of the editors or publisher. Errors brought to the attention of the publisher and verified to the satisfaction of the publisher will be corrected in future editions.

Gale
27500 Drake Rd.
Farmington Hills, MI 48331-3535

ISBN-13: 978-0-7876-5103-9 (set)
ISBN-13: 978-1-4144-4121-4

ISBN-10: 0-7876-5103-6 (set)
ISBN-10: 1-4144-4121-5

ISSN 1532-1185

This title is also available as an e-book.
ISBN-13: 978-1-4144-7003-0 (set)
ISBN-10: 1-4144-7003-7 (set)
Contact your Gale sales representative for ordering information.

Printed in the United States of America
1 2 3 4 5 6 7 14 13 12 11 10

TABLE OF CONTENTS

PREFACE

Minorities: Race and Ethnicity in America is part of the *Information Plus Reference Series*. The purpose of each volume of the series is to present the latest facts on a topic of pressing concern in modern American life. These topics include the most controversial and studied social issues in the 21st century: abortion, capital punishment, care for the elderly, crime, the environment, health care, immigration, social welfare, women, world poverty, youth, and many more. Even though this series is written especially for high school and undergraduate students, it is an excellent resource for anyone in need of factual information on current affairs.

By presenting the facts, it is the intention of Gale, Cengage Learning to provide its readers with everything they need to reach an informed opinion on current issues. To that end, there is a particular emphasis in this series on the presentation of scientific studies, surveys, and statistics. These data are generally presented in the form of tables, charts, and other graphics placed within the text of each book. Every graphic is directly referred to and carefully explained in the text. The source of each graphic is presented within the graphic itself. The data used in these graphics are drawn from the most reputable and reliable sources, such as from the various branches of the U.S. government and from major organizations and associations. Every effort has been made to secure the most recent information available. Readers should bear in mind that many major studies take years to conduct and that additional years often pass before the data from these studies are made available to the public. Therefore, in many cases the most recent information available in 2010 is dated from 2007 or 2008. Older statistics are sometimes presented as well, if they are landmark studies or of particular interest and no more-recent information exists.

Even though statistics are a major focus of the *Information Plus Reference Series*, they are by no means its only content. Each book also presents the widely held positions and important ideas that shape how the book's subject is discussed in the United States. These positions are explained in detail and, where possible, in the words of their proponents. Some of the other material to be found in these books includes historical background, descriptions of major events related to the subject, relevant laws and court cases, and examples of how these issues play out in American life. Some books also feature primary documents or have pro and con debate sections that provide the words and opinions of prominent Americans on both sides of a controversial topic. All material is presented in an even-handed and unbiased manner; readers will never be encouraged to accept one view of an issue over another.

HOW TO USE THIS BOOK

Race and ethnicity have acted as some of the most divisive factors in U.S. history. Many people, from all racial and ethnic backgrounds, have struggled, sometimes at great peril to themselves, to provide equality for all people in the United States. Nevertheless, it is an undeniable fact that African-Americans, Hispanics, Native Americans, Asian-Americans, and other minority groups have a different experience living in the United States than do whites. This book reports on and examines the differences between minority groups and white Americans across the economic, political, and social spectrums.

Minorities: Race and Ethnicity in America consists of eight chapters and three appendixes. Each chapter is devoted to a particular aspect of minorities. For a summary of the information covered in each chapter, please see the synopses provided in the Table of Contents. Chapters generally begin with an overview of the basic facts and background information on the chapter's topic, then proceed to examine subtopics of particular interest. For example, Chapter 2: Family Life and Living Arrangements begins with an overview of how fundamental shifts in family life in the United States, away from the nuclear family and toward single men and women living alone, cohabitation before marriage, and single-parent families, have affected minority groups. Next, the chapter examines teenage pregnancy among minority groups, as well as the living arrangements of children. In conclusion, the chapter examines homeownership in minority communities and the impact of the global economic recession that began in late 2007. Readers can find their way through a chapter by looking for the section and subsection headings, which are clearly set off from the text. They can also refer to the book's extensive index if they already know what they are looking for.

Statistical Information

The tables and figures featured throughout *Minorities: Race and Ethnicity in America* will be of particular use to readers in learning about this issue. These tables and figures represent an extensive collection of the most recent and important statistics on minorities, as well as related issues—for example, graphics cover the number of different minority peoples living in the United States overall and in specific regions, their average earnings as compared to whites, the rates at which they are the victims of various crimes, and the health problems that disproportionately afflict certain minority groups. Gale, Cengage Learning believes that making this information available to readers is the most important way to fulfill the goal of this book: to help readers understand the issues and controversies surrounding minorities and reach their own conclusions about them.

Each table or figure has a unique identifier appearing above it, for ease of identification and reference. Titles for the tables and figures explain their purpose. At the end of each table or figure, the original source of the data is provided.

To help readers understand these often complicated statistics, all tables and figures are explained in the text. References in the text direct readers to the relevant statistics. Furthermore, the contents of all tables and figures are fully indexed. Please see the opening section of the index at the back of this volume for a description of how to find tables and figures within it.

Appendixes

Besides the main body text and images, *Minorities: Race and Ethnicity in America* has three appendixes. The first is the Important Names and Addresses directory. Here, readers will find contact information for a number of government and private organizations that can provide further information on aspects of minorities. The second appendix is the Resources section, which can also assist readers in conducting their own research. In this section, the author and editors of *Minorities: Race and Ethnicity in America* describe some of the sources that were most useful during the compilation of this book. The final appendix is the index.

ADVISORY BOARD CONTRIBUTIONS

The staff of Information Plus would like to extend its heartfelt appreciation to the Information Plus Advisory Board. This dedicated group of media professionals provides feedback on the series on an ongoing basis. Their comments allow the editorial staff who work on the project to continually make the series better and more user-friendly. The staff's top priority is to produce the highest-quality and most useful books possible, and the Information Plus Advisory Board's contributions to this process are invaluable.

The members of the Information Plus Advisory Board are:

- Kathleen R. Bonn, Librarian, Newbury Park High School, Newbury Park, California

- Madelyn Garner, Librarian, San Jacinto College, North Campus, Houston, Texas

- Anne Oxenrider, Media Specialist, Dundee High School, Dundee, Michigan

- Charles R. Rodgers, Director of Libraries, Pasco-Hernando Community College, Dade City, Florida

- James N. Zitzelsberger, Library Media Department Chairman, Oshkosh West High School, Oshkosh, Wisconsin

COMMENTS AND SUGGESTIONS

The editors of the *Information Plus Reference Series* welcome your feedback on *Minorities: Race and Ethnicity in America*. Please direct all correspondence to:

Editors
Information Plus Reference Series
27500 Drake Rd.
Farmington Hills, MI 48331-3535

CHAPTER 1
WHO ARE MINORITIES?

MINORITIES ARE A GROWING PERCENTAGE OF THE NATION

The U.S. Census Bureau reports that in 2008 the U.S. population totaled 304.1 million people. (See Table 1.1.) Of that number, 199.5 million (65.6%) people identified themselves as non-Hispanic white alone. The other 34.4% were members of one or more minority racial or ethnic groups. Even though women are a majority of the nation's population (154.1 million women versus 149.9 million men), women are often considered a "minority" in social issues because they have been historically discriminated against in American society. In this publication, however, women are treated only in relation to racial or ethnic minority groups.

Minority populations are growing faster than is the non-Hispanic white population. Between 2000 and 2050 the non-Hispanic white population is expected to grow by only 4%, whereas the African-American population is projected to grow by 51%, the Asian-American population is expected to grow by 220%, and the Hispanic population is expected to grow by 273%. (See Table 1.2.) The Census Bureau predicts in "U.S. Interim Projections by Age, Sex, Race, and Hispanic Origin" (March 18, 2004, http://www .census.gov/population/www/projections/usinterimproj/ natprojtab01a.pdf) that by 2020, 61.3% of Americans will be non-Hispanic white and 38.7% will belong to a minority group. Projections indicate that the proportion of non-Hispanic white Americans will shrink to only a bare majority (50.1%) by 2050. In that year, the Census Bureau projects that 49.9% of Americans will belong to a minority racial or ethnic group. The nation is increasingly diverse due to the growth in immigration and interracial marriages.

CHANGING RACIAL AND ETHNIC ORIGIN CLASSIFICATIONS

For the 1980 and 1990 censuses the Census Bureau divided the U.S. population into the four racial categories identified by the Office of Management and Budget— White, Black, American Indian/Alaskan Native, and Asian/Pacific Islander—and added the category "Some Other Race." The U.S. government uses these race and ethnic origin data to make decisions, among other things, about funding and making laws. For example, federal programs use the race information to monitor and ensure that the civil rights of African-Americans and other minority groups are not violated, and states use the data to ensure compliance with political redistricting requirements.

As ethnic identity becomes more complex because of immigration and interracial marriages and births, a growing number of people object to categories based on race. It is no longer unusual to find Americans whose backgrounds include two or more races.

Katherine K. Wallman explains in "Data on Race and Ethnicity: Revising the Federal Standard" (*American Statistician*, vol. 52, no. 1, 1998) that these standards came under attack because many Americans believed they did not accurately reflect the diversity of the nation's population. Between 1993 and 1995 the Census Bureau conducted hearings and invited public comment on the proposal under consideration to add new choices to the categories that had been used in the 1990 census. Among the Census Bureau's findings were that Arab-Americans were unhappy with their official designation as "white, non-European." This group included people from the Middle East, Turkey, and North Africa. In addition, many indigenous Hawaiians wanted to be recategorized from Pacific Islander to Native American, reflecting historical accuracy and giving them access to greater minority benefits.

Some Hispanics wanted the Census Bureau to identify them as a race and not as an ethnic origin, and to replace the word *Hispanic* with *Latino*. They asserted that *Hispanic* recalled the colonization of Latin America by Spain and Portugal and argued that the term was as offensive as the term *Negro* is for African-Americans.

TABLE 1.1

Population by sex, race, and Hispanic origin, 2008

Sex, race, and Hispanic origin	Population July 1, 2008
Both sexes	**304,059,724**
One race	298,892,695
White	242,639,242
Black	39,058,834
AIAN	3,083,434
Asian	13,549,064
NHPI	562,121
Two or more races	5,167,029
Race alone or in combination:*	
White	247,112,954
Black	41,126,808
AIAN	4,861,963
Asian	15,480,349
NHPI	1,112,297
Not Hispanic	**257,116,111**
One race	252,664,449
White	199,491,458
Black	37,171,750
AIAN	2,328,982
Asian	13,237,698
NHPI	434,561
Two or more races	4,451,662
Race alone or in combination:*	
White	203,336,299
Black	38,915,749
AIAN	3,827,922
Asian	14,956,889
NHPI	899,371
Hispanic	**46,943,613**
One race	46,228,246
White	43,147,784
Black	1,887,084
AIAN	754,452
Asian	311,366
NHPI	127,560
Two or more races	715,367
Race alone or in combination:*	
White	43,776,655
Black	2,211,059
AIAN	1,034,041
Asian	523,460
NHPI	212,926
Male	**149,924,604**
One race	147,369,737
White	120,326,022
Black	18,639,632
AIAN	1,544,661
Asian	6,573,734
NHPI	285,688
Two or more races	2,554,867
Race alone or in combination:*	
White	122,545,020
Black	19,651,276
AIAN	2,410,335
Asian	7,540,644
NHPI	559,750

TABLE 1.1

Population by sex, race, and Hispanic origin, 2008 [CONTINUED]

Sex, race, and Hispanic origin	Population July 1, 2008
Not Hispanic	**125,670,207**
One race	123,472,302
White	97,978,191
Black	17,708,252
AIAN	1,148,428
Asian	6,418,554
NHPI	218,877
Two or more races	2,197,905
Race alone or in combination:*	
White	99,882,419
Black	18,559,060
AIAN	1,874,527
Asian	7,280,319
NHPI	450,389
Hispanic	**24,254,397**
One race	23,897,435
White	22,347,831
Black	931,380
AIAN	396,233
Asian	155,180
NHPI	66,811
Two or more races	356,962
Race alone or in combination:*	
White	22,662,601
Black	1,092,216
AIAN	535,808
Asian	260,325
NHPI	109,361
Female	**154,135,120**
One race	151,522,958
White	122,313,220
Black	20,419,202
AIAN	1,538,773
Asian	6,975,330
NHPI	276,433
Two or more races	2,612,162
Race alone or in combination:*	
White	124,567,934
Black	21,475,532
AIAN	2,451,628
Asian	7,939,705
NHPI	552,547
Not Hispanic	**131,445,904**
One race	129,192,147
White	101,513,267
Black	19,463,498
AIAN	1,180,554
Asian	6,819,144
NHPI	215,684
Two or more races	2,253,757
Race alone or in combination:*	
White	103,453,880
Black	20,356,689
AIAN	1,953,395
Asian	7,676,570
NHPI	448,982

However, when Hispanics were surveyed, the results showed they preferred to be identified by their families' country of origin, such as Puerto Rican, Colombian, Cuban, or sometimes just American.

A number of African-Americans wanted the Census Bureau to retire the term *Black*. Nevertheless, there was some difference of opinion. For example, people from the Caribbean preferred to be labeled by their families' country of origin, such as Jamaican-American or Haitian-American.

Africans who were not American also found the term inaccurate. Even though the term *African-American* has become more prominent in spoken English in recent years, lack of agreement and the length of the term have been significant factors in preventing its adoption by the government.

The 2000 Census

Conforming to revised standards issued by the Office of Management and Budget, the 2000 census recategorized

TABLE 1.1

Population by sex, race, and Hispanic origin, 2008 [CONTINUED]

Sex, race, and Hispanic origin	Population July 1, 2008
Hispanic	**22,689,216**
One race	22,330,811
White	20,799,953
Black	955,704
AIAN	358,219
Asian	156,186
NHPI	60,749
Two or more races	358,405
Race alone or in combination:*	
White	21,114,054
Black	1,118,843
AIAN	498,233
Asian	263,135
NHPI	103,565

*In combination' means in combination with one or more other races. The sum of the five race groups adds to more than the total population because individuals may report more than one race.
Note: The April 1, 2000 Population Estimates base reflects changes to the Census 2000 population from the Count Question Resolution program and geographic program revisions. Hispanic origin is considered an ethnicity, not a race. Hispanics may be of any race. Abbreviations: Black = Black or African American; AIAN = American Indian and Alaska Native; NHPI = Native Hawaiian and other Pacific Islander. The original race data from Census 2000 are modified to eliminate the "some other race" category.

SOURCE: Adapted from "Table 3. Annual Estimates of the Resident Population by Sex, Race, and Hispanic Origin for the United States: April 1, 2000 to July 1, 2008," in *National Population Estimates—National Characteristics*, U.S. Census Bureau, Population Division, May 14, 2009, http://www.census.gov/popest/national/asrh/NC-EST2008-srh.html (accessed December 1, 2009)

the races into White, Black/African-American/Negro, American Indian/Alaskan Native, Native Hawaiian/Other Pacific Islander, and Asian. The Census Bureau also added a sixth category: Some Other Race. In addition, the Census Bureau included two ethnic categories: Hispanic/Latino and Not Hispanic/Not Latino. To provide an accurate count of multiracial Americans, the 2000 census allowed Americans to select more than one race. Write-in spaces allowed Native Americans to record their tribal affiliation, and individuals of Hispanic origin could write in a national affiliation other than the major groups of Mexican, Cuban, and Puerto Rican.

In "Impact of Census' Race Data Debated" (*USA Today*, March 12, 2001), Martin Kasindorf and Haya El Nasser explain that many Americans thought that the official recognition of multiracial Americans would profoundly change how Americans thought about race in the long term. Some believed that racial lines would blur until racial differences no longer became so important in American life. Others took a more pessimistic view, arguing that because African-Americans marry outside their racial categories less than other minorities, the difference between an "expanded majority" of whites and the African-American minority group would harden further.

For the 2010 census, the U.S. government announced the inclusion of even more specific racial categories. The Population Reference Bureau notes in "The 2010 Census Questionnaire: Seven Questions for Everyone" (April 2009, http://www.prb.org/Articles/2009/questionnaire.aspx) that there were 15 race categories: White; Black, African-American, or Negro; American Indian or Alaskan Native; Asian Indian; Japanese; Native Hawaiian; Chinese; Korean; Guamanian or Chamorro; Filipino; Vietnamese; Samoan; other Asian; other Pacific Islander; and "Some Other Race." The 2010 census also considers Hispanic origin separately from race, with Hispanics able to identify with any race. In addition, the census also allowed respondents to choose more than one race.

A more in-depth discussion of the major race and ethnic groups follows.

HISPANICS

Hispanic is a broad term used to describe a varied ethnic group of individuals who trace their cultural heritage to Spain or to Spanish-speaking countries in Latin America. The term can also refer to people whose Spanish ancestors were residents of the southwestern region of the United States that was formerly under Spanish or Mexican control.

The Census Bureau indicates that in 2008, 46.9 million Hispanics lived in the United States. (See Table 1.1.) As 15.4% of the population, they were the largest minority group in the nation. Frank Hobbs and Nicole Stoops of the Census Bureau indicate in *Demographic Trends in the 20th Century* (November 2002, http://www.census.gov/prod/2002pubs/censr-4.pdf) that in 1980 Hispanics represented 14.6 million people (6.4% of the total U.S. population). In 1990 Hispanics totaled about 22.4 million people (9% of the total U.S. population). The 2000 census counted 35.3 million Hispanics (12.5% of the total U.S. population) living in the United States. The Hispanic population within the country increased by 141.7% between 1980 and 2000. The Census Bureau predicts in "U.S. Interim Projections by Age, Sex, Race, and Hispanic Origin" that by 2050 there will be 102.6 million Hispanics (24.4% of the total U.S. population) living in the United States.

Immigration and high birth rates are two major reasons for the large growth of the Hispanic population. In *Estimates of the Unauthorized Immigrant Population Residing in the United States: January 2008* (February 2009, http://www.lb9.uscourts.gov/webcites/09documents/Mendoza_statistics.pdf), Michael Hoefer, Nancy Rytina, and Bryan C. Baker of the U.S. Department of Homeland Security (DHS) estimate that as of January 2008 approximately 11.6 million illegal aliens lived in the United States, up from 8.5 million in January 2000 but down from 11.8 million in January 2007. Seven million (61%) of these illegal immigrants came from Mexico, and El Salvador and Guatemala were the next leading source countries, with 570,000 (5%) and 430,000 (4%), respectively.

TABLE 1.2

Projected change in population size by race and Hispanic origin, 2000–50

(Resident population as of July 1. Numbers in thousands)

Race and Hispanic origin[a]	2000–2050		2000–2025		2025–2050	
	Numerical	Percent	Numerical	Percent	Numerical	Percent
Total population	156,852	56	75,294	27	81,558	23
One race	144,602	52	70,605	25	73,997	21
White	96,202	42	47,683	21	48,519	18
Black	21,127	59	10,777	30	10,350	22
AIAN	2,786	104	1,363	51	1,423	35
Asian	23,729	222	10,439	98	13,290	63
NHPI	757	163	343	74	414	51
Two or more races	12,250	311	4,687	119	7,563	88
Race alone or in combination:[b]						
White	107,482	46	51,931	22	55,551	20
Black	28,468	76	13,391	36	15,077	30
AIAN	4,349	102	2,099	49	2,250	35
Asian	28,484	235	12,283	101	16,201	66
NHPI	1,664	182	730	80	934	57
Not Hispanic	**59,689**	**24**	**35,151**	**14**	**24,538**	**9**
One race	49,783	20	31,278	13	18,505	7
White	7,576	4	10,891	6	−3,315	−2
Black	17,535	51	9,289	27	8,246	19
AIAN	1,254	60	726	35	528	19
Asian	22,982	220	10,155	97	12,827	62
NHPI	434	118	216	59	218	37
Two or more races	9,906	288	3,873	113	6,033	83
Race alone or in combination:[b]						
White	16,714	8	14,404	7	2,310	1
Black	23,703	67	11,506	32	12,197	26
AIAN	2,166	62	1,204	35	962	21
Asian	26,921	230	11,736	100	15,185	65
NHPI	1,071	142	510	67	561	44
Hispanic	**97,163**	**273**	**40,143**	**113**	**57,020**	**75**
One race	94,819	270	39,328	112	55,491	75
White	88,626	270	36,793	112	51,833	74
Black	3,592	256	1,488	106	2,104	73
AIAN	1,533	268	638	112	895	74
Asian	746	317	283	120	463	89
NHPI	323	336	127	132	196	88
Two or more races	2,344	472	814	164	1,530	117
Race alone or in combination:[b]						
White	90,768	273	37,527	113	53,241	75
Black	4,764	294	1,884	116	2,880	82
AIAN	2,183	281	895	115	1,288	77
Asian	1,563	412	547	144	1,016	110
NHPI	593	378	220	140	373	99

[a]Hispanics may be of any race.
[b]In combination' means in combination with one or more other races. The sum of the five race groups adds to more than the total change because individuals may report more than one race.
Black = Black or African American; AIAN = American Indian and Alaska Native; NHPI = Native Hawaiian and Other Pacific Islander.
Note: The original race data from Census 2000 are modified to eliminate the "some other race" category. This modification is used for all Census Bureau projections products.

SOURCE: "Table 7. Projected Change in Population Size by Race and Hispanic Origin for the United States: 2000 to 2050," in *National Population Projections*, U.S. Census Bureau, August 14, 2008, http://www.census.gov/population/www/projections/summarytables.html (accessed December 1, 2009)

The Census Bureau collected information on the Hispanic population in the 2008 Current Population Survey. It found that 12.995 million of the 17.847 million foreign-born Hispanics, or 72.8%, were not citizens as of 2008. (See Table 1.3.) About 61.2% of all Hispanics had been born in the United States, and another 10.5% had become naturalized citizens. This varied by country of origin, however. Almost all Puerto Ricans had been born in the United States, because Puerto Rico is a U.S. territory. As of 2008 more Mexicans than any other foreign group had been born in the United States: 62.1% of Mexicans, 40.4% of Cubans, 32.5% of Central Americans, and 31.7% of South Ameri-

cans had been born in the United States. Cubans had the highest proportion of those who had become naturalized citizens: 32.4% of Cubans, 27.3% of South Americans, 19.7% of Central Americans, and only 8% of Mexicans had become naturalized citizens. Central Americans had the highest percent of residents who were not citizens (47.8%), followed by South Americans (41%), Mexicans (29.9%), and Cubans (27.1%).

Hispanic Origins

Hispanic-Americans trace their origins to a number of countries. The Census Bureau reports that in 2008,

TABLE 1.3

Nativity and citizenship status by sex and Hispanic origin type, 2008

[Numbers in thousands. Civilian noninstitutionalized population[a]]

	Hispanic origin type[b]													
	Total Hispanic		Mexican		Puerto Rican		Cuban		Central American		South American		Other Hispanic[c]	
Sex, nativity, and citizenship status[d]	Number	Percent	Number	Percent	Number	Percent	Number	Percent	Number	Percent	Number	Percent	Number	Percent
Both sexes	46,026	100.0	30,272	100.0	4,030	100.0	1,612	100.0	3,520	100.0	2,526	100.0	4,066	100.0
Native	28,179	61.2	18,788	62.1	4,011	99.5	652	40.4	1,144	32.5	800	31.7	2,784	68.5
Foreign born	17,847	38.8	11,484	37.9	19	0.5	960	59.6	2,376	67.5	1,726	68.3	1,282	31.5
Naturalized citizen	4,852	10.5	2,429	8.0	13	0.3	523	32.4	692	19.7	690	27.3	505	12.4
Not a citizen	12,995	28.2	9,055	29.9	6	0.2	437	27.1	1,684	47.8	1,036	41.0	777	19.1
Male	23,652	100.0	15,748	100.0	1,973	100.0	823	100.0	1,887	100.0	1,245	100.0	1,976	100.0
Native	14,071	59.5	9,392	59.6	1,964	99.5	343	41.7	603	31.9	386	31.0	1,383	70.0
Foreign born	9,581	40.5	6,355	40.4	9	0.5	479	58.3	1,284	68.1	860	69.0	593	30.0
Naturalized citizen	2,279	9.6	1,207	7.7	6	0.3	227	27.5	315	16.7	316	25.4	209	10.6
Not a citizen	7,302	30.9	5,149	32.7	3	0.2	253	30.7	970	51.4	544	43.6	384	19.4
Female	22,374	100.0	14,524	100.0	2,057	100.0	790	100.0	1,633	100.0	1,280	100.0	2,091	100.0
Native	14,108	63.1	9,395	64.7	2,047	99.5	309	39.1	541	33.2	414	32.4	1,402	67.0
Foreign born	8,266	36.9	5,129	35.3	10	0.5	481	60.9	1,092	66.8	866	67.6	689	33.0
Naturalized citizen	2,573	11.5	1,222	8.4	7	0.4	296	37.6	378	23.1	374	29.2	296	14.2
Not a citizen	5,693	25.4	3,907	26.9	3	0.1	184	23.4	714	43.7	492	38.4	393	18.8

[a]Plus armed forces living off post or with their families on post.

[b]Hispanic refers to people whose origin is Mexican, Puerto Rican, Cuban, Spanish-speaking Central or South American countries, or other Hispanic/Latino, regardless of race. Central American totals exclude Mexican.

[c]This category includes Dominicans and people who responded "Hispanic," "Lat no," or provided other genera terms.

[d]Native includes anyone who was a U.S. citizen or U.S. national at birth. Conversely, fore gn born includes anyone who was not a U.S. citizen or U.S. national at birth.

SOURCE: "Table 31. Regional Distribution of the Population by Sex, Hispanic Origin, and Race: 2008," in *The Hispanic Population in the United States: 2008 Detailed Tables*, U.S. Census Bureau, September 2009, http://www.census.gov/population/www/socdemo/hispanic/cps2008.html (accessed December 1, 2009)

30.3 million of the 46 million Hispanics living in the United States, or 65.8%, were of Mexican heritage. (See Table 1.3.) Another 4 million, or 8.8%, were of Puerto Rican heritage; 3.5 million, or 7.6%, were of Central America heritage; 2.5 million, or 5.5%, were of South American heritage; and 1.6 million, or 3.5%, were of Cuban heritage. Another 4.1 million, or 8.8%, were from other parts of the world. The differences in origin can often mean significant variations in where Hispanics live in the United States and in their educational attainment, income, and living conditions.

Geographic Distribution

Different areas of the United States have more Hispanics living in them. Roberto R. Ramirez and G. Patricia de la Cruz of the Census Bureau note in *The Hispanic Population in the United States: March 2002* (June 2003, http://www.census.gov/prod/2003pubs/p20-545.pdf) that the likelihood of Hispanics living in a particular region depends primarily on their country of origin. In 2008 more Hispanics lived in the West (42%) than in any other region, followed by the South (35.8%), the Northeast (13.4%) and the Midwest (8.7%). (See Table 1.4.) In *The American Community—Hispanics: 2004* (February 2007, http://www.census.gov/prod/2007pubs/acs-03.pdf), the Census Bureau reports that New Mexico had the highest Hispanic population; 43.4% of its residents in 2004 were Hispanic, followed by 34.9% of the residents of both Texas and California, 28.1% of the residents of Arizona, and 22.9% of the residents of Nevada. Even though New Mexico had the highest proportion of Hispanic residents, 30.3% of all Hispanic people living in the United States lived in California in 2004.

Mexican-Americans

Many Hispanic-Americans are descendants of the Spanish and Mexican people who lived in the West and Southwest when these regions were controlled by Spain (starting in the 1500s) and later by Mexico (after Mexico gained its independence from Spain in 1821). Their forebears were absorbed into the United States when Texas revolted, broke away from Mexico, became a republic, and then finally joined the United States during the 1840s. The Mexican-American War (1846–1848) added California, Arizona, New Mexico, Utah, Colorado, and territories north of the Rio Grande to the United States with the signing of the Treaty of Guadalupe Hidalgo in 1848. As a result, Hispanics living in these areas became Americans.

The Mexican-origin population, which more than doubled in the last two decades of the 20th century, continues to grow in the 21st century. According to the Census Bureau, 30.3 million people, or 10.1% of the U.S. population, were of Mexican origin in 2008. (See Table 1.3.) Mexican-Americans represented 65.8% of the Hispanic population in the United States in 2008. The DHS indicates in *Yearbook of Immigration Statistics, 2008* (August 2009, http://www.dhs.gov/xlibrary/assets/statistics/yearbook/2008/ois_yb_2008.pdf) that by far the largest number of legal

TABLE 1.4

Regional distribution of the population by sex, Hispanic origin, and race, 2008

[Numbers in thousands. Civilian noninstitutionalized population[a]]

					Hispanic origin and race[b]					
							Non-Hispanic			
	Total		Hispanic		Total		White alone		All other races	
Sex and region[c]	Number	Percent	Number	Percent	Number	Percent	Number	Percent	Number	Percent
Both sexes	299,106	100.0	46,026	100.0	253,079	100.0	196,768	100.0	56,312	100.0
Northeast	54,031	18.1	6,190	13.4	47,841	18.9	38,427	19.5	9,415	16.7
Midwest	65,480	21.9	4,016	8.7	61,464	24.3	52,016	26.4	9,448	16.8
South	109,710	36.7	16,481	35.8	93,229	36.8	67,742	34.4	25,487	45.3
West	69,883	23.4	19,339	42.0	50,545	20.0	38,583	19.6	11,962	21.2
Male	146,855	100.0	23,652	100.0	123,203	100.0	96,613	100.0	26,591	100.0
Northeast	26,266	17.9	3,086	13.0	23,180	18.8	18,787	19.4	4,392	16.5
Midwest	32,113	21.9	2,020	8.5	30,092	24.4	25,610	26.5	4,482	16.9
South	53,627	36.5	8,574	36.2	45,053	36.6	33,138	34.3	11,915	44.8
West	34,850	23.7	9,972	42.2	24,878	20.2	19,077	19.7	5,801	21.8
Female	152,250	100.0	22,374	100.0	129,876	100.0	100,155	100.0	29,721	100.0
Northeast	27,766	18.2	3,104	13.9	24,662	19.0	19,639	19.6	5,023	16.9
Midwest	33,368	21.9	1,996	8.9	31,372	24.2	26,406	26.4	4,965	16.7
South	56,083	36.8	7,907	35.3	48,176	37.1	34,604	34.6	13,572	45.7
West	35,034	23.0	9,367	41.9	25,667	19.8	19,506	19.5	6,161	20.7

[a]Plus armed forces living off post or with their families on post.
[b]Hispanic refers to people whose origin is Mexican, Puerto Rican, Cuban, Spanish-speaking Central or South American countries, or other Hispanic/Latino, regardless of race.
[c]Regions are described in the CPS glossary of subject concepts at www.census.gov/population/www/cps/cpsdef.html.

SOURCE: "Table 8. Nativity and Citizenship Status by Sex and Hispanic Origin Type: 2008," in *The Hispanic Population in the United States: 2008 Detailed Tables*, U.S. Census Bureau, September 2009, http://www.census.gov/population/www/socdemo/hispanic/cps2008.html (accessed December 1, 2009) immigrants comes from Mexico each year; in 2008, 189,989 Mexicans legally immigrated to the United States, with many more coming illegally. In the fact sheet "Hispanics of Mexican Origin in the United States, 2007" (September 16, 2009, http://pewhispanic .org/files/factsheets/49.pdf), the Pew Hispanic Center notes that most Mexicans live either in California (37.6%) or in Texas (25%).

Puerto Ricans

The situation of Puerto Ricans is unique in American society. The Caribbean island of Puerto Rico, formerly a Spanish colony, became a U.S. commonwealth after it was ceded to the United States by the Treaty of Paris in 1898, which ended the Spanish-American War (1898). In 1917 the Revised Organic Act (the Jones Act) granted the island a bill of rights and its own legislature. It also conferred U.S. citizenship to all Puerto Ricans.

Ruth Glasser states in "Tobacco Valley: Puerto Rican Farm Workers in Connecticut" (*Hog River Journal*, vol. 1, no. 1, 2002) that following World War II (1939–1945) an industrialization program was launched in Puerto Rico. Even though the program benefited many, it sharply reduced the number of agricultural jobs on the island, driving many rural residents to the cities. Combined with a high birth rate, this led to unemployment, overcrowding, and poverty. These conditions forced many Puerto Ricans to move to the mainland United States, particularly New York City. Since 1993, when President Bill Clinton (1946–) eliminated tax exemptions for manufacturing firms in Puerto Rico, industries have moved away from the island in search of cheaper labor, further compounding the economic problems of Puerto Rico. According to Virginia E. Sánchez Korrol, in *From Colonia to Community: The History of Puerto Ricans in New York City* (1994), in 1940 fewer than 70,000 Puerto Ricans lived in the contiguous United States. The Census Bureau notes that by 2008, over 4 million Puerto Ricans called the United States home. (See Table 1.3.) Partly because of the relative ease with which Puerto Ricans can travel in the United States, many move freely back and forth between the United States and Puerto Rico.

Joseph Berger explains in "A Puerto Rican Rebirth in El Barrio; After Exodus, Gentrification Changes Face of East Harlem" (*New York Times*, December 10, 2002) that most of the first Puerto Ricans who arrived in the United States settled in New York City in the Manhattan neighborhood of East Harlem, which came to be known as El Barrio (the Neighborhood). Eventually, Puerto Rican immigrants moved in greater numbers to other boroughs of the city and into New Jersey.

According to the Pew Hispanic Center, in the fact sheet "Hispanics of Puerto Rican Origin in the United States, 2007" (July 13, 2009, http://pewhispanic.org/files/factsheets/48.pdf), by 2007 more Puerto Ricans lived in the United States than in Puerto Rico. In 2008 Puerto Ricans represented 8.8% of the Hispanic population living in the United States. (See Table 1.3.) The Pew Hispanic Center finds that Puerto Ricans were concentrated in New York and Florida. Ramirez and de la Cruz state that in 2002 Puerto Ricans were even more likely than other Hispanic groups to reside inside central cities in metropolitan areas—57.4% of them lived in these areas.

Cuban-Americans

According to the Pew Hispanic Center, in the fact sheet "Cubans in the United States" (August 25, 2006, http://pewhispanic.org/files/factsheets/23.pdf), many Cubans fled Cuba during the early 1960s after the Fulgencio Batista y Zaldivar (1901–1973) regime was overthrown by Fidel Castro (1926–). Cuban immigrants tended to settle in Miami, Florida, and in the surrounding Dade County. Most of these political refugees were older, middle class, and educated. Many fled to maintain a capitalist way of life, and many succeeded in achieving economic prosperity in the United States. A second phase of Cuban immigration took place from about 1965 to 1974, legally bringing middle- and working-class Cubans to the United States through Cuban and U.S. government programs.

In "Mariel Boatlift" (April 27, 2005, http://www.global security.org/military/ops/mariel-boatlift.htm), John Pike reports that in 1980, 125,000 people seeking refuge from Castro's government fled Cuba in what became known as the Mariel Boatlift, named after the town in Cuba from which they sailed. Because most of these new immigrants were from less wealthy and less educated backgrounds than their predecessors, and some were actually criminals or people who were mentally ill, many had difficulty fitting into the existing Cuban communities in the United States. Also, unlike the Cubans who came before them, they had spent 20 years living under a dictatorship that was vastly different from the democratic government they encountered in the United States. This difference led to further difficulties in adjustment to their new home.

Mireya Navarro reports in "Last of Refugees from Cuba in '94 Flight Now Enter U.S." (*New York Times*, February 1, 1996) that in 1994 more than 29,000 Cubans tried to enter the United States after fleeing a severe economic crisis in their own country. Most attempted the trip by boats and rafts but were intercepted by the U.S. Coast Guard and taken back to Cuba, where they were detained at Guantánamo Bay, the U.S. naval base. By January 1996 most detainees had been allowed to enter the United States, and the detention camps were closed. The Pew Hispanic Center notes that under current U.S. policy, Cubans who are able to reach the United States are allowed to stay, whereas those intercepted at sea are returned to Cuba.

Even though language differences cause initial difficulties for Cuban immigrants, the Pew Hispanic Center explains in the fact sheet "Hispanics of Cuban Origin in the United States, 2007" (September 16, 2009, http://pewhispanic.org/files/factsheets/50.pdf) that most adapt well and that Cubans have a higher level of educational attainment and are the most economically successful of the Hispanic ethnic groups. Unlike Americans of Mexican and Puerto Rican backgrounds, who began migrating throughout the country during the 1990s, the Cuban population has generally remained concentrated in Florida (68.7% of them live there), even though large numbers also live in New Jersey, New York, and California. Cubans continue to come to the United States. In *Yearbook of Immigration Statistics, 2008*, the DHS notes that 49,500 Cubans immigrated to the United States in 2008.

AFRICAN-AMERICANS

In 1619 the first Africans arrived in colonial North America. Subsequently, their numbers increased rapidly to fill the growing demand for slave labor in the new land. The first slaves were brought into this country by way of the West Indies, but as demand increased, they were soon brought directly to the English colonies on the mainland in North America. Most were delivered to the South and worked on plantations, where they supplied cheap labor.

The vast majority of African-Americans in the United States were kept as slaves until the Civil War (1861–1865). According to the 1860 census (http://www2.census.gov/prod2/decennial/documents/1860a-02.pdf), the states that made up the Confederacy in the South at the outbreak of hostilities had a slave population of 3.5 million, compared with a white population of nearly 5.5 million. By contrast, the Union states and territories in the North had a white population of 21.5 million, with slaves numbering 432,650.

In 1863 President Abraham Lincoln (1809–1865) issued the Emancipation Proclamation, which technically freed slaves in the Confederate states, although those states did not recognize the legality of the proclamation. In 1865 the 13th Amendment to the U.S. Constitution abolished slavery throughout the United States. In 1868 the 14th Amendment afforded former slaves and other African-Americans equal protection under the law, and in 1870 the 15th Amendment granted them the right to vote. The present population of African-Americans in the United States includes not only those descended from former slaves but also those who have since emigrated from Africa, the West Indies, and Central and South America.

According to the Census Bureau, in 2008, 39.1 million people who identified their race as non-Hispanic, black alone lived in the United States; 41.1 million people identified their race as black alone or in combination with one or more other races. (See Table 1.1.) Generally, even mixed-race individuals in the United States identify as African-American due to the rigid politics of race in the nation. In 2008 African-Americans made up 13.5% of the population, up from 12.3% in 2000, as reported by the Census Bureau in *Profiles of General Demographic Characteristics 2000* (May 2001, http://www.census.gov/prod/cen2000/dp1/2kh00.pdf).

Geographic Distribution

Few African-Americans voluntarily migrated from the southern farms and plantations that had been their homes in the first decades after the abolition of slavery. As a result, at the beginning of the 20th century a large majority of African-Americans still lived in the South. However, when World War I (1914–1918) interrupted the flow of migrant labor from Europe, large numbers of African-Americans migrated from the rural South to northern industrial cities to take advantage of new work opportunities there. Compared with the oppressive system of segregation in the South, economic and social conditions were better in the North for many African-Americans, thereby encouraging a continuous flow of migrants. According to the article "North by South: The African American Great Migration" (August 28, 2005, http://northbysouth.kenyon.edu/), between 1900 and 1960, 4.8 million African-Americans left the South and settled in northern cities such as Chicago, Detroit, Cleveland, Pittsburgh, and New York. The African-American migrations following World War I and World War II are among the largest voluntary internal migrations in U.S. history.

Most African-Americans moved to the Northeast and Midwest, although after 1940 significant numbers also moved West. The traditional migration from the South to the North dwindled dramatically in the 1970s. In fact, after 1975, largely due to the favorable economic conditions developing in the booming Sunbelt cities, African-Americans started migrating in droves to the South. In 2004, five out of the six states whose populations were more than 25% African-American were in the deep South: Mississippi (37.5%), Louisiana (31.9%), Georgia (30%), South Carolina (28.1%), and Alabama (26.2%). As Figure 1.1 shows, the deep South had the highest proportions of African-Americans, whereas states in the Midwest and Northwest had lower proportions of African-Americans.

White Flight

African-Americans are significantly more likely than non-Hispanic whites to live in metropolitan areas, inside of central cities. According to Jesse McKinnon of the Census Bureau, in *The Black Population in the United States: March 2002* (April 2003, http://www.census.gov/prod/2003pubs/p20-541.pdf), 51.5% of African-Americans lived in these areas in 2002, compared with only 21.1% of non-Hispanic whites. In contrast, a higher proportion of whites lived inside metropolitan areas, but outside of

FIGURE 1.1

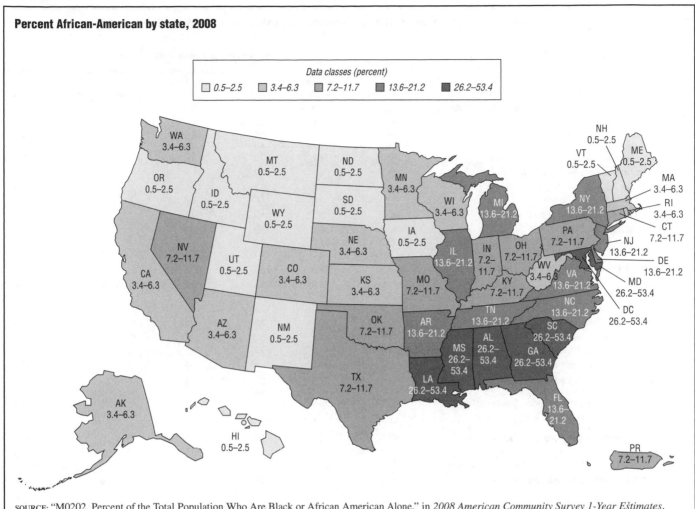

Percent African-American by state, 2008

Data classes (percent)

☐ 0.5–2.5　☐ 3.4–6.3　☐ 7.2–11.7　■ 13.6–21.2　■ 26.2–53.4

SOURCE: "M0202. Percent of the Total Population Who Are Black or African American Alone," in *2008 American Community Survey 1-Year Estimates*, U.S. Census Bureau, 2009, http://factfinder.census.gov/servlet/ThematicMapFramesetServlet?_bm=y&-geo_id=01000US&-tm_name=ACS_2008_1YR_G00_M00628&-ds_name=ACS_2008_1YR_G00_&-_lang=en&-format=&-CONTEXT=tm#?479,199 (accessed December 1, 2009)

central cities, than did African-Americans (56.8% and 36%, respectively), as well as in nonmetropolitan areas (22.1% and 12.5%, respectively).

Cities with particularly high proportions of African-Americans in 2003 included New York–White Plains–Wayne (24.7%), Philadelphia (22.3%), Washington, D.C.–Arlington–Alexandria (30.1%), Atlanta–Sandy Springs–Marietta (29.2%), and Baltimore–Towson (27.3%). (See Table 1.5.) However, the suburban areas around these metropolitan areas have lower proportions of African-Americans. For example, only 9.8% of the population of Nassau and Suffolk counties, the suburbs of New York City, was African-American, compared with 24.7% of New York City itself. Even though Chicago was 19.7% African-American, its suburbs in Lake and Kenosha counties were only 6.9% African-American.

Eric Bickford of the University of California, Berkeley, explains in "White Flight: The Effect of Minority Presence on Post World War II Suburbanization" (Sep-

tember 1999, http://eh.net/Clio/Publications/flight.shtml) that a primary reason for the high proportion of African-Americans in central cities has been "white flight." Beginning in the 1950s, as African-Americans moved to northeastern and midwestern cities, whites who were economically able to do so moved to suburban areas. Before the Civil Rights Act of 1964, which prohibited discrimination in housing, African-Americans were not given the same opportunities to move away from cities, whether or not they were economically able to do so. As wealthier whites abandoned city neighborhoods, taking their tax dollars with them, city neighborhoods rapidly deteriorated, leaving poor and nonwhite residents to deal with increasing crime and neighborhood deterioration.

ASIAN-AMERICANS

The term *Asian-American* is a catchall term that did not gain currency until the late 1960s and early 1970s. It was not until 1980 that the Census Bureau created the "Asian and Pacific Islander" category, a departure from the previous

TABLE 1.5

Population of twenty largest metropolitan statistical areas with metropolitan divisions, by race and Hispanic origin, 2003

Rank	Metropolitan statistical area/metropolitan division	White alone	Black or African American alone	Asian alone	American Indian, Alaska Native alone	Native Hawaiian and other Pacific Islander alone	Hispanic or Latino (any race)
				Population characteristics, 2003 (percent)			
1	**New York-Northern New Jersey-Long Island, NY-NJ-PA**	69.2	20.2	8.6	0.5	0.1	20.9
	Edison, NJ	82.2	7.8	8.7	0.2	0	10
	Nassau-Suffolk, NY	84.3	9.8	4.5	0.3	0.1	12.1
	Newark-Union, NJ-PA	71.6	22.7	4.4	0.3	0.1	14.4
	New York-White Plains-Wayne, NY-NJ	62.5	24.7	10.3	0.6	0.1	26.4
2	**Los Angeles-Long Beach-Santa Ana, CA**	75.6	8.1	13.2	1	0.3	43
	Los Angeles-Long Beach-Glendale, CA	74.3	9.9	12.7	1.1	0.3	46.3
	Santa Ana-Anaheim-Irvine, CA	80	1.8	14.9	0.9	0.3	32.1
3	**Chicago-Naperville-Joliet, IL-IN-WI**	75.1	18.5	4.9	0.3	0.1	17.9
	Chicago-Naperville-Joliet, IL	73.5	19.7	5.3	0.4	0.1	18.9
	Gary, IN	79.2	18.5	0.9	0.3	0.1	10.3
	Lake County-Kenosha County, IL-WI	87	6.9	4.3	0.4	0.1	15
4	**Philadelphia-Camden-Wilmington, PA-NJ-DE-MD**	74.2	20.6	3.8	0.2	0	5.4
	Camden, NJ	78.6	16.5	3.2	0.2	0.1	6.8
	Philadelphia, PA	72.1	22.3	4.3	0.2	0	4.9
	Wilmington, DE-MD-NJ	78	17.9	2.6	0.3	0	5.1
5	**Dallas-Fort Worth-Arlington, TX**	79.7	14	4.3	0.6	0.1	24.3
	Dallas-Plano-Irving, TX	78.1	15.2	4.8	0.6	0.1	26.1
	Fort Worth-Arlington, TX	82.8	11.6	3.5	0.6	0.1	20.8
6	**Miami-Fort Lauderdale-Miami Beach, FL**	75.7	20.9	1.9	0.3	0.1	36.8
	Fort Lauderdale-Pompano Beach-Deerfield Beach, FL	71.3	24.3	2.7	0.3	0.1	20.2
	Miami-Miami Beach-Kendall, FL	76.2	20.9	1.4	0.3	0.1	60.5
	West Palm Beach-Boca Raton-Boynton Beach, FL	80.8	15.9	1.8	0.4	0.1	14.9
7	**Houston-Sugar Land-Baytown, TX**	76.1	16.8	5.4	0.5	0.1	31.1
8	**Washington-Arlington-Alexandria, DC-VA-MD-WV**	63.5	26.4	7.7	0.4	0.1	10.1
	Bethesda-Gaithersburg-Frederick, MD	73.6	13.3	10.8	0.3	0.1	10.6
	Washington-Arlington-Alexandria, DC-VA-MD-WV	60.6	30.1	6.9	0.4	0.1	10
9	**Atlanta-Sandy Springs-Marietta, GA**	65.6	29.2	3.7	0.3	0.1	7.7
10	**Detroit-Warren-Livonia, MI**	72.4	23	2.9	0.3	0	3.1
	Detroit-Livonia-Dearborn, MI	53.6	42.4	2.1	0.4	0	4.2
	Warren-Farmington Hills-Troy, MI	87.8	7	3.5	0.3	0	2.3
11	**Boston-Cambridge-Quincy, MA-NH**	85.6	7.5	5.4	0.3	0.1	7
	Boston-Quincy, MA	79.9	12.9	5.6	0.3	0.1	7.7
	Cambridge-Newton, Framingham, MA	87.1	4	7.6	0.2	0	4.8
	Essex County, MA	90.3	4.7	2.8	0.3	0.1	13.2
	Rockingham County-Strafford County, NH	96.8	0.7	1.4	0.2	0.1	1.2
12	**San Francisco-Oakland-Fremont, CA**	65.2	9.5	20.9	0.6	0.7	18.9
	Oakland-Fremont-Hayward, CA	64.2	12.5	18.6	0.7	0.6	20.2
	San Francisco-San Mateo-Redwood City, CA	66.7	5.2	24.3	0.5	0.8	17.1
13	**Riverside-San Bernardino-Ontario, CA**	83.1	8.2	4.6	1.4	0.4	40.9
14	**Phoenix-Mesa-Scottsdale, AZ**	89.4	4	2.4	2.5	0.2	28.1
15	**Seattle-Tacoma-Bellevue, WA**	79.8	5.5	9.5	1.2	0.6	6.2
	Seattle-Bellevue-Everett, WA	79.7	4.9	10.7	1.1	0.5	6.1
	Tacoma, WA	80.3	7.3	5.4	1.5	0.9	6.3
16	**Minneapolis-St. Paul-Bloomington, MN-WI**	86.9	5.9	4.7	0.7	0.1	3.8
17	**San Diego-Carlsbad-San Marcos, CA**	80.3	5.9	9.4	1	0.5	28.7
18	**St. Louis, MO-IL**	78.8	18.1	1.7	0.2	0	1.7
19	**Baltimore-Towson, MD**	68	27.3	3.1	0.3	0.1	2.1
20	**Tampa-St. Petersburg-Clearwater, FL**	84.8	11.2	2.2	0.4	0.1	12

SOURCE: Adapted from "Table 1. Annual Estimates of the Population of Metropolitan and Micropolitan Statistical Areas: April 1, 2000 to July 1, 2006," in *Metropolitan and Micropolitan Statistical Area Estimates*, U.S. Census Bureau, April 2007, http://www.census.gov/population/www/estimates/CBSA-est2006-annual.html, and "Table B-3. Metropolitan Areas—Population by Age, Race, and Sex," in *State and Metropolitan Area Data Book: 2006*, U.S. Census Bureau, July 2006, http://www.census.gov/prod/2006pubs/smadb/smadb-06tableb.pdf (accessed December 12, 2009).

practice of counting several Asian groups separately. Even though seemingly a geographic description, "Asian and Pacific Islander" contains racial overtones, given that natives of Australia and New Zealand are not included, nor are whites born in the Asian region of the former Soviet Union. In 2008, 13.5 million Asian-Americans lived in the

United States, making up 4.5% of the country's population. (See Table 1.1.) Native Hawaiians and Pacific Islanders had a population of 562,121, making up 0.2% of the total U.S. population. According to the Census Bureau (December 2009, http://www.census.gov/population/socdemo/foreign/cps2008/tab3-2008.pdf), in 2008 nearly 10 million residents of the United States had been born in Asia.

Chinese Immigration in the 1800s

In "Chinese Immigration" (February 2010, http://www.loc.gov/teachers/classroommaterials/presentationsandactivities/presentations/immigration/chinese.html), the Library of Congress explains that the first major immigration of people from Asia to the United States involved the Chinese. From the time of the California gold rush of 1849 until the early 1880s, it is estimated that as many as 250,000 Chinese immigrated to the United States, with the vast majority coming from the Pearl River delta of Guangdong Province. Many hoped to strike it rich in California, the "Golden Mountain," and then return home. A few fulfilled that dream, but most stayed in the United States, two-thirds in California, where they faced intense discrimination. They became the object of political posturing that portrayed "cheap Chinese labor" as a threat to U.S. workers.

After the Civil War, when most African-Americans were able to gain citizenship with the adoption of the 14th Amendment in 1868, an exception was carved out for Asian immigrants. They were designated "aliens ineligible to citizenship." The Chinese Exclusion Act of 1882 then stopped the entry of Chinese into the country altogether, except for a few merchants and students. As a result, China became the source of the United States' first illegal aliens. Claire Lui states in "How Illegal Immigration Was Born" (May 7, 2007, http://www.americanheritage.com/) that besides jumping ship or illegally crossing borders, many Chinese immigrants took advantage of the 1906 earthquake in San Francisco, which destroyed the city's vital statistics records, to gain legal status by forging U.S. birth certificates. By law, any male of Chinese heritage born in the United States had the right to return to China for any children he fathered (although he could not bring back the alien mother). As a result, many of these fraudulent U.S. citizens escorted to the United States a host of "paper sons." Despite this traffic and other means of illegal entry, the Chinese-American population declined from the 1880s to the 1920s. Laws regulating Chinese immigration to the United States did not change until World War II, when China became an ally. President Franklin D. Roosevelt (1882–1945) persuaded Congress to repeal the Chinese Exclusion Act in 1943.

People of other nationalities that make up the Asian-American category also began immigrating to the United States before World War II. The Japanese first came to the United States in significant numbers during the 1890s,

although many laborers had previously settled in Hawaii. Like the Chinese, the Japanese mostly lived in the western United States. There was some call for a "Japanese Exclusion Act," but because Japan was an emerging Pacific power, such legislation was never passed. Overall, Japanese immigrants fared better than their Chinese counterparts and soon outpaced them in population. However, the Library of Congress notes in "Japanese Immigration" (February 2010, http://www.loc.gov/teachers/classroommaterials/presentationsandactivities/presentations/immigration/japanese.html) that when Japan and the United States went to war in 1941, over 100,000 Americans of Japanese descent, including many who were native-born U.S. citizens, were removed from their homes and confined in detention camps. By 1945 approximately 125,000 people of Japanese descent had been sent to these camps. It is noteworthy that even though the United States was also at war with Germany and Italy, citizens of German and Italian descent or birth were not subject to incarceration due to their heritage.

Before World War II, Filipinos, Asian-Indians, and Koreans represented a negligible share of the Asian-American population. In *Historical Census Statistics on Population Totals by Race, 1790 to 1990, and by Hispanic Origin, 1970 to 1990, for the United States, Regions, Divisions, and States* (September 2002, http://www.census.gov/population/www/documentation/twps0056/twps0056.html), Campbell Gibson and Kay Jung of the Census Bureau state that in 1940 there were 254,918 Asian-Americans living in the United States; 126,947 were Japanese, 77,504 were Chinese, and 45,563 were Filipino. Asian-Indians totaled some 2,405, and Koreans numbered even fewer. As was the case with Puerto Ricans, Filipinos began immigrating to the United States in the years following the Spanish-American War, when their country was annexed and eventually granted commonwealth status. Designated "American nationals," Filipinos held a unique position: They were not eligible for citizenship, but they also could not be prevented from entering the United States. Many Filipinos immigrated during the 1920s looking for work, but the Great Depression of the 1930s stemmed this flow.

Asian-Indians had come to the United States in small numbers, generally settling in New York City and other eastern ports, but it was not until the early years of the 20th century that they began immigrating to the West Coast, generally entering through western Canada. Koreans came to the United States from Hawaii, where several thousand had immigrated between 1903 and 1905. Both Asian-Indians and Koreans lost their eligibility to enter the United States following the Immigration Act of 1917, which accounted for their small populations before World War II. Once the Chinese Exclusion Act was repealed, however, the door was also open for Filipinos and Asian-Indians to gain entry to the United States as well as to earn citizenship during the postwar years. The Korean War (1950–1953) led to a long-term U.S. military presence in

Korea, resulting in a number of Korean-born wives of military personnel relocating to the United States. In addition, many Korean-born children were adopted and brought to the United States. A larger influx of Korean families immigrated during the mid-1960s.

Sharp Rise in Immigration

Asian immigration during the 1980s can be divided into two "streams." The first stream came from Asian countries that already had large populations in the United States (such as the People's Republic of China, Korea, and the Philippines). These immigrants, many of whom were highly educated, came primarily for family reunification and through employment provisions of the immigration laws. The second stream consisted primarily of immigrants and refugees from the war-torn countries of Southeast Asia (Vietnam, Laos, and Cambodia). They were admitted under U.S. policies that supported political refugees after the Vietnam War (1954–1975), as well as those escaping unstable economic and political conditions in neighboring countries. In "Southeast Asian Communities" (February 2010, http://www.searac.org/commun.html), the Southeast Asia Resource Action Center notes that between 1975 and 2002 an estimated 1.1 million refugees arrived in the United States from Southeast Asia.

According to the DHS, in *Yearbook of Immigration Statistics, 2008*, China was the top Asian country of origin for Asian immigrants in 2008—in that year 80,271 immigrants from China made their way to the United States. India was second, with 63,352 immigrants; 31,497 Vietnamese immigrants and 26,666 Korean immigrants made their way to the United States that same year.

Geographic Distribution

According to the Census Bureau (2004, http://www.census.gov/population/socdemo/race/api/ppl-184/tab20.pdf), Asian-Americans are much more likely than non-Hispanic whites to live in the West—47.9% of Asian-Americans, compared with 19.4% of non-Hispanic whites, lived in the West in 2004. In 2008 California had the highest population of Asian-Americans in the continental United States, at 12.3%. In addition to California, as Figure 1.2 shows, New York, New Jersey, Massachusetts, Maryland, Virginia, Washington, D.C., Illinois, Washington, Nevada, Alaska, and Hawaii all had greater than average populations of Asian-Americans.

In *The Asian and Pacific Islander Population in the United States: March 2002* (May 2003, http://www.census.gov/prod/2003pubs/p20-540.pdf), Terrance Reeves and Claudette Bennett of the Census Bureau report that in 2002, 95% of Asians and Pacific Islanders lived in metropolitan areas, whereas only 78% of non-Hispanic whites lived in metropolitan areas. Jessica S. Barnes and Claudette E. Bennett of the Census Bureau state in

The Asian Population: 2000 (February 2002, http://www.census.gov/prod/2002pubs/c2kbr01-16.pdf) that in 2000 New York, Los Angeles, and San Jose, California, were the three cities with the largest populations of Asian-Americans. Likewise, Elizabeth M. Grieco of the Census Bureau notes in *The Native Hawaiian and Other Pacific Islander Population: 2000* (December 2001, http://www.census.gov/prod/2001pubs/c2kbr01-14.pdf) that Honolulu, Los Angeles, and San Diego, California, were the three cities with the largest Native Hawaiian and Pacific Islander populations in 2000.

NATIVE AMERICANS

Most archaeologists agree that the people known as Native Americans and Alaskan Natives arrived in North America from northeast Asia at least 30,000 years ago during the last of the Ice Age glaciations (coverings of large areas of Earth with ice). At that time the two continents were connected by a land bridge over what is currently the Bering Strait. However, according to Charles W. Petit, in "Rediscovering America: The New World May Be 20,000 Years Older Than Experts Thought" (*U.S. News and World Report*, October 12, 1998), some archaeologists dispute this theory by citing evidence that indicates that migrants may have actually arrived many thousands of years earlier, perhaps by boat. For example, the article "New Evidence Puts Man in North America 50,000 Years Ago" (*ScienceDaily*, November 18, 2004) notes that artifacts have been discovered along the Savannah River in Allendale County, South Carolina, that date back to at least 50,000 years ago. The article indicates that "the findings are significant because they suggest that humans inhabited North America well before the last ice age more than 20,000 years ago, a potentially explosive revelation in American archaeology."

Migrants who settled on the northern coast of Alaska and the Yukon River valley, which were free of ice barriers, became known as Eskimos and Aleuts. Those who ventured farther south followed the eastern slope of the Rocky Mountains and continued along the mountainous spine of North America into South America. They eventually moved east throughout the central plains and eastern highlands of both continents and were later erroneously named Indians by exploring Spaniards. The misnomer is attributed to Christopher Columbus (1451–1506), who, on landing in the Bahamas in 1492, thought he had reached the islands off the eastern region of Asia, called the Indies. He therefore greeted the inhabitants as "Indians." In the 21st century many descendants of the original settlers prefer to be called Native Americans.

Most Native American groups have had a close relationship with Earth. Some specialized in farming, whereas others focused on hunting and/or fishing. The arrival of the Europeans eventually changed the Native Americans' way of life. Devastating wars, diseases, the annihilation of the buffalo,

FIGURE 1.2

Percent Asian by state, 2008

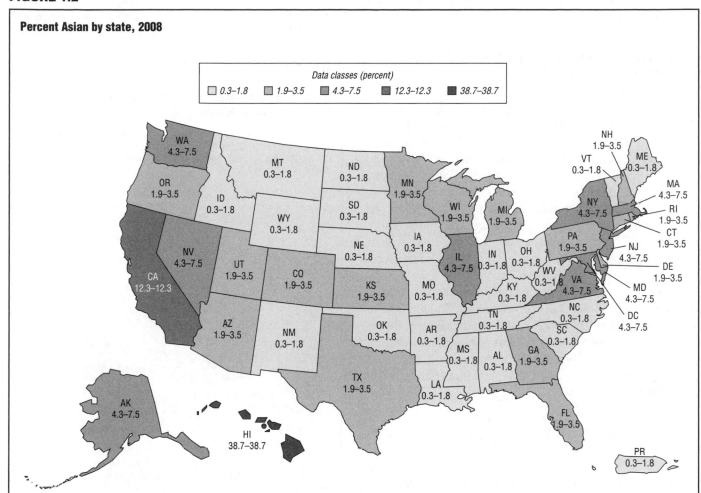

SOURCE: "M0204. Percent of the Total Population Who Are Asian Alone," in *2006–2008 American Community Survey 3-Year Estimates*, U.S. Census Bureau, 2009, http://factfinder.census.gov/servlet/ThematicMapFramesetServlet?_bm=y&-context=tm&-PANEL_ID=tm_result&-_MapEvent= displayBy&-tm_name=ACS_2008_3YR_G00_M00630&-ds_name=ACS_2008_3YR_G00_&-tm_config=lb=50ll=enlt=3308lzf=0.0lms=thm_defldw= 1.9557697048764706E7ldh=1.4455689123E7ldt=gov.census.aff.domain.map.LSRMapExtentlif=giflcx=−1159354.4733499996lcy=7122022.5lzl=10lpz= 10lbo=lbl=lft=350:349:335:389:388:332:331lfl,=403:381:204:380:369:379:368lg=01000USlds=ACS_2008_3YR_G00_lsb=48ltud=falseldb=040lmn=0.3l mx=38.7lcc=1lcm=1lcn=5lcb=lum=Percentlpr=1lth=ACS_2008_3YR_G00_M00630lsf=Nlsg=&-CONTEXT=tm&-tree_id=308&-keyword=Asian &-errMsg=&-redoLog=false&-geo_id=01000US&-_dBy=040&-format= (accessed December 1, 2009)

and the loss of land fit for cultivation to Europeans led to the elimination of much of their population.

In 2008, 3.1 million Native Americans and Alaskan Natives lived in the United States, making up approximately 1% of the population; 4.9 million people identified their race as Native American and Alaskan Native alone or in combination with one or more other races. (See Table 1.1.)

Geographic Distribution

The Census Bureau reports in American FactFinder (2010, http://factfinder.census.gov/) that during the period from 2006 to 2008 Alaska, South Dakota, and New Mexico had the highest proportion of Native Americans and Alaskan Natives among their populations. Over one out of 10 (13.4%) of Alaska's residents were Native American or Alaskan Native, as were 9.3% of New Mexico's residents and 8.4%

of South Dakota's residents. Other states with high concentrations of Native Americans and Alaskan Natives were Oklahoma (6.7%), Montana (6.1%), North Dakota (5.3%), and Arizona (4.5%).

Many Native Americans live on or near reservations and are members of groupings called tribes. Stella U. Ogunwole of the Census Bureau notes in *The American Indian and Alaska Native Population: 2000* (February 2002, http://www.census.gov/prod/2002pubs/c2kbr01-15.pdf) that in 2000 the largest tribal groupings were the Cherokee, with 729,533 members, followed by the Navajo, with 298,197 members, and the Latin Native Americans, with 180,940 members. Many Alaskan Natives are also members of such groups. The largest tribal groupings of Alaskan Natives in 2000 were the Eskimos, with 54,761 members, followed by the Tlingit-Haida, with 22,365 members, the Alaska

Athabascan, with 18,838 members, and the Aleut, with 16,978 members.

RELATIONS BETWEEN WHITES AND MINORITY GROUPS

In *U.S. Waiting for Race Relations to Improve under Obama* (November 9, 2009, http://www.gallup.com/poll/124181/U.S.-Waiting-Race-Relations-Improve-Obama.aspx), Lydia Saad of the Gallup Organization reports on a 2009 poll about whether relations between racial and ethnic groups have improved under Barack Obama (1961–), the nation's first African-American president. Overall, 41% of Americans believed that race relations have gotten better under the Obama administration. More than half (53%) of African-Americans and 39% of non-Hispanic whites believed that race relations have improved, but only 11% of African-Americans and 7% of non-Hispanic whites believed that race relations have "gotten a lot better." (See Figure 1.3.) Nevertheless, 79% of African-Americans and 58% of non-Hispanic whites believed that in the coming years of the Obama administration race relations will improve. (See Figure 1.4.) Only 6% of African-Americans and 15% of non-Hispanic whites believed that race relations will get worse.

Saad notes in *Whites May Exaggerate Black-Hispanic Tensions* (July 17, 2008, http://www.gallup.com/poll/108868/Whites-May-Exaggerate-BlackHispanic-Tensions.aspx) that in 2008, 81% of Americans said they believe relations between whites and Asian-Americans are "very/somewhat good," 68% believed relations between whites and African-Americans are "very/somewhat good," and 65% believed relations between whites and Hispanics are "very/somewhat good." (See Table 1.6.) Non-Hispanic whites were significantly more likely than African-Americans to perceive relations between whites and African-Americans as being good (70% and 61%, respectively).

FIGURE 1.4

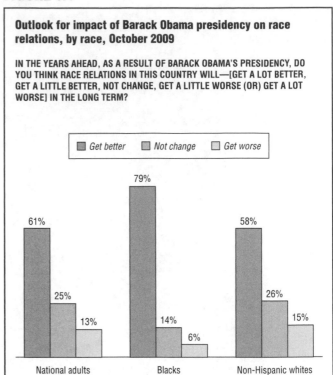

Outlook for impact of Barack Obama presidency on race relations, by race, October 2009

IN THE YEARS AHEAD, AS A RESULT OF BARACK OBAMA'S PRESIDENCY, DO YOU THINK RACE RELATIONS IN THIS COUNTRY WILL—[GET A LOT BETTER, GET A LITTLE BETTER, NOT CHANGE, GET A LITTLE WORSE (OR) GET A LOT WORSE] IN THE LONG TERM?

SOURCE: Lydia Saad, "Current Outlook for Impact of Barack Obama Presidency on Race Relations," in *U.S. Waiting for Race Relations to Improve under Obama*, The Gallup Organization, November 9, 2009, http://www.gallup.com/poll/124181/U.S.-Waiting-Race-Relations-Improve-Obama.aspx (accessed December 1, 2009). Copyright © 2009 by The Gallup Organization. Reproduced by Permission of The Gallup Organization.

FIGURE 1.3

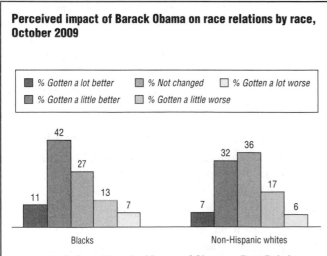

Perceived impact of Barack Obama on race relations by race, October 2009

SOURCE: Lydia Saad, "Perceived Impact of Obama on Race Relations—by Race," in *U.S. Waiting for Race Relations to Improve under Obama*, The Gallup Organization, November 9, 2009, http://www.gallup.com/poll/124181/U.S.-Waiting-Race-Relations-Improve-Obama.aspx (accessed December 1, 2009). Copyright © 2009 by The Gallup Organization. Reproduced by Permission of The Gallup Organization.

TABLE 1.6

Public opinion on state of relations between different groups, June–July 2008

NEXT, WE'D LIKE TO KNOW HOW YOU WOULD RATE RELATIONS BETWEEN VARIOUS GROUPS IN THE UNITED STATES THESE DAYS. WOULD YOU SAY RELATIONS BETWEEN—[RANDOM ORDER]—ARE VERY GOOD, SOMEWHAT GOOD, SOMEWHAT BAD, OR VERY BAD?

	National adults %	Non-Hispanic whites %	Non-Hispanic blacks %	Hispanics %
Whites and Asians	81	83	73	71
Whites and blacks	68	70	61	57
Whites and Hispanics	65	65	58	71
Blacks and Hispanics	49	43	67	60

SOURCE: Lydia Saad, "Next, We'd Like to Know How You Would Rate Relations between Various Groups in the United States These Days. Would You Say Relations between—[RANDOM ORDER]—Are Very Good, Somewhat Good, Somewhat Bad, or Very Bad?" in *Whites May Exaggerate Black-Hispanic Tensions*, The Gallup Organization, July 17, 2008, http://www.gallup.com/poll/108868/Whites-May-Exaggerate-Black-Hispanic-Tensions.aspx (accessed December 1, 2009). Copyright © 2008 by The Gallup Organization. Reproduced by Permission of The Gallup Organization.

CHAPTER 2
FAMILY LIFE AND LIVING ARRANGEMENTS

Historically, the family has been regarded as the cornerstone of society in the United States. For many years, particularly when the nation was primarily an agricultural society, extended families (multiple generations living in the same household) were common. As the culture became more urban and mobile, nuclear families (two parents and their children) became the American norm.

However, the makeup of families and their role in society have been undergoing a massive change. Shifts in economics, employment, moral values, and social conditions have led to an increasing number of single men and women living alone, cohabitations without marriage, and single-parent families. A growing number of children, especially minority children, are being raised by only one parent or by neither parent, as in the case of children being raised by grandparents or foster parents. How these changes affect minorities in the United States can be best understood through a detailed look at minority families.

MARITAL STATUS

The U.S. Census Bureau reports in *America's Families and Living Arrangements: 2008* (February 25, 2009, http://www.census.gov/population/www/socdemo/hh-fam/cps2008.html) that in 2008, 123.7 million Americans (aged 15 years and older) were married, up from 95.3 million in 1970 and 112.6 million in 1990 but down from 127.1 million in 2005. This figure includes both people who did and people who did not live with their spouses. However, the proportion of people of marriage age who were married has decreased steadily since 1960, even though the absolute numbers of married people have increased until quite recently. In 1960, 67.6% of the population aged 15 years and older was married, dropping to 64.2% in 1970, 60.9% in 1980, 58.7% in 1990, 56.2% in 2000, and to a low of 51.9% in 2008. The proportion of African-Americans who were married has been lower than the proportion of married adults in the general population

since 1960 and has dropped faster as well. Of all African-Americans aged 15 years and older, 60.3% in 1960, 55.4% in 1970, 46.5% in 1980, 42.4% in 1990, and 39.2% in 2000 were married. By 2008 only 32.6% of African-Americans aged 15 years and older were married. (See Table 2.1.) That same year, 60.5% of Asian-Americans, 55.5% of non-Hispanic whites, and 49.3% of Hispanics aged years 15 and older were married.

Never Married

Racial differences among never-married people are also significant. Among those over the age of 15, African-Americans are far more likely than non-Hispanic whites, Hispanics, or Asian-Americans to have never married. In 2008, 45.6% of African-Americans had never been married, compared with 36.8% of Hispanics, 29.2% of Asian-Americans, and 25.8% of non-Hispanic whites. (See Table 2.1.)

One reason that the proportion of never-married individuals aged 15 years and older has increased over time is that the age at first marriage has steadily risen since 1970 for all races and ethnic groups. The median age (half of all people below the median value and half of all people above the median value) of first marriage for women rose from 20.8 in 1970 to 25.9 in 2008. (See Figure 2.1.) The median age of first marriage for men rose from 23.2 in 1970 to 27.6 in 2008. This rise in the age at first marriage accounts for some of the decreases in the proportion of adults who have ever married.

Another reason that the proportion of never-married individuals has risen is the rise in cohabitation. The Census Bureau reports that in 2008, 6.8 million unmarried couples cohabited in the United States. Unlike in the past, the birth of children does not necessarily lead to parents marrying. In 2007, 1.5 million cohabiting couples had children. (See Table 2.2.) In that year, 1.8% of family groups were unmarried parent couples.

TABLE 2.1

Marital status of people 15 years and over, by sex, race, and Hispanic origin, 2008

[Numbers in thousands, except for percentages.]

	Total Number	Married spouse present Number	Married spouse absent Number	Widowed Number	Divorced Number	Separated Number	Never married Number	Total Percent	Married spouse present Percent	Married spouse absent Percent	Widowed Percent	Divorced Percent	Separated Percent	Never married Percent
All races														
Total 15+	237,993	120,258	3,413	14,314	23,346	5,183	71,479	100.0	50.5	1.4	6.0	9.8	2.2	30.0
Male Total 15+	115,599	60,129	1,944	2,916	9,782	2,144	38,685	100.0	52.0	1.7	2.5	8.5	1.9	33.5
Female Total 15+	122,394	60,129	1,470	11,398	13,564	3,039	32,794	100.0	49.1	1.2	9.3	11.1	2.5	26.8
White, non-Hispanic														
Total 15+	162,522	88,816	1,438	10,881	16,951	2,501	41,936	100.0	54.6	0.9	6.7	10.4	1.5	25.8
Male Total 15+	79,043	44,570	681	2,242	7,309	1,099	23,142	100.0	56.4	0.9	2.8	9.2	1.4	29.3
Female Total 15+	83,479	44,246	757	8,639	9,642	1,401	18,794	100.0	53.0	0.9	10.3	11.6	1.7	22.5
Black alone														
Total 15+	28,493	8,813	475	1,711	3,180	1,321	12,993	100.0	30.9	1.7	6.0	11.2	4.6	45.6
Male Total 15+	12,878	4,504	222	332	1,190	508	6,121	100.0	35.0	1.7	2.6	9.2	3.9	47.5
Female Total 15+	15,615	4,309	254	1,378	1,990	813	6,872	100.0	27.6	1.6	8.8	12.7	5.2	44.0
Asian alone														
Total 15+	10,776	6,163	357	499	444	162	3,152	100.0	57.2	3.3	4.6	4.1	1.5	29.2
Male Total 15+	5,106	2,873	201	79	138	63	1,751	100.0	56.3	3.9	1.6	2.7	1.2	34.3
Female Total 15+	5,670	3,289	156	419	305	99	1,400	100.0	58.0	2.7	7.4	5.4	1.8	24.7
Hispanic														
Total 15+	32,677	15,002	1,109	1,068	2,330	1,147	12,021	100.0	45.9	3.4	3.3	7.1	3.5	36.8
Male Total 15+	16,832	7,445	820	228	945	438	6,955	100.0	44.2	4.9	1.4	5.6	2.6	41.3
Female Total 15+	15,845	7,557	288	839	1,385	709	5,066	100.0	47.7	1.8	5.3	8.7	4.5	32.0

Notes: Hispanics may be of any race. Prior to 2001, this table included group quarters people.

SOURCE: Adapted from "Table A1. Marital Status of People 15 Years and over, by Age, Sex, Personal Earnings, Race, and Hispanic Origin, 2008," in *America's Families and Living Arrangements: 2008*, U.S. Census Bureau, January 2009, http://www.census.gov/population/www/socdemo/hh-fam/cps2008.html (accessed December 1, 2009)

FIGURE 2.1

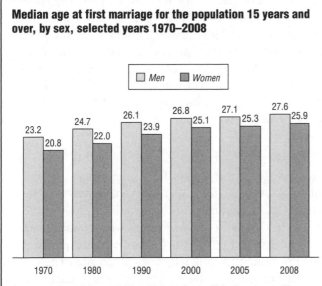

Median age at first marriage for the population 15 years and over, by sex, selected years 1970–2008

□ Men ■ Women

1970: Men 23.2, Women 20.8
1980: Men 24.7, Women 22.0
1990: Men 26.1, Women 23.9
2000: Men 26.8, Women 25.1
2005: Men 27.1, Women 25.3
2008: Men 27.6, Women 25.9

SOURCE: Adapted from "Table MS-2. Estimated Median Age at First Marriage, by Sex: 1890 to the Present," in *Families and Living Arrangements*, U.S. Census Bureau, January 2009, http://www.census .gov/population/www/socdemo/hh-fam.html (accessed December 1, 2009)

Interracial Marriage

Laws that prohibited interracial marriage were on the books in many states until 1967. In that year the U.S. Supreme Court unanimously decided in *Loving v. Virginia* (388 U.S. 1) that prohibitions against interracial marriage were unconstitutional. However, interracial marriages were rare even into the 1970s. After 1980 interracial marriages became much more common. The Census Bureau reports that the number of interracial married couples more than tripled between 1980 and 2007. (See Table 2.3.) For example, in 1980 there were 167,000 African-American–white interracial married couples; by 2007 there were 464,000 African-American–white interracial married couples. In 1980 there were 450,000 married couples with one white spouse and one spouse of a race other than white or African-American, such as Native American or Asian and Pacific Islander; in 2007 nearly 1.7 million married couples fit this description. Even though the proportion of interracial married couples is rising, the vast majority of married couples continue to be made up of two spouses of the same race. In 1980, 651,000 married couples were interracial; by 2007 there were 2.3 million.

TABLE 2.2

Family groups by race and Hispanic origin of reference person, 2007

[Numbers in thousands]

Type of family group	Total	White alone	White alone, non-Hispanic	Black alone	Asian alone	Hispanic (any race)
Total	**82,746**	**67,120**	**56,613**	**10,081**	**3,669**	**11,280**
Number						
Married couples	60,676	52,020	45,124	4,512	2,995	7,284
With children under 18	26,802	22,519	18,152	2,182	1,519	4,628
Without children under 18	33,874	29,500	26,972	2,330	1,477	2,656
Unmarried parent couple[a]	1,474	1,127	804	222	49	356
Mother only with children under 18[b]	9,965	6,358	4,586	3,068	184	1,988
Father only with children under 18[b]	1,742	1,354	1,154	289	42	221
Householder and other relative(s)[c]	8,888	6,262	4,944	1,990	399	1,431
Grandparent householder with grandchildren under 18	1,126	690	520	390	11	194
Householder with adult children	4,785	3,483	2,923	1,080	123	595
Householder with young adult children aged 18 to 24	1,956	1,382	1,138	474	59	267
Householder with parent	2,072	1,411	1,016	421	173	435
Percent						
Married couples	73.3	77.5	79.7	44.8	81.6	64.6
With children under 18	32.4	33.6	32.1	21.6	41.4	41.0
Without children under 18	40.9	44.0	47.6	23.1	40.3	23.5
Unmarried parent couple[a]	1.8	1.7	1.4	2.2	1.3	3.2
Mother only with children under 18[b]	12.0	9.5	8.1	30.4	5.0	17.6
Father only with children under 18[b]	2.1	2.0	2.0	2.9	1.1	2.0
Householder and other relative(s)[c]	10.7	9.3	8.7	19.7	10.9	12.7
Grandparent householder with grandchildren under 18	1.4	1.0	0.9	3.9	0.3	1.7
Householder with adult children	5.8	5.2	5.2	10.7	3.4	5.3
Householder with young adult children aged 18 to 24	2.4	2.1	2.0	4.7	1.6	2.4
Householder with parent	2.5	2.1	1.8	4.2	4.7	3.9

[a]These couples have at least one joint never-married child under 18.
[b]Parent may have a cohabiting partner, but none of his or her children are also identified as the child of his or her cohabiting partner.
[c]Subcategories of "householder and other relative(s)" are not mutually exclusive—915,000 family groups overlap among the subcategories; and 1,844,000 family groups fall under "householder and other relative(s)" but not in the subcategories listed.

SOURCE: Rose M. Kreider and Diana B. Elliott, "Table 2. Family Groups by Race and Hispanic Origin of Reference Person: 2007," in *America's Families and Living Arrangements: 2007*, U.S. Census Bureau, September 2009, http://www.census.gov/population/www/socdemo/hh-fam/p20–561.pdf (accessed December 2, 2009)

TABLE 2.3

Married couples by race and Hispanic origin of spouses, selected years 1980–2007

[In thousands (49,714 represents 49,714,000). As of March. Persons 15 years old and over. Persons of Hispanic origin may be any race. Based on Current Population Survey.]

Race and origin of spouses	1980	1990	2000	2007
Married couples, total[a]	49,714	53,256	56,497	60,676
Interracial married couples, total	651	964	1,464	2,281
White[b]/black[b]	167	211	363	464
Black husband/white wife	122	150	268	338
White husband/black wife	45	61	95	126
White[b]/other race[c]	450	720	1,051	1,688
Black[b]/other race[c]	34	33	50	129
Hispanic origin				
Hispanic/Hispanic	1,906	3,085	4,739	6,261
Hispanic/other origin (not Hispanic)	891	1,193	1,743	2,241
All other couples (not of Hispanic origin)	46,917	48,979	50,015	52,173

[a]Includes other married couples not shown separately.
[b]Beginning with the 2003 Current Population Survey (CPS), respondents could choose more than one race. Beginning 2005, data shown represent persons who selected this race group only and exclude persons reporting more than one race. The CPS prior to 2003 only allowed respondents to report one race group.
[c]"Other race," is any race other than white or black, such as American Indian, Japanese, Chinese, etc. This total excludes combinations of other races by other races.

SOURCE: "Table 59. Married Couples by Race and Hispanic Origin of Spouses: 1980 to 2007," in *Statistical Abstract of the United States: 2009*, 128th ed., U.S. Census Bureau, 2008, http://www.census.gov/compendia/statab/2009/2009edition.html (accessed December 3, 2009)

Why is the number of interracial and interethnic marriage rising? Michael J. Rosenfeld of Stanford University argues in "The Steady Rise of Non-traditional Romantic Unions" (March 8, 2007, http://www.contemporaryfamilies.org/marriage-partnership-divorce/unions.html) that the rise in immigration from Asian and Hispanic countries is partially responsible, because neither of these groups is as segregated from white society as African-Americans have historically been in the United States. He also cites a rising marriage age, greater acceptance of diversity, and improving race relations as reasons marriages between whites and African-Americans have increased.

In fact, considerable progress has been made in the public acceptance of interracial marriage. According to Joseph Carroll of the Gallup Organization, in *Most Americans Approve of Interracial Marriages* (August 16, 2007, http://www.gallup.com/poll/28417/Most-Americans-Approve-Interracial-Marriages.aspx), in 1958 only 4% of Americans were accepting of marriage between couples of different races, and as late as 1994, 48% of all Americans approved. By 2007, however, 77% of Americans said they approved of marriages between African-Americans and whites. Support for interracial marriages was higher among African-Americans (85%) than among whites (75%). Younger Americans were more accepting of interracial marriages than older Americans—85% of people between the ages of 18 and 49 approved, whereas among adults over the age of 50 only 67% approved. These numbers indicate that the trend toward increasing acceptance of interracial marriage is likely to continue.

MIXED-RACE CHILDREN. The number of mixed-race births has kept pace with increases in interracial marriage and cohabitation. The change in the question of race for the 2000 census, which enabled people to identify themselves by multiple races, made it easier to track mixed-race Americans. According to the 2000 census, 3.9 million Americans identified themselves as belonging to two or more races. (See Table 2.4.) By 2007 this number had grown to nearly 4.9 million Americans, an increase of 24.6%.

Members of some groups were more likely to report being mixed race than others. For example, an estimated 1.4 million Native Americans and Alaskan Natives were multiracial in 2007, virtually unchanged since 2000. In 2000 there were 375,000 Asian-Americans who reported that they were multiracial; by 2007 the Census Bureau reported there were 1.6 million multiracial Asian-Americans. The groups with the smallest proportion claiming a multiracial heritage in the 2000 census were non-Hispanic African-Americans (1.2 million, which increased to 1.7 million in 2007) and non-Hispanic whites (2.9 million, which increased to 3.6 million in 2007). The rigid politics of race in the United States probably leads to an underreporting of mixed-race backgrounds among these two groups.

Divorce

The Census Bureau reports that in 2008, 23.3 million adults aged 15 years and older were divorced. (See Table 2.1.) In other words, nearly one out of 10 (9.8%) of all people aged 15 years and older were divorced and had not remarried at the time of the survey—thus, the proportion of ever-divorced people is much higher. A similar proportion of African-Americans (11.2%) and non-Hispanic whites (10.4%) were divorced, whereas a much lower proportion of Hispanics (7.1%) and Asian-Americans (4.1%) were divorced. In *Marital Status and Living Arrangements: March 1994* (February 1996, http://www.census.gov/prod/1/pop/p20-484.pdf), Arlene F. Saluter of the Census Bureau reports that divorce for most groups rose sharply from 1970 to the 1990s, when 4.4% of African-Americans, 3.9% of Hispanics, and 3.1% of whites were divorced. The divorce rate leveled off in the 1990s, according to Jason Fields of the Census Bureau, in *America's Families and Living Arrangements: 2003* (November 2004, http://www.census .gov/prod/2004pubs/p20-553.pdf).

Because men are considerably more likely than women to remarry following a divorce, there are significantly higher proportions of currently divorced women than currently divorced men. In 2008, 1.2 million (9.2%) African-American men were currently divorced, compared with 2 million (12.7%) African-American women; and 7.3 million (9.2%) non-Hispanic white men were divorced, compared with 9.6 million (11.6%) non-Hispanic white women. (See Table 2.1.) Among those of Hispanic origin, 945,000 (5.6%) men and 1.4 million (8.7%) women were

TABLE 2.4

Resident population by race and Hispanic origin, 2000 and 2007

[281,425 represents 281,425,000. As of July, except as noted. Data shown are modified race counts.]

Characteristic	Number (1,000) 2000[a] (April 1)	Number (1,000) 2007	Percent change, 2000 to 2007
Both sexes			
Total	**281,425**	**301,621**	**7.2**
One race	277,527	296,765	6.9
White	228,107	241,167	5.7
Black or African American	35,705	38,756	8.5
American Indian and Alaska Native	2,664	2,938	10.3
Asian	10,589	13,366	26.2
Native Hawaiian and other Pacific Islander	463	537	16.1
Two or more races	3,898	4,856	24.6
Race alone or in combination:[b]			
White	231,436	245,374	6.0
Black or African American	37,105	40,744	9.8
American Indian and Alaska Native	4,225	4,537	7.4
Asian	12,007	15,165	26.3
Native Hawaiian and other Pacific Islander	907	1,019	12.4
Not Hispanic	**246,118**	**256,117**	**4.1**
One race	242,712	251,912	3.8
White	195,577	199,092	1.8
Black or African American	34,314	37,037	7.9
American Indian and Alaska Native	2,097	2,287	9.0
Asian	10,357	13,080	26.3
Native Hawaiian and other Pacific Islander	367	417	13.6
Two or more races	3,406	4,205	23.4
Race alone or in combination: [b]			
White	198,477	202,720	2.1
Black or African American	35,499	38,717	9.1
American Indian and Alaska Native	3,456	3,658	5.9
Asian	11,632	14,688	26.3
Native Hawaiian and other Pacific Islander	752	832	10.6
Hispanic[c]	**35,306**	**45,504**	**28.9**
One race	34,815	44,853	28.8
White	32,530	42,075	29.3
Black or African American	1,391	1,719	23.6
American Indian and Alaska Native	566	652	15.1
Asian	232	287	23.3
Native Hawaiian and other Pacific Islander	95	120	25.8
Two or more races	491	651	32.6
Race alone or in combination:[b]			
White	32,959	42,654	29.4
Black or African American	1,606	2,027	26.2
American Indian and Alaska Native	770	879	14.2
Asian	375	477	27.3
Native Hawaiian and other Pacific Islander	155	188	21.1
Male			
Total	**138,056**	**148,659**	**7.7**
One race	136,146	146,263	7.4
White	112,478	119,549	6.3
Black or African American	16,972	18,487	8.9
American Indian and Alaska Native	1,333	1,471	10.4
Asian	5,128	6,482	26.4
Native Hawaiian and other Pacific Islander	235	273	16.2
Two or more races	1,910	2,396	25.4
Race alone or in combination:[b]			
White	114,116	121,632	6.6
Black or African American	17,644	19,458	10.3
American Indian and Alaska Native	2,088	2,245	7.5
Asian	5,834	7,381	26.5
Native Hawaiian and other Pacific Islander	456	512	12.3
Not Hispanic	119,894	125,135	4.4
Hispanic[c]	18,162	23,524	29.5

divorced. In the Asian-American community, 138,000 (2.7%) men and 305,000 (5.4%) women were divorced. Many more women of each race and ethnicity remained divorced than men.

Death of a Spouse

In 2008, 14.3 million (6%) people aged 15 years and older in the United States were widowed. (See Table 2.1.) Across all racial and ethnic groups, more women than

TABLE 2.4

Resident population by race and Hispanic origin, 2000 and 2007 [CONTINUED]

[281,425 represents 281,425,000. As of July, except as noted. Data shown are modified race counts.]

Characteristic	Number (1,000) 2000ª (April 1)	2007	Percent change, 2000 to 2007
Female			
Total	143,368	152,962	6.7
One race	141,381	150,502	6.5
White	115,628	121,617	5.2
Black or African American	18,733	20,269	8.2
American Indian and Alaska Native	1,331	1,467	10.2
Asian	5,461	6,884	26.1
Native Hawaiian and other Pacific Islander	227	264	16.0
Two or more races	1,987	2,460	23.8
Race alone or in combination:ᵇ			
White	117,321	123,742	5.5
Black or African American	19,461	21,286	9.4
American Indian and Alaska Native	2,137	2,292	7.3
Asian	6,173	7,784	26.1
Native Hawaiian and other Pacific Islander	451	507	12.5
Not Hispanic	126,224	130,982	3.8
Hispanicᶜ	17,144	21,981	28.2

ªThe April 1, 2000, population estimates base reflects changes to the Census 2000 population from the Count Question Resolution program.
ᵇIn combination with one or more other races. The sum of the five race groups adds to more than the total population because individuals may report more than one race.
ᶜPersons of Hispanic origin may be any race.

SOURCE: Adapted from "Table 6. Resident Population by Sex, Race, and Hispanic-Origin Status: 2000 to 2007," in *Statistical Abstract of the United States: 2009*, 128th ed., U.S. Census Bureau, 2008, http://www.census.gov/compendia/statab/2009/2009edition.html (accessed December 3, 2009)

men were widowed because of the shorter average life span of men, the tendency of wives to be younger than their husbands, and the greater likelihood that men will remarry. This was particularly pronounced in the white and African-American communities. Over 8.6 million (10.3%) non-Hispanic white women were widowed, compared with only 2.2 million (2.8%) non-Hispanic white men. A similar proportion of African-American women (1.4 million, or 8.8%) were widowed, compared with 332,000 (2.6%) African-American men. Among Asian-Americans, 419,000 (7.4%) women were widowed, compared with only 79,000 (1.6%) men. Among Hispanics, 839,000 (5.3%) women were widowed, compared with 228,000 (1.4%) men.

TEENAGE PREGNANCY

Over the generations, a major change in American attitudes has removed much of the social stigma from unwed motherhood. Unmarried women of all ages are having children openly and with a regularity that was unheard of just a few generations ago. Many women do not feel the need to marry immediately when they become pregnant. Joyce A. Martin et al. of the Centers for Disease Control and Prevention (CDC) indicate in "Births: Final Data for 2006" (*National Vital Statistics Reports*, vol. 57, no. 7, January 7, 2009) that in 2006, 1.6 million babies were born to single mothers—the highest number ever recorded; 38.5% of all births were to unmarried mothers in that year. However, even though the proportion of all births to unmarried mothers has risen, between 1990 and 2006 the birth rate to unmarried

teenagers decreased. (See Figure 2.2.) For example, among 15- to 17-year-olds, the birth rate decreased from 30 births per 1,000 women in 1990 to 20 births per 1,000 women in 2006. However, Brady E. Hamilton, Joyce A. Martin, and Stephanie J. Ventura of the CDC note in "Births: Preliminary Data for 2007" (*National Vital Statistics Reports*, vol. 57, no. 12, March 18, 2009) that the birth rate for teenagers rose markedly between 2005 and 2007, the first increase since 1991. The birth rate for teenagers 15 to 17 years old increased 4% to 22.2 births per 1,000 females in 2007, and for teenagers aged 18 to 19 the rate increased 6% to 73.9 per 1,000 births. (See Figure 2.3.)

Experts offer many possible explanations for the high rates of teenage motherhood. Among them are lack of access to birth control, lack of education, and little hope for the future, including absence of educational goals. What is certain is that the health of the babies born to teenagers is at risk. According to Xi-Kuan Chen et al., in "Teenage Pregnancy and Adverse Birth Outcomes: A Large Population Based Retrospective Cohort Study" (*International Journal of Epidemiology*, vol. 36, no. 2, April 2007), teenage pregnancy is associated with higher rates of pre-term delivery, low birth weight, and neonatal mortality regardless of the socioeconomic status of the mother, adequate prenatal care, amount of education, or other known risk factors. These adverse outcomes are even more pronounced among minority teens. Shih-Chen Chang et al. note in "Characteristics and Risk Factors for Adverse

FIGURE 2.2

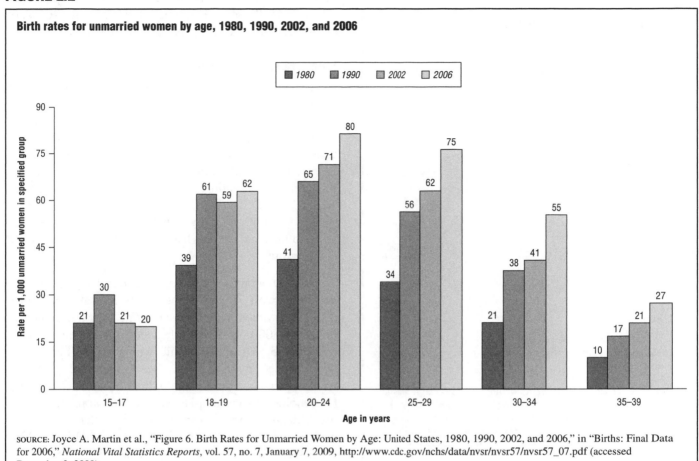

Birth rates for unmarried women by age, 1980, 1990, 2002, and 2006

source: Joyce A. Martin et al., "Figure 6. Birth Rates for Unmarried Women by Age: United States, 1980, 1990, 2002, and 2006," in "Births: Final Data for 2006," *National Vital Statistics Reports*, vol. 57, no. 7, January 7, 2009, http://www.cdc.gov/nchs/data/nvsr/nvsr57/nvsr57_07.pdf (accessed December 2, 2009)

Birth Outcomes in Pregnant Black Adolescents" (*Journal of Pediatrics*, vol. 143, no. 2, August 2003) that African-American teenagers are twice as likely as white teenagers to deliver low birth weight babies and 1.5 times more likely to have premature babies. Both low birth weight and premature babies experience a number of serious health and developmental problems. In general, babies born to teenage mothers of all races suffer a higher risk of low birth weight, preterm delivery, and infant mortality when compared with babies born to older mothers.

The largest decline in teen birth rates between 1991 and 2006 was among non-Hispanic African-American teens; the birth rate for this group fell from 118.2 to 60.9 births per 1,000 females in 2005 before rising to 63.7 in 2006. (See Figure 2.4 and Table 2.5.) Non-Hispanic African-American teens had the highest birth rate in 1991, but by 2006 they had the second-highest birth rate. Even though the teen Hispanic birthrate had fallen from 104.6 births per 1,000 women in 1991 to 83 births per 1,000 women in 2006, these teens had the highest birthrate in 2006. In 2006 Native American or Alaskan Native teens had a birthrate of 55, 4% higher than the year before, non-Hispanic white teens had a birthrate of 26.6, 3% higher than the year before, and Asian or Pacific Islander teens had a birthrate of 17,

unchanged from 2005. Preliminary data for 2007 suggest that birthrates among teenagers rose between 2006 and 2007 for all teenagers aged 15 to 19 years old, except among Hispanics, whose birthrate decreased by 2%.

MINORITY FAMILY STRUCTURE
Married-Couple Families

The Census Bureau defines a family as two or more people living together who are related by birth, marriage, or adoption. A household, however, can be family or nonfamily and is simply all people who occupy a housing unit. The proportion of married-couple families among all households declined from 1970 to 2008. According to Fields, 70.6% of all households in 1970 were married-couple families. By 2008 the Census Bureau (2009, http://www.census.gov/compendia/statab/2010/tables/10s0059.pdf) reports that the proportion of households that were married-couple families had dropped to 49.9%.

The proportion of married-couple families among all family households declined between 1970 and 2007 for all races and ethnicities. In *Household and Family Characteristics: March 1994* (September 1995, http://www.census.gov/prod/1/pop/p20-483.pdf), Steve Rawlings and Arlene F. Saluter of the Census Bureau report numbers

FIGURE 2.3

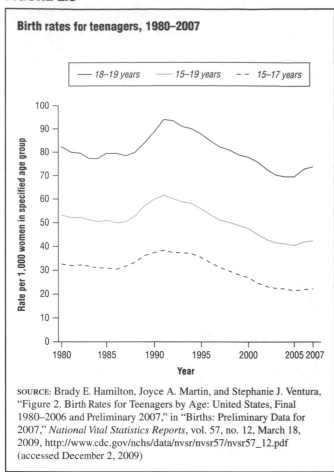

Birth rates for teenagers, 1980–2007

— 18–19 years   — 15–19 years   - - 15–17 years

SOURCE: Brady E. Hamilton, Joyce A. Martin, and Stephanie J. Ventura, "Figure 2. Birth Rates for Teenagers by Age: United States, Final 1980–2006 and Preliminary 2007," in "Births: Preliminary Data for 2007," *National Vital Statistics Reports*, vol. 57, no. 12, March 18, 2009, http://www.cdc.gov/nchs/data/nvsr/nvsr57/nvsr57_12.pdf (accessed December 2, 2009)

from 1970 and 1980, which here are compared with numbers from 2007 reported by Rose M. Kreider and Diana B. Elliott of the Census Bureau in *America's Families and Living Arrangements, 2007* (September 2009, http://www.census.gov/population/www/socdemo/hh-fam/p20-561.pdf). In 1970, 88.9% of non-Hispanic white families were married-couple families, compared with 80.7% in 2007. Asian-Americans also maintained a proportion of married-couple families comparable to that among the non-Hispanic white community. In 1980, 84.5% of Asian-American family households were headed by married couples; by 2007 this proportion had decreased to 81.2%. A high proportion of Hispanic families were headed by a married couple in 1970 (80.6%), but by 2007 this proportion had decreased more significantly (to 64.7%) than had the proportion of married-couple families among either non-Hispanic whites or Asian-Americans. However, the percentage of married-couple families was the lowest, and had decreased the most dramatically, among African-Americans between 1970 and 2007. In 1970, 68.3% of African-American families were married-couple families; by 2007 this proportion had dropped to 44.7%.

By 2008 only 50.5% of all people aged 15 years and older lived with a spouse. (See Table 2.1.) In comparison to this average, 57.2% of all Asian-Americans and 54.6%

of all adult non-Hispanic whites lived with a spouse. In contrast, 45.9% of all Hispanic adults and only 30.9% of all African-American adults lived with a spouse.

Single-Parent Households

In 1970 there were 2.9 million families headed by a single mother, accounting 10% of all family households with children. (See Figure 2.5.) By 2007 there were 10 million single-mother families, 23% of all families with children. Single-father families increased from 341,000 in 1970 to 1.7 million in 2007, increasing from 1% to 5% of families with children. Most single-parent households in the United States continue to be headed by women. The proportion of family households headed by women with no husband present has grown among all racial and ethnic groups.

In 2007 Asian-Americans and non-Hispanic whites had the lowest proportion of family households headed by single women. Among Asian-American family households, 369,000 (11%) were headed by a female, and 7.4 million (13.5%) non-Hispanic white family households were headed by a female. (See Table 2.6.) Hispanic women were over one and a half times as likely to head households as were non-Hispanic white women, and single African-American women were more than three times as likely as white women to head households. In 2007 there were 2.4 million (24.1%) Hispanic families headed by a female and 4.1 million (43.7%) African-American families headed by a female. Hispanic and African-American female-headed families were also more likely to contain children than female-headed families of other races and ethnic groups. Two-thirds of Hispanic, female-headed families (67%) and African-American, female-headed families (64%) contained children under 18 years old, compared with 55% of non-Hispanic white and 41% of Asian-American female-headed families.

Living Arrangements of Children

Changes in the marital circumstances of adults naturally affect the living arrangements of children. High divorce rates, an increased delay in first marriages, and more out-of-wedlock births have resulted in fewer children living with two parents. In 2008, 51.8 million (69.9%) children under the age of 18 were living with two parents (not necessarily both birth parents), meaning that three out of 10 (30.1%) of children were living with either a single parent or no parents. (See Table 2.7.) African-American children and Hispanic children, to a lesser extent, have been particularly affected by these changes. (See Figure 2.6.)

The Census Bureau notes in *America's Families and Living Arrangements: 2006* (August 27, 2008, http://www.census.gov/population/www/socdemo/hh-fam/cps2006.html) that divorced single women are on average older

FIGURE 2.4

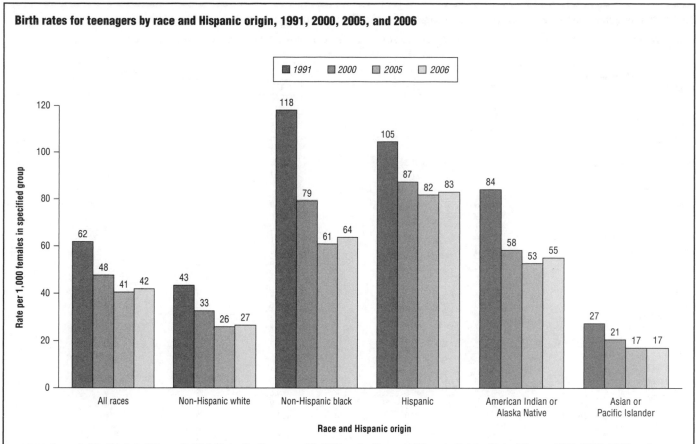

Birth rates for teenagers by race and Hispanic origin, 1991, 2000, 2005, and 2006

SOURCE: Joyce A. Martin et al., "Figure 3. Birth Rates for Teenagers 15–19 Years by Race and Hispanic Origin: United States, 1991, 2000, 2005, and 2006," in "Births: Final Data for 2006," *National Vital Statistics Reports*, vol. 57, no. 7, January 7, 2009, http://www.cdc.gov/nchs/data/nvsr/nvsr57/nvsr57_07.pdf (accessed December 2, 2009)

than never-married women and that they tend to have more education and higher incomes as well—leading their children to have an advantage over the children of never-married women. In 2006 African-American single mothers were the most likely to have never married (1.9 million, 63.1%) and the least likely to be divorced (595,000, 18.9%). Hispanic single mothers were more likely to have never married (908,000, 46.4%) than to be divorced (521,000, 26.6%). Non-Hispanic white single mothers were the most likely to be divorced (2.8 million, 42.2%) and only a third had never married (2.4 million, 35.8%). Asian-American single mothers were the least likely to have never married (63,000, 28.9%) but also less likely than non-Hispanic white women to be divorced (76,000, 34.7%), perhaps because of the high proportion of Asian-American single mothers who were separated but not yet divorced (60,000, 27.5%). As a group, then, the children of non-Hispanic white single mothers tend to have an economic advantage over the children of Hispanic or African-American single mothers, whereas the children of African-American single mothers, on average, tend to be the most economically disadvantaged of all minority groups.

AFRICAN-AMERICAN CHILDREN. In 2008, 4.3 million (37.5%) African-American children under the age of 18 lived with two parents, whereas 5.8 million (51.1%) lived with their mothers only. (See Table 2.7.) A higher proportion of African-American children lived with neither parent (919,000, or 8.1%) than lived with their fathers only (376,000, or 3.3%). The Census Bureau (September 21, 2006, http://www.census.gov/population/socdemo/hh-fam/ch3.pdf) reports that in 1970 the proportions of African-American children who lived with one parent (31.7%) or two parents (58.6%) were virtually the reverse of their living arrangements in 2008.

A large number of African-American children live with neither parent. A disproportionate number of them are in foster care. In *AFCARS Report* (October 2009, http://www.acf.hhs.gov/programs/cb/stats_research/afcars/tar/report16.pdf), the U.S. Department of Health and Human Services reports that on September 30, 2008, 31% of children in foster care were African-American. According to the Census Bureau, in "National Population Estimates—Characteristics" (December 22, 2009, http://www.census.gov/popest/national/asrh/natasrh.html/), if the number of African-American children in foster care

TABLE 2.5

Birth rates for young women aged 15–19 years, by age, race, and Hispanic origin, selected years 1991–2007

[Data for 2007 are based on a continuous file of records received from the states. Rates are per 1,000 women in the specified age and race and Hispanic origin group]

Age and race and—Hispanic origin of mother	Year				Percent change		
	2007	2006	2005	1991	2006–2007	2005–2007	1991–2005
10–14 years							
All races and origins[a]	0.6	0.6	0.7	1.4	0	−14	−50
Non-Hispanic white[b]	0.2	0.2	0.2	0.5	0	0	−60
Non-Hispanic black[b]	1.5	1.6	1.7	4.9	−6	−12	−65
American Indian or Alaska Native total[b, c]	0.9	0.9	0.9	1.6	0	0	−44
Asian or Pacific Islander total[b, c]	0.2	0.2	0.2	0.8	0	0	−75
Hispanic[d]	1.2	1.3	1.3	2.4	−8	−8	−46
15—19 years							
All races and origins[a]	42.5	41.9	40.5	61.8	1	5	−34
Non-Hispanic white[b]	27.2	26.6	25.9	43.4	2	5	−40
Non-Hispanic black[b]	64.3	63.7	60.9	118.2	1	6	−48
American Indian or Alaska Native total[b, c]	59.0	55.0	52.7	84.1	7	12	−37
Asian or Pacific Islander total[b, c]	17.3	17.0	17.0	27.3	2	2	−38
Hispanic[d]	81.7	83.0	81.7	104.6	−2	0	−22
15–17 years							
All races and origins[a]	22.2	22.0	21.4	38.6	1	4	−45
Non-Hispanic white[b]	11.8	11.8	11.5	23.6	0	3	−51
Non-Hispanic black[b]	35.8	36.2	34.9	86.1	−1	3	−59
American Indian or Alaska Native total[b, c]	31.7	30.7	30.5	51.9	3	4	−41
Asian or Pacific Islander total[b, c]	8.4	8.8	8.2	16.3	−5	2	−50
Hispanic[d]	47.8	47.9	48.5	69.2	0	−1	−30
18–19 years							
All races and origins[a]	73.9	73.0	69.9	94.0	1	6	−26
Non-Hispanic white[b]	50.5	49.3	48.0	70.6	2	5	−32
Non-Hispanic black[b]	109.3	108.4	103.0	162.2	1	6	−36
American Indian or Alaska Native total[b, c]	101.3	93.0	87.6	134.2	9	16	−35
Asian or Pacific Islander total[b, c]	30.7	29.5	30.1	42.2	4	2	−29
Hispanic[d]	137.1	139.7	134.6	155.5	−2	2	−13

[a]Includes origin not stated.
[b]Race and Hispanic origina are reported separately on birth certificates. Persons of Hispanic origin may be of any race. Race categories are consistent with the 1977 Office of Management and Budget (OMB) standards. In 2007, 27 states reported multiple-race data. The multiple-race data for these states were bridged to the single-race categories of the 1977 OMB standards for comparability with other states.
[c]Data for persons of Hispanic origin are included for this race group.
[d]Includes all persons of Hispanic origin of any race.

SOURCE: Brady E. Hamilton, Joyce A. Martin, and Stephanie J. Ventura, "Table 3. Birth Rates for Women Aged 15–19 Years, by Age and Race and Hispanic Origin of Mother: United States, Final 1991, 2005, and 2006, and Preliminary 2007; and Percentage of Change in Rates, 1991–2005, 2005–2007, and 2006–2007," in "Births: Preliminary Data for 2007," *National Vital Statistics Reports*, vol. 57, no. 12, March 18, 2009, http://www.cdc.gov/nchs/data/nvsr/nvsr57/nvsr57_12.pdf (accessed December 2, 2009)

reflected their proportion in the general population, only 7.5% of children in foster care would be African-American.

HISPANIC CHILDREN. In 2008 a higher proportion of Hispanic children (10.9 million, or 69.7%) than African-American children were living with two parents, but this proportion was still lower than the proportion of non-Hispanic white children who lived with two parents (32.7 million, or 77.8%). (See Table 2.7.) Almost 3.8 million (24%) Hispanic children lived with a single mother and 367,000 (2.3%) lived with a single father. This proportion was considerably higher than among non-Hispanic whites—6.5 million (15.5%) non-Hispanic white children lived with a single mother and 1.7 million (4.1%) lived with a single father—but well below the proportion of African-American children living with a single parent. Approximately 610,000 (3.9%) Hispanic children lived with neither parent. Some of these children likely lived with other relatives, such as grandparents, or with foster parents.

ASIAN-AMERICAN CHILDREN. The Asian-American family is typically a close-knit unit, and members are traditionally respectful of the authority of the elder members of the family. As the younger generation becomes more assimilated into American culture, however, the unchallenged role of elders may not remain as strong. Even so, family tradition and honor are still held in high regard. In 2008, 2.5 million (85.1%) Asian-American children were living with both parents, a proportion higher than that of whites. (See Table 2.7.) About 305,000 (10.2%) Asian-American children lived with a single mother and 68,000 (2.3%) lived with a single father. Approximately 72,000 (2.4%) lived with neither parent.

HOUSING GRANDCHILDREN. Because of many factors, including the high cost of housing, substance abuse, and the inability of some parents to care for their children, many children are living with their grandparents. It is especially common in the African-American community

FIGURE 2.5

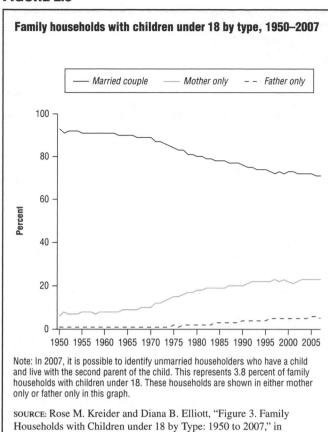

Family households with children under 18 by type, 1950–2007

— Married couple ⋯ Mother only – – Father only

Note: In 2007, it is possible to identify unmarried householders who have a child and live with the second parent of the child. This represents 3.8 percent of family households with children under 18. These households are shown in either mother only or father only in this graph.

SOURCE: Rose M. Kreider and Diana B. Elliott, "Figure 3. Family Households with Children under 18 by Type: 1950 to 2007," in *America's Families and Living Arrangements: 2007*, U.S. Census Bureau, September 2009, http://www.census.gov/population/www/socdemo/hh-fam/p20–561.pdf (accessed December 2, 2009)

for children to live with their grandparents, with or without one or both of their parents present. In *America's Families and Living Arrangements: 2008*, the Census Bureau states that in 2008, 571,000 (5%) African-American children lived in a grandparent's home without either of their parents present. The proportion of children who lived in a grandparent's home is significantly higher when children who lived with one or both parents in the home of a grandparent are added to this total. More than one out of 10 (1.3 million, or 11.3%) African-American children lived in the home of a grandparent, with or without a parent present, in 2008. In other words, more than one out of 10 African-American children were living in the home of a grandparent in 2008, and one out of 20 were being raised exclusively by a grandparent.

Only 235,000 (1.5%) Hispanic children lived in the home of a grandparent with neither parent present in 2008. This number jumps to 883,000 (5.6%) when children who lived with one or both parents in the home of a grandparent are added. Among Asian-Americans, 17,000 (0.5%) children under the age of 18 lived in the home of a grandparent with neither parent present in 2008. This number climbs to 122,000 (4.1%) when children who lived with one or both parents in the home of a grand-

parent are counted. Among non-Hispanic whites, only 617,000 (1.5%) children lived in the home of a grandparent with neither parent present in 2008; 1.9 million (4.4%) white children lived in the home of a grandparent with or without a parent present. African-American children, then, were the most likely to be living in the home of a grandparent, with or without a parent present, whereas Asian-American children were the least likely to be living with a grandparent. Children of all races and ethnicities were significantly more likely to be living with their mother in their grandparents' home rather than with the father in their grandparents' home.

HOMEOWNERSHIP

Owning one's home has traditionally been the American dream. However, for many Americans, especially minorities, purchasing a home can be difficult or impossible. The Census Bureau's Housing Vacancy Survey calculates homeownership rates by race and ethnicity of householder (the rate is computed by dividing the number of owner households by the total number of households). In 2008 the rate for non-Hispanic white householders who owned their home was 75%, for Asian or Pacific Islander householders it was 59.5%, for Native American or Alaskan Native householders it was 56.5%, for Hispanic householders it was 49.1%, and for African-American householders it was 47.4%. (See Table 2.8.)

Subprime Mortgage Crisis

Even though compared with non-Hispanic white homeownership the proportion of minority homeownership is low, these numbers actually reflect significant growth in the purchase of homes by minorities. Homeownership rates rose for all groups between 1994 and 2008, but they rose faster among minority groups. (See Table 2.8.) A number of factors were responsible for the growth of minority homeownership in the 1990s. The administration of President Bill Clinton (1946–) provided more lending opportunities for minorities by revitalizing the Federal Housing Administration and improving enforcement of the Community Reinvestment Act, which was passed by Congress in 1977 to encourage banks and other lending institutions to invest in the communities in which they operate. Furthermore, the U.S. Department of Housing and Urban Development pressured the Federal National Mortgage Association (Fannie Mae) and the Federal Home Loan Mortgage Corporation (Freddie Mac) to initiate programs to help minority and low-income borrowers in securing mortgages. Fannie Mae is a private company that was created by Congress in 1938 to improve the housing industry during the Great Depression. Its smaller counterpart, Freddie Mac, is a shareholder-owned company created by Congress in 1970 to support homeownership. Both Fannie Mae and Freddie Mac buy mortgages, package them into

TABLE 2.6

Families by number of own children under 18 years old, by race and Hispanic origin, 2000, 2005, and 2007

[As of March (72,025 represents 72,025,000). Based on Current Population Survey.]

Race, Hispanic origin, and year	Number of families (1,000)					Percent distribution				
	Total	No children	One child	Two children	Three or more children	Total	No children	One child	Two children	Three or more children
All families[a]										
2000	72,025	37,420	14,311	13,215	7,080	100	52	20	18	10
2005	76,858	40,647	15,069	13,741	7,400	100	53	20	18	10
2007, total	78,425	41,668	15,651	13,815	7,292	100	53	20	18	9
Married couple	58,945	32,787	10,127	10,497	5,534	100	56	17	18	9
Male householder[b]	5,063	3,049	1,243	553	218	100	60	25	11	4
Female householder[b]	14,416	5,832	4,280	2,765	1,540	100	40	30	19	11
White families[c]										
2000	60,251	32,144	11,496	10,918	5,693	100	53	19	18	9
2005	63,079	34,255	11,872	11,127	5,825	100	54	19	18	9
2007, total	64,091	34,993	12,231	11,115	5,752	100	55	19	17	9
Married couple	50,729	28,741	8,419	8,866	4,704	100	57	17	17	9
Male householder[b]	3,806	2,236	977	434	159	100	59	26	11	4
Female householder[b]	9,556	4,017	2,835	1,815	890	100	42	30	19	9
Black families[c]										
2000	8,664	3,882	2,101	1,624	1,058	100	45	24	19	12
2005	8,902	4,077	2,059	1,641	1,125	100	46	23	18	13
2007, total	9,272	4,215	2,282	1,686	1,089	100	45	25	18	12
Married couple	4,358	2,225	868	784	480	100	51	20	18	11
Male householder[b]	864	535	200	89	40	100	62	23	10	5
Female householder[b]	4,050	1,454	1,214	813	568	100	36	30	20	14
Asian families[c]										
2005	3,142	1,535	730	646	230	100	49	23	21	7
2007, total	3,346	1,676	722	721	226	100	50	22	22	7
Married couple	2,754	1,277	618	655	204	100	46	22	24	7
Male householder[b]	223	181	23	14	5	100	81	10	6	2
Female householder[b]	369	218	81	53	17	100	59	22	14	5
Hispanic families[d]										
2000	7,561	2,747	1,791	1,693	1,330	100	36	24	22	18
2005	9,521	3,528	2,130	2,163	1,699	100	37	22	23	18
2007, total	10,152	3,796	2,354	2,401	1,601	100	37	23	24	16
Married couple	6,762	2,370	1,451	1,768	1,173	100	35	21	26	17
Male householder[b]	945	627	172	94	51	100	66	18	10	5
Female householder[b]	2,445	798	731	539	377	100	33	30	22	15
Non-Hispanic white families[c, d]										
2005	54,257	30,965	9,924	9,151	4,217	100	57	18	17	8
2007, total	54,632	31,418	10,091	8,871	4,252	100	58	18	16	8
Married couple	44,327	26,478	7,076	7,188	3,584	100	60	16	16	8
Male householder[b]	2,921	1,641	820	345	114	100	56	28	12	4
Female householder[b]	7,384	3,298	2,195	1,337	553	100	45	30	18	7

[a]Includes other races not shown separately.
[b]No spouse present.
[c]Beginning with the 2003 Current Population Survey (CPS), respondents could choose more than one race. Beginning 2005, data represent persons who selected this race group only and exclude persons reporting more than one race. The CPS prior to 2003 only allowed respondents to report one race group.
[d]Hispanic persons may be any race.

SOURCE: "Table 63. Families by Number of Own Children under 18 Years Old: 2000 to 2007," in *Statistical Abstract of the United States: 2009*, 128th ed., U.S. Census Bureau, 2008, http://www.census.gov/compendia/statab/2009/2009edition.html (accessed December 3, 2009)

bonds backed by the government, and sell them to investors, thereby freeing up money for additional mortgage lending. Besides these efforts, minority homeownership was also helped by a considerably strong economy and a robust stock market during the 1990s and by low mortgage rates during the first few years of the first decade of the 21st century.

President George W. Bush (1946–) also made minority homeownership a priority of his administration. His administration announced several initiatives to help minority and low-income Americans buy homes. Arguing that many Americans could afford a monthly mortgage payment but lacked the funds for a down payment, in 2003 Bush signed the American Dream Downpayment Assistance Act, authorizing $200 million per year in down payment assistance to at least 40,000 low-income families.

However, expanding mortgages to low and moderate income borrowers at high interest rates—called the "subprime market"—seriously undermined the American economy by

TABLE 2.7

Living arrangements of children and marital status of parents, by age, race, and Hispanic origin, 2008

[Numbers in thousands]

	Total	Living with both parents		Living with mother only					Living with father only					Living with neither parent
		Married to each other	Not married to each other	Married spouse absent	Widowed	Divorced	Separated	Never married	Married spouse absent	Widowed	Divorced	Separated	Never married	No parent present
All children	74,104	49,426	2,360	821	642	5,578	2,611	7,236	149	128	1,315	413	610	2,818
Age of child														
Under 1 year	4,254	2,880	441	37	5	52	74	593	—	—	8	5	26	134
1–2 years	8,396	5,613	575	107	28	240	235	1,151	24	7	44	32	116	224
3–5 years	12,286	8,284	503	119	42	606	412	1,584	25	8	144	62	138	359
6–8 years	12,040	8,164	298	112	86	862	460	1,227	12	22	193	74	95	434
9–11 years	11,774	7,987	221	156	97	1,077	445	1,044	19	20	214	48	73	372
12–14 years	12,192	8,107	163	134	153	1,219	474	878	40	21	308	85	81	526
15–17 years	13,162	8,389	159	156	230	1,520	511	758	28	49	404	107	81	769
Race														
White alone	56,482	41,158	1,772	532	417	4,231	1,689	2,994	93	93	1,142	312	402	1,647
Black alone	11,342	3,911	345	189	176	978	741	3,707	33	24	87	76	156	919
Asian alone	2,980	2,489	46	57	26	80	46	96	11	7	25	5	20	72
All remaining single races and all race combinations	3,301	1,867	197	42	23	288	135	440	12	3	61	20	32	180
Race														
Hispanic	15,644	10,046	855	278	112	915	810	1,649	35	7	111	68	146	610
White alone, Non-Hispanic	42,051	31,700	1,012	278	314	3,388	974	1,568	67	86	1,043	247	274	1,101
All remaining single races and all race combinations, non-hispanic	16,408	7,679	493	265	216	1,274	826	4,019	47	34	160	98	190	1,107

Dash "—" represents or rounds to zero.

Notes: Excludes children in group quarters, and those who are a family reference person or spouse. Hispanics may be of any race.

SOURCE: Adapted from "Table C3. Living Arrangements of Children under 18 Years and Marital Status of Parents, by Age, Sex, Race, and Hispanic Origin and Selected Characteristics of the Child for All Children: 2008," in *America's Families and Living Arrangements: 2008*, U.S. Census Bureau, February 25, 2009, http://www.census.gov/population/www/socdemo/hh-fam/cps2008.html (accessed December 4, 2009)

FIGURE 2.6

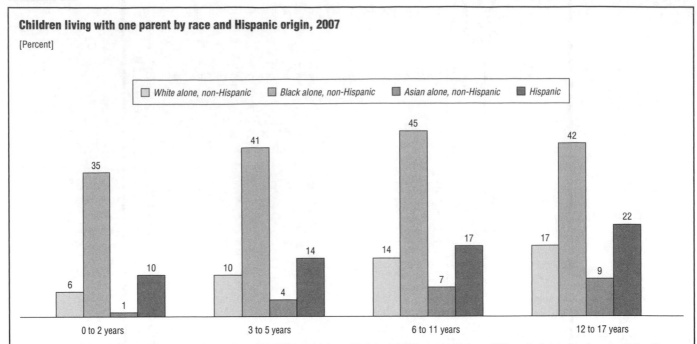

Children living with one parent by race and Hispanic origin, 2007

[Percent]

SOURCE: Rose M. Kreider and Diana B. Elliott, "Figure 11. Children Living with Sole Adult Parent by Race and Hispanic Origin," in *America's Families and Living Arrangements: 2007*, U.S. Census Bureau, September 2009, http://www.census.gov/population/www/socdemo/hh-fam/p20–561.pdf (accessed December 2, 2009)

the end of the first decade of the 21st century. Fannie Mae and Freddie Mac took on increasingly risky mortgage loans during this period. By 2007 an increasing number of borrowers were unable to meet their mortgage payments and home foreclosures skyrocketed. As foreclosures added to the available housing stock and credit tightened, home prices declined. Securities backed by subprime mortgages, which were widely owned by financial firms, lost their value, leading to a precipitous decline in the capital of banks as well as to a worldwide credit crisis and plunging the nation into a deep recession.

By mid-2008 Fannie Mae and Freddie Mac were nearly in ruins. In September 2008 the director of the Federal Housing Finance Agency announced that Fannie Mae and Freddie Mac, which together guaranteed about half of the U.S. mortgage market, would be put into a conservatorship of the agency. Dawn Kopecki and Alison Vekshin note in "Frank to Recommend

Replacing Fannie Mae, Freddie Mac" (*Bloomberg News*, January 22, 2010) that the companies, which were essentially bailed-out by the federal government, received $110.6 billion in taxpayer-funded aid between 2008 and 2009.

In January 2010 the U.S. representative Barney Frank (1940–; D-MA), the chairperson of the House Financial Services Committee, announced that he would push to abolish Fannie Mae and Freddie Mac and put in place a new mortgage system. According to Kopecki and Vekshin, Frank stated, "We're going to look at the whole question of housing finance. . . . I don't know anybody who thinks Fannie and Freddie should continue." At the same time, Frank suggested a "subsidy for affordability" that could replace the mandate to increase minority homeownership in the future. Subprime mortgage lending to low-income people, including minorities, had seemingly come to an end as a result of the economic crisis.

TABLE 2.8

Homeownership rates by race and Hispanic origin of householder, 1994–2008

	1994	1995	1996ᵃ	1997	1998	1999	2000	2001	2002	2002	2003	2004	2005	2006	2007	2008
U.S. total	**64.0**	**64.7**	**65.4**	**65.7**	**66.3**	**66.8**	**67.4**	**67.8**	**67.9**	**67.9**	**68.3**	**69.0**	**68.9**	**68.8**	**68.1**	**67.8**
White, total	67.7	68.7	69.1	69.3	70.0	70.5	71.1	71.6	71.8	71.7	72.1	72.8	72.7	72.6	72.0	71.7
Non-Hispanic white	70.0	70.9	71.7	72.0	72.6	73.2	73.8	74.3	74.5	74.7	75.4	76.0	75.8	75.8	75.2	75.0
Black, total	42.3	42.7	44.1	44.8	45.6	46.3	47.2	47.7	47.3	47.4	48.1	49.1	48.2	47.9	47.2	47.4
All other races, total	47.7	47.2	51.0	52.5	53.0	53.7	53.5	54.2	54.7	54.5	56.0	58.6	59.2	59.9	59.2	58.5
American Indian or Alaskan Native	51.7	55.8	51.6	51.7	54.3	56.1	56.2	55.4	54.6	54.0	54.3	55.6	58.2	58.2	56.9	56.5
Asian or Native Hawaiian/Pacific Islander	51.3	50.8	50.8	52.8	52.6	53.1	52.8	53.9	54.7	54.6	56.3	59.8	60.1	60.8	60.0	59.5
Other	36.1	37.4	NA	NA	NA	NA	NA	NA	NA	NA	NA	NA	NA	NA	NA	NA
Hispanic or Latino	41.2	42.1	42.8	43.3	44.7	45.5	46.3	47.3	48.2	47.0	46.7	48.1	49.5	49.7	49.7	49.1
Non-Hispanic	65.9	66.7	67.4	67.8	68.3	68.9	69.5	69.9	70.0	70.2	70.8	71.5	71.2	71.2	70.5	70.3

ᵃBeginning in 1996 to 2002, those answering 'other' for race were allocated to one of the 4 race categories—white, black, American Indian, aleut or eskimo (one category), or Asian or Native Hawaiian.
ᵇAsian, Native Hawaiian or other Pacific Islander, American Indian or Alaska Native (only one race reported) and two or more races.
NA - Not Applicable.

SOURCE: "Table 22. Homeownership Rates by Race and Ethnicity of Householder: 1994 to 2008," in *Housing Vacancies and Homeownership Annual Statistics: 2008*, U.S. Census Bureau, March 5, 2009, www.census.gov/hhes/www/housing/hvs/annual08/ann08t22.xls (accessed December 4, 2009)

CHAPTER 3
EDUCATION

In *The Condition of Education, 2005* (June 2005, http://nces.ed.gov/pubs2005/2005094.pdf), the National Center for Education Statistics (NCES) reports that two factors—rising immigration and the baby boom echo—boosted public school enrollment from the latter part of the 1980s to the first few years of the first decade of the 21st century. According to Michael Planty et al., in *The Condition of Education, 2009* (June 2009, http://nces.ed.gov/pubs2009/2009081.pdf), enrollment was projected to reach 50 million in 2010 and then set new public-school enrollment records each year through 2018, with a projected enrollment of 53.9 million in that year.

Along with this increase in enrollment came an increase in the proportion of public school students who were considered to be part of a minority group, due largely to the growth in the Hispanic public school population. In 2007, 44.1% of public school students enrolled in kindergarten through 12th grade belonged to a minority group. (See Table 3.1.) Hispanics (20.9%) and African-Americans (15.3%) accounted for the largest number of minority students in public schools. These figures represented a significant increase since 1972, when white students made up 77.8% and minority students only 22.2% of the public school population. However, minority enrollment in public schools differed from region to region. In 2007 the Midwest had the lowest proportion of minority students (28%) and the West had the highest (56.6%). (See Figure 3.1.) Nearly four out of 10 (39.1%) students in the West were Hispanic, whereas nearly a quarter (24.3%) of students in the South were African-American.

RISK FACTORS IN EDUCATION

In the United States, education is often viewed as a way out of poverty to a better life. Many observers believe education is the key to narrowing the economic gap between the races. Even though many individual minority students strive for, and achieve, great educational success, on average minority students perform less well than white students in school and are generally more likely than their white counterparts to drop out of school. Asian-Americans are the exception to this rule. Many Asian-American students accomplish stunning academic achievements. Educators point with pride to these high-achieving students, who have often overcome both language and cultural barriers. Why are some groups more at risk of failure, and other groups more likely to succeed in school?

The Early Childhood Longitudinal Study, Birth Cohort, a study by the NCES, attempts to begin answering this question by assessing preschoolers' readiness for school. The study collected information on a cohort (a group of individuals with several characteristics in common) of children born in 2001 and followed them through 2007, focusing on the children's early development and how parents prepared their children for school. Even though at nine months of age little variation in mental and motor skills was found by race or ethnic group, several demographic characteristics were related to the likelihood of families engaging in activities that help prepare children for school. These activities include reading or telling children stories, singing to them, taking them on errands, playing peek-a-boo, and allowing them to play outside. The NCES indicates in *Condition of Education, 2005* that in 2001–02 Asian-American families were more likely than other minority groups to read to their children (26%), tell them stories (25%), and play peek-a-boo (73%), although they were less likely to facilitate outside playing (43%) and significantly less likely to take their children on errands (38%) than were other minority families.

In contrast, both African-American and Hispanic families were less likely to read to (23% and 21%, respectively) and tell their children stories (24% and 21%, respectively), and more likely to sing to them (73% and 70%, respectively) and play peek-a-boo (61% and 64%,

TABLE 3.1

Number and percentage distribution of the race and Hispanic origin of public school students in kindergarten through 12th grade, 1972–2007

October of year	Total (in thousands)	White	Other racial/ethnic groups							
			Total	Black	Hispanic	Asian	Pacific Islander	American Indian/ Alaska Native	More than one race	Other
1972	45,343	77.8	22.2	14.8	6.0	—	—	—	—	1.4
1973	44,945	78.1	21.9	14.7	5.7	—	—	—	—	1.4
1974	44,958	76.8	23.2	15.4	6.3	—	—	—	—	1.5
1975	44,524	76.2	23.8	15.4	6.7	—	—	—	—	1.7
1976	44,264	76.2	23.8	15.5	6.5	—	—	—	—	1.7
1977	43,154	76.1	23.9	15.8	6.2	—	—	—	—	1.9
1978	42,123	75.5	24.5	16.0	6.5	—	—	—	—	2.1
1979	—	—	—	—	—	—	—	—	—	—
1980	—	—	—	—	—	—	—	—	—	—
1981	41,022	72.4	27.6	16.0	8.7	—	—	—	—	2.9
1982	40,259	71.9	28.1	16.0	8.9	—	—	—	—	3.2
1983	39,806	71.3	28.7	16.1	9.2	—	—	—	—	3.4
1984	39,901	71.7	28.3	16.1	8.5	—	—	—	—	3.6
1985	39,890	69.6	30.4	16.8	10.1	—	—	—	—	3.5
1986	40,344	69.1	30.9	16.6	10.8	—	—	—	—	3.6
1987	40,887	68.5	31.5	16.6	10.8	—	—	—	—	4.0
1988	41,045	68.3	31.7	16.5	11.0	—	—	—	—	4.2
1989	41,259	68.0	32.0	16.6	11.4	3.0*	(*)	0.9	—	0.1
1990	41,862	67.6	32.4	16.5	11.7	3.0*	(*)	0.9	—	0.3
1991	42,366	67.1	32.9	16.8	11.8	3.2*		0.8	—	0.2
1992	42,943	66.8	33.2	16.9	12.0	3.3*	(*)	0.8	—	0.2
1993	43,848	67.0	33.0	16.6	12.1	3.3*	(*)	0.8	—	0.2
1994	44,948	65.8	34.2	16.7	13.7	2.5*	(*)	0.8	—	0.5
1995	45,308	65.5	34.5	16.9	14.1	2.3*	(*)	0.6	—	0.6
1996	45,619	63.7	36.3	16.6	14.5	4.1*	(*)	1.2	—	—
1997	47,212	63.0	37.0	16.9	14.9	3.9*	(*)	1.2	—	—
1998	46,552	62.4	37.6	17.2	15.4	4.0*	(*)	1.1	—	—
1999	47,069	61.9	38.1	16.5	16.2	4.5*	(*)	1.0	—	—
2000	46,981	61.3	38.7	16.6	16.6	4.2*	(*)	1.3	—	—
2001	47,689	61.3	38.7	16.5	16.6	4.3*	(*)	1.3	—	—
2002	47,973	60.7	39.3	16.5	17.6	4.0*	(*)	1.2	—	—
2003	48,087	58.3	41.7	16.1	18.6	3.7*	0.3	0.6	2.4	—
2004	48,081	57.4	42.6	16.0	19.3	3.9*	0.2	0.8	2.4	—
2005	48,356	57.6	42.4	15.6	19.7	3.7*	0.2	0.7	2.5	—
2006	48,590	56.9	43.1	15.6	20.2	3.8*	0.2	0.7	2.7	—
2007	48,512	55.9	44.1	15.3	20.9	4.1*	0.3	0.8	2.6	—

—Not available.

*From 1989 through 2002, data on Asian and Pacific Islander students were not reported separately; therefore, Pacific Islander students are included with Asian students during this period.

Note: Estimates include all public school students enrolled in kindergarten through 12th grade. Race categories exclude persons of Hispanic ethnicity. Over time, the Current Population Survey (CPS) has had different response options for race/ethnicity.

SOURCE: Michael Planty et al., "Table A-7-1.Number and Percentage Distribution of the Race/Ethnicity of Public School Students Enrolled in Kindergarten through 12th Grade: October 1972–October 2007," in *The Condition of Education 2009*, U.S. Department of Education, National Center for Education Statistics, June 2009, http://nces.ed.gov/pubs2009/2009081.pdf (accessed December 9, 2009)

respectively) than were non-Hispanic white families in the period from 2001 to 2002. This may be partly because poor families are much less likely to read to their children or tell them stories than are nonpoor families, and African-American and Hispanic families are disproportionately poor. African-American families, non-Hispanic white families, and Hispanic families were about equally likely to take their children on errands and facilitate outside playing.

In its third wave, the Early Childhood Longitudinal Study, Birth Cohort, collected more specific information about the readiness of preschoolers for school. Researchers assessed children between the ages of 48 and 57 months. In *Preschool: First Findings from the Preschool Follow-up of the Early Childhood Longitudinal Study, Birth*

Cohort (October 2007, http://nces.ed.gov/pubs2008/2008025.pdf), Jodi Jacobson Chernoff et al. note that children's language knowledge—or ability to understand words or retell a story—varied by race and ethnicity, with non-Hispanic white children (9.2) scoring the highest, followed by non-Hispanic African-American children (8), Asian-American children (7.9), Native American and Alaskan Native children (7.9), and Hispanic children (7.4). Overall literacy, such as letter recognition and understanding aspects of reading such as reading from left to right, also varied by race and ethnicity. Non-Hispanic white children (14.2) scored high on the overall literacy score, although Asian-American children (17.5) scored higher, followed by non-Hispanic African-American children (12), Hispanic children (10.7), and Native American and Alaskan Native children (9.6). Asian-American

FIGURE 3.1

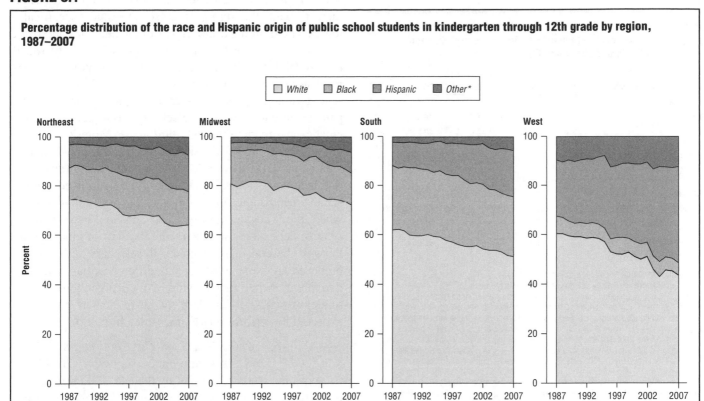

Percentage distribution of the race and Hispanic origin of public school students in kindergarten through 12th grade by region, 1987–2007

☐ White ☐ Black ☐ Hispanic ■ Other*

Northeast   Midwest   South   West

Percent

Year   Year   Year   Year

*"Other" includes all students who identified themselves as being Asian, Hawaiian, American Indian, or two or more races.
Note: Estimates include all public school students enrolled in kindergarten through 12th grade. Race categories exclude persons of Hispanic ethnicity. Over time, the Current Population Survey (CPS) has had different response options for race/ethnicity.

SOURCE: Michael Planty et al., "Figure 7-2. Percentage Distribution of the Race/Ethnicity of Public School Students Enrolled in Kindergarten through 12th Grade, by Region: October 1987–October 2007," in *The Condition of Education 2009*, U.S. Department of Education, National Center for Education Statistics, June 2009, http://nces.ed.gov/pubs2009/2009081.pdf (accessed December 9, 2009)

preschoolers (26.3) scored the highest on mathematics knowledge and skills, followed by non-Hispanic white preschoolers (24.2), non-Hispanic African-American preschoolers (20.6), Hispanic preschoolers (20.1), and Native American and Alaskan Native preschoolers (17.6). Therefore, overall, Native American and Alaskan Native, Hispanic, and non-Hispanic African-American children were less prepared for school than were either non-Hispanic white or Asian-American children.

Kristin Denton Flanagan and Cameron McPhee note in *The Children Born in 2001 at Kindergarten Entry: First Findings from the Kindergarten Data Collections of the Early Childhood Longitudinal Study, Birth Cohort* (October 2009, http://nces.ed.gov/pubs2010/2010005.pdf) that by the time these children entered school, the average early reading scale scores varied considerably by race and ethnicity. Asian-American children (51.9) scored the highest, followed by non-Hispanic white children (46.4), non-Hispanic African-American children (41.1), Hispanic children (39.4), and Native American and Alaskan Native children (37.1). Mathematics scale scores also varied by race and ethnic group, although less dramatically. Asian-American children (48.7) scored the highest

and non-Hispanic white children (46.5) scored the second highest. Non-Hispanic African-American children (40.4), Hispanic children (40.3), and Native American and Alaskan Native children (37.3) scored substantially lower.

Preprimary Education

One activity that can help preschoolers prepare for elementary school is attending center-based early childhood programs. Angelina KewalRamani et al. state in *Status and Trends in the Education of Racial and Ethnic Minorities* (September 2007, http://nces.ed.gov/pubs2007/2007039.pdf) that "research has suggested that intensive, high-quality preschool programs can have positive effects on the cognitive and academic development of low-income minority children, both in the short- and long-term." In 2005, 57.2% of all three- to five-year-olds who were not yet enrolled in kindergarten were enrolled in center-based preschools. (See Table 3.2.) However, non-poor children were more likely than poor children to be enrolled in these programs (59.9% and 47.2%, respectively). Among nonpoor preschoolers, Asian and Pacific Islander preschoolers were the most likely to be enrolled (73.4%), followed by African-American preschoolers

TABLE 3.2

Percentage of 3- to 5-year-olds enrolled in center-based preprimary programs, by poverty status, race and Hispanic origin, 1995, 1999, 2001, and 2005

Poverty status and race/ethnicity	1995	1999	2001	2005
Total	55.1	59.7	56.4	57.2
Poor*	45.6	51.9	46.4	47.2
White	43.6	42.9	46.2	44.6
Black	55.3	72.7	57.7	64.8
Hispanic	32.0	41.7	35.4	36.0
Asian/Pacific Islander	‡	‡	‡	‡
American Indian/Alaska Native	‡	‡	‡	‡
Nonpoor*	58.5	62.2	59.6	59.9
White	59.6	62.7	61.1	61.0
Black	65.4	73.7	68.0	67.8
Hispanic	42.3	46.5	43.0	47.8
Asian/Pacific Islander	58.1	64.2	75.9	73.4
American Indian/Alaska Native	‡	‡	‡	53.1

‡Reporting standards not met. Sample size too small.
*Total includes race/ethnicity categories not separately shown.
Note: Estimates are based on children who have yet to enter kindergarten. Center-based programs include day care centers, Head Start program, preschool, prekindergarten, and other early childhood programs. "Poor" is defined to include those families below the poverty threshold; "nonpoor" is defined as 100 percent or more than the poverty threshold. As the 2005 poverty thresholds were not yet available at the time this table was prepared, an approximation was used for analyses using National Household Education Survey (NHES):2005 data. Race categories exclude persons of Hispanic origin.

SOURCE: Angelina KewalRamani et al., "Table 6. Percentage of 3- to 5-Year-Olds Enrolled in Center-Based Preprimary Programs, by Poverty Status and Race/Ethnicity: Selected Years, 1995–2005," in *Status and Trends in the Education of Racial and Ethnic Minorities*, U.S. Department of Education, National Center for Education Statistics, Institute of Education Sciences, September 2007, http://nces.ed.gov/pubs2007/2007039.pdf (accessed December 9, 2009)

(67.8%), white preschoolers (61%), Native American and Alaskan Native preschoolers (53.1%), and Hispanic students (47.8%). Among poor preschoolers, African-American children were the most likely to be enrolled (64.8%), followed by white students (44.6%) and Hispanic students (36%).

In *Digest of Education Statistics, 2008* (March 2009, http://nces.ed.gov/pubs2009/2009020.pdf), Thomas D. Snyder, Sally A. Dillow, and Charlene M. Hoffman report data on the distribution of children in low-, medium-, and high-quality child care arrangements. In the 2005–06 school year Hispanic children were the most likely to be enrolled in a high-quality center-based program (39.8%), followed by non-Hispanic whites (36.1%) and Asian-Americans (32%). (See Table 3.3.) African-American children were the most likely to be enrolled in a low-quality center-based program (14.7%). Among children in home-based care provided by a relative or a nonrelative, Hispanic children (62.5%) and African-American children (52.8%) were significantly more likely than non-Hispanic white children (29.9%) to be enrolled in low-quality care.

Educational Progress

The Early Childhood Longitudinal Study, Kindergarten Class of 1998–99, another research study conducted by the NCES, collected information on a cohort of children who began kindergarten in the fall of 1998 and followed them through the spring of 2004. The study specifically looked at children's achievement in mathematics and reading as they progressed through school. The study found that several family risk factors (such as poverty, non-English primary home language, mother's lack of a high school diploma/general education diploma, or a single-parent household) were inversely related to gains in mathematics and reading through third grade. Minority children had higher numbers of risk factors than did non-Hispanic white children. However, even when controlling for family risk factors, African-American children had lower average achievement scores than other racial and ethnic groups when they began kindergarten, and the gap in these achievement scores widened from the start of kindergarten through the end of third grade. Researchers have not yet proposed an explanation for this difference, but it may be due to entrenched racism within American culture and the school system—if children of a particular group are expected to perform poorly, they may in fact do so.

According to the NCES, in *The Condition of Education, 2004* (June 2004, http://nces.ed.gov/pubs2004/2004077.pdf), the study found that by the end of third grade the mean (average) scale scores for reading achievement were highest for non-Hispanic whites (112) and Asians and Pacific Islanders (111), followed by Hispanics (105) and African-Americans (98). The same pattern held true in mathematics. The mean scale scores for mathematics achievement were highest for non-Hispanic whites (89) and Asians and Pacific Islanders (88), followed by Hispanics (82) and African-Americans (73). From the start of kindergarten through third grade, non-Hispanic whites, Asians and Pacific Islanders, and Hispanics made similar gains in both reading and mathematics; however, African-Americans lagged behind in both areas.

READING PERFORMANCE. The ability to read is fundamental to most aspects of education. When students cannot read well, they usually cannot succeed in other subject areas and will eventually have additional problems in a society requiring increasingly sophisticated job skills.

The National Assessment of Educational Progress (NAEP) measures reading and mathematics proficiency on a scale from 0 to 500. The NAEP finds that the average reading scale scores of students in fourth, eighth, and 12th grades vary by race and ethnicity, with non-Hispanic white and Asian-American students scoring higher than other groups. In 2007, fourth-grade Asian-American (232) and non-Hispanic white (231) students scored significantly higher than Hispanic (205), African-American (203), and Native Americans and Alaskan Native (203) students. (See Table 3.4.) This difference persisted as children moved through higher grades in school.

SCIENCE AND MATHEMATICS PERFORMANCE. In a time when science and technology are considered vital

TABLE 3.3

Percentage distribution of quality rating of child care arrangements of children at about 4 years of age, by type of arrangement and selected child and family characteristics, 2005–06

Quality rating of primary type of child care arrangement[a]

Selected characteristic	Home-based relative and nonrelative care[b,c] — Low	Medium	High	Head Start and other center-based programs[d] — Low	Medium	High	All center-based programs — Head Start[d] — Low	Medium	High	Center-based care other than Head Start[d,e] — Low	Medium	High
Total	42.6 (4.01)	47.9 (4.22)	9.5 (2.37)	9.5 (1.40)	55.8 (2.43)	34.7 (2.57)	3.2 (0.78)	56.7 (3.27)	40.1 (3.33)	11.6 (1.74)	55.5 (3.04)	32.9 (3.09)
Sex of child												
Male	45.5 (5.48)	44.1 (5.58)	10.4 (3.88)	6.4 (1.48)	53.3 (3.33)	40.3 (3.29)	2.2 (0.96)	56.5 (3.93)	41.3 (3.93)	7.9 (1.83)	52.2 (4.05)	39.9 (4.07)
Female	39.3 (5.23)	52.2 (5.83)	8.5 (2.45)	12.7 (2.32)	58.2 (3.32)	29.1 (3.23)	4.3 (1.14)	56.9 (4.83)	38.8 (4.88)	15.2 (2.83)	58.6 (3.98)	26.2 (3.70)
Race/ethnicity of child												
White	29.9 (4.72)	55.3 (5.34)	14.9 (4.09)	9.3 (1.79)	54.6 (3.76)	36.1 (3.68)	4.0 (1.92)	47.6 (8.27)	48.5 (8.28)	10.2 (1.94)	55.8 (3.99)	34.1 (3.82)
Black	52.8 (8.64)	47.2 (8.64)	‡ (†)	14.7 (3.72)	59.9 (4.52)	25.4 (3.89)	6.8 (1.57)	67.1 (4.41)	26.1 (4.61)	20.7 (6.22)	54.4 (6.72)	24.8 (4.23)
Hispanic	62.5 (8.53)	33.4 (8.03)	4.1 (2.31)	7.2 (2.79)	52.9 (4.25)	39.8 (4.77)	‡ (†)	56.2 (5.54)	43.4 (5.47)	11.7 (4.47)	50.8 (6.82)	37.6 (7.31)
Asian	‡ (†)	‡ (†)	‡ (†)	7.2 (3.52)	60.8 (3.13)	32.0 (7.99)	‡ (†)	‡ (†)	‡ (†)	7.8 (3.78)	63.7 (8.19)	28.6 (7.83)
Pacific Islander	‡ (†)	‡ (†)	‡ (†)	‡ (†)	‡ (†)	‡ (†)	‡ (†)	‡ (†)	‡ (†)	‡ (†)	‡ (†)	‡ (†)
American Indian/Alaska Native	‡ (†)	‡ (†)	‡ (†)	‡ (†)	73.5 (7.69)	23.5 (7.02)	‡ (†)	‡ (†)	‡ (†)	‡ (†)	67.3 (9.09)	20.4 (7.10)
More than one race	‡ (†)	‡ (†)	‡ (†)	8.6 (4.86)	65.7 (7.78)	25.7 (6.77)	‡ (†)	‡ (†)	‡ (†)	12.3 (6.65)	—	—
Age of child												
Less than 48 months	31.8 (7.35)	64.3 (7.24)	‡ (†)	10.2 (2.45)	56.8 (5.35)	33.0 (5.47)	‡ (†)	62.3 (8.56)	35.3 (8.44)	13.1 (3.62)	54.8 (7.33)	32.1 (7.16)
48 to 52 months	40.3 (6.19)	47.2 (6.86)	12.5 (4.19)	12.3 (2.58)	54.8 (4.11)	32.9 (3.71)	0.9 (0.49)	55.6 (6.30)	43.5 (6.33)	16.1 (3.22)	54.6 (4.99)	29.3 (4.36)
53 to 57 months	46.6 (6.49)	42.5 (6.69)	10.9 (3.14)	7.3 (1.66)	56.5 (3.22)	36.2 (3.36)	3.8 (1.34)	57.5 (4.02)	38.7 (4.06)	8.4 (2.07)	56.2 (4.22)	35.4 (4.29)
58 or more months	‡ (†)	‡ (†)	‡ (†)	7.2 (3.64)	55.0 (4.80)	37.8 (4.55)	14.8 (9.46)	46.1 (13.15)	39.1 (11.33)	5.0 (3.81)	57.5 (5.77)	37.5 (5.88)
Mother's employment status												
Full-time (35 hours or more)	36.6 (4.34)	56.6 (4.50)	6.9 (2.52)	14.9 (2.83)	55.3 (3.72)	29.8 (3.66)	4.9 (1.16)	47.7 (5.16)	47.4 (5.53)	17.7 (3.45)	57.4 (4.44)	25.0 (4.44)
Part-time (less than 35 hours)	48.9 (7.47)	35.1 (7.08)	16.0 (4.61)	5.7 (1.80)	60.9 (4.64)	33.4 (4.72)	3.2 (2.59)	59.8 (8.26)	37.0 (7.97)	6.5 (2.17)	61.2 (6.14)	32.3 (5.97)
Looking for work	‡ (†)	‡ (†)	‡ (†)	14.0 (5.16)	53.7 (6.25)	32.4 (6.61)	‡ (†)	73.4 (8.27)	24.2 (8.12)	22.4 (8.52)	39.2 (8.58)	38.4 (9.45)
Not in labor force	‡ (†)	‡ (†)	‡ (†)	3.5 (1.31)	53.3 (4.80)	43.2 (4.98)	1.7 (1.23)	58.9 (5.58)	39.4 (5.60)	4.2 (1.73)	51.2 (6.71)	44.7 (7.02)
No mother in household	‡ (†)	‡ (†)	‡ (†)	# (†)	50.6 (39.00)	49.4 (39.00)	‡ (†)	‡ (†)	‡ (†)	‡ (†)	‡ (†)	‡ (†)
Parents' highest level of education												
Less than high school	‡ (†)	‡ (†)	‡ (†)	12.5 (4.50)	59.1 (6.95)	28.3 (5.83)	‡ (†)	56.9 (7.43)	40.9 (7.36)	20.6 (7.95)	60.9 (10.59)	18.5 (7.52)
High school completion	63.0 (5.71)	31.8 (5.75)	5.1 (2.57)	6.0 (1.69)	49.9 (3.34)	44.1 (3.92)	4.9 (1.33)	54.9 (5.91)	40.3 (6.01)	6.7 (2.39)	47.2 (4.45)	46.1 (5.29)
Some college/vocational	40.1 (6.76)	52.3 (6.89)	7.6 (3.54)	16.1 (2.95)	58.8 (3.05)	25.1 (2.82)	2.8 (1.51)	60.4 (4.54)	36.8 (4.41)	22.4 (3.80)	58.1 (4.04)	19.5 (3.54)
Bachelor's degree	29.9 (8.51)	62.1 (8.63)	8.0 (4.86)	6.7 (2.43)	59.8 (6.64)	33.4 (6.78)	‡ (†)	‡ (†)	‡ (†)	7.3 (2.64)	60.2 (7.18)	32.6 (7.32)
Any graduate education	10.3 (5.73)	61.3 (8.63)	28.3 (7.99)	5.0 (2.52)	53.6 (7.44)	41.4 (7.48)	‡ (†)	‡ (†)	‡ (†)	5.3 (2.66)	54.5 (7.47)	40.2 (7.47)

TABLE 3.3

Percentage distribution of quality rating of child care arrangements of children at about 4 years of age, by type of arrangement and selected child and family characteristics, 2005–06 [CONTINUED]

	Quality rating of primary type of child care arrangement[a]											
	Home-based relative and nonrelative care[b,c]			Head Start and other center-based programs[d]			All center-based programs					
							Head Start[d]			Center-based care other than Head Start[d,e]		
Selected characteristic	Low	Medium	High	Low	Medium	High	Low	Medium	High	Low	Medium	High
Poverty status[f]												
Below poverty threshold	68.1 (6.76)	28.3 (6.86)	3.6 (2.03)	9.2 (2.38)	59.1 (3.17)	31.7 (3.47)	2.6 (1.10)	57.9 (4.15)	39.6 (4.35)	15.4 (4.16)	60.2 (5.63)	24.4 (5.10)
At or above poverty threshold	35.8 (4.32)	53.2 (4.79)	11.1 (2.70)	9.6 (1.46)	54.7 (3.18)	35.7 (3.29)	3.8 (1.35)	55.5 (4.74)	40.6 (4.69)	10.8 (1.73)	54.5 (3.61)	34.7 (3.72)
Socioeconomic status[g]												
Lowest 20 percent	71.2 (7.12)	26.4 (7.02)	2.4 (1.80)	6.7 (2.19)	58.7 (4.31)	34.7 (4.41)	3.4 (1.25)	53.7 (5.22)	42.9 (5.54)	9.8 (3.99)	63.5 (7.31)	26.6 (6.57)
Middle 60 percent	43.3 (5.26)	49.7 (5.50)	7.0 (2.57)	11.3 (1.84)	56.3 (2.70)	32.4 (2.70)	3.2 (1.24)	59.3 (4.14)	37.5 (4.11)	14.1 (2.28)	55.2 (3.35)	30.7 (3.36)
Highest 20 percent	7.8 (4.79)	66.3 (7.41)	25.9 (6.85)	7.3 (2.54)	52.2 (6.28)	40.5 (6.20)	‡	‡ (†)	‡ (†)	7.5 (2.61)	52.7 (6.34)	39.8 (6.21)

†Not applicable.

#Rounds to zero.

‡Reporting standards not met.

[a]Primary type of care arrangement is the type of nonparental care in which the child spent the most hours.

[b]Care provider in the child's home or in another private home by a relative (excluding parents) or by a person unrelated to the child.

[c]Quality rating based on the Family Day Care Rating Scale (FDCRS). Low quality = score of 1 but less than 3. Medium quality = score of 3 but less than 5. High quality = score of 5 to 7.

[d]Quality rating based on the Early Childhood Environment Rating Scale (ECERS). Low quality = score of 1 but less than 3. Medium quality = score of 3 but less than 5. High quality = score of 5 to 7.

[e]Care provided in places such as early learning centers, nursery schools, and preschools, not classified as Head Start.

[f]Poverty status based on Census Bureau guidelines from 2002, which identify a dollar amount determined to meet a household's needs, given its size and composition. In 2002, a family of four was considered to live below the poverty threshold if its income was less than or equal to $18,392.

[g]Socioeconomic status (SES) was measured by a composite score on parental education and occupations, and family income.

Note: Estimates pertain to children assessed between 44 months and 65 months of age. Rating is for child's primary type of care arrangement, which was the type of nonparental care in which the child spent the most hours. Children who were primarily cared for by parents or in multiple arrangements are not included in this table. Ratings of care arrangement quality using both the FDCRS and ECERS scales were based on interviewer observations of children's interactions with adults and peers, children's exposure to materials and activities, the extent to which and the manner in which routine care needs were met, and the furnishings and displays in the classroom. The FDCRS and ECERS metrics are designed to be equivalent. Race categories exclude persons of Hispanic ethnicity. Detail may not sum to totals because of rounding and suppression of cells that do not meet standards. Standard errors appear in parentheses.

SOURCE: Thomas D. Snyder, Sally A. Dillow, and Charlene M. Hoffman, "Table 47. Percentage Distribution of Quality Rating of Child Care Arrangements of Children at about 4 Years of Age, by Type of Arrangement and Selected Child and Family Characteristics: 2005–06," in *Digest of Education Statistics, 2008*, U.S. Department of Education, National Center for Education Statistics, March 2009, http://nces.ed.gov/programs/digest/d08/tables/dt08_047.asp (accessed December 9, 2009)

TABLE 3.4

Average reading scale scores by sex, grade, race and Hispanic origin, selected years 1992–2007

Grade, race/ethnicity, and percentile	1992*	1994*	1998	2000	2002	2003	2005 Total	2005 Male	2005 Female	2007 Total	2007 Male	2007 Female
1	2	3	4	5	6	7	8	9	10	11	12	13
All students												
4th grade	217	214	215	213	219	218	219	216	222	221	218	224
8th grade	260	260	263	—	264	263	262	257	267	263	258	268
12th grade	292	287	290	—	287	—	286	279	292	—	—	—
Race/ethnicity												
4th grade												
White	224	224	225	224	229	229	229	226	232	231	228	234
Black	192	185	193	190	199	198	200	195	205	203	199	208
Hispanic	197	188	193	190	201	200	203	200	205	205	202	208
Asian/Pacific Islander	216	220	215	225	224	226	229	225	232	232	228	236
American Indian/Alaska Native	‡	211	‡	214	207	202	204	199	209	203	200	206
8th grade												
White	267	267	270	—	272	272	271	266	277	272	267	277
Black	237	236	244	—	245	244	243	237	249	245	238	251
Hispanic	241	243	243	—	247	245	246	242	251	247	242	251
Asian/Pacific Islander	268	265	264	—	267	270	271	266	275	271	266	275
American Indian/Alaska Native	‡	248	‡	—	250	246	249	244	254	247	242	253
12th grade												
White	297	293	297	—	292	—	293	285	300	—	—	—
Black	273	265	269	—	267	—	267	261	272	—	—	—
Hispanic	279	270	275	—	273	—	272	266	277	—	—	—
Asian/Pacific Islander	290	278	287	—	286	—	287	282	292	—	—	—
American Indian/Alaska Native	‡	274	‡	—	‡	—	279	‡	‡	—	—	—

—Not available. Data not collected.
‡Reporting standards not met.
*Accommodations were not permitted for this assessment.
Note: Scale ranges from 0 to 500. Includes public and private schools. Excludes persons not enrolled in school and those who were unable to be tested due to limited proficiency in English or due to a disability. Race categories exclude persons of Hispanic ethnicity.

SOURCE: Adapted from Thomas D. Snyder, Sally A. Dillow, and Charlene M. Hoffman, "Table 118. Average Reading Scale Score by Sex, Grade, Race/Ethnicity, and Percentile: Selected Years, 1992 through 2007," in *Digest of Education Statistics, 2008*, U.S. Department of Education, National Center for Education Statistics, March 2009, http://nces.ed.gov/programs/digest/d08/tables/dt08_118.asp (accessed December 9, 2009)

to the nation's economy and position in the international community, education observers are concerned about the generally poor American performance in mathematics and science. Since 1971 the NAEP has tested students to determine their mathematical knowledge, skills, and aptitudes. The measurement assesses students in five content areas: number sense, properties, and operations; measurement; geometry and spatial sense; data analysis, statistics, and probability; and algebra and functions. The NAEP also tests students on their knowledge of facts, understanding of concepts, and ability to reason in the life, physical, and earth sciences.

In 2007 Asians and Pacific Islanders outperformed all other racial and ethnic groups in mathematics for each grade reported. The average scale score for Asian and Pacific Islander fourth graders was 253, and the average scale score for non-Hispanic whites was 248. (See Table 3.5.) By contrast, Native American and Alaskan Native fourth graders averaged 228, Hispanic fourth graders averaged 227, and African-American fourth graders averaged just 222. The differences in average mathematics scale scores persisted throughout the school years.

Results were similar in the NAEP science assessment, although non-Hispanic white students consistently scored slightly higher than did Asian and Pacific Islander students. Non-Hispanic white fourth graders averaged the highest scale score of 162 in 2005, followed by Asian and Pacific Islander fourth graders, who averaged 158. (See Table 3.6.) Native Americans averaged 138, Hispanics averaged 133, and African-Americans averaged 129. These differences persisted through 12th grade.

Dropping Out

When students drop out or fail to complete high school, both the individual and society suffer. Dropping out of school often results in limited occupational and economic opportunities for these individuals. KewalRamani et al. note that individuals who drop out of school have higher unemployment rates and lower earnings than individuals who graduate from high school. For society, high dropout rates may result in increased costs of government assistance programs for these individuals and their families, costly public training programs, and higher crime rates.

In 2007, 8.7% of all 16- to 24-year-olds had dropped out of high school. (See Table 3.7.) The dropout rate was highest among Hispanics (21.4%), followed by African-Americans (8.4%) and non-Hispanic whites (5.3%).

TABLE 3.5

Average mathematics scale scores by sex, grade, race and Hispanic origin, selected years, 1990–2007

Selected student or school characteristic	1990*	1992*	1996	2000	2003	2005	2007
4th-graders, all students	213	220	224	226	235	238	240
Sex							
Male	214	221	224	227	236	239	241
Female	213	219	223	224	233	237	239
Race/ethnicity							
White	220	227	232	234	243	246	248
Black	188	193	198	203	216	220	222
Hispanic	200	202	207	208	222	226	227
Asian/Pacific Islander	225	231	229	‡	246	251	253
American Indian/Alaska Native	‡	‡	217	208	223	226	228
8th-graders, all students	263	268	270	273	278	279	281
Sex							
Male	263	268	271	274	278	280	282
Female	262	269	269	272	277	278	280
Race/ethnicity							
White	270	277	281	284	288	289	291
Black	237	237	240	244	252	255	260
Hispanic	246	249	251	253	259	262	265
Asian/Pacific Islander	275	290	‡	288	291	295	297
American Indian/Alaska Native	‡	‡	‡	259	263	264	264
12th-graders, all students	294	299	302	300	—	—	—
Sex							
Male	297	301	303	302	—	—	—
Female	291	298	300	299	—	—	—
Race/ethnicity							
White	300	305	309	307	—	—	—
Black	268	275	275	273	—	—	—
Hispanic	276	286	284	282	—	—	—
Asian/Pacific Islander	311	312	305	315	—	—	—
American Indian/Alaska Native	‡	‡	‡	294	—	—	—

—Not available.
‡Reporting standards not met.
*Accommodations were not permitted for this assessment.
Notes: Scale ranges from 0 to 500. Includes public and private schools. Excludes persons not enrolled in school and those who were unable to be tested due to limited proficiency in English or due to a disability. Race categories exclude persons of Hispanic ethnicity. Some data have been revised from previously published figures.

SOURCE: Adapted from Thomas D. Snyder, Sally A. Dillow, and Charlene M. Hoffman, "Table 136. Average Mathematics Scale Scores of 4th-, 8th-, and 12th-Graders, by Selected Student and School Characteristics: Selected Years, 1990 through 2007," in *Digest of Education Statistics, 2008*, U.S. Department of Education, National Center for Education Statistics, March 2009, http://nces.ed.gov/programs/digest/d08/tables/dt08_136.asp (accessed December 9, 2009)

However, since 1994 the percentage of dropouts in this age group has decreased for all race and ethnic groups. (See Figure 3.2.)

More detailed statistics are available for 2005. In that year, Asians were the least likely to drop out (3.5%), followed by non-Hispanic whites (7.2%), African-Americans (11.6%), Native Americans and Alaskan Natives (15.5%), and Hispanics (22.8%). (See Table 3.8.) However, the dropout rate varied greatly depending on the place of birth. Overall, only 8.6% of native-born 16- to 24-year-olds had dropped out of high school, whereas a quarter (25.2%) of foreign-born individuals of that age group had. This discrepancy was particularly true among Hispanic students; 34% of foreign-born Hispanic students dropped out of school in 2007, three times more than any other group. (See Figure 3.3.) In addition, among Hispanics, individuals from some countries were more likely to drop out when compared with others. Nearly a third (32.6%) of individuals with

Central American ancestry had dropped out, as had a quarter (25.5%) of individuals with Mexican roots, although the dropout rate was much lower among those born in the United States than among immigrants. (See Table 3.8.) By contrast, individuals with South American ancestry had a dropout rate of only 9.1% in that year.

One reason for the high dropout rate among foreign-born Hispanic young adults may be their undocumented immigration status. Some Hispanic youth who were brought to the United States as children see little benefit in graduating from high school as "illegal" residents. Beginning in 2001 advocacy groups urged Congress to pass the Development, Relief, and Education for Alien Minors Act. The act would have allowed students to remain in the United States for up to six years after high school graduation, as long as they either attended college or joined the military. The act would also have allowed these students to pay in-state tuition rates for college in

TABLE 3.6

Average science scale scores by sex, grade, race and Hispanic origin, 1996, 2000, and 2005

Selected characteristic, percentile, and achievement level	4th-graders			8th-graders			12th-graders		
	1996[a]	2000	2005	1996[a]	2000	2005	1996[a]	2000	2005
All students	**147**	**147**	**151**	**149**	**149**	**149**	**150**	**146**	**147**
Sex									
Male	148	149	153	150	153	150	154	148	149
Female	146	145	149	148	146	147	147	145	145
Race/ethnicity									
White	158	159	162	159	161	160	159	153	156
Black	120	122	129	121	121	124	123	122	120
Hispanic	124	122	133	128	127	129	131	128	128
Asian/Pacific Islander	144	‡	158	151	153	156	147	149	153
American Indian	129	135	138	148	147	128	144	151	139
	Percent attaining science achievement levels								
Achievement level									
Below basic	37	37	32	40	41	41	43	48	46
At or above basic[b]	63	63	68	60	59	59	57	52	54
At or above proficient[c]	28	27	29	29	30	29	21	18	18
At advanced[d]	3	3	3	3	4	3	3	2	2

‡Reporting standards not met.
[a]Testing accommodations (e.g., extended time, small group testing) for children with disabilities and limited-English-proficient students were not permitted on the 1996 science assessment.
[b]Basic denotes partial mastery of the knowledge and skills that are fundamental for proficient work.
[c]Proficient represents solid academic performance. Students reaching this level have demonstrated competency over challenging subject matter.
[d]Advanced signifies superior performance.
Note: The National Assessment of Education Progress (NAEP) science scale ranges from 0 to 300. Race categories exclude persons of Hispanic ethnicity.

SOURCE: Adapted from Thomas D. Snyder, Sally A. Dillow, and Charlene M. Hoffman, "Table 138. Average Science Scale Scores and Percentage of 4th-, 8th-, and 12th-Graders Attaining Science Achievement Levels, by Selected Student Characteristics and Percentile: 1996, 2000, and 2005," in *Digest of Education Statistics, 2008*, U.S. Department of Education, National Center for Education Statistics, March 2009, http://nces.ed.gov/programs/digest/d08/tables/dt08_138.asp (accessed December 9, 2009)

the state in which they had resided for at least five years. At the end of this period, students who completed the two-year college or military requirement would be allowed to become permanent residents. In 2006 the act passed the U.S. Senate as part of the Comprehensive Immigration Reform Act of 2006; however, in October 2007 it fell eight votes short of the 60 votes necessary to bring the bill up for full debate. The act was introduced again in the 110th Congress, where it died in committee, and in the 111th Congress, where it was again referred to committee. However, prospects for the bill's passage looked somewhat better under the administration of Barack Obama (1961–) than it had under the administration of George W. Bush (1946–).

MINORITY STUDENTS IN SCHOOL
Asian-American Students Often Excel

Jamie Lew of Rutgers University, in "Burden of Acting Neither White nor Black: Asian American Identities and Achievement in Urban Schools" (*Urban Review*, vol. 38, no. 5, December 2006), and Stacey J. Lee of the University of Wisconsin, Madison, in "Additional Complexities: Social Class, Ethnicity, Generation, and Gender in Asian American Student Experiences" (*Race Ethnicity and Education*, vol. 9, no. 1, March 2006), indicate that Asian-American students often excel at school, sometimes performing better than their non-Hispanic white peers.

Asian-American students generally have fewer family risk factors than do other minority children, including living below the poverty level, living in a household where the primary language is not English, having a mother whose highest education is less than a high school diploma or equivalent, and living in a single-parent household. When these risk factors are present, they affect the performance of Asian-American students as well as students from all racial and ethnic backgrounds.

Progress for African-American Students

Even though the average academic performance of African-American students, in general, remains below that of non-Hispanic white students, high school graduation rates among African-Americans rose considerably in the second half of the 20th century. Snyder, Dillow, and Hoffman indicate that 42.6% of African-American students and 38.5% of Hispanic students graduated from high school in 1975. The graduation rate has increased more dramatically for African-American students since 1975 than it has for Hispanic students. In 2008 African-Americans aged 25 years and older were less likely than non-Hispanic whites to have earned a high school diploma, but they were more likely than Hispanics to have received a diploma. More than four out of five (83.5%) African-Americans of this age had received a high school diploma.

TABLE 3.7

Percentage of 16- to 24-year-olds who were high school dropouts, by sex, race and Hispanic origin, selected years 1970–2007

Year	Total status dropout rate				Male status dropout rate				Female status dropout rate			
	All races[a]	White	Black	Hispanic	All races[a]	White	Black	Hispanic	All races[a]	White	Black	Hispanic
1970[c]	15.0 (0.29)	13.2 (0.30)	27.9 (1.22)	— (†)	14.2 (0.42)	12.2 (0.42)	29.4 (1.82)	— (†)	15.7 (0.41)	14.1 (0.42)	26.6 (1.65)	— (†)
1975	13.9 (0.27)	11.4 (0.27)	22.9 (1.06)	29.2 (2.02)	13.3 (0.37)	11.0 (0.38)	23.0 (1.56)	26.7 (2.84)	14.5 (0.38)	11.8 (0.39)	22.9 (1.44)	31.6 (2.86)
1980	14.1 (0.26)	11.4 (0.27)	19.1 (0.97)	35.2 (1.89)	15.1 (0.39)	12.3 (0.40)	20.8 (1.47)	37.2 (2.72)	13.1 (0.36)	10.5 (0.37)	17.7 (1.28)	33.2 (2.61)
1985	12.6 (0.27)	10.4 (0.29)	15.2 (0.92)	27.6 (1.93)	13.4 (0.40)	11.1 (0.42)	16.1 (1.37)	29.9 (2.76)	11.8 (0.37)	9.8 (0.39)	14.3 (1.23)	25.2 (2.68)
1990	12.1 (0.29)	9.0 (0.30)	13.2 (0.94)	32.4 (1.91)	12.3 (0.42)	9.3 (0.44)	11.9 (1.30)	34.3 (2.71)	11.8 (0.41)	8.7 (0.42)	14.4 (1.34)	30.3 (2.70)
1995	12.0 (0.27)	8.6 (0.28)	12.1 (0.74)	30.0 (1.15)	12.2 (0.38)	9.0 (0.40)	11.1 (1.05)	30.0 (1.59)	11.7 (0.37)	8.2 (0.39)	12.9 (1.05)	30.0 (1.66)
2000[d]	10.9 (0.26)	6.9 (0.26)	13.1 (0.78)	27.8 (1.08)	12.0 (0.38)	7.0 (0.37)	15.3 (1.20)	31.8 (1.56)	9.9 (0.35)	6.9 (0.37)	11.1 (1.00)	23.5 (1.48)
2005[d, e]	9.4 (0.22)	6.0 (0.23)	10.4 (0.66)	22.4 (0.87)	10.8 (0.33)	6.6 (0.34)	12.0 (1.02)	26.4 (1.26)	8.0 (0.29)	5.3 (0.31)	9.0 (0.86)	18.1 (1.16)
2006[d, e]	9.3 (0.22)	5.8 (0.23)	10.7 (0.66)	22.1 (0.86)	10.3 (0.33)	6.4 (0.33)	9.7 (0.91)	25.7 (1.25)	8.3 (0.30)	5.3 (0.31)	11.7 (0.96)	18.1 (1.15)
2007[d, e]	8.7 (0.21)	5.3 (0.22)	8.4 (0.59)	21.4 (0.83)	9.8 (0.32)	6.0 (0.32)	8.0 (0.82)	24.7 (1.22)	7.7 (0.29)	4.5 (0.28)	8.8 (0.84)	18.0 (1.13)

—Not available.

†Not applicable.

[a]Includes other racial/ethnic categories not separately shown.

[b]Based on the April 1960 decennial census.

[c]White and black include persons of Hispanic ethnicity.

[d]Because of changes in data collection procedures, data may not be comparable with figures for years prior to 1992.

[e]White and black exclude persons identifying themselves as more than one race.

Note: "Status" dropouts are 16- to 24-year-olds who are not enrolled in school and who have not completed a high school program, regardless of when they left school. People who have received General Educational Diploma (GED) credentials are counted as high school completers. All data except for 1960 are based on October counts. Data are based on sample surveys of the civilian noninstitutionalized population, which excludes persons in prisons, persons in the military, and other persons not living in households. Race categories exclude persons of Hispanic ethnicity except where otherwise noted. Standard errors appear in parentheses.

SOURCE: Adapted from Thomas D. Snyder, Sally A. Dillow, and Charlene M. Hoffman, "Table 109. Percentage of High School Dropouts among Persons 16 through 24 Years Old (Status Dropout Rate), by Sex and Race/Ethnicity: Selected Years, 1960 through 2007," in *Digest of Education Statistics, 2008,* U.S. Department of Education, National Center for Education Statistics, March 2009, http://nces.ed.gov/programs/digest/d08/tables/dt08_109.asp (accessed December 9, 2009)

FIGURE 3.2

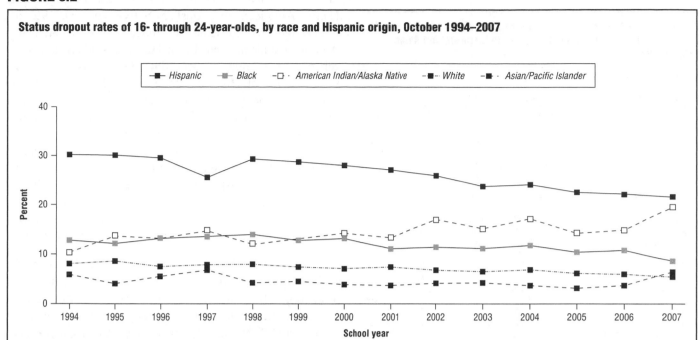

Status dropout rates of 16- through 24-year-olds, by race and Hispanic origin, October 1994–2007

Note: The status dropout rate is the percentage of 16- through 24-year-olds who are not enrolled in high school and who have not earned a high school credential (either a diploma or equivalency credential such as General Equivalency Diploma [GED] certificate). The status dropout rate includes all dropouts regardless of when they last attended school. Data for American Indians/Alaska Natives in 1999 have been suppressed due to unstable estimates.

SOURCE: Michael Planty et al., "Figure 20-2. Status Dropout Rates of 16- through 24-Year-Olds in the Civilian, Noninstitutionalized Population, by Race/Ethnicity: October Current Population Survey 1994–2007," in *The Condition of Education 2009*, U.S. Department of Education, National Center for Education Statistics, June 2009, http://nces.ed.gov/pubs2009/2009081.pdf (accessed December 9, 2009)

Snyder, Dillow, and Hoffman note that the percent of African-American high school graduates who enrolled in college within a 12-month period fluctuated throughout the period from 1972 to 2007, from a low of 32.5% in 1973 to a high of 62.5% in 2004. In 2007 more than half (55.7%) of African-American students who had completed high school or earned a general education diploma in the past 12 months enrolled in college.

SCHOOL SEGREGATION. One reason African-American children have historically lagged behind non-Hispanic white children in educational achievement has been the separate and inferior schools that they have been forced to attend. In 1954, in *Brown v. Board of Education of Topeka, Kansas* (347 U.S. 483), the U.S. Supreme Court declared that separate schools for African-American children were inherently unequal and that schools had to desegregate. Over 50 years later, more and more school districts are questioning whether the federal courts need to continue supervising desegregation. However, despite regulations and busing, many inner-city schools are still not integrated, and academic achievement for African-American children is still lagging. Many non-Hispanic white students have moved (with their family's tax dollars) to the suburbs or transferred to private schools to avoid inner-city schools with high populations of minority students. For example, KewalRamani et al. indicate that between 1993 and 2003 the percentage of central city public school students who were

non-Hispanic white decreased from 44.3% to 35.2%, whereas the proportion of minority students increased from 55.7% to 64.8%. The percentage of African-American students in central city public schools stayed relatively stable during this period, whereas the percentage of Hispanic students rose dramatically. In the 2006–07 school year, 33% of African-American students were in high-poverty schools, compared with 4% of non-Hispanic whites; almost half (46%) of urban African-American students were in high-poverty schools, compared with 10% of non-Hispanic whites. (See Figure 3.4.) In fact, segregation increased between the 1990–91 school year and the 2006–07 school year. In 1990–91, 45% of African-American students attended schools with a 75% minority enrollment; by 2006–07, 52% attended such schools. (See Figure 3.5.)

Half a century after *Brown*, the Supreme Court restricted the use of plans that use race as a factor in assigning students to schools in an effort to promote racial diversity. The two cases, decided in June 2007, are: *Parents Involved in Community Schools v. Seattle School District* (No. 05-908) and *Meredith v. Jefferson County* (No. 05-915). The court did not, however, declare that race could never be used to achieve diversity. Regardless, Robert Barnes reports in "Divided Court Limits Use of Race by School Districts" (*Washington Post*, June 29, 2007) that experts observe that many school districts will abandon policies designed to achieve racial diversity as a result of this ruling.

TABLE 3.8

Percentage of 16- to 24-year-olds who were high school dropouts, by nativity, race and Hispanic origin with Hispanic and Asian subgroups, 2005

Race/ethnicity and subgroup	Number	Total	Native	Foreign-born
Total*	34,602,000	10.5	8.6	25.2
White	21,163,000	7.2	7.2	6.3
Black	4,786,000	11.6	11.8	8.5
Hispanic	6,190,000	22.8	13.2	38.1
Mexican	4,150,000	25.5	13.8	41.9
Puerto Rican	502,000	16.9	16.9	‡
Dominican	172,000	14.2	10.6!	17.7
Central American	469,000	32.6	9.9!	43.7
South American	267,000	9.1	4.8!	11.8
Other Hispanic or Latino	629,000	10.9	9.7	17.8
Asian	1,423,000	3.5	2.9	4.0
Asian Indian	236,000	3.1!	1.6!	4.0!
Chinese	297,000	2.2!	0.6!	3.8!
Filipino	266,000	3.2!	2.8!	3.6!
Japanese	55,000	2.1!	2.8!	#
Korean	167,000	2.0!	3.7!	1.0!
Vietnamese	166,000	2.0!	1.9!	5.6!
Other Asian	236,000	6.9	6.6!	7.2!
Native Hawaiian/Pacific Islander	53,000	9.8!	7.7!	18.2!
American Indian/Alaska Native	286,000	15.5	15.6	‡

#Rounds to zero.
!Interpret data with caution.
‡Reporting standards not met. Sample size too small.
*Total includes other race/ethnicity categories not separately shown.
Note: The data presented here represent status dropout rates, which is the percentage of civilian, non-institutionalized 16- to 24-year-olds who are not in high school and who have not earned a high school credential (either a diploma or equivalency credential such as a GED). The status dropout rate includes all dropouts regardless of when they last attended school, as well as individuals who may have never attended school in the United States, such as immigrants who did not complete a high school diploma in their home country. Another way of calculating dropout rates is the event dropout rate, which is the percentage of 15- to 24-year-olds who dropped out of grades 10 through 12 in the 12 months preceding the fall of each data collection year. Race categories exclude persons of Hispanic origin.

SOURCE: Angelina KewalRamani et al., "Table 17b. Percentage of 16- to 24-Year-Olds Who Were High School Status Dropouts, by Nativity and Race/Ethnicity with Hispanic and Asian Subgroups: 2005," in *Status and Trends in the Education of Racial and Ethnic Minorities*, U.S. Department of Education, National Center for Education Statistics, Institute of Education Sciences, September 2007, http://nces.ed.gov/pubs2007/2007039.pdf (accessed December 9, 2009)

Resegregation began in the 1990s and most likely will accelerate as a result of the Supreme Court decision. In *Historic Reversals, Accelerating Resegregation, and the Need for New Integration Strategies* (August 2007, http://www.civilrightsproject.ucla.edu/research/deseg/reversals_reseg_need.pdf), Gary Orfield and Chungmei Lee of the Civil Rights Project state that "the trends . . . are those of increasing isolation and profound inequality." They note that the June 2007 Supreme Court decision was a dramatic reversal of the gains made during the Civil Rights Movement (1954–1971): "On average, segregated minority schools are inferior in terms of the quality of their teachers, the character of the curriculum, the level of competition, average test scores, and graduation rates."

In the 2006–07 school year 64% of non-Hispanic white students attended public elementary or secondary schools where the percent of minority enrollment was less than 25%. (See Figure 3.6.) By contrast, only 24% of Native American and Alaskan Native students, 19% of Asian and Pacific Islander students, 9% of African-American students, and 8% of Hispanic students attended schools where minority enrollment was this low. Conversely, 57% of Hispanic students and 52% of African-American students attended schools where minorities made up 75% or more of the student population. A third (33%) of Asian and Pacific Islander students and 29% of Native American and Alaskan Native students attended schools with such high minority enrollment. However, only 3% of non-Hispanic white students attended schools where minorities made up 75% or more of the student population. These figures attest to the continued segregation of minority students in the U.S. public school system.

CRITICAL RACE THEORY. Bree Picower of New York University argues in "The Unexamined Whiteness of Teaching: How White Teachers Maintain and Enact Dominant Racial Ideologies" (*Race Ethnicity and Education*, vol. 12, no. 2, July 2009) that the ideas about race brought into the classroom by white teachers are entrenched and difficult to change and that these ideas negatively affect students of color. In fact, the idea that racism is pervasive and permanent is a basic premise of critical race theory; racism's pervasiveness and permanency translates into achievement gaps in the classroom.

Structural racism works against African-American students in the classroom. Gregg D. Beratan of the University of London posits in "The Song Remains the Same: Transposition and the Disproportionate Representation of Minority Students in Special Education" (*Race Ethnicity and Education*, vol. 11, no. 4, December 2008) that such ideas have resulted in the "legal" segregation of students of color into special education classrooms in the aftermath of the *Brown* decision. He writes, "The disproportionate representation of minority students in special education is as clear an example of a racist outcome as one can find." According to Sabina E. Vaught and Angelina E. Castagno, in "'I Don't Think I'm a Racist': Critical Race Theory, Teacher Attitudes, and Structural Racism" (*Race Ethnicity and Education*, vol. 11, no. 2, July 2008), achievement gaps are structural—not individual—and remedying these gaps will therefore require systemic, rather than individual, change.

Hispanic Educational Attainment Holds Steady

Even though Hispanics made modest gains in education in the 1990s, low educational attainment has been a major hindrance to their economic advancement in the United States. Snyder, Dillow, and Hoffman find that, in 2008, Hispanics continued to trail behind other groups in high school graduation rates in 2008. Only 62.3% of Hispanics aged 25 years and older had received high school diplomas, compared with 91.5% of non-Hispanic whites

FIGURE 3.3

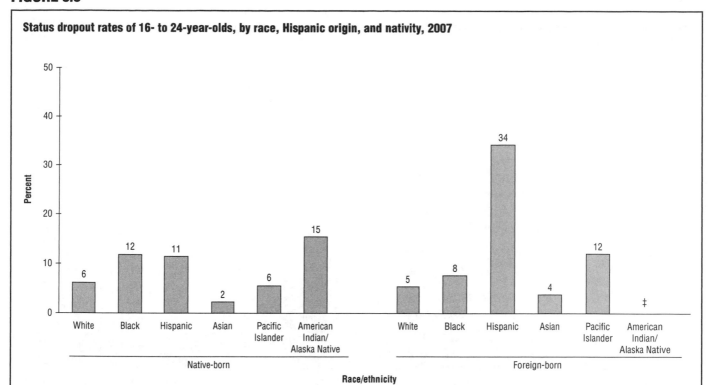

Status dropout rates of 16- to 24-year-olds, by race, Hispanic origin, and nativity, 2007

‡ Reporting standards not met (too few cases).

Note: The status dropout rate is the percentage of 16- through 24-year-olds who are not enrolled in high school and who have not earned a high school credential (either a diploma or equivalency credential such as a General Equivalency Diploma [GED] certificate). The status dropout rate includes all dropouts regardless of when they last attended school.

SOURCE: Michael Planty et al., "Figure 20-1. Status Dropout Rates of 16- through 24-Year-Olds, by Race/Ethnicity and Nativity: American Community Survey 2007," in *The Condition of Education 2009*, U.S. Department of Education, National Center for Education Statistics, June 2009, http://nces.ed.gov/pubs2009/2009081.pdf (accessed December 9, 2009)

and 83.3% of African-Americans. Not surprisingly, in 2008, Asians and Pacific Islanders, non-Hispanic whites, and African-Americans were more likely to have graduated from college than were Hispanics. (See Figure 3.7.)

Why do Hispanics trail other racial and ethnic groups in educational attainment? A language barrier may be one reason. In 2007, 7.1 million (68.3%) out of 10.4 million Hispanic students in kindergarten through 12th grade spoke Spanish at home. (See Table 3.9.) Almost one out of five (18.1%) Hispanic students spoke English with difficulty.

However, there are some signs that the Hispanic population is making slow but steady progress in educational attainment in the United States. Snyder, Dillow, and Hoffman indicate that the proportion of Hispanic adults with a high school diploma rose from 50.8% in 1990 to 62.3% in 2008. Likewise, the proportion of Hispanics with a bachelor's degree also rose, from 9.2% in 1990 to 13.3% in 2008. The proportion of Hispanics aged 25 to 29 years with a high school diploma was higher than the proportion of all Hispanics over the age of 25 with a diploma (68.3% and 62.3%, respectively), indicating that fewer young Hispanic adults than in previous generations are dropping out of school.

Native American Educational Attainment Remains Low

Native Americans have the lowest educational attainment of all minority groups, which is attributable in part to a high dropout rate. According to Catherine Freeman and Mary Ann Fox, in *Status and Trends in the Education of American Indians and Alaska Natives* (August 2005, http://nces.ed.gov/pubs2005/2005108.pdf), 45,828 students attended Bureau of Indian Affairs schools and tribal schools in 2003–04. In 2002, 624,298 Native American and Alaskan Native students attended public schools.

Kristin Denton Flanagan and Jen Park indicate in *American Indian and Alaska Native Children: Findings from the Base Year of the Early Childhood Longitudinal Study, Birth Cohort* (August 2005, http://nces.ed.gov/pubs2005/2005116.pdf) that a high proportion of Native American children have certain risk factors that may affect their educational attainment. The Early Childhood Longitudinal Study, Birth Cohort, oversampled Native American children to better study their educational experiences. Fully a third (34%) of Native American children lived below the poverty line, compared with 23% of all children. A quarter (24%) of all Native American children lived with a single parent, compared with 20% of all

FIGURE 3.4

Percentage of public elementary and secondary school students in high-poverty schools, by race and Hispanic origin and locale, 2006–07

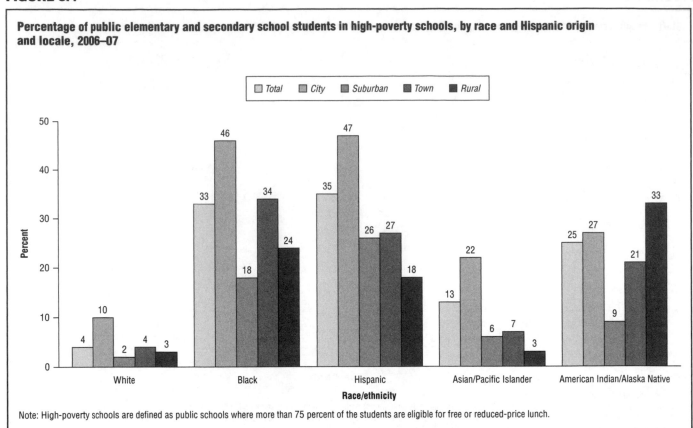

Note: High-poverty schools are defined as public schools where more than 75 percent of the students are eligible for free or reduced-price lunch.

SOURCE: Michael Planty et al., "Figure 25-1. Percentage of Public Elementary and Secondary School Students in High-Poverty Schools, by Race/Ethnicity and Locale: School Year 2006–07," in *The Condition of Education 2009*, U.S. Department of Education, National Center for Education Statistics, June 2009, http://nces.ed.gov/pubs2009/2009081.pdf (accessed December 9, 2009)

children. In addition, Native American parents had low educational attainment. A third (34%) of the mothers and 27% of the fathers had not completed high school, compared with 27% of all mothers and 17% of all fathers. Furthermore, only 9% of Native American mothers and 6% of Native American fathers had earned a bachelor's degree or higher, compared with 24% of all mothers and 24% of all fathers.

In 2005 Native American and Alaskan Native eighth graders had the highest rate of absences of any race or ethnic group in the month preceding the study—66% of Native American and Alaskan Native students had been absent, and 30% had been absent three or more times in the past month. (See Table 3.10.) A smaller proportion of Hispanic students (58%), non-Hispanic white students (56%), African-American students (56%), and Asian and Pacific Islander students (38%) had been absent in the past month, whereas only 25% of African-American students, 24% of Hispanic students, 20% of non-Hispanic white students, and 12% of Asian and Pacific Islander students had been absent three or more times in the past month. High rates of absenteeism were associated with lower rates of achieving at least a "Basic" level of achievement on the NAEP mathematics assessment. Only 41% of Native American and Alaskan Native students

who had been absent three or more times achieved Basic or above, compared with 56% of students who had been absent one or two times and 62% of students who had not been absent at all.

REFORMING THE PUBLIC SCHOOL SYSTEM
No Child Left Behind

In January 2002 President Bush signed into law the No Child Left Behind (NCLB) Act, which was intended to improve the U.S. public school system and provide educational choice, especially for minority families. The law mandated that all public school students be proficient in reading and math by 2014, with progress measured by the administration of annual standardized tests. In addition, all subgroups (those with certain racial backgrounds, limited English proficiency, or disabilities or from low-income families) must meet the same performance standards as all students. Failure to make adequate yearly progress may result in escalating sanctions against the school, including the payment of transportation costs for students who wished to transfer to better-performing schools, extra tutoring for low-income students, replacement of the school staff, and potentially converting the school to a charter school or even turning to a private company to operate the school.

FIGURE 3.5

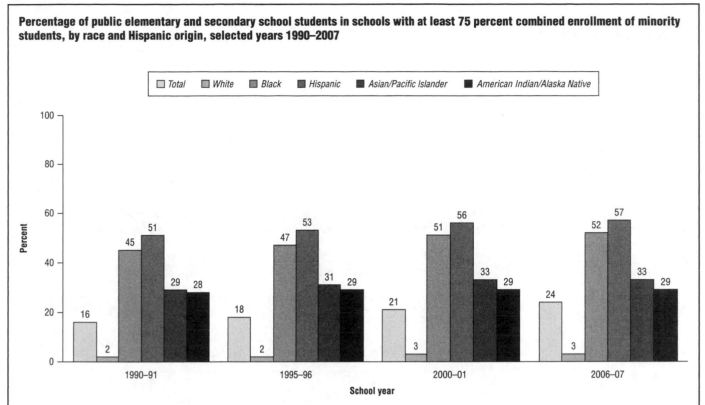

Percentage of public elementary and secondary school students in schools with at least 75 percent combined enrollment of minority students, by race and Hispanic origin, selected years 1990–2007

Legend: □ Total ▨ White ▨ Black ▨ Hispanic ■ Asian/Pacific Islander ■ American Indian/Alaska Native

SOURCE: Michael Planty et al., "Figure 26-2. Percentage of Public Elementary and Secondary School Students in Schools with at Least 75 Percent Combined Enrollment of Black, Hispanic, Asian/Pacific Islander, and American Indian/Alaska Native Students, by Year and Race/Ethnicity: Selected School Years, 1990–91 to 2006–07," in *The Condition of Education 2009*, U.S. Department of Education, National Center for Education Statistics, June 2009, http://nces.ed.gov/pubs2009/2009081.pdf (accessed December 9, 2009)

Even though the NCLB was passed with bipartisan support, critics quickly emerged, including those who charged that the mandate was underfinanced by the Bush administration. Another problem was that because of the strict testing requirements, many schools that were regarded as successful by almost all objective measures found themselves designated as failed schools. In some cases a school failed to meet its goal simply because two or three students in a subgroup failed to take a standardized test. A further problem was that minority students who attended schools that were unquestionably substandard found that even if by law they had the right to transfer to another school, there were few places to go. In *Holding NCLB Accountable: Achieving Accountability, Equity, and School Reform* (2008), a multipart study that was conducted by the Civil Rights Project at Harvard University and edited by Gail L. Sunderman, the researchers find that no districts are able to approve all transfer requests. However well intentioned, the NCLB is proving difficult to implement, demonstrating once again that there are no easy answers to improving the U.S. educational system, especially for minority and low-income students.

In the meantime, students performing at the highest levels suffered under the act. Sam Dillon, in "Schools

Cut Back Subjects to Push Reading and Math" (*New York Times*, March 26, 2006), and Jennifer Booher-Jennings of Columbia University, in "Below the Bubble: 'Educational Triage' and the Texas Accountability System" (*American Educational Research Journal*, vol. 42, no. 2, 2005), report that many critics consider the law inflexible and so flawed that it actually undercuts the goals it seeks to achieve. Some question the reliance on high-stakes standardized tests, which force schools to spend a considerable amount of time preparing students to take the tests, an effort that produces no lasting educational benefit and requires a reallocation of resources. In many cases gifted students' programs have been cut back. Because low-income, minority gifted students lack the options of their white counterparts, they are left to languish in classes that fail to stimulate them.

Even the law's own accountability systems show little progress since its implementation. Jihyun Lee, Wendy S. Grigg, and Patricia L. Donahue indicate in *The Nation's Report Card: Reading 2007* (September 2007, http://nces.ed.gov/nationsreportcard/pdf/main2007/2007496.pdf) that despite small gains in reading scores of fourth and eighth graders between 1992 and 2007, the achievement gap between white and minority students had not narrowed. The NCES notes in *The Nation's Report Card: Mathematics*

FIGURE 3.6

Percentage distribution of public elementary and secondary school students of each racial/ethnic group, by percent minority enrollment in school, 2006–07

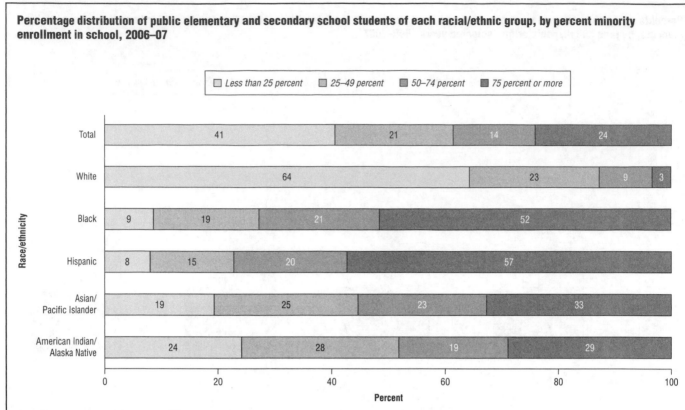

Note: Race categories exclude persons of Hispanic ethnicity.

SOURCE: Michael Planty et al., "Figure 26-1. Percentage Distribution of Public Elementary and Secondary School Students of Each Racial/Ethnic Group, by Percent Combined Enrollment of Black, Hispanic, Asian/Pacific Islander, and American Indian/Alaska Native Students in School: School Year 2006–07," in *The Condition of Education 2009*, U.S. Department of Education, National Center for Education Statistics, June 2009, http://nces.ed.gov/pubs2009/2009081.pdf (accessed December 9, 2009)

2009 (October 2009, http://nces.ed.gov/nationsreportcard/pdf/main2009/2010451.pdf) that the same was true in mathematics. Even though the achievement gap between African-American and non-Hispanic white fourth graders had narrowed somewhat between 1990 and 2009, among eighth graders the gap had not narrowed at all. In addition, Bobby D. Rampey, Gloria S. Dion, and Patricia L. Donahue find in *The Nation's Report Card: Trends in Academic Progress in Reading and Mathematics 2008* (April 2009, http://nces.ed.gov/nationsreportcard/pdf/main2008/2009479.pdf) that the NCLB had no effect on closing the gap between the performance of non-Hispanic white students and African-American and Hispanic students between 2004 and 2008 in either math or reading.

The Forum on Educational Accountability was formed by several organizations that oppose certain provisions of the NCLB and that want changes in the law's pending reauthorization. Among the changes the forum advocates are those proposed in the "Joint Organizational Statement on No Child Left Behind Act" (October 21, 2004, http://www.edaccountability.org/Joint_Statement.html), which as of June 1, 2009, had 151 organizational signers:

- Replace arbitrary proficiency targets with achievement targets based on the success rates in the best public schools

- Measure progress by students' progress rather than by point-in-time tests

- Increase accountability of school districts and state governments to the federal government

- Use a variety of measures of student performance, not only standardized testing

- Institute funding for research into effective accountability systems

- Develop effective accountability systems

- Decrease testing burden by testing only selected grades

- Train teachers better and encourage ongoing professional development

- Reform the system of sanctioning underperforming schools to better support the goal of improved student achievement

- Increase funding

FIGURE 3.7

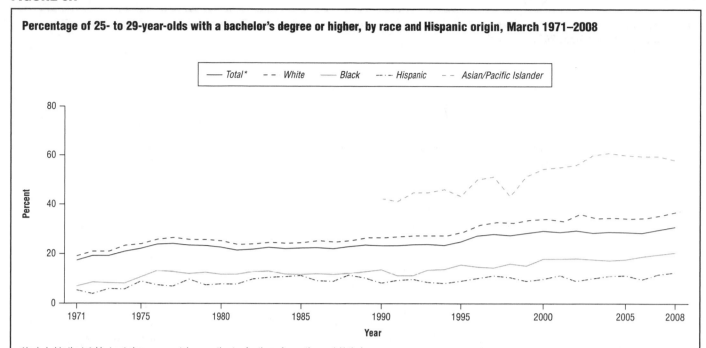

Percentage of 25- to 29-year-olds with a bachelor's degree or higher, by race and Hispanic origin, March 1971–2008

*Included in the total but not shown separately are estimates for those from other racial/ethnic groups.
Note: Data for Asians/Pacific Islanders were only available from 1990. Data prior to 1992 were for completing 4 years of college: beginning in 1992, data were for earning a bachelor's degree.

SOURCE: Michael Planty et al., "Figure 23-2. Percentage of 25- to 29-Year-Olds with a Bachelor's Degree or Higher, by Race/Ethnicity: March 1971–2008," in *The Condition of Education 2009*, U.S. Department of Education, National Center for Education Statistics, June 2009, http://nces.ed.gov/pubs2009/2009081.pdf (accessed December 9, 2009)

Critics of the NCLB found an ally in the new Obama administration. According to the U.S. Department of Education, in the press release "Secretary Duncan Says Rewrite of 'No Child Left Behind' Should Start Now; Reauthorization Can't Wait" (September 24, 2009, http://www.ed.gov/news/pressreleases/2009/09/09242009.html), in September 2009 Arne Duncan (1964–), the U.S. secretary of education, stressed that the NCLB needed to be reformed by pointing out many of its flaws, including its overemphasis on standardized testing, the unfair labeling of many schools as failures, and the law's failure to use student progress as part of its accountability system. Duncan said, "The biggest problem with NCLB is that it doesn't encourage high learning standards. In fact, it inadvertently encourages states to lower them. The net effect is that we are lying to children and parents by telling kids they are succeeding when they are not."

School "Choice"

Planty et al. find that the percentage of parents who enrolled their children in chosen public schools, rather than in their assigned public schools, increased from 11% in 1993 and to 15.5% in 2007. Nearly half (46.2%) the parents surveyed reported that they had the option to send their children to a chosen public school. Among those parents, 66.8% sent their children to their assigned public school, whereas 24.5% sent their children to a chosen

public school. In 2007 African-American students were the most likely to attend a chosen public school (36.2%) and non-Hispanic whites were the least likely to attend one (20.3%), probably because whites were less likely to be assigned to schools in high-poverty areas and were more likely to attend chosen private schools.

SCHOOL VOUCHERS. Despite the Supreme Court's rejection of segregated schools, many minority students have been relegated to failing neighborhood public schools with little diversity. One proposed solution to this problem is the school voucher, a concept pioneered by the Nobel Prize–winning economist Milton Friedman (1912–2006) in 1955. The Friedman Foundation for Educational Choice explains in "School Choice" (2010, http://www.friedmanfoundation.org/friedman/schoolchoice/) that the voucher program provides parents with a predetermined amount of money—in essence the tax dollars already collected by a community to be used for education—and allows parents to present that voucher to the public or private school of their choice. Proponents for vouchers believe that not only will minority children benefit but also that public schools, fearful of losing tax revenues, will gain an incentive to improve. Opponents of vouchers, such as the National Educational Association (NEA), in "Vouchers" (2010, http://www.nea.org/home/16378.htm), maintain that choice will simply drain money from the public schools and worsen their condition, while not providing

TABLE 3.9

Number and percentage of children ages 5–17 who spoke a language other than English at home and who spoke English with difficulty, by selected characteristics, 2007

[Numbers in thousands]

				Spoke a language other than English at home					
						Spoke English with difficulty			
				Total		Ages 5–9		Ages 10–17	
Characteristic	Total population	Number	Percent of total population	Number	Percent of total population	Number	Percent of population[a]	Number	Percent of population[a]
Total	**53,217**	**10,850**	**20.4**	**2,739**	**5.2**	**1,368**	**6.9**	**1,371**	**4.1**
Language spoken at home									
Spanish	7,826	7,826	100.0	2,060	26.3	1,048	35.4	1,012	20.8
Other Indo-European[b]	1,455	1,455	100.0	287	19.7	134	24.9	153	16.7
Asian/Pacific Islander[c]	1,174	1,174	100.0	320	27.3	151	34.2	169	23.1
Other	395	395	100.0	72	18.3	35	22.8	37	15.4
Race/ethnicity[d]									
White	30,825	1,729	5.6	371	1.2	141	1.3	230	1.2
Black	7,719	413	5.4	96	1.3	39	1.4	57	1.2
Hispanic	10,438	7,133	68.3	1,886	18.1	1,005	24.2	882	14.0
Mexican	7,163	5,103	71.2	1,486	20.8	819	28.0	667	15.7
Puerto Rican	946	456	48.2	76	8.0	27	7.8	49	8.2
Cuban	231	159	69.2	30	12.9	12	15.0	17	11.6
Dominican	268	233	86.9	48	17.8	20	21.7	27	15.7
Central American	664	543	81.8	133	20.1	70	27.0	63	15.6
South American	416	326	78.4	57	13.8	27	17.6	30	11.5
Other Hispanic	749	312	41.7	56	7.5	28	9.7	28	6.2
Asian	2,060	1,312	63.7	338	16.4	162	20.0	177	14.1
Asian Indian	399	264	66.2	41	10.3	23	13.1	18	8.2
Chinese	438	306	69.9	88	20.0	43	24.9	44	16.8
Filipino	352	118	33.5	29	8.3	11	8.7	18	8.1
Japanese	60	31	51.8	13	22.7	8	34.9	6	15.2
Korean	218	161	73.7	44	20.0	15	21.7	28	19.2
Vietnamese	265	209	78.7	64	24.1	34	29.8	30	19.9
Other Asian	328	223	68.0	59	18.0	27	22.0	32	15.6
Pacific Islander	79	27	34.4	5	6.8	3	10.1	3	5.1
American Indian/Alaska Native	416	65	15.6	11	2.5	4	2.7	7	2.5
More than one race	1,508	114	7.6	17	1.1	7	1.1	10	1.2
Citizenship									
U.S.-born citizen	50,548	8,619	17.1	1,842	3.6	1,070	5.6	771	2.5
Naturalized U.S. citizen	558	342	61.3	71	12.8	18	13.7	53	12.5
Non-U.S. citizen	2,110	1,888	89.5	826	39.1	279	48.8	547	35.6
Poverty status[e]									
Poor	8,833	2,678	30.3	857	9.7	451	12.7	407	7.7
Near-poor	10,889	3,267	30.0	892	8.2	460	10.8	432	6.5
Nonpoor	32,570	4,759	14.6	939	2.9	430	3.7	509	2.4

[a]Percentage of the total subgroup population for that particular subgroup. For example, 2.7 percent of all American Indians/Alaska Natives ages 5–9 spoke a language other than English at home and spoke English with difficulty.
[b]An Indo-European language other than Spanish (e.g., French, German, Portuguese, etc.)
[c]Any native language spoken by Asians or Pacific Islanders, which linguists classify variously as Sino-Tibetan, Austroasiatic, or Austronesian languages.
[d]Race categories exclude persons of Hispanic ethnicity. Totals may include some racial/ethnic categories not shown separately.
[e]Poor is defined to include families below the poverty threshold, near-poor is defined to include families at 100–199 percent of the poverty threshold, and nonpoor is defined to include families at 200 percent or more than the poverty threshold. Detail may not sum to totals because of missing values for poverty.
Note: Respondents were asked whether each child in the household spoke a language other than English at home. If they answered "yes," they were asked how well each child could speak English using the following categories: "very well," "well," "not well," and "not at all." All those who reported speaking English less than "very well" were considered to have difficulty speaking English. A Spanish-language version of the American Community Survey (ACS) was available to respondents.

SOURCE: Michael Planty et al., "TableA-8-2. Number and Percentage of Children Ages 5–17 Who Spoke a Language Other Than English at Home and Who Spoke English with Difficulty, by Selected Characteristics: 2007," in *The Condition of Education 2009*, U.S. Department of Education, National Center for Education Statistics, June 2009, http://nces.ed.gov/pubs2009/2009081.pdf (accessed December 9, 2009)

real choice for students from impoverished or low-income families.

Vouchers have been used on an experimental basis around the country. The main programs are in Milwaukee, Wisconsin, enacted in 1990, and in Cleveland, Ohio, enacted in 1995; also, a program for children with disabilities was enacted in Florida in 1999. More recent programs have been established on a smaller scale, including a special education voucher program in Georgia, enacted in 2007, and programs in Arizona, enacted in 2006 but under court challenge, and in New Orleans, Louisiana, enacted in 2008. The article "Topic A: Obama's Compromise on D.C.'s School Vouchers Program" (*Washington Post*, May 10, 2009) indicates that President Obama essentially ended the Washington, D.C., voucher

TABLE 3.10

Percentage distribution of 8th-graders and percentage at or above *Basic* on the National Assessment of Educational Progress mathematics assessment, by race and Hispanic origin and number of days absent from school in the past month, 2005

Race/ethnicity	Total	No absences	1–2 absences	3 or more absences
		Percentage distribution		
Total*	100	45	34	21
White	100	44	36	20
Black	100	44	31	25
Hispanic	100	42	34	24
Asian/Pacific Islander	100	62	26	12
American Indian/Alaska Native	100	34	36	30
		Percentage at or above *basic*		
Total	69	75	71	56
White	80	85	81	69
Black	42	49	43	30
Hispanic	52	58	52	40
Asian/Pacific Islander	81	86	81	64
American Indian/Alaska Native	53	62	56	41

*Total includes other race/ethnicity categories not separately shown.
Note: Race categories exclude persons of Hispanic origin. Detail may not sum to totals because of rounding.

SOURCE: Angelina KewalRamani et al., "Table 15. Percentage Distribution of 8th-Graders and Percentage at or above *Basic* on the NAEP Mathematics Assessment, by Race/Ethnicity and Number of Days Absent from School in the Past Month: 2005," in *Status and Trends in the Education of Racial and Ethnic Minorities*, U.S. Department of Education, National Center for Education Statistics, Institute of Education Sciences, September 2007, http://nces.ed.gov/pubs2007/2007039.pdf (accessed December 9, 2009)

program, established in 2004, when he signed a spending bill in 2009 that prevented new students from entering the program.

These programs have produced mixed results. Even though some minority children have been able to use vouchers to escape inferior schools, many families still lack the money necessary to educate their children outside of the public school system. The value of the vouchers, ranging from $1,250 to $3,700, is simply too small to cover the tuition for most traditional private schools, leading a number of parents to opt for Catholic schools, which can be less expensive. However, the funding of religious education may not hold up to constitutional scrutiny. In "Vouchers Are Constitutionally Suspect" (2001, http://www.adl.org/vouchers/vouchers_constit_suspect.asp), the Anti-Defamation League states that "voucher programs ... would force citizens—Christians, Jews, Muslims and atheists—to pay for the religious indoctrination of school children at schools with narrow parochial agendas. In many areas, 80 percent of vouchers would be used in schools whose central mission is religious training."

Moreover, parents using vouchers incur additional costs, such as transportation and school lunches, that many have found they cannot afford. According to Andrew Stephen, in "America—Andrew Stephen on Magic Solutions for US Schools" (*New Statesman*, December 9, 2002), in Florida "a quarter of the kids who were signed up for vouchers this school year have already found themselves back in the public system." In these cases, voucher programs end up not helping low-income children at all but segregating them further in neighborhood public schools while children from higher-income families who can afford the additional costs use the vouchers to attend private schools.

The voucher movement suffered a serious setback in January 2006, when the Florida Supreme Court struck down that state's Opportunity Scholarship voucher system, saying that it violated the constitutional requirement of a uniform system of free public schools. With this argument, the court avoided the controversial issue of whether public school dollars could be used to fund parochial education. The NEA reports in "Florida High Court Rules against Vouchers" (January 2006, http://www.nea.org/home/16987.htm) that even supporters of the voucher system in Florida admitted that the court's decision most likely threatened the two other voucher programs in use in the state. In "Utah Voters Resoundingly Defeat School Voucher Ballot Issue" (December 7, 2007, http://www.nsba.org/), the National School Boards Association notes that a further setback occurred in Utah in November 2007, when voters rejected a statewide voucher program. In general, taxpayers do not support voucher programs. The National School Boards Association notes in "The Case against Private School Vouchers" (February 20, 2009, http://www.nsba.org/) that when put before voters, voucher programs have been defeated in all 11 referenda since 1990.

CHARTER SCHOOLS. Like vouchers, the idea of charter schools has also found proponents in the minority community. A charter school is publicly financed but operates independent of school districts, thereby combining the advantages of a private school with the free tuition of a public school. Parents, teachers, and other groups receive a charter from a state legislature to operate these schools, which in effect exist as independent school districts. They receive public funds and are accountable for both their financing and educational standards.

According to Robin J. Lake and Paul T. Hill, in *Hopes, Fears, and Reality: A Balanced Look at American Charter Schools in 2005* (November 2005, http://www.ncsrp.org/downloads/HopesandFears2005_report.pdf), the charter school experiment started in Minnesota in 1992. The NCES reports in *Condition of Education, 2007* (2007, http://nces.ed.gov/programs/coe/2007/pdf/32_2007.pdf) that by the 2004–05 school year, 3,294 charter schools taught 887,243 students in 40 states and the District of Columbia. As with vouchers, results have been uneven, with a number of successes offset by charter schools that failed to improve student achievement.

Overall, however, the charter school movement has stood the test of time, and these schools have provided some parents with real options for their children's education. In 2009 the charter school movement gained even more momentum with the support of the Obama administration, which pressured states to lift restrictions on the establishment and growth of charter schools by using discretionary education funds contained in the American Recovery and Reinvestment Act, signed into law in February 2009.

However, one unintended consequence of charter schools is that they are more segregated than public schools. The NCES reports that 31.3% of charter school students are African-American, compared with 16.9% of conventional public school students; 21.8% of charter school students are Hispanic, compared with 19.4% of conventional public school students; and 42% of charter school students are non-Hispanic white, compared with 58% of conventional public school students. In "Charter Schools and Race: A Lost Opportunity for Integrated Education" (*Education Policy Analysis Archives*, vol. 11, no. 32, September 5, 2003), Erica Frankenberg and Chungmei Lee state that "seventy percent of all black charter school students attend intensely segregated minority schools compared with 34% of black public school students.... The pattern for Latino segregation is mixed; on the whole, Latino charter school students are less segregated than their black counterparts." Amy Stambach and Natalie Crow Becker note in "Finding the Old in the New: On Race and Class in U.S. Charter School Debates" (*Race Ethnicity and Education*, vol. 9, no. 2, July 2006) that the "political and social processes surrounding charter school formation can promote racial exclusion and class stratification" rather than overcome socioeconomic stratification within the public school system, as their founders often intend.

HIGHER EDUCATION
Preparation for College

HIGH SCHOOL COURSE-TAKING. High school students are better prepared for college-level coursework if they take advanced courses while still in high school. Asian-American students are more likely than other students to take advanced math and science courses in high school. Non-Hispanic white students, while less likely to take these courses than Asian-American students, are significantly more likely than most minority students to take these courses. According to the College Board (August 18, 2009, http://professionals.collegeboard.com/profdownload/cbs-2009-Graph-8_2009-Seniors-Taking-Physics-Precalc-Calc-Race-Ethnicity.pdf), 53% of all college-bound seniors had taken physics, 53% had taken precalculus, and 28% had taken calculus in 2009. Among Asian-American students, 66% took physics, 69% took precalculus, and 48%

took calculus. More than half (54%) of non-Hispanic white students took physics, while 55% took precalculus and 30% took calculus. However, only 44% of African-American students took physics, 36% took precalculus, and 14% took calculus. Even though higher proportions of Hispanic and Native American students took these upper-level courses than did African-American students, non-Hispanic white students were more likely to have taken them.

Asian and Pacific Islander students were more likely to achieve the highest academic levels in science and mathematics in 2005. More than four out of 10 (42.8%) completed biology, chemistry, and physics, compared with 29% of non-Hispanic white students, 21.3% of African-American students, 18.9% of Hispanic students, and 14.1% of Native American and Alaskan Native students. (See Table 3.11.) Nearly three out of 10 (29.8%) Asian and Pacific Islander students completed a calculus course, compared with 15.3% of non-Hispanic white students, 7.9% of Native American and Alaskan Native students, 6.3% of Hispanic students, and 5.5% of African-American students.

However, Hispanic students earned more credits in English, on average, than did other students, perhaps because they were the most likely to speak English as a second language. In 2005 Hispanic students earned, on average, 4.8 credits in English, African-American and Asian and Pacific Islander students each earned 4.5 credits, Native American and Alaskan Native students earned 4.4 credits, and non-Hispanic white students earned 4.3 credits. (See Table 3.12.) By contrast, Hispanic students earned the fewest history credits, on average, with 3.8 credits, whereas Asian and Pacific Islander students earned 3.9 credits, African-American and non-Hispanic white students each earned 4 credits, and Native American and Alaskan Native students earned 4.1 credits. Asian and Pacific Islander students earned far more foreign language credits, on average, than did other students (2.4), compared with 2 credits for non-Hispanic white students, 1.9 credits for Hispanic students, 1.7 credits for African-American students, and 1.4 credits for Native American and Alaskan Native students.

Asian and Pacific Islander students were the most likely to take the toughest course load in high school in 2005. More than four out of 10 (42.9%) Asian and Pacific Islander students took the toughest load of four English courses, three social science courses, three science courses, three math courses, half a year of computer science, and two language courses. (See Table 3.13.) African-American students (39.9%) were the next most likely to take this course load, followed by non-Hispanic white students (35.8%) and Native American and Alaskan Native students (24.5%).

Advanced placement courses are college-level courses offered to students in high school. The College

TABLE 3.11

Percentage of public and private high school graduates taking selected mathematics and science courses in high school, by sex, race and Hispanic origin, selected years 1982–2005

							2005								
								Sex				Race/ethnicity			
Course (Carnegie units)	1982	1987	1990	1994	1998	2000	Total	Male	Female	White	Black	Hispanic	Asian/Pacific Islander	American Indian/Alaska Native	Other
1	2	3	4	5	6	7	8	9	10	11	12	13	14	15	16
Mathematics[a]															
Any mathematics (1.0)	98.5	98.9	99.9	99.8	99.8	99.8	99.9	99.9	100.0	99.9	100.0	99.9	100.0	100.0	100.0
Algebra I (1.0)[b]	55.2	58.8	63.7	65.8	62.8	61.7	62.8	61.5	64.1	60.9	71.8	65.6	58.0	67.9	69.3
Geometry (1.0)	47.1	58.6	63.2	70.0	75.1	78.3	83.3	81.4	85.2	83.4	84.7	80.5	86.1	74.2	89.2
Algebra II (0.5)[c]	39.9	49.0	52.9	61.1	61.7	67.8	70.3	67.1	73.3	71.2	69.2	62.7	78.3	67.5	81.8
Trigonometry (0.5)	8.1	11.5	9.6	11.7	8.9	7.5	8.3	8.1	8.6	9.6	3.9	4.8	9.4	10.4	13.9
Analysis/pre-calculus (0.5)	6.2	12.8	13.3	17.3	23.1	26.7	29.5	28.0	30.8	32.0	17.9	20.5	48.8	15.9	31.6
Statistics/probability (0.5)	1.0	1.1	1.0	2.0	3.7	5.7	7.7	7.7	7.8	8.5	5.8	3.4	13.0	2.8	12.0
Calculus (1.0)	5.0	6.1	6.5	9.3	11.0	11.6	13.5	14.0	13.2	15.3	5.5	6.3	29.8	7.9	16.6
AP calculus (1.0)	1.6	3.4	4.1	7.0	6.7	7.9	9.2	9.8	8.7	10.1	2.9	5.0	24.6	2.8	10.9
Science[a]															
Any science (1.0)	96.4	97.8	99.3	99.5	99.5	99.5	99.6	99.5	99.6	99.7	99.7	99.1	99.3	98.3	100.0
Biology (1.0)	77.4	86.1	90.9	93.2	92.7	91.2	92.3	90.8	93.7	92.6	93.6	89.1	92.1	92.1	93.9
AP/honors biology (1.0)	10.0	9.4	10.1	11.9	16.2	16.3	16.0	13.9	18.0	17.0	12.0	11.8	24.0	8.3	21.6
Chemistry (1.0)	32.1	44.2	48.9	55.8	60.4	62.0	66.2	62.5	69.7	67.1	63.6	59.2	79.4	49.3	77.8
AP/honors chemistry (1.0)	3.0	3.5	3.5	3.9	4.7	5.8	7.6	7.6	7.6	8.0	4.0	5.7	17.2	4.8	10.5
Physics (1.0)	15.0	20.0	21.5	24.5	28.8	31.4	32.7	34.8	30.8	34.6	25.8	23.3	49.9	18.2	42.7
AP/honors physics (1.0)	1.2	1.8	2.0	2.7	3.0	3.9	5.3	6.6	4.1	5.6	2.5	3.4	14.2	1.5	8.3
Engineering (1.0)	1.2	2.6	4.2	4.5	6.7	3.9	4.3	4.6	4.0	4.4	4.8	3.3	3.7	3.8	4.2
Astronomy (0.5)	1.2	1.0	1.2	1.7	1.9	2.8	2.8	2.9	2.7	3.3	1.4	1.2	3.1	3.5	1.2
Geology/earth science (0.5)	13.6	13.4	24.7	22.9	20.7	17.4	23.1	23.9	22.4	24.0	24.3	19.6	16.2	22.7	23.2
Biology and chemistry (2.0)	29.3	41.4	47.5	53.7	59.0	59.4	64.3	60.3	68.0	65.3	62.0	57.2	75.5	48.0	73.9
Biology, chemistry, and physics (3.0)	11.2	16.5	18.8	21.4	25.4	25.1	27.3	28.2	26.5	29.0	21.3	18.9	42.8	14.1	33.2

†Not applicable.

[a]These data only report the percentage of students who earned the indicated credit (0.5 = one semester; 1.0 = one academic year) in each course while in high school and do not count those students who took these courses prior to entering high school.

[b]Excludes pre-algebra.

[c]Includes algebra/trigonometry and algebra/geometry.

Notes: The Carnegie unit is a standard of measurement that represents one credit for the completion of a 1-year course. Data differ slightly from figures appearing in other National Center for Education Statistics (NCES) reports because of differences in taxonomies and case exclusion criteria. Some data have been revised from previously published figures. Race categories exclude persons of Hispanic ethnicity.
AP = Advanced Placement

SOURCE: Thomas D. Snyder, Sally A. Dillow, and Charlene M. Hoffman, "Table 149. Percentage of Public and Private High School Graduates Taking Selected Mathematics and Science Courses in High School, by Sex and Race/Ethnicity: Selected Years, 1982 through 2005," in *Digest of Education Statistics, 2008*, U.S. Department of Education, National Center for Education Statistics, March 2009, http://nces.ed.gov/programs/digest/d08/tables/dt08_149.asp (accessed December 9, 2009)

TABLE 3.12

Average number of Carnegie units earned by public high school graduates in various subject fields, by selected student characteristics, selected years 1982–2005

Graduation year and selected student characteristic	Total	English	History/ social studies	Mathematics			Science					Foreign languages	Arts	Career/ technical education[a]	Personal use[b]	Computer related[c]
				Total	Less than algebra	Algebra or higher	Total	General science	Biology	Chemistry	Physics					
1	2	3	4	5	6	7	8	9	10	11	12	13	14	15	16	17
1982 graduates	21.58	3.93	3.16	2.63	0.90	1.74	2.20	0.73	0.94	0.34	0.17	0.99	1.47	4.62	2.58	0.12
Sex																
Male	21.40	3.88	3.16	2.71	0.94	1.77	2.27	0.76	0.91	0.36	0.23	0.80	1.29	4.60	2.69	0.14
Female	21.75	3.98	3.15	2.57	0.86	1.71	2.13	0.71	0.97	0.33	0.12	1.17	1.63	4.64	2.48	0.11
Race/ethnicity																
White	21.69	3.90	3.19	2.68	0.77	1.91	2.27	0.73	0.97	0.38	0.20	1.06	1.53	4.53	2.52	0.13
Black	21.15	4.08	3.08	2.61	1.36	1.25	2.06	0.81	0.90	0.26	0.09	0.72	1.26	4.75	2.60	0.12
Hispanic	21.23	3.94	3.00	2.33	1.21	1.12	1.80	0.75	0.81	0.16	0.07	0.77	1.29	5.22	2.87	0.08
Asian/Pacific Islander	22.46	4.01	3.16	3.15	0.71	2.44	2.64	0.51	1.11	0.61	0.42	1.79	1.31	3.34	3.05	0.22
American Indian/Alaska Native	21.45	3.98	3.25	2.35	1.23	1.12	2.04	0.67	0.84	0.42	0.12	0.48	1.72	4.77	2.84	0.06
Academic track																
Academic[d]	21.75	4.11	3.32	3.04	0.73	2.30	2.65	0.73	1.13	0.53	0.26	1.54	1.91	2.55	2.62	0.10
Career/technical[e]	20.21	3.44	2.63	1.80	1.09	0.71	1.32	0.69	0.57	0.04	0.02	0.18	0.59	7.74	2.51	0.12
Both[f]	22.89	4.04	3.33	2.69	1.02	1.67	2.17	0.79	0.94	0.29	0.14	0.75	1.41	6.03	2.47	0.18
Neither[g]	18.73	3.58	2.70	1.73	1.08	0.65	1.33	0.69	0.59	0.03	0.02	0.22	0.85	5.23	3.06	0.05
1987 graduates	23.00	4.12	3.32	3.01	0.86	2.14	2.55	0.76	1.10	0.47	0.21	1.35	1.44	4.55	2.67	0.47
Sex																
Male	22.88	4.08	3.29	3.05	0.91	2.14	2.59	0.79	1.05	0.47	0.26	1.16	1.24	4.64	2.83	0.47
Female	23.12	4.15	3.35	2.96	0.82	2.15	2.52	0.74	1.14	0.47	0.17	1.53	1.63	4.47	2.51	0.47
Race/ethnicity																
White	23.11	4.08	3.29	3.01	0.74	2.27	2.61	0.75	1.12	0.50	0.23	1.38	1.50	4.65	2.60	0.49
Black	22.40	4.22	3.34	2.99	1.40	1.59	2.33	0.90	1.01	0.31	0.10	1.08	1.20	4.52	2.73	0.39
Hispanic	22.84	4.30	3.22	2.81	1.30	1.50	2.24	0.78	1.07	0.29	0.10	1.25	1.34	4.49	3.19	0.42
Asian/Pacific Islander	24.47	4.37	3.65	3.71	0.53	3.18	3.14	0.59	1.17	0.87	0.50	2.07	1.18	3.11	3.23	0.58
American Indian/Alaska Native	23.23	4.22	3.18	2.98	1.35	1.63	2.44	0.81	1.22	0.32	0.09	0.75	1.68	4.92	3.06	0.39
Academic track																
Academic[d]	23.20	4.26	3.55	3.33	0.65	2.68	2.97	0.73	1.23	0.68	0.32	1.92	1.87	2.57	2.73	0.38
Career/technical[e]	21.07	3.62	2.59	2.00	1.29	0.71	1.48	0.74	0.70	0.03	0.01	0.18	0.47	8.07	2.67	0.39
Both[f]	23.53	4.11	3.29	2.93	0.97	1.96	2.37	0.81	1.07	0.35	0.14	1.01	1.20	6.09	2.53	0.64
Neither[g]	19.56	3.55	2.45	2.11	1.62	0.49	1.47	0.84	0.59	0.03	0.00	0.18	0.76	5.10	3.93	0.17
1990 graduates	23.53	4.19	3.47	3.15	0.90	2.25	2.75	0.85	1.14	0.53	0.23	1.54	1.55	4.19	2.68	0.54
Sex																
Male	23.35	4.13	3.45	3.16	0.96	2.20	2.78	0.88	1.11	0.52	0.28	1.33	1.31	4.32	2.87	0.50
Female	23.69	4.25	3.50	3.14	0.85	2.29	2.73	0.83	1.17	0.53	0.19	1.72	1.76	4.08	2.51	0.57
Race/ethnicity																
White	23.54	4.12	3.46	3.13	0.80	2.33	2.80	0.84	1.15	0.55	0.25	1.58	1.61	4.22	2.61	0.52
Black	23.40	4.34	3.49	3.20	1.25	1.95	2.68	0.98	1.11	0.42	0.16	1.20	1.34	4.41	2.74	0.60
Hispanic	23.83	4.51	3.42	3.13	1.30	1.83	2.50	0.83	1.10	0.42	0.14	1.57	1.48	4.12	3.10	0.58
Asian/Pacific Islander	24.07	4.50	3.70	3.52	0.70	2.82	2.97	0.68	1.12	0.74	0.42	2.06	1.29	3.07	2.96	0.54
American Indian/Alaska Native	22.64	4.08	3.34	3.04	1.03	2.01	2.48	0.83	1.09	0.42	0.15	1.15	1.11	4.62	2.81	0.60

TABLE 3.12

Average number of Carnegie units earned by public high school graduates in various subject fields, by selected student characteristics, selected years 1982–2005 [CONTINUED]

Graduation year and selected student characteristic	Total	English	History/ social studies	Mathematics			Science					Foreign languages	Arts	Career/ technical education[a]	Personal use[b]	Computer related[c]
				Total	Less than algebra	Algebra or higher	Total	General science	Biology	Chemistry	Physics					
1	2	3	4	5	6	7	8	9	10	11	12	13	14	15	16	17
Academic track																
Academic[d]	23.53	4.30	3.65	3.37	0.68	2.70	3.06	0.81	1.23	0.70	0.32	2.02	1.93	2.41	2.78	0.42
Career/technical[e]	21.73	3.60	2.58	2.07	1.54	0.53	1.62	0.87	0.71	0.03	0.01	0.17	0.42	8.68	2.59	0.46
Both[f]	23.92	4.14	3.38	3.02	1.12	1.90	2.51	0.92	1.09	0.36	0.14	1.07	1.17	6.10	2.53	0.73
Neither[g]	19.81	3.63	2.59	2.01	1.57	0.44	1.47	0.79	0.60	0.04	0.03	0.21	0.79	5.81	3.29	0.36
1994 graduates	24.17	4.29	3.55	3.33	0.76	2.57	3.04	0.88	1.26	0.62	0.28	1.71	1.66	3.96	2.63	0.64
Sex																
Male	23.79	4.26	3.51	3.32	0.85	2.48	3.03	0.91	1.20	0.59	0.32	1.49	1.43	4.13	2.83	0.63
Female	24.11	4.32	3.59	3.34	0.68	2.66	3.06	0.86	1.31	0.64	0.24	1.93	1.87	3.80	2.44	0.65
Race/ethnicity																
White	24.08	4.23	3.56	3.36	0.70	2.66	3.13	0.89	1.29	0.65	0.30	1.76	1.74	3.96	2.61	0.63
Black	23.28	4.36	3.51	3.23	1.09	2.14	2.80	0.92	1.21	0.49	0.17	1.35	1.36	4.29	2.69	0.64
Hispanic	23.71	4.61	3.45	3.28	0.96	2.32	2.69	0.83	1.19	0.49	0.17	1.73	1.51	3.87	2.93	0.76
Asian/Pacific Islander	23.84	4.60	3.66	3.66	0.67	2.98	3.35	0.80	1.22	0.81	0.48	2.09	1.32	3.01	2.78	0.71
American Indian/Alaska Native	23.40	4.27	3.57	3.11	0.94	2.17	2.82	0.91	1.28	0.50	0.13	1.30	2.01	4.27	3.12	0.53
Academic track																
Academic[d]	23.86	4.37	3.69	3.52	0.58	2.94	3.32	0.83	1.34	0.77	0.37	2.14	2.05	2.28	2.71	0.50
Career/technical[e]	21.20	3.70	2.49	2.20	1.56	0.64	1.69	0.80	0.83	0.03	0.02	0.14	0.34	8.64	2.41	0.55
Both[f]	24.41	4.23	3.45	3.17	0.96	2.21	2.78	0.96	1.19	0.45	0.17	1.24	1.21	6.01	2.52	0.85
Neither[g]	20.56	3.54	2.24	2.25	1.71	0.54	1.53	0.82	0.63	0.05	0.02	0.19	0.56	6.51	4.47	0.33
1998 graduates	25.14	4.25	3.74	3.40	0.67	2.73	3.12	0.89	1.26	0.66	0.31	1.85	1.90	3.99	2.89	0.74
Sex																
Male	24.64	4.19	3.68	3.37	0.74	2.64	3.09	0.93	1.20	0.62	0.33	1.62	1.61	4.25	3.12	0.78
Female	25.04	4.31	3.80	3.42	0.62	2.80	3.17	0.87	1.32	0.70	0.28	2.06	2.15	3.77	2.67	0.71
Race/ethnicity																
White	24.87	4.19	3.77	3.40	0.57	2.84	3.18	0.87	1.28	0.69	0.33	1.90	2.00	3.97	2.80	0.73
Black	24.37	4.28	3.69	3.42	0.90	2.53	3.03	0.97	1.24	0.58	0.22	1.58	1.57	4.33	2.94	0.84
Hispanic	24.69	4.51	3.60	3.28	1.05	2.23	2.81	0.97	1.13	0.50	0.20	1.78	1.78	3.97	3.36	0.71
Asian/Pacific Islander	24.67	4.37	3.92	3.62	0.65	2.97	3.43	0.81	1.26	0.83	0.51	2.29	1.52	3.15	2.95	0.67
American Indian/Alaska Native	23.81	4.18	3.67	3.10	0.90	2.20	2.68	0.98	1.07	0.49	0.15	1.45	1.94	4.02	3.40	0.67
Academic track																
Academic[d]	24.61	4.33	3.87	3.54	0.53	3.00	3.34	0.84	1.33	0.78	0.38	2.24	2.41	2.22	2.97	0.52
Career/technical[e]	22.10	3.46	2.55	2.17	1.30	0.87	1.69	1.05	0.59	0.03	0.01	0.14	0.47	9.12	3.01	0.81
Both[f]	25.38	4.20	3.66	3.30	0.81	2.49	2.94	0.96	1.20	0.54	0.23	1.45	1.31	6.06	2.73	1.03
Neither[g]	20.39	3.21	2.32	2.19	1.59	0.60	1.58	0.88	0.58	0.04	0.08	0.20	0.55	5.64	5.82	0.51
2000 graduates	26.05	4.39	3.83	3.56	0.61	2.95	3.20	0.85	1.29	0.69	0.36	1.95	2.03	4.21	2.88	0.83
Sex																
Male	26.23	4.31	3.76	3.53	0.68	2.86	3.16	0.88	1.20	0.65	0.40	1.71	1.75	4.60	3.09	0.93
Female	26.46	4.46	3.89	3.58	0.55	3.03	3.25	0.82	1.36	0.73	0.33	2.18	2.30	3.82	2.69	0.74

TABLE 3.12

Average number of Carnegie units earned by public high school graduates in various subject fields, by selected student characteristics, selected years 1982–2005 [CONTINUED]

Graduation year and selected student characteristic	Total	English	History/ social studies	Mathematics			Science					Foreign languages	Arts	Career/ technical education[a]	Personal use[b]	Computer related[c]
				Total	Less than algebra	Algebra or higher	Total	General science	Biology	Chemistry	Physics					
1	2	3	4	5	6	7	8	9	10	11	12	13	14	15	16	17
Race/ethnicity																
White	26.57	4.32	3.86	3.56	0.58	2.98	3.24	0.84	1.30	0.70	0.38	1.98	2.12	4.34	2.79	0.81
Black	26.28	4.43	3.75	3.54	0.72	2.82	3.13	0.91	1.26	0.65	0.27	1.70	1.95	4.29	2.98	0.85
Hispanic	25.91	4.69	3.77	3.42	0.74	2.68	2.87	0.85	1.19	0.58	0.24	1.90	1.77	3.83	3.21	0.89
Asian/Pacific Islander	26.66	4.57	3.77	3.96	0.35	3.61	3.71	0.71	1.36	0.96	0.65	2.51	1.79	2.82	3.09	0.92
American Indian/Alaska Native	26.03	4.12	3.75	3.29	0.91	2.38	2.88	0.98	1.25	0.45	0.19	1.40	1.99	4.79	2.89	0.96
Academic track																
Academic[d]	25.82	4.47	3.93	3.70	0.49	3.21	3.39	0.81	1.35	0.80	0.42	2.32	2.52	2.28	2.96	0.54
Career/technical[e]	24.13	3.33	2.62	2.11	1.28	0.82	1.61	0.84	0.65	0.06	0.05	0.15	0.57	9.56	3.50	1.17
Both[f]	27.16	4.33	3.76	3.45	0.74	2.71	3.04	0.89	1.24	0.59	0.30	1.56	1.47	6.46	2.74	1.20
Neither[g]	22.41	3.50	1.86	2.27	1.76	0.51	1.59	1.04	0.48	0.04	0.02	0.20	0.93	5.52	5.72	0.29
2005 graduates	26.68	4.42	3.98	3.67	0.49	3.19	3.34	0.95	1.28	0.74	0.35	1.97	2.05	4.01	3.23	0.93
Sex																
Male	26.50	4.36	3.91	3.65	0.54	3.10	3.29	0.97	1.19	0.70	0.39	1.76	1.71	4.35	3.47	1.09
Female	26.84	4.48	4.05	3.70	0.44	3.26	3.40	0.92	1.37	0.78	0.32	2.16	2.38	3.68	3.00	0.79
Race/ethnicity																
White	26.87	4.32	4.02	3.69	0.44	3.24	3.43	0.96	1.31	0.76	0.38	2.01	2.17	4.12	3.10	0.90
Black	26.57	4.54	3.98	3.71	0.63	3.08	3.21	0.99	1.27	0.68	0.27	1.71	1.77	4.11	3.53	1.07
Hispanic	25.91	4.80	3.75	3.49	0.65	2.83	2.92	0.92	1.11	0.63	0.24	1.88	1.78	3.69	3.62	1.00
Asian/Pacific Islander	26.32	4.51	3.94	3.90	0.27	3.62	3.63	0.74	1.31	0.97	0.56	2.43	1.80	2.91	3.21	0.94
American Indian/Alaska Native	26.48	4.44	4.06	3.53	0.69	2.84	3.02	1.04	1.28	0.52	0.17	1.44	2.44	4.20	3.36	0.82
Other	26.09	4.39	3.87	3.72	0.26	3.46	3.50	0.93	1.35	0.81	0.37	2.31	2.12	2.93	3.26	0.72
Academic track																
Academic[d]	26.53	4.48	4.09	3.78	0.42	3.36	3.50	0.92	1.35	0.82	0.40	2.20	2.29	2.92	3.27	0.80
Career/technical[e]	24.01	3.56	2.78	2.42	0.96	1.45	1.87	0.90	0.75	0.16	0.05	0.50	1.32	8.16	3.40	0.77
Both[f]	27.93	4.36	3.90	3.63	0.61	3.02	3.17	1.06	1.19	0.62	0.29	1.51	1.34	7.01	3.00	1.42
Neither[g]	22.73	4.08	2.92	2.44	0.87	1.57	2.01	0.84	0.85	0.21	0.09	1.02	2.35	3.86	4.05	0.64

[a]Includes general labor market preparation, consumer and home-making education, and occupational education in agriculture, business, marketing, health, occupational home economics, trade and industry, and technical courses.

[b]Includes general skills, personal health and physical education, religion, military sciences, special education, and other courses not included in other subject fields.

[c]Though shown separately here, computer-related courses are also included in the mathematics and career/technical categories.

[d]Includes students who complete at least 12 Carnegie units in academic courses, but less than 3 Carnegie units in any occupational education field.

[e]Includes students who complete at least 3 Carnegie units in an occupational education field, but less than 12 Carnegie units in academic courses.

[f]Includes students who complete at least 12 Carnegie units in academic courses and at least 3 Carnegie units in an occupational education field.

[g]Includes students who complete less than 12 Carnegie units in academic courses and less than 3 Carnegie units in an occupational education field.

Notes: The Carnegie unit is a standard of measurement that represents one credit for the completion of a 1-year course. Data differ slightly from figures appearing in other National Center for Educations Statistics (NCES) reports because of differences in taxonomies and case exclusion criteria. Race categories exclude persons of Hispanic ethnicity. Detail may not sum to totals because of rounding.

SOURCE: Thomas D. Snyder, Sally A. Dillow, and Charlene M. Hoffman, "Table 147. Average Number of Carnegie Units Earned by Public High School Graduates in Various Subject Fields, by Selected Student Characteristics: Selected Years, 1982 through 2005," in Digest of Education Statistics, 2008, U.S. Department of Education, National Center for Education Statistics, March 2009, http://nces.ed.gov/programs/digest/d08/tables/dt08_147.asp (accessed December 9, 2009)

TABLE 3.13

Percentage of public and private high school graduates earning minimum credits in selected combinations of academic courses, by sex and race and Hispanic origin, selected years 1982–2005

Year of graduation and course combination taken[a]	All students		Sex				White		Black		Hispanic		Asian/ Pacific Islander		American Indian/ Alaska Native		Other	
			Male		Female													
1982 graduates																		
4 Eng, 3 SS, 3 Sci, 3 Math, .5 Comp, and 2 FL[b]	2.0	(0.22)	2.3	(0.31)	1.8	(0.27)	2.4	(0.28)	0.7	(0.28)	0.6	(0.22)	5.8	(1.72)	1.1	(0.77)	—	(†)
4 Eng, 3 SS, 3 Sci, 3 Math, and 2 FL	9.5	(0.57)	9.1	(0.70)	9.9	(0.71)	10.9	(0.69)	5.2	(1.02)	3.9	(0.57)	17.0	(2.49)	3.3	(1.68)	—	(†)
4 Eng, 3 SS, 3 Sci, 3 Math	14.3	(0.66)	15.2	(0.86)	13.4	(0.79)	15.9	(0.79)	11.0	(1.39)	6.7	(0.79)	21.1	(2.65)	8.1	(3.02)	—	(†)
4 Eng, 3 SS, 2 Sci, 2 Math	31.5	(1.07)	31.7	(1.26)	31.3	(1.22)	32.4	(1.21)	30.8	(2.32)	25.6	(1.76)	32.0	(3.40)	23.6	(5.39)	—	(†)
1987 graduates																		
4 Eng, 3 SS, 3 Sci, 3 Math, .5 Comp, and 2 FL[b]	10.6	(0.73)	11.5	(1.01)	9.8	(0.65)	11.3	(0.97)	6.6	(0.91)	5.5	(1.03)	20.5	(2.57)	2.5	(0.86)	—	(†)
4 Eng, 3 SS, 3 Sci, 3 Math, and 2 FL	18.1	(0.91)	18.0	(1.13)	18.3	(1.01)	19.0	(1.10)	12.7	(1.15)	10.8	(1.70)	35.7	(4.49)	4.9	(1.40)	—	(†)
4 Eng, 3 SS, 3 Sci, 3 Math	24.8	(1.03)	25.9	(1.27)	23.7	(1.07)	26.1	(1.21)	19.6	(1.99)	14.5	(1.69)	39.8	(4.51)	24.3	(3.69)	—	(†)
4 Eng, 3 SS, 2 Sci, 2 Math	48.1	(1.74)	48.0	(2.22)	48.4	(1.56)	48.1	(2.15)	48.3	(2.63)	43.9	(1.92)	57.9	(4.82)	61.8	(5.56)	—	(†)
1990 graduates																		
4 Eng, 3 SS, 3 Sci, 3 Math, .5 Comp, and 2 FL[b]	18.0	(1.06)	17.8	(1.16)	18.2	(1.09)	18.6	(1.21)	15.1	(1.66)	17.8	(2.42)	23.3	(2.23)	7.8	(3.33)	—	(†)
4 Eng, 3 SS, 3 Sci, 3 Math, and 2 FL	29.9	(1.26)	28.8	(1.38)	31.0	(1.36)	31.7	(1.46)	22.9	(2.27)	25.4	(2.41)	42.6	(2.95)	9.9	(3.70)	—	(†)
4 Eng, 3 SS, 3 Sci, 3 Math	38.2	(1.50)	38.5	(1.69)	37.9	(1.54)	39.2	(1.63)	39.0	(3.57)	29.8	(2.51)	47.4	(3.04)	19.2	(4.70)	—	(†)
4 Eng, 3 SS, 2 Sci, 2 Math	65.5	(1.96)	64.3	(2.09)	66.4	(1.98)	64.9	(2.28)	71.3	(3.00)	63.7	(3.01)	69.1	(3.90)	46.3	(6.39)	—	(†)
1994 graduates																		
4 Eng, 3 SS, 3 Sci, 3 Math, .5 Comp, and 2 FL[b]	25.1	(1.05)	23.4	(0.93)	26.8	(1.32)	26.4	(1.19)	19.0	(1.45)	27.1	(3.75)	35.5	(2.84)	12.9	(3.09)	—	(†)
4 Eng, 3 SS, 3 Sci, 3 Math, and 2 FL	39.0	(1.12)	35.0	(1.11)	42.7	(1.33)	41.6	(1.32)	29.6	(1.52)	35.6	(2.94)	50.1	(2.39)	22.5	(4.31)	—	(†)
4 Eng, 3 SS, 3 Sci, 3 Math	49.3	(1.45)	47.0	(1.45)	51.5	(1.58)	52.4	(1.67)	43.7	(2.39)	40.3	(3.25)	54.9	(2.46)	46.0	(3.30)	—	(†)
4 Eng, 3 SS, 2 Sci, 2 Math	73.9	(1.50)	71.2	(1.63)	76.4	(1.46)	75.1	(1.69)	74.5	(2.32)	74.7	(2.61)	72.3	(3.62)	76.3	(3.60)	—	(†)
1998 graduates																		
4 Eng, 3 SS, 3 Sci, 3 Math, .5 Comp, and 2 FL[b]	28.6	(1.72)	27.6	(2.12)	30.1	(1.90)	29.6	(1.99)	27.9	(3.36)	20.4	(2.44)	38.6	(4.61)	16.5	(4.65)	—	(†)
4 Eng, 3 SS, 3 Sci, 3 Math, and 2 FL	44.2	(1.92)	40.5	(2.19)	48.2	(2.05)	46.2	(2.16)	40.0	(3.41)	32.0	(2.94)	57.8	(4.51)	28.3	(4.53)	—	(†)
4 Eng, 3 SS, 3 Sci, 3 Math	55.0	(2.44)	52.9	(2.64)	57.8	(2.48)	56.8	(2.69)	55.6	(4.39)	40.0	(3.28)	66.1	(5.69)	40.0	(4.73)	—	(†)
4 Eng, 3 SS, 2 Sci, 2 Math	74.5	(2.18)	72.8	(2.34)	77.0	(2.14)	74.7	(2.64)	76.0	(3.21)	70.1	(2.57)	79.5	(4.76)	76.4	(5.21)	—	(†)
2000 graduates																		
4 Eng, 3 SS, 3 Sci, 3 Math, .5 Comp, and 2 FL[b]	31.0	(1.53)	28.6	(1.59)	33.2	(1.73)	31.5	(1.55)	28.9	(1.65)	28.4	(5.50)	37.8	(5.45)	16.2	(2.69)	—	(†)
4 Eng, 3 SS, 3 Sci, 3 Math, and 2 FL	46.5	(1.46)	40.3	(1.59)	52.1	(1.60)	47.8	(1.56)	44.2	(2.14)	38.4	(5.05)	56.5	(3.13)	25.6	(3.40)	—	(†)
4 Eng, 3 SS, 3 Sci, 3 Math	57.2	(1.58)	52.9	(1.65)	61.1	(1.70)	58.1	(1.70)	62.4	(2.44)	46.4	(5.46)	61.1	(3.11)	40.9	(5.56)	—	(†)
4 Eng, 3 SS, 2 Sci, 2 Math	77.6	(1.58)	74.2	(1.86)	80.6	(1.44)	77.9	(1.84)	81.2	(2.23)	74.1	(3.24)	74.5	(3.05)	71.2	(4.44)	—	(†)
2005 graduates																		
4 Eng, 3 SS, 3 Sci, 3 Math, .5 Comp, and 2 FL[b]	36.2	(1.00)	34.6	(0.97)	37.7	(1.23)	35.8	(1.22)	39.9	(1.72)	33.0	(1.86)	42.9	(2.34)	24.5	(3.48)	36.8	(5.09)
4 Eng, 3 SS, 3 Sci, 3 Math, and 2 FL	52.1	(1.00)	46.8	(1.16)	57.2	(1.01)	53.3	(1.20)	51.4	(1.88)	41.8	(2.07)	63.6	(2.19)	36.2	(3.40)	65.7	(3.12)
4 Eng, 3 SS, 3 Sci, 3 Math	64.7	(1.07)	61.1	(1.26)	68.0	(0.99)	65.9	(1.32)	69.6	(1.83)	49.8	(2.29)	69.1	(2.20)	59.3	(3.30)	72.4	(3.44)
4 Eng, 3 SS, 2 Sci, 2 Math	81.8	(1.02)	79.2	(1.18)	84.3	(0.97)	81.2	(1.33)	88.7	(0.93)	77.2	(1.33)	83.7	(1.72)	81.0	(3.18)	87.2	(2.71)

—Not available.

†Not applicable.

[a]Eng = English; SS = social studies; Sci = science; Comp = computer science; and FL = foreign language.

[b]The National Commission on Excellence in Education recommended that all college-bound high school students take these courses as a minimum.

Note: Data differ slightly from figures appearing in other National Center for Education Statistics (NCES) reports because of differences in taxonomies and case exclusion criteria. Race categories exclude persons of Hispanic ethnicity. Standard errors appear in parentheses.

SOURCE: Thomas D. Snyder, Sally A. Dillow, and Charlene M. Hoffman, "Table 151. Percentage of Public and Private High School Graduates Earning Minimum Credits in Selected Combinations of Academic Courses, by Sex and Race/Ethnicity: Selected Years, 1982 through 2005," in *Digest of Education Statistics, 2008*, U.S. Department of Education, National Center for Education Statistics, March 2009, http://nces.ed.gov/programs/digest/d08/tables/dt08_151 .asp (accessed December 9, 2009)

Board developed 37 courses in 20 subjects; college credit can be awarded for a qualifying score of 3.0 or better on a five-point scale. Between 1997 and 2005 the number of students taking advanced placement examinations

TABLE 3.14

Number and percent change of students taking Advanced Placement (AP) examinations, by race and Hispanic origin, 1997–2005

Race/ethnicity	1997	1998	1999	2000	2001	2002	2003	2004	2005	Percent change 1997 to 2005
Total*	566,720	618,257	685,981	747,922	820,880	913,251	998,329	1,081,102	1,197,439	111
White	371,606	403,553	445,880	504,600	549,065	607,816	660,225	702,489	762,548	105
Total minority*	154,046	170,054	194,557	225,825	250,230	280,276	315,046	350,425	398,243	159
Black	24,469	27,054	31,023	36,158	40,078	45,271	51,160	57,001	67,702	177
Hispanic	47,626	53,627	62,853	74,852	86,018	98,495	114,246	130,042	148,960	213
Asian/Asian American	63,528	68,109	75,875	85,756	92,762	102,653	111,704	121,038	135,815	114
American Indian/Alaska Native	2,520	2,761	3,136	3,584	3,472	3,896	4,530	4,974	5,654	124
Missing	41,068	44,650	45,544	17,497	21,585	25,159	23,058	28,188	36,648	−11

*Total includes other race/ethnicity categories not separately shown.
Note: Data reported are for all students who completed an AP exam. The College Board collects racial/ethnic information based on the categories American Indian/Alaska Native; Asian/Asian American; black/Afro-American; Latino: Chicano/Mexican, Puerto Rican, other Latino; white; and other. Hispanic refers to the sum of all Latino subgroups. Race categories exclude persons of Hispanic ethnicity.

SOURCE: Michael Planty, Stephen Provasnik, and Bruce Daniel, "Table 3. Number and Percent Change of Students Taking Advanced Placement (AP) Examinations, by Race/Ethnicity: 1997–2005," in *High School Coursetaking: Findings from The Condition of Education 2007*, U.S. Department of Education, National Center for Education Statistics, June 2007, http://nces.ed.gov/programs/coe/2007/analysis/2007065.pdf (accessed December 11, 2009)

increased by 111%. (See Table 3.14.) The participation of minority students increased more than the participation of non-Hispanic white students. For example, the participation of Hispanic students increased by 213%, the participation of African-American students increased by 177%, the participation of Native American and Alaskan Native students increased by 124%, and the participation of Asian and Pacific Islander students increased by 114%, whereas the participation of non-Hispanic white students increased by 105%. However, Michael Planty, Stephen Provasnik, and Bruce Daniel explain in *High School Coursetaking: Findings from the Condition of Education, 2007* (June 2007, http://nces.ed.gov/programs/coe/2007/analysis/2007065.pdf) that even though the average scores of non-Hispanic white and Asian-American students remained relatively stable during this period, at 3.0 and 3.1, respectively, the scores of other minority students declined. This lack of preparation for college coursework could affect these students' acceptance to and success in college.

GRADE POINT AVERAGE. Most groups of minority students, except for Asian-American students, are at a disadvantage when applying to college because of low grades in high school. In *College-Bound Seniors 2009* (July 2009, http://professionals.collegeboard.com/profdownload/cbs-2009-national-TOTAL-GROUP.pdf), the College Board notes that in 2009 the average grade point average (GPA) of most minority groups who took the Scholastic Assessment Test (SAT) was lower than 3.32, the average GPA of all students who took the SAT. The average GPA of African-American students was 0.32 lower than the average GPA, the average of Puerto Rican students was 0.21 lower, the average of Mexican-American students was 0.1 lower, and the average of other Hispanic students was 0.14 lower.

Only Native American students narrowed the gap between their average GPA and the overall average GPA from 1999 to 2009.

Asian-American students' average GPA remained higher than the average GPA of all students and higher than the GPA of non-Hispanic white students in 2009—Asian-American students' GPAs were 0.14 higher than the average, whereas non-Hispanic white students' GPAs were 0.08 higher than the average.

SAT and ACT Scores

Students wishing to enter most colleges and universities in the United States must take the SAT or the ACT Assessment (formerly the American College Test). These are standardized tests intended to measure verbal and mathematical ability to determine readiness for college-level work. Most students take the SAT. Performance on the SAT is measured in three areas, each on a scale of 200 to 800: critical reading, mathematics, and a written essay portion that was added to the SAT in 2005.

Historically, minority students have not scored as well on the SAT as non-Hispanic white students, but gains have been made by some groups since 1999. The College Board indicates in *College-Bound Seniors 2009* that in 2009 the average score for the critical reading portion of the SAT among non-Hispanic whites was 528, compared with 516 for Asians or Pacific Islanders, 486 for Native Americans or Alaskan Natives, and 429 for African-Americans. Among Hispanic subgroups, Mexican-Americans averaged 453 on the critical reading portion of the test, Puerto Ricans averaged 452, and the rest of the Hispanic subgroups combined for an average of 455. The College Board states that the average critical reading scores for minority groups generally

TABLE 3.15

Enrollment rates of 18- to 24-year-olds in degree-granting institutions, by type of institution, sex, and race and Hispanic origin of student, selected years 1975–2007

Year	Enrollment as a percent of all 18- to 24-year-olds[a]							
	All students			Sex		Race/ethnicity		
	Total	2-year	4-year	Male	Female	White	Black	Hispanic
1975	26.3	9.0	17.3	29.0	23.7	27.4	20.4	20.4
1980	25.7	7.1	18.6	26.4	25.0	27.3	19.4	16.1
1985	27.8	7.4	20.4	28.4	27.2	30.0	19.6	16.9
1990	32.0	8.7	23.3	32.3	31.8	35.1	25.4	15.8
1995	34.3	8.9	25.4	33.1	35.5	37.9	27.5	20.7
2000	35.5	9.4	26.0	32.6	38.4	38.7	30.5	21.7
2005[b]	38.9	9.6	29.2	35.3	42.5	42.8	33.1	24.8
2006[b]	37.3	9.6	27.8	34.1	40.6	41.0	32.6	23.6
2007[b]	38.8	10.9	27.9	35.5	42.1	42.6	33.1	26.6

[a]Includes students who were enrolled in college, but did not report high school completion.
[b]White and black data exclude persons identifying themselves as multiracial.
Note: Data are based on sample surveys of the civilian noninstitutional population. Percents based on 18- to 24-year-old high school completers for 1992 and later years use a slightly different definition of completion and may not be precisely comparable with figures for other years. All college students are counted as high school completers. Totals include other racial/ethnic groups not separately shown. Race categories exclude persons of Hispanic ethnicity except where otherwise noted.

SOURCE: Adapted from Thomas D. Snyder, Sally A. Dillow, and Charlene M. Hoffman, "Table 204. Enrollment Rates of 18- to 24-Year-Olds in Degree-Granting Institutions, by Type of Institution and Sex and Race/Ethnicity of Student: 1967–2007," in *Digest of Education Statistics, 2008*, U.S. Department of Education, National Center for Education Statistics, March 2009, http://nces.ed.gov/programs/digest/d08/tables/dt08_204.asp (accessed December 9, 2009)

held steady from 1999 to 2009. Asians or Pacific Islanders were the only group who experienced the largest increase, from 498 to 516. The average scores of Native Americans or Alaskan Natives also improved marginally, from 484 to 486. Mexican-Americans' scores held steady at 453, whereas Puerto Rican scores declined from 455 to 452. African-Americans' average score decreased from 434 in 1999 to 429 in 2009. Likewise, other Hispanics' average score also decreased, from 463 in 1999 to 455 in 2009.

According to the College Board, mathematics scores were better in 2009 than they were in 1999 for all minority groups except other Hispanics. In 2009 Asians or Pacific Islanders scored the highest by far on the math portion of the test, with an average score of 587, up from 560 in 1999. Non-Hispanic whites scored an average of 536, up from 528 in 1999. Native Americans or Alaskan Natives scored 493, up from 481 in 1999. Mexican-Americans scored 463 and Puerto Ricans scored 450, up from 456 and 448, respectively, in 1999. African-Americans scored 426, up from 422 in 1999. Other Hispanics dropped from 464 in 1999 to 461 in 2009.

The writing portion of the SAT was a relatively new part of the test in 2009, having only been added by the College Board in 2005. In 2009 Asians or Pacific Islanders and non-Hispanic whites did the best on this portion of the test, at 520 and 517, respectively. Native Americans or Alaskan Natives averaged 469, Mexican-Americans averaged 446, Puerto Ricans averaged 443, other Hispanics averaged 448, and African-Americans scored an average of 421.

Minority College Attendance

Generally, minority enrollment in colleges and universities has grown ever since racial and ethnic enrollment statistics were first reported in 1975. Even though these gains are encouraging, they must be viewed in the context of overall participation rates in higher education and degree completion rates.

KewalRamani et al. note that in 2004, 60.3% of Asians and Pacific Islanders aged 18 to 24 years were enrolled in colleges and universities, the largest proportion of all racial and ethnic groups, compared with 41.7% of non-Hispanic white young adults aged 18 to 24. Other minority groups have significantly lower enrollment rates. In 2007 about one-third (33.1%) of African-Americans and 26.6% of Hispanics in this age group were enrolled in colleges and universities, compared with 42.6% of non-Hispanic whites. (See Table 3.15.)

Earning a Bachelor's Degree

College participation rates are telling, but so, too, are college completion rates. A number of students begin college, only to drop out before receiving a bachelor's degree. In 2008 only 20.4% of African-Americans between the ages of 25 and 29 had earned a bachelor's degree or higher. (See Figure 3.7.) Among Hispanics in this age group, only 12.4% had received a bachelor's degree or higher. Among Asians and Pacific Islanders in this age group, 57.9% had received a bachelor's degree or higher—the highest completion rate of any race or ethnic group.

College completion rates among Asian-Americans and Hispanics vary according to their country of origin. KewalRamani et al. report that among Hispanics aged 25 to 29 in 2005, those who traced their roots to South America had the highest completion rate, at 30.7%. Almost one out of five (18%) Dominicans in this age group had a bachelor's degree, and 16.4% of Puerto Ricans had a bachelor's degree. Not even one out of 10 Hispanics who traced their roots to Mexico (8.3%) or Central America (8.6%) had earned a bachelor's degree by age 29.

Among those of Asian origin, 25- to 29-year-olds who traced their roots to India had the highest percentage of bachelor's degrees, whereas those who traced their roots to Vietnam had the lowest percentage. Four out of five (80%) Indians in this age group had bachelor's degrees, compared with 71.4% of Chinese, 67.2% of Koreans, 57% of Japanese, 42% of Filipinos, and 37.7% of Vietnamese. However, the percentage of those who traced their roots to Vietnam who held bachelor's degrees was still more than twice as high as the percentage of African-Americans (17.2%) in the same age group with bachelor's degrees.

Affirmative Action in Higher Education

In the landmark 1978 affirmative action case *Regents of the University of California v. Bakke* (438 U.S. 265), the Supreme Court allowed race and ethnicity to be considered in college admissions in the interest of racial and ethnic diversity on U.S. college campuses. This led many schools to take special steps to boost the number of minorities that they admitted, a process commonly called affirmative action.

Over time, many people came to see affirmative action as a negative policy. Their reasons varied, but a common complaint was that affirmative action allowed some minority students to get into colleges even when their test scores and high school grades were below what those colleges would accept from non-Hispanic white students. In June 1996 Pete Wilson (1933–), the governor of California, urged California voters to support the California Civil Rights Initiative (Proposition 209), a proposal to eliminate affirmative action in higher-education enrollment. In November 1996 California voters approved Proposition 209, which prohibited public universities from considering race and ethnicity when deciding on admissions. Sheila O'Rourke of the University of California (UC) reports in "Strategies for Achieving Faculty Diversity at the University of California in a Post-Proposition 209 Legal Climate" (2002, http://www.oma.umn.edu/kof/pdf/209.pdf) that in 1997, the last year that UC considered race and ethnicity in its admissions process, 17.9% of the students who were admitted were from underrepresented minority groups (Native Americans, African-Americans, and Hispanics). In 1998, the first year of admissions after Proposition 209 went into effect, the proportion of underrepresented minorities dropped to 15.5%.

In *Hopwood v. Texas* (78 F.3d 932 [1996]), the Fifth Circuit Court of Appeals unanimously ruled that the University of Texas (UT) School of Law was discriminating against non-Hispanic white students by using race and ethnicity as a factor in admissions. Four non-Hispanic white applicants charged that less-qualified African-American and Hispanic students had been accepted instead of them because of racial preference on the part of UT. The appeals court ruled that colleges could not give preferences to minority students—even for what it called "the wholesome practice of correcting perceived racial imbalance in the student body." In the opinion of the appeals court, "any consideration of race or ethnicity by the law school for the purpose of achieving a diverse student body is not a compelling interest under the Fourteenth Amendment." The *Hopwood* decision applied to all public universities in Texas, Louisiana, and Mississippi. In Texas, Dan Morales (1956–), the attorney general of Texas, applied the admissions ruling to include financial aid and scholarships.

This decision negatively affected the number of underrepresented minority students at the UT School of Law. According to Lydia Lum, in "Minority Rolls Cut by Hopwood" (*Houston Chronicle*, September 1997), in 1997, following the decision affecting the law school, out of 500 incoming students, only 4 African-American students and 26 Mexican-Americans were enrolled, down from 31 African-Americans and 42 Mexican-Americans the previous year. At the undergraduate level, public universities throughout Texas also saw a drop in minority applications. Texas A&M University registered nearly 15% fewer Hispanics and 23% fewer African-Americans that year.

PUBLIC UNIVERSITIES RESPOND. In 1998 the UT system became the first public university to grant automatic admission to first-time freshmen based on class rank. Under Texas Education Code 51.803, students who graduate in the top 10% of their class from an accredited Texas high school are guaranteed admission to UT. Because some high schools have large minority populations, state officials hoped that more minority students would be admitted to state universities. After initial declines in minority enrollment, UT announced in early 2003 that Hispanic enrollment had returned to the pre-*Hopwood* level and that African-American enrollment was nearing its 1996 level. However, James C. McKinley Jr. reports in "Texas Vote Curbs a College Admission Guarantee Meant to Bolster Diversity" (*New York Times*, May 30, 2009) that in 2009 Texas legislators limited automatic college admissions to 75% of the incoming freshman class, even though some state senators argued that such a limit would again depress minority enrollment. McKinley explains that this limit was put in place to give admissions officials more "latitude in putting together a class" and to lessen the so-called brain drain of students attending colleges and universities outside of the state.

In March 1999 UC regents approved a similar admission policy called Eligibility in the Local Context (ELC). According to the article "Freshman Eligibility in the Local Context (ELC)" (November 17, 2003, http://www

.universityofcalifornia.edu/news/compreview/freshmanelc .pdf), under the ELC students graduating in the top 4% of their class in California high schools are eligible for admission to one of UC's undergraduate campuses. The ELC was implemented starting with freshmen applicants in the fall of 2001. According to Rebecca Trounson, in "Admissions Studies Find Flaws" (*Los Angeles Times*, February 11, 2003), early reports did not find evidence, however, that the program boosted minority enrollment.

Catherine L. Horn and Stella M. Flores note in *Percent Plans in College Admissions: A Comparative Analysis of Three States' Experiences* (February 7, 2003, http:// www.civilrightsproject.ucla.edu/research/affirmativeaction/ tristate.pdf) that in November 1999 Florida implemented a similar plan called the Talented 20. Horn and Flores reviewed the three admission plans by Texas, California, and Florida and concluded that "any increases in racial/ ethnic diversity on these campuses cannot be singularly attributed to percent plans because they have happened in the context of the extensive race-attentive efforts made by these schools."

Supreme Court Affirms Racial Preferences

In June 2003 the Supreme Court made two separate rulings on the admission practices at the University of Michigan's undergraduate college and law school. The undergraduate college used a point system in an effort to achieve diversity in the student body, awarding 20 points on a scale of 150 to African-Americans, Hispanics, and Native Americans. The court rejected this system, maintaining that it was too broad and too much like a quota, and ruled that it violated the equal protection clause in the 14th Amendment of the U.S. Constitution. By contrast, the University of Michigan law school weighed race and ethnicity along with a number of other admissions factors. The court deemed this approach legal in *Grutter v. Bollinger* (539 U.S. 306 [2003]), because it furthered "a compelling interest in obtaining the educational benefits that flow from a diverse student body." As a result, the court upheld the concept of race-conscious admissions, but the nuanced approach to admissions that the court found acceptable left the door open for further lawsuits. Even though smaller schools can devote more time and attention to individual applicants, larger institutions still face the problem of how to use race and ethnicity as a factor in screening many applications without assigning a numerical value to an individual's minority status.

Views of Educational Opportunities for African-Americans

African-Americans are less likely than non-Hispanic whites to say that their children have the same opportunity as white children to get a good education. A Gallup poll (http://www.gallup.com/poll/1687/Race-Relations .aspx#2) in June 2008 found that 49% of African-Americans

believed their children "have as good a chance as white children" of receiving a good education. This figure had declined from a high of 68% in 1990. Nevertheless, a large majority of non-Hispanic whites (80%) and Hispanics (74%) believed that African-American children "have as good a chance" as their white peers to get a good education.

This racial divide in perceptions of educational opportunities for African-American children continued into discussions of higher education. In *Blacks Convinced Discrimination Still Exists in College Admission Process* (August 24, 2007, http://www.gallup.com/poll/28507/ Blacks-Convinced-Discrimination-Still-Exists-College-Admission-Process.aspx), Frank Newport of the Gallup Organization reports on a 2007 poll, in which respondents were asked: "If two equally qualified students, one white and one black, applied to a major U.S. college or university, who do you think would have the better chance of being accepted to the college—the white student, the black student—or would they have the same chance?" Nearly half (48%) of non-Hispanic white respondents believed the two students would have the same chance, another quarter (26%) believed the African-American student would have the better chance, and one out of five (20%) believed the white student would have the better chance. African-Americans responded differently. Only 28% believed the two students would have the same chance, whereas 61% believed the white student would have the better chance. One out of 20 (5%) African-American respondents believed the African-American student would have the better chance for college admission. Newport notes that African-Americans who themselves had a college education felt most strongly that the white student would have the advantage.

Tribal Colleges

Special postsecondary institutions, collectively known as tribal colleges, were established to prepare Native American and Alaskan Native students with the skills most needed on reservations, while at the same time preserving their culture. Usually situated in areas where the students cannot otherwise pursue education beyond high school without leaving the community, these colleges all offer associate's degrees. In addition, some offer bachelor's and master's degrees. Tribal colleges and universities are located in Alaska, Arizona, Kansas, Michigan, Minnesota, Montana, Nebraska, New Mexico, North Dakota, Oklahoma, South Dakota, Washington, Wisconsin, and Wyoming.

Tribal colleges offer courses ranging from teaching and nursing to secretarial skills and computer science that meet the needs of specific communities. Besides tribal languages, traditional subjects are a part of the curricula. For example, in *Salish Kootenai College Course Catalog, 2008–2010* (May 2008, http://ecampus.skc.edu/ics/icsfs/ 2008_-_10_catalog.pdf?target=72dafc3f-8630-4b22-9481-

5bd021f181fc), Salish Kootenai College in Montana indicates that a variety of tribal language and culture courses are offered, including "Coyote Stories," which covers morality tales that have important lessons of Indian life. These stories can only be told during the winter. "Tipi Setup" teaches students various techniques used by Montana tribes to erect tipis; "Hide Tanning" teaches students how to tan a fresh deer, elk, moose, or buffalo hide and turn it into buckskin; and "Stickgame" introduces students to the rules and techniques of this Native American game.

The AIHEC (September 21, 2007, http://www.aihec .org/colleges/TCUstudents.cfm) reports that in the fall of 2005, 16,986 students were enrolled in tribal colleges— 79% of them were Native American or Alaskan Native. Freeman and Fox state that in 2002, 8% of all Native American and Alaskan Native college students were enrolled in tribally controlled colleges. They also note that enrollment in tribally controlled colleges increased at a faster rate between 1997 and 2002 (32%) than did Native American and Alaskan Native enrollment in college generally (16%). As a result, these rising enrollment figures suggest that tribal colleges do meet the unique needs of Native American and Alaskan Native students.

Black Colleges and Universities

According to the U.S. Department of Education, in "List of HBCUs—White House Initiative on Historically Black Colleges and Universities" (January 4, 2010, http:// www2.ed.gov/about/inits/list/whhbcu/edlite-list.html), there were 104 historically black colleges and universities located in the United States in 2010. Alabama had the largest number of historically black colleges, at 15.

North Carolina had 11 institutions, Georgia had 10, Texas had 9, and South Carolina had 8. The NCES reports in "Fall Enrollment in Degree-Granting Historically Black Colleges and Universities, by Type and Control of Institution and Race/Ethnicity of Student: Selected Years, 1976–2004" (June 2006, http://nces.ed.gov/sur veys/AnnualReports/historicallyblack.asp) that in 2004, 269,208 minority students, 257,545 of them African-American, were enrolled in these institutions.

Historically black colleges and universities often offer unique courses and programs of study to students. For example, Howard University (May 15, 2008, http://www .coas.howard.edu/afroamerican/courses.html), a traditional black college founded in Washington, D.C., in 1867, has an Afro-American studies department that offers a major and a minor. Courses include "Black Philosophies of Education," which explores historical and contemporary theories of education of African-American students; "Commercial Exploitation of the Third World," which examines colonial and imperialistic economies and explores the political and economic forces that influence people of color around the world; and both 19th- and 20th-century "Black Social and Political Thought," which examines influential political and social ideas that were supported by African-American leaders in U.S. history. Florida A&M University (2007, http://www.famu.edu/histpol/African%20American%20 Studies%20BS%20-%20 Evaluation%20Form.pdf), which was founded in Tallahassee in 1887, also has an African-American studies program. Majors are required to take two African-American history courses, two African history courses, "Blacks and the Political Process," "African-American Novel," and "Psychology of Race and Prejudice," among other courses.

CHAPTER 4
MINORITIES IN THE LABOR FORCE

A HISTORICAL PERSPECTIVE

Members of minority groups have always been an important part of the U.S. labor force. In many instances groups were allowed and encouraged or even forced to immigrate to the United States (or, what would eventually become the United States) to fill specific labor needs. Perhaps the most obvious example is the involuntary immigration of Africans, who provided slave labor for southern plantations as early as the 17th century. Later, Asians and Hispanics were employed to mine resources, farm land, and build railroads.

African-Americans

Since 1619, with the arrival of the first slave ships to North American shores, African-Americans have been part of the labor force. Even though most worked as unpaid slaves on southern plantations, a few were allowed to work for pay to purchase their freedom and that of their family, an effort that often took many years. Besides laboring on farms and in households, some enslaved people developed talents in masonry, music, or other skills and were hired out by their owners.

On January 1, 1863, during the Civil War (1861–1865), President Abraham Lincoln (1809–1865) issued the Emancipation Proclamation. This freed all slaves in the Confederacy, although Confederate states did not recognize the authority of the Union government, and blacks in the South remained enslaved. The proclamation did not free slaves held in Northern states, where slavery remained legal. On January 31, 1865, Congress passed the 13th Amendment, which abolished slavery in the entire United States; it was ratified after the war. Then, on July 9, 1868, the 14th Amendment was ratified by three-fourths of the U.S. states, providing citizenship to African Americans, as it did to all immigrants born or naturalized in the United States. However, when the period of Reconstruction (1865–1877) came to an end, many southern states enacted "black codes," which were new laws that restricted the freedom of African-Americans living in the South. These codes included provisions that forbade African-Americans from leaving their jobs without permission. African-Americans in the South labored under these codes for decades.

The Library of Congress (LOC) explains in "African Immigration" (February 2010, http://www.loc.gov/teachers/classroommaterials/presentationsandactivities/presentations/immigration/african.html) that because the best job prospects were in urban areas in the North and because the obstacles created by racial discrimination were the least burdensome there, hundreds of thousands of African-Americans left their rural southern homes and migrated north and west before and during World War I (1914–1918) in search of unskilled work in factories and homes. During the 1940s arms production for World War II (1939–1945) again attracted hundreds of thousands of African-Americans to the North, bringing about a moderate increase in the number of African-American workers in these factories. These migrations of African-Americans from the South to the North following both world wars were the largest movements of people within the United States in the country's history and did much to influence its future.

Asian-Americans

In "Chinese and Westward Expansion" (May 23, 2003, http://memory.loc.gov/ammem/award99/cubhtml/theme1.html), the LOC notes that Chinese immigrants came to the United States not only because of the California gold rush but also to work on railroads, on farms, and in construction and manufacturing. The LOC states in "Japanese Immigration" (February 2010, http://www.loc.gov/teachers/classroommaterials/presentationsandactivities/presentations/immigration/japanese.html) that between 1886 and 1911 more than 400,000 Japanese immigrants came to the United States, often to work on the rapidly expanding sugarcane plantations in Hawaii or on the fruit and vegetable farms in California. However, the Gentleman's Agreement of 1907 between President Theodore Roosevelt (1858–1919) and the Japanese government stopped the flow of Japanese workers to the United States by withholding passports, thus cutting the flow to a trickle.

The most recent wave of Asians came to the United States in the 1970s and 1980s, when hundreds of thousands of refugees were admitted from Vietnam, Laos, and Cambodia following the Vietnam War (1954–1975). The Southeast Asia Resource Action Center reports in "Southeast Asian Communities" (February 2010, http://www.searac.org/commun.html) that the first wave of refugees came from Vietnam when Saigon fell to the North Vietnamese Communists in April 1975. Over 100,000 Vietnamese who had worked for the U.S. military during the war fled Vietnam for the United States, where they were resettled in communities around the nation. Subsequent waves of refugees fled Vietnam legally and illegally over the decades. As of February 2010, the largest number of Vietnamese lived in California, Illinois, Massachusetts, Minnesota, New York, Pennsylvania, Texas, Washington, and Washington, D.C. When the Laotian government was toppled by a Communist regime after the fall of South Vietnam in 1975, Laotian and Hmong refugees fled to Thailand and were then resettled in the United States. Likewise, when Cambodia was taken over by the Khmer Rouge in 1976, Cambodian refugees fled to Thailand and were then resettled in other countries, including the United States.

Hispanics

Many Hispanics can trace their roots to the time when the southwestern states were still a part of Mexico. However, the ancestors of most Hispanics arrived after Mexico surrendered much of its territory following its defeat in the Mexican-American War (1846–1848). The U.S. policy toward Hispanic workers (mainly from Mexico) has alternately encouraged and discouraged immigration, reflecting the nation's changing needs for labor. In "Mexican Immigration" (February 2010, http://www.loc.gov/teachers/classroommaterials/presentationsandactivities/presentations/immigration/mexican.html), the LOC notes that before the 20th century, when there was little demand in the Southwest for Mexican labor, Mexicans moved back and forth across completely open borders to work in mines, on ranches, and on railroads.

However, as the Southwest began to develop and as Asian immigration slowed, the demand for Mexican labor increased. According to the LOC, "Between 1910 and 1930, the number of Mexican immigrants counted by the U.S. census tripled from 200,000 to 600,000." The need for Mexican labor was so great that during World War I the Immigration and Naturalization Service exempted many Mexicans from meeting most immigration conditions, such as head taxes (paying a small amount to enter the country) and literacy requirements. Even though legal immigration rose, a large amount of illegal immigration also occurred. Historians estimate that during the 1920s there were as many illegal as legal Mexican immigrants in the country.

The LOC explains that during the Great Depression of the 1930s, when jobs became scarce, many Americans believed the nation's unemployment situation was significantly compounded by illegal aliens working in the United States. As a result, hundreds of thousands of Mexican immigrants, both legal immigrants and illegal aliens, were repatriated (sent back) to Mexico.

Following the outbreak of World War II, the United States needed workers to help in its role as a supplier to the Allied countries. When the lure of better-paying factory jobs brought many rural workers to the city, the nation looked to Mexico to fill the need for agricultural workers. The Bracero Program (1942–1964) permitted the entry of Mexican farm workers on a temporary contractual basis with U.S. employers. Even though the program was considered an alternative to illegal immigration, it likely contributed to it because there were more workers who wanted to participate in the program than there were openings. According to the LOC, more than 5 million Mexican immigrants came to the United States during and after the war as part of the Bracero Program, and hundreds of thousands stayed.

Marc Perry et al. of the U.S. Census Bureau estimate in *Evaluating Components of International Migration: Legal Migrants* (December 2001, http://www.census.gov/population/www/documentation/twps0059/twps0059.html) that over 1 million undocumented Hispanics entered the United States in the early 1980s. A major downturn in the Mexican economy led to a surge in Mexican immigrants, and hundreds of thousands of other Hispanics arrived from Central America, most notably from El Salvador and Guatemala, to escape bloody civil wars and repressive regimes. Overall, Hispanics accounted for approximately one out of every three legal immigrants to the United States during this period. In 1986 the Immigration Reform and Control Act gave more than 2 million Mexicans legal status in the United States. Since that time, Hispanics from Cuba, Central and South America, and Mexico have continued to enter the United States, legally and illegally.

"GET TOUGH" POLICY. To stem the flow of undocumented workers, a "get tough" policy was initiated in 1994, but many critics believed that the money spent on installing infrared sensors, cameras, and stadium-level lighting along the Mexican border was essentially wasted. Instead of crossing at more populated and better-secured areas, illegal immigrants crossed into the United States through mountains and deserts, facing dangerous conditions, and many died as a result. In September 2006 Congress passed a bill authorizing the construction of a 700-mile (1,100-km) fence along the U.S.-Mexican border in California, Arizona, New Mexico, and Texas, and the installation of a high-tech surveillance system to keep illegal Mexican immigrants from crossing into the United States. Jonathan Weisman reports in "With Senate Vote, Congress Passes Border Fence Bill" (*Washington Post*, September 30, 2006) that the fence would cost $6 billion to construct. Critics charged that the fence, as planned, would be impossible to construct across the rugged terrain and the borders of the Tohono O'odham Nation, which opposed the bill. According to the U.S. Government Accountability Office (GAO), in *Secure Border Initiative: Technology Deployment Delays Persist and the Impact of Border Fencing Has Not Been Assessed* (September 2009, http://www.gao.gov/new.items/d09896.pdf), by June 2009, 661 miles (1,064 km) of the still-unfinished fence had been completed at a cost of $2.4 billion. The new fencing has been breached 3,363 times, requiring an average $1,300 repair for each breach, and the GAO estimates that the new fencing will cost $6.5 billion to maintain through 2029.

Even though arrests of illegal aliens along the southwestern border increased after 1994, enforcement in the workplace was rare. In fact, the U.S. economy became so dependent on a pool of low-wage workers that mass deportation of undocumented workers was not a realistic option. In "Temporary Worker Program Is Explained" (*Washington Post*, October 19, 2005), Darryl Fears and Michael A. Fletcher state that in January 2004 President George W. Bush (1946–) proposed a guest-worker program that would grant a three-year work permit to millions of undocumented workers. This permit would be renewable for at least three more years, with a chance to apply for a green card to gain permanent residency. In addition, workers in other countries could apply for work permits to take jobs that no U.S. citizen wanted. That program was not approved, and since then various types of guest-worker programs have been introduced by many lawmakers.

Guest-worker programs have come under criticism because opponents argue they leave foreign workers vulnerable to exploitation. For example, the article "Broad Opposition to Guest Worker Program" (Associated Press, October 21, 2009) notes that a 2009 lawsuit alleged that a Tennessee company, Cumberland Environmental Resources Company, abused the nonagricultural guest-worker program by lying about the availability of U.S. workers and failing to pay immigrants the prevailing wage required by law. The article also reports that a survey undertaken by the Economic Policy Institute in 2008 found that 98% of temporary workers "were paid less than the prevailing wage in occupations they commonly filled." According to Julia Preston, in "Suit Points to Guest Worker Program Flaws" (*New York Times*, February 1, 2010), a 2007 lawsuit against a marine oil-rig company located in Mississippi alleged that Indian workers had been abused and discriminated against.

Farmworkers Justice reports in "Labor Department Reverses Bush Administration Changes to H-2A Guest-worker Program" (February 11, 2010, http://www.fwjustice.org/Immigration_Labor/h2anews.htm) that the Bush administration, having failed to expand the guest-worker programs already in place while in office, issued rules in its final days that reversed regulations, which had somewhat protected foreign workers in the H-2A program. These rules slashed minimum wages and reduced government oversight of the program. One year later, however, the Obama administration restored the older minimum wage formula, restored the requirement that employers pay employees' transportation costs, and reinstated several government oversight regulations.

LABOR FORCE PARTICIPATION AND UNEMPLOYMENT

Participation in the labor force means that a person is either employed or actively seeking employment. Those who are not looking for work because they are "going to school" or "unable to work" are not considered part of the labor force. The labor force increases with the long-term growth of the population. It responds to economic forces and social trends, and its size changes with the seasons.

To be classified as unemployed, a person must:

- Not have worked in the week specified for the survey
- Have actively sought work sometime during the four weeks preceding the survey
- Be currently available to take a suitable job

Due to the global economic recession that began in 2007, unemployment rates hit double digits in October 2009 for the first time since 1983. In December 2009 the unemployment rate was 10% overall. However, some groups were harder hit than others.

In November 2009, 2.8 million (15.6%) African-Americans in the civilian labor force were unemployed. Their unemployment rate was 68% higher than that of the white population, at 9.3% (11.6 million). (See Table 4.1.) Nearly 2.9 million (12.7%) Hispanics in the civilian labor force were unemployed. (See Table 4.2.) The lowest unemployment rate was among Asian-Americans. Approximately 514,000 Asian-Americans in the civilian labor force were unemployed in November 2009, with an unemployment rate of 7.3%. (See Table 4.1.)

African-Americans

Historically, African-American workers have participated in the labor force in larger proportions than whites, primarily because African-American women were more likely to be working than their white counterparts. However, the increased entry of white women into the labor force since the 1970s has narrowed the gap between the

TABLE 4.1

Employment status of the civilian population, by race, sex, and age, 2008–09

[Numbers in thousands]

Employment status, race, sex, and age	Not seasonally adjusted			Seasonally adjusted[a]					
	Nov. 2008	Oct. 2009	Nov. 2009	Nov. 2008	July 2009	Aug. 2009	Sept. 2009	Oct. 2009	Nov. 2009
White									
Civilian noninstitutional population	190,221	191,394	191,516	190,221	190,944	191,086	191,244	191,394	191,516
Civilian labor force	126,057	125,339	125,170	126,029	125,997	126,118	125,599	125,694	125,393
Participation rate	66.3	65.5	65.4	66.3	66.0	66.0	65.7	65.7	65.5
Employed	118,721	114,469	114,403	118,226	115,123	114,922	114,251	113,803	113,755
Employment—population ratio	62.4	59.8	59.7	62.2	60.3	60.1	59.7	59.5	59.4
Unemployed	7,336	10,870	10,767	7,803	10,874	11,197	11,349	11,891	11,639
Unemployment rate	5.8	8.7	8.6	6.2	8.6	8.9	9.0	9.5	9.3
Not in labor force	64,165	66,056	66,346	64,193	64,947	64,968	65,645	65,700	66,123
Men, 20 years and over									
Civilian labor force	65,681	65,313	65,286	65,762	65,643	65,674	65,609	65,634	65,502
Participation rate	76.0	75.0	74.9	76.1	75.6	75.6	75.4	75.4	75.2
Employed	61,995	59,555	59,438	61,761	59,701	59,576	59,329	59,109	59,059
Employment—population ratio	71.7	68.4	68.2	71.5	68.8	68.6	68.2	67.9	67.8
Unemployed	3,686	5,758	5,848	4,001	5,941	6,098	6,281	6,525	6,443
Unemployment rate	5.6	8.8	9.0	6.1	9.1	9.3	9.6	9.9	9.8
Women, 20 years and over									
Civilian labor force	55,131	55,217	55,165	54,810	54,987	55,045	54,770	54,947	54,931
Participation rate	60.8	60.5	60.4	60.4	60.4	60.4	60.0	60.2	60.1
Employed	52,454	51,288	51,334	52,014	51,245	51,250	50,914	50,875	50,874
Employment—population ratio	57.8	56.2	56.2	57.3	56.3	56.2	55.8	55.7	55.7
Unemployed	2,677	3,928	3,831	2,796	3,742	3,796	3,856	4,072	4,058
Unemployment rate	4.9	7.1	6.9	5.1	6.8	6.9	7.0	7.4	7.4
Both sexes, 16 to 19 years									
Civilian labor force	5,245	4,809	4,719	5,457	5,367	5,399	5,220	5,113	4,960
Participation rate	40.0	37.0	36.3	41.6	41.2	41.5	40.1	39.3	38.2
Employed	4,272	3,626	3,631	4,451	4,176	4,096	4,008	3,819	3,822
Employment—population ratio	32.6	27.9	28.0	34.0	32.0	31.5	30.8	29.4	29.4
Unemployed	973	1,183	1,088	1,006	1,191	1,303	1,212	1,294	1,138
Unemployment rate	18.6	24.6	23.0	18.4	22.2	24.1	23.2	25.3	23.0
Black or African American									
Civilian noninstitutional population	28,021	28,369	28,404	28,021	28,252	28,290	28,330	28,369	28,404
Civilian labor force	17,683	17,491	17,606	17,708	17,684	17,584	17,442	17,509	17,664
Participation rate	63.1	61.7	62.0	63.2	62.6	62.2	61.6	61.7	62.2
Employed	15,705	14,816	14,938	15,703	15,111	14,929	14,755	14,760	14,903
Employment—population ratio	56.0	52.2	52.6	56.0	53.5	52.8	52.1	52.0	52.5
Unemployed	1,979	2,675	2,667	2,005	2,573	2,655	2,687	2,749	2,760
Unemployment rate	11.2	15.3	15.2	11.3	14.5	15.1	15.4	15.7	15.6
Not in labor force	10,338	10,879	10,798	10,313	10,568	10,706	10,888	10,860	10,740
Men, 20 years and over									
Civilian labor force	7,957	7,909	7,911	7,954	7,896	7,921	7,809	7,897	7,921
Participation rate	70.6	69.1	69.0	70.5	69.4	69.5	68.3	69.0	69.1
Employed	7,013	6,603	6,637	6,989	6,645	6,578	6,518	6,544	6,585
Employment—population ratio	62.2	57.7	57.9	62.0	58.4	57.7	57.0	57.2	57.4
Unemployed	944	1,306	1,274	965	1,251	1,343	1,291	1,353	1,336
Unemployment rate	11.9	16.5	16.1	12.1	15.8	17.0	16.5	17.1	16.9
Women, 20 years and over									
Civilian labor force	9,069	8,904	8,999	9,069	9,045	8,955	8,942	8,912	9,001
Participation rate	64.5	62.5	63.1	64.5	63.8	63.1	62.9	62.6	63.1
Employed	8,234	7,803	7,942	8,249	7,988	7,889	7,828	7,806	7,944
Employment—population ratio	58.6	54.8	55.7	58.7	56.3	55.5	55.0	54.8	55.7
Unemployed	836	1,100	1,057	820	1,057	1,066	1,114	1,106	1,057
Unemployment rate	9.2	12.4	11.7	9.0	11.7	11.9	12.5	12.4	11.7
Both sexes, 16 to 19 years									
Civilian labor force	657	678	696	685	744	708	691	700	742
Participation rate	24.4	25.3	26.0	25.5	27.7	26.4	25.8	26.2	27.8
Employed	457	409	359	464	479	462	409	411	375
Employment—population ratio	17.0	15.3	13.4	17.3	17.8	17.2	15.3	15.4	14.0
Unemployed	199	269	337	221	265	246	282	289	367
Unemployment rate	30.4	39.7	48.4	32.2	35.7	34.7	40.8	41.3	49.4

two races. The U.S. Bureau of Labor Statistics (BLS; February 5, 2010, http://www.bls.gov/webapps/legacy/cpsatab2.htm) reports that in November 1972, 26.1 million (42.6%) white women participated in the labor force, compared with 3.6 million (51.8%) African-American women. By November 2009, 54.9 million (60.1%) white women over the age of 20 were in the civilian labor force, which was still proportionately lower than the 9 million

TABLE 4.1

Employment status of the civilian population, by race, sex, and age, 2008–09 [CONTINUED]

[Numbers in thousands]

Employment status, race, sex, and age	Not seasonally adjusted			Seasonally adjusted[a]					
	Nov. 2008	Oct. 2009	Nov. 2009	Nov. 2008	July 2009	Aug. 2009	Sept. 2009	Oct. 2009	Nov. 2009
Asian[b]									
Civilian noninstitutional population	10,811	10,841	10,879	—	—	—	—	—	—
Civilian labor force	7,134	7,051	7,080	—	—	—	—	—	—
Participation rate	66.0	65.0	65.1	—	—	—	—	—	—
Employed	6,791	6,520	6,566	—	—	—	—	—	—
Employment-population ratio	62.8	60.1	60.4	—	—	—	—	—	—
Unemployed	343	531	514	—	—	—	—	—	—
Unemployment rate	4.8	7.5	7.3	—	—	—	—	—	—
Not in labor force	3,677	3,790	3,799	—	—	—	—	—	—

[a]The population figures are not adjusted for seasonal variation; therefore, identical numbers appear in the unadjusted and seasonally adjusted columns.
[b]Adults aged 16 years and older.
— Data not available.
Note: Updated population controls are introduced annually with the release of January data.

SOURCE: "Table A-2. Employment Status of the Civilian Population by Race, Sex, and Age," in *The Employment Situation—November 2009*, U.S. Department of Labor, Bureau of Labor Statistics, December 4, 2009, http://www.bls.gov/news.release/pdf/empsit.pdf (accessed December 11, 2009)

TABLE 4.2

Employment status of the Hispanic population by sex and age, 2008–09

[Number in thousands]

Employment status, sex, and age	Not seasonally adjusted			Seasonally adjusted[a]					
	Nov. 2008	Oct. 2009	Nov. 2009	Nov. 2008	July 2009	Aug. 2009	Sept. 2009	Oct. 2009	Nov. 2009
Hispanic or Latino ethnicity									
Civilian noninstitutional population	32,558	33,202	33,291	32,558	32,926	33,017	33,110	33,202	33,291
Civilian labor force	22,137	22,481	22,622	22,074	22,526	22,341	22,469	22,497	22,566
Participation rate	68.0	67.7	68.0	67.8	68.4	67.7	67.9	67.8	67.8
Employed	20,263	19,688	19,860	20,168	19,745	19,433	19,625	19,555	19,694
Employment-population ratio	62.2	59.3	59.7	61.9	60.0	58.9	59.3	58.9	59.2
Unemployed	1,874	2,792	2,762	1,906	2,781	2,908	2,844	2,942	2,872
Unemployment rate	8.5	12.4	12.2	8.6	12.3	13.0	12.7	13.1	12.7
Not in labor force	10,421	10,721	10,669	10,484	10,400	10,675	10,641	10,705	10,725
Men, 20 years and over									
Civilian labor force	12,760	12,863	12,862	[b]	[b]	[b]	[b]	[b]	[b]
Participation rate	84.1	83.2	83.0	[b]	[b]	[b]	[b]	[b]	[b]
Employed	11,777	11,333	11,374	[b]	[b]	[b]	[b]	[b]	[b]
Employment-population ratio	77.7	73.3	73.4	[b]	[b]	[b]	[b]	[b]	[b]
Unemployed	983	1,531	1,488	[b]	[b]	[b]	[b]	[b]	[b]
Unemployment rate	7.7	11.9	11.6	[b]	[b]	[b]	[b]	[b]	[b]
Women, 20 years and over									
Civilian labor force	8,362	8,628	8,767	[b]	[b]	[b]	[b]	[b]	[b]
Participation rate	58.5	59.1	59.9	[b]	[b]	[b]	[b]	[b]	[b]
Employed	7,745	7,718	7,838	[b]	[b]	[b]	[b]	[b]	[b]
Employment-population ratio	54.2	52.9	53.5	[b]	[b]	[b]	[b]	[b]	[b]
Unemployed	618	909	929	[b]	[b]	[b]	[b]	[b]	[b]
Unemployment rate	7.4	10.5	10.6	[b]	[b]	[b]	[b]	[b]	[b]
Both sexes, 16 to 19 years									
Civilian labor force	1,015	990	993	[b]	[b]	[b]	[b]	[b]	[b]
Participation rate	32.8	31.4	31.5	[b]	[b]	[b]	[b]	[b]	[b]
Employed	741	637	649	[b]	[b]	[b]	[b]	[b]	[b]
Employment-population ratio	24.0	20.2	20.6	[b]	[b]	[b]	[b]	[b]	[b]
Unemployed	274	353	344	[b]	[b]	[b]	[b]	[b]	[b]
Unemployment rate	27.0	35.6	34.7	[b]	[b]	[b]	[b]	[b]	[b]

[a]The population figures are not adjusted for seasonal variation; therefore, identical numbers appear in the unadjusted and seasonally adjusted columns.
[b]Data not available.
Notes: Persons whose ethnicity is identified as Hispanic or Latino may be of any race. Updated population controls are introduced annually with the release of January data.

SOURCE: "Table A-3. Employment Status of the Hispanic or Latino Population by Sex and Age," in *The Employment Situation—November 2009*, U.S. Department of Labor, Bureau of Labor Statistics, December 4, 2009, http://www.bls.gov/news.release/pdf/empsit.pdf (accessed December 11, 2009)

(63.1%) African-American women over the age of 20 who participated in the labor force. (See Table 4.1.)

Conversely, the labor force participation rate of African-American men 20 years and older has declined since the 1970s. The BLS notes that in November 1972, 4.4 million (78.1%) African-American men 20 years and older were in the civilian labor force; in November 2009, 7.9 million (69.1%) were in the labor force. (See Table 4.1.) In comparison, 44.3 million (81.7%) white men were employed in November 1972; in November 2009, 65.5 million (75.2%) white men 20 years and older were in the civilian labor force. The overall participation rate for all African-Americans (men and women) was 62.2% (17.7 million) in November 2009, compared with a participation rate of 65.5% (125.4 million) for all whites.

Even though unemployment rates rise and fall with the strength of the economy, for several decades the unemployment rates for African-Americans have been nearly twice the rates for whites. Often having fewer marketable skills and less education than do whites, besides facing long-standing discrimination in the labor force, African-Americans are more likely to remain unemployed for longer periods, especially during a recession. As a result, they are more likely to be labeled as "long-term unemployed" (those without work for at least 27 weeks).

In November 2009 the unemployment rate for African-American men 20 years and older was 16.9% (1.3 million), which was 72% higher than that of white men of the same age, 9.8% (6.4 million). (See Table 4.1.) African-American women aged 20 years and older had an unemployment rate of 11.7% (1.1 million), which was 54% higher than the unemployment rate of white women 20 years and older, 7.4% (4.1 million).

Hispanics

The BLS began maintaining annual employment data on Hispanics in 1973. In November 2009, 22.6 million (67.8%) Hispanics were employed or actively looking for work. (See Table 4.2.) As of the third quarter of 2009, Mexican-Americans had the highest overall participation rate among the three largest Hispanic groups in the United States. More than two out of three Mexican-Americans (14.1 million, or 68.3%) participated in the civilian labor force, followed by Puerto Ricans (1.8 million, 61.7%) and Cuban-Americans (872,000, or 61.1%). (See Table 4.3.)

Men 20 years and older in all three groups had a much higher labor force participation rate than did women of the same age. This difference in rates of labor force participation was especially pronounced for Mexican-Americans. Among Mexican-Americans, 8.4 million (84.9%) men and nearly 5 million (56.9%) women participated in the labor force. (See Table 4.3.) Among Cuban-Americans, 485,000 (71.9%) men and 358,000

(52.5%) women participated in the labor force. Among Puerto Ricans, 909,000 (72.3%) men and 794,000 (58.3%) women participated in the labor force.

The unemployment rate for Hispanics in November 2009 was 12.7% (2.9 million). (See Table 4.2.) According to the BLS (February 5, 2010, http://www.bls.gov/webapps/legacy/cpsatab3.htm), this rate had more than doubled from the rate of 5.8% (1.3 million) in November 2007 because of the global economic recession. The unemployment rate varies among Hispanic people depending on the country of origin. In the third quarter of 2009 the Puerto Rican–origin population had the highest rate of unemployment at 13.8% (249,000). (See Table 4.3.) Cuban-Americans had a lower unemployment rate of 13.2% (115,000), and Mexican-Americans had the lowest unemployment rate of the Hispanic subgroups at 12.7% (1.8 million).

Asian-Americans

In November 2009, 7.1 million (65.1%) Asian-Americans aged 16 years and older were in the civilian labor force. (See Table 4.1.) In 2008, 3.3 million (61.5%) Asian-American women and 3.8 million (78.7%) Asian-American men aged 20 years and older were in the labor force. (See Table 4.4.) In that year, a higher percentage of Asian-American men aged 20 years and older was participating in the labor force than either white men (65.5 million, or 76.1%) or African-American men (8 million, or 71.1%). Among women aged 20 years and older, a higher percentage of African-American women (9 million, or 64.3%) were participating in the labor force than were Asian-American women (3.3 million, or 61.5%). However, both groups of minority women were participating in the labor force at rates higher than white women (54.5 million, or 60.3%) in that year.

Unemployment figures for Asian-Americans are similar to those for non-Hispanic whites. In November 2009 the unemployment rate for Asian-Americans was 7.3% (514,000), up from 3.6% (262,000) two years before. (See Table 4.1.) The Asian-American unemployment rate was two percentage points lower than the unemployment rate of 9.3% (11.6 million) for the white population, suggesting that the Asian-American community was not hit quite as hard as the white community by the unemployment crisis resulting from the global economic recession. The low rate of unemployment among Asian-Americans can be attributed, in part, to their high educational attainment and their commitment to small family businesses.

Older Asian-Americans tend to work longer because of the strong work ethic in Asian cultures and frequently because of economic need. Often, they are employed in family businesses that do not offer retirement benefits. Depending on the time of their immigration and their work history, Asian-Americans aged 65 years and older may not be entitled to adequate Social Security benefits. Also, some may have immigrated under circumstances that prevented them from

TABLE 4.3

Employment status of the Mexican, Puerto Rican, and Cuban population, by sex and age, 2008–09

[Numbers in thousands]

	Hispanic or Latino ethnicity							
	Total[a]		Mexican		Puerto Rican		Cuban	
Employment status, sex, and age	III 2008	III 2009	III 2008	III 2009	III 2008	III 2009	III 2008	III 2009
Total								
Civilian noninstitutional population	32,274	33,018	20,744	20,716	2,811	2,936	1,415	1,427
Civilian labor force	22,205	22,508	14,238	14,140	1,787	1,811	886	872
Percent of population	68.8	68.2	68.6	68.3	63.6	61.7	62.6	61.1
Employed	20,487	19,680	13,158	12,350	1,592	1,562	813	757
Unemployed	1,718	2,828	1,080	1,790	195	249	73	115
Unemployment rate	7.7	12.6	7.6	12.7	10.9	13.8	8.2	13.2
Not in labor force	10,069	10,509	6,506	6,576	1,024	1,125	529	555
Men, 16 years and over								
Civilian noninstitutional population	16,595	16,964	10,865	10,942	1,389	1,422	687	709
Civilian labor force	13,358	13,451	8,886	8,806	970	963	495	502
Percent of population	80.5	79.3	81.8	80.5	69.8	67.7	72.0	70.8
Employed	12,365	11,732	8,259	7,684	853	817	448	444
Unemployed	993	1,719	627	1,122	117	146	47	58
Unemployment rate	7.4	12.8	7.1	12.7	12.1	15.2	9.6	11.5
Not in labor force	3,236	3,514	1,979	2,136	419	459	192	207
Men, 20 years and over								
Civilian noninstitutional population	15,034	15,366	9,799	9,859	1,238	1,258	645	675
Civilian labor force	12,711	12,807	8,443	8,372	911	909	467	485
Percent of population	84.5	83.3	86.2	84.9	73.6	72.3	72.4	71.9
Employed	11,884	11,297	7,928	7,396	816	779	426	428
Unemployed	826	1,510	515	976	94	129	40	57
Unemployment rate	6.5	11.8	6.1	11.7	10.4	14.2	8.6	11.8
Not in labor force	2,323	2,559	1,356	1,486	327	349	178	190
Women, 16 years and over								
Civilian noninstitutional population	15,679	16,053	9,878	9,774	1,422	1,514	728	718
Civilian labor force	8,847	9,058	5,351	5,334	817	848	391	370
Percent of population	56.4	56.4	54.2	54.6	57.4	56.0	53.7	51.5
Employed	8,122	7,948	4,899	4,665	739	745	365	313
Unemployed	725	1,109	453	669	78	103	26	57
Unemployment rate	8.2	12.2	8.5	12.5	9.6	12.1	6.5	15.5
Not in labor force	6,832	6,996	4,527	4,440	605	666	337	349
Women, 20 years and over								
Civilian noninstitutional population	14,183	14,517	8,846	8,768	1,272	1,362	689	682
Civilian labor force	8,322	8,531	4,977	4,985	771	794	378	358
Percent of population	58.7	58.8	56.3	56.9	60.6	58.3	54.9	52.5
Employed	7,723	7,577	4,618	4,425	705	707	356	301
Unemployed	598	954	358	561	66	87	22	57
Unemployment rate	7.2	11.2	7.2	11.2	8.6	11.0	5.8	16.0
Not in labor force	5,861	5,986	3,869	3,782	501	568	310	324
Both sexes, 16 to 19 years								
Civilian noninstitutional population	3,057	3,135	2,099	2,090	301	316	82	70
Civilian labor force	1,173	1,170	818	783	105	108	41	28
Percent of population	38.4	37.3	39.0	37.5	34.8	34.2	49.8	40.3
Employed	879	806	611	529	70	76	30	28
Unemployed	294	364	206	254	34	33	11	—
Unemployment rate	25.1	31.1	25.2	32.4	32.7	30.1	(b)	(b)
Not in labor force	1,884	1,964	1,281	1,307	196	208	41	42

[a]Includes persons of Central or South American origin and of other Hispanic or Latino ethnicity, not shown separately.
[b]Data not shown where base is less than 60,000.
Note: Persons whose ethnicity is identified as Hispanic or Latino may be of any race. Updated population controls are introduced annually with the release of January data. Dash indicates no data or data that do not meet publication criteria. Figures current as of 3rd quarter 2008 and 2009.

SOURCE: "Table D-12. Employment Status of the Hispanic or Latino Population by Sex, Age, and Detailed Ethnic Group," in *Employment and Earnings*, U.S. Department of Labor, Bureau of Labor Statistics, 2009, http://www.bls.gov/web/cpseed12.pdf (accessed December 11, 2009)

retaining any wealth they might have accumulated in their native lands.

Native Americans and Alaskan Natives

Gathering accurate statistical data on the labor force participation rates of Native Americans is difficult. They are often counted as "other" in BLS and Census Bureau data, making specific information hard to obtain. In addition, the concepts that guide the assessment of labor force participation nationally are considered to be inappropriate for Native American population groups. For example, because few jobs are available on many reservations, many adults do

TABLE 4.4

Employment status of the civilian noninstitutional population, by sex, age, and race, 2007–08

[Numbers in thousands]

Employment status, sex, and age	Total 2007	Total 2008	White 2007	White 2008	Black or African American 2007	Black or African American 2008	Asian 2007	Asian 2008
Total								
Civilian noninstitutional population	231,867	233,788	188,253	189,540	27,485	27,843	10,633	10,751
Civilian labor force	153,124	154,287	124,935	125,635	17,496	17,740	7,067	7,202
Percent of population	66.0	66.0	66.4	66.3	63.7	63.7	66.5	67.0
Employed	146,047	145,362	119,792	119,126	16,051	15,953	6,839	6,917
Unemployed	7,078	8,924	5,143	6,509	1,445	1,788	229	285
Unemployment rate	4.6	5.8	4.1	5.2	8.3	10.1	3.2	4.0
Not in labor force	78,743	79,501	63,319	63,905	9,989	10,103	3,566	3,549
Men, 16 years and over								
Civilian noninstitutional population	112,173	113,113	92,073	92,725	12,361	12,516	5,052	5,112
Civilian labor force	82,136	82,520	68,158	68,351	8,252	8,347	3,796	3,852
Percent of population	73.2	73.0	74.0	73.7	66.8	66.7	75.1	75.3
Employed	78,254	77,486	65,289	64,624	7,500	7,398	3,677	3,692
Unemployed	3,882	5,033	2,869	3,727	752	949	119	160
Unemployment rate	4.7	6.1	4.2	5.5	9.1	11.4	3.1	4.1
Not in labor force	30,036	30,593	23,915	24,374	4,110	4,169	1,256	1,260
Men, 20 years and over								
Civilian noninstitutional population	103,555	104,453	85,420	86,056	11,057	11,194	4,737	4,787
Civilian labor force	78,596	79,047	65,214	65,483	7,867	7,962	3,718	3,767
Percent of population	75.9	75.7	76.3	76.1	71.2	71.1	78.5	78.7
Employed	75,337	74,750	62,806	62,304	7,245	7,151	3,608	3,621
Unemployed	3,259	4,297	2,408	3,179	622	811	110	146
Unemployment rate	4.1	5.4	3.7	4.9	7.9	10.2	3.0	3.9
Not in labor force	24,959	25,406	20,206	20,573	3,189	3,232	1,019	1,021
Women, 16 years and over								
Civilian noninstitutional population	119,694	120,675	96,180	96,814	15,124	15,328	5,581	5,639
Civilian labor force	70,988	71,767	56,777	57,284	9,244	9,393	3,271	3,350
Percent of population	59.3	59.5	59.0	59.2	61.1	61.3	58.6	59.4
Employed	67,792	67,876	54,503	54,501	8,551	8,554	3,162	3,225
Unemployed	3,196	3,891	2,274	2,782	693	839	110	125
Unemployment rate	4.5	5.4	4.0	4.9	7.5	8.9	3.4	3.7
Not in labor force	48,707	48,908	39,403	39,531	5,879	5,934	2,310	2,289
Women, 20 years and over								
Civilian noninstitutional population	111,330	112,260	89,790	90,400	13,788	13,974	5,265	5,333
Civilian labor force	67,516	68,382	53,925	54,508	8,828	8,991	3,194	3,278
Percent of population	60.6	60.9	60.1	60.3	64.0	64.3	60.7	61.5
Employed	64,799	65,039	51,996	52,124	8,240	8,260	3,096	3,162
Unemployed	2,718	3,342	1,930	2,384	588	732	99	116
Unemployment rate	4.0	4.9	3.6	4.4	6.7	8.1	3.1	3.5
Not in labor force	43,814	43,878	35,864	35,892	4,960	4,982	2,071	2,055
Both sexes, 16 to 19 years								
Civilian noninstitutional population	16,982	17,075	13,043	13,084	2,640	2,676	631	630
Civilian labor force	7,012	6,858	5,795	5,644	801	787	155	157
Percent of population	41.3	40.2	44.4	43.1	30.3	29.4	24.5	24.9
Employed	5,911	5,573	4,990	4,697	566	541	135	134
Unemployed	1,101	1,285	805	947	235	246	20	23
Unemployment rate	15.7	18.7	13.9	16.8	29.4	31.2	12.7	14.6
Not in labor force	9,970	10,218	7,248	7,440	1,839	1,889	476	473

Note: Estimates for the above race groups will not sum to totals because data are not presented for all races. Updated population controls are introduced annually with the release of January data.

SOURCE: "5. Employment Status of the Civilian Noninstitutional Population by Sex, Age, and Race," in *Employment and Earnings*, U.S. Department of Labor, Bureau of Labor Statistics, 2009, http://www.bls.gov/cps/cpsaat5.pdf (accessed December 11, 2009)

not actively seek work—but to exclude these individuals from the statistics on the labor force results in a serious underestimation of unemployment of Native Americans.

In *We the People: American Indians and Alaska Natives in the United States* (February 2006, http://www.census.gov/prod/2006pubs/censr-28.pdf), Stella U. Ogunwole of the Census Bureau indicates that in 2000, 33.5% of Native Ameri-

cans and Alaskan Natives lived in "American Indian areas"—that is, reservations or trust lands. In *American Indian Population and Labor Force Report, 2005* (September 2008, http://www.bia.gov/idc/groups/public/documents/text/idc-001719.pdf), the Bureau of Indian Affairs notes that in 2005 unemployment rates on reservations averaged 49%, but varied greatly among reservations. In some places, nine out of 10 people in the labor force or more were out of work, such as in Arctic Village (90%), Pechanga Band of Luigero Mission (91%), Beaver Village (93%), Nooryik Native Community (93%), the Native Village of Tyonek (93%), Sokaogon Chippewa Community (93%), Soboba Band of Luiseno Mission Indians (94%), the Native Village of Unga (94%), the Native Village of Elim (95%), the Native Village of Kanatak (96%), as well as the tiny villages of the Ramona Band, the Village of Chuilla, and Telida Village, where 100% of the workforce was unemployed. In contrast, a few villages had a 0% unemployment rate, such as Blue Lake Rancheria, Buena Vista Rancheria of Me-Wuk, the California Valley Miwok Tribe, the Native Village of Chignik Lagoon, the Coeur D'Alene Tribe, the Iowa Tribe, the Mescolero Apache Tribe, the Paiute Indian Tribe, the Baskenta Band of Nomiaki Indians, the Potter Valley Rancheria, the Pueblo of Taos, the Pueblo of Zia, the San Pasqual Band of Diegueno Mission Indians, and the Seneca Nation. Regardless, many tribes had unemployment rates well over 50%.

In many cases reservations do not generate the jobs necessary to support Native American families. Even when Native Americans are employed, the Bureau of Indian Affairs notes that fully a third (32%) of employed individuals earns wages below the poverty guidelines. This fact helps explain why Native American tribes have been so willing to introduce or expand casino gambling on their reservations. William N. Evans and Julie H. Topoleski of the University of Maryland note in *The Social and Economic Impact of Native American Casinos* (September 2002) that the 310 gaming operations run by more than 200 tribes have increased employment by 26%. At the same time, it has increased tribal population by about 12% (as Native Americans who left the reservation in search of jobs elsewhere return), resulting in a 12% increase in the employment-to-population ratio. In addition, the proportion of adults who work but earn wages below the poverty guidelines decreased by 14%. In "Lands of Opportunity: Social and Economic Effects of Tribal Gaming on Localities" (*Policy Matters*, vol. 1, no. 4, Summer 2007), Mindy Marks and Kate Spilde Contreras of the University of California, Riverside, come to similar conclusions regarding tribal gaming in California, noting that the economic benefits often help the people most in need. The researchers state that "tribal governments with gaming are concentrating employment opportunity in areas that are economically worse off than areas without gaming reservations."

DISCRIMINATORY EMPLOYMENT PRACTICES

Under Title VII of the Civil Rights Act of 1964, employers may not intentionally use race, skin color, age, gender, religious beliefs, or national origin as the basis for decisions relating to almost any aspect of the employment relationship, including hiring. Despite this law, African-Americans, Hispanics, and other minority groups continue to suffer from discriminatory hiring practices as well as other race- and ethnicity-based obstacles to finding employment.

In one of the highest profile workplace discrimination cases in recent years, civil rights attorneys filed a class action lawsuit in June 2003 against Abercrombie & Fitch, one of the nation's largest clothing retailers, for discriminating against people of Hispanic, Asian-American, and African-American descent. The young adults were represented by the Mexican American Legal Defense and Educational Fund, the Asian Pacific American Legal Center, the National Association for the Advancement of Colored-People's Legal Defense and Educational Fund, and the law firm of Lieff Cabraser Heimann & Bernstein LLP. According to Lieff Cabraser Heimann & Bernstein, in the press release "Lieff Cabraser and Civil Rights Organizations Announce Abercrombie & Fitch Charged with Employment Discrimination in Federal Class Action Lawsuit" (June 17, 2003, http://www.afjustice.com/press_release_01.htm), Thomas A. Saenz of the Mexican American Legal Defense and Educational Fund said, "Through means both subtle and direct, Abercrombie has consistently reinforced to its store managers that they must recruit and maintain an overwhelmingly white workforce." In the press release "$40 Million Payment, Detailed Plan for Diversity in Employment Discrimination Suit against Retail Giant Abercrombie & Fitch" (November 16, 2004, http://www.afjustice.com/press_release_02.htm), Lieff Cabraser Heimann & Bernstein states that the lawsuit was settled in November 2004. The company agreed to pay $40 million to the applicants and employees who charged the company with discrimination and to comply with provisions related to the recruitment, hiring, job assignment, training, and promotion of minority employees. This was a prominent case brought to court; however, in general, discriminatory employment practices are difficult to prosecute effectively and remain pervasive in the United States.

In 2006 the federal government filed a lawsuit against a medical clinic in California because a manager used racial code words, including "reggin," which Barbara Feder Ostrov explains in "Discrimination at Work Growing Subtle" (*San Jose Mercury News*, August 12, 2006) is an "infamous racial slur spelled backward." An African-American file clerk was fired from her job after she complained about the racial slurs. The case underscored the changing nature of racial and ethnic discrimination in the workplace, as methods of intimidation become more subtle. This kind of subtle discrimination does not always lead to lawsuits. In fact, the Level Playing Field Institute reports in *The Cost of Employee Turnover Due Solely to Unfairness in the Workplace* (June 22, 2007, http://www.lpfi.org/docs/cl-executive-summary.pdf) that each year 2 million professionals and managers leave their jobs because they are "pushed out by cumulative small comments, whispered jokes and not-so-funny emails."

In another high-profile case, the U.S. Equal Employment Opportunity Commission (EEOC) won a settlement in a racial harassment lawsuit against Lockheed Martin in 2008. In the press release "Lockheed Martin to Pay $2.5 Million to Settle Racial Harassment Lawsuit" (January 2, 2008, http://www.eeoc.gov/eeoc/newsroom/release/1-2-08.cfm), the EEOC notes that Charles Daniels, an African-American electrician, was awarded $2.5 million after being harassed at job sites nationwide, including being threatened with lynching and other physical harm. Coworkers and a supervisor reportedly told Daniels that "we should do to blacks what Hitler did to the Jews" and "if the South had won then this would be a better country." The company failed to discipline the harassers when it was made aware of the situation.

U.S. Equal Employment Opportunity Commission

In May 2000 the EEOC issued new guidelines to facilitate the settlement of federal-sector discrimination complaints, including claims brought under Title VII. Under the administration of Chairperson Ida L. Castro (1953–), the EEOC sought to reform its complaint process for federal employees. The new directive authorizes federal agencies to enter into settlement of bias claims, including monetary payment.

In fiscal year (FY) 2008 the EEOC received 33,937 charges under Title VII alleging race-based discrimination. (See Table 4.5.) That same year, the EEOC resolved 28,321 charges (some of these cases were carried over from the previous year). Of those, 3,069 (10.8%) were settled, with payments totaling $79.3 million to the charging parties. The percent of cases settled was up substantially from FY 1997, when only 3.3% (1,206) were settled. In FY 2008 another 1,061 (3.7%) of the claims were found to have reasonable cause; 355 (1.3%) of these were charges with reasonable cause that closed after successful conciliation and 706 (2.5%) of them were charges with reasonable cause that closed after unsuccessful conciliation. Another 1,435 (5.1%) cases were withdrawn by the charging party on receipt of desired benefits ("withdrawals with benefits"). In other words, 5,565 cases of racial discrimination were found to have reasonable cause or were settled or withdrawn after the employer admitted culpability and submitted to a monetary settlement. Countless other incidents of racial discrimination in the workplace are never brought to the attention of the EEOC. Instead, victims suffer silently or leave their places of employment, as found by the Level Playing Field Institute Survey.

Views of Economic Opportunities

Whites are much more likely than African-Americans to believe that members of minority groups have equal job opportunities in the United States. In a 2008 Gallup poll, 82% of whites, including Hispanics, believed African-Americans have as good a chance as whites to get a job that they are qualified for, whereas only 49% of African-Americans thought so. (See Figure 4.1.) An earlier Gallup poll surveyed Hispanics, as well. In *Whites, Minorities Differ in Views of Economic Opportunities in U.S.* (July 10, 2006, http://www.gallup.com/poll/23617/Whites-Minorities-Differ-Views-Economic-Opportunities-US.aspx), Joseph Carroll of the Gallup Organization reports on a June 2006 poll that asked the question: "Do you feel that racial minorities in this country have equal job opportunities as whites, or not?" There were stark differences in the responses of non-Hispanic whites and members of minority groups. Over half (53%) of non-Hispanic whites surveyed believed members of minority groups have equal job opportunities. By contrast, only a third (34%) of Hispanics surveyed believed this was true, down significantly from 46% in June 2001. Only 17% of African-Americans surveyed believed the job opportunities for minorities are equal to those of whites, down from 23% the previous year but basically unchanged from June 2001.

WORKFORCE PROJECTIONS FOR 2016

In 2008 the percent of the workforce of Hispanic origin (14.3%) was higher than the percent of the workforce that was African-American (11.5%). (See Table 4.6.) In addition, more Hispanics than African-Americans or non-Hispanic whites will enter the workforce through 2018, causing the group to make up an increasingly larger part of the workforce. The proportion of African-Americans in the labor force is expected to increase slightly to 12.1% in 2018, whereas the proportion of non-Hispanic whites is expected to actually decrease from 68.2% in 2008 to 64% in 2018. As recently as 1988, non-Hispanic whites made up nearly four-fifths (79%) of the workforce. The proportion of Hispanics in the workforce is expected to increase from 14.3% in 2008 to 17.6% in 2018. The growth of Hispanics in the workforce can be attributed to higher birth rates among that group and to increased immigration.

Asian-Americans are another fast-growing group in the labor force. The proportion of Asian-Americans in the workforce is expected to increase from 4.7% in 2008 to 5.6% in 2018. (See Table 4.6.) As with most other minority groups, increases reflect continued high immigration and higher fertility rates among some minority populations. By contrast, the non-Hispanic white population is decreasing its share of the labor force due to lower birth rates among the majority group, relatively low immigration of non-Hispanic whites to the United States, and declining labor force participation by non-Hispanic white men, which is a reflection of the aging of the white male labor force.

OCCUPATIONS
African-Americans and Jobs

African-Americans are much less likely than whites or Asian-Americans to hold the jobs requiring the most

TABLE 4.5

Race-based charges filed and resolved under Title VII of the Civil Rights Act of 1964, fiscal years 1997–2008

	Fiscal year 1997	Fiscal year 1998	Fiscal year 1999	Fiscal year 2000	Fiscal year 2001	Fiscal year 2002	Fiscal year 2003	Fiscal year 2004	Fiscal year 2005	Fiscal year 2006	Fiscal year 2007	Fiscal year 2008
Receipts	29,199	28,820	28,819	28,945	28,912	29,910	28,526	27,696	26,740	27,238	30,510	33,937
Resolutions	36,419	35,716	35,094	33,188	32,077	33,199	30,702	29,631	27,411	25,992	25,882	28,321
Resolutions by type												
Settlements	1,206	1,460	2,138	2,802	2,549	3,059	2,890	2,927	2,801	3,039	2,945	3,069
	3.3%	4.1%	6.1%	8.4%	7.9%	9.2%	9.4%	9.9%	10.2%	11.7%	11.4%	10.8%
Withdrawals w/benefits	912	823	1,036	1,150	1,203	1,200	1,125	1,088	1,167	1,177	1,235	1,435
	2.5%	2.3%	3.0%	3.5%	3.8%	3.6%	3.7%	3.7%	4.3%	4.5%	4.8%	5.1%
Administrative closures	8,395	7,871	7,213	5,727	5,626	5,043	4,759	4,261	3,674	3,436	3,931	3,964
	23.1%	22.0%	20.6%	17.3%	17.5%	15.2%	15.5%	14.4%	13.4%	13.2%	15.2%	14.0%
No reasonable cause	24,988	24,515	23,148	21,319	20,302	21,853	20,506	20,166	18,608	17,324	16,773	18,792
	68.6%	68.6%	66.0%	64.2%	63.3%	65.8%	66.8%	68.1%	67.9%	66.7%	64.8%	66.4%
Reasonable cause	918	1,047	1,559	2,190	2,397	2,044	1,422	1,189	1,161	1,016	998	1,061
	2.5%	2.9%	4.4%	6.6%	7.5%	6.2%	4.6%	4.0%	4.2%	3.9%	3.9%	3.7%
Successful conciliations	248	287	382	529	691	580	392	330	377	292	285	355
	0.7%	0.8%	1.1%	1.6%	2.2%	1.7%	1.3%	1.1%	1.4%	1.1%	1.1%	1.3%
Unsuccessful conciliations	670	760	1,177	1,661	1,706	1,464	1,030	859	784	724	713	706
	1.8%	2.1%	3.4%	5.0%	5.3%	4.4%	3.4%	2.9%	2.9%	2.8%	2.8%	2.5%
Merit resolutions	3,036	3,330	4,733	6,142	6,149	6,303	5,437	5,204	5,129	5,232	5,178	5,565
	8.3%	9.3%	13.5%	18.5%	19.2%	19.0%	17.7%	17.6%	18.7%	20.1%	20.0%	19.6%
Monetary benefits (millions)*	$41.8	$32.2	$53.2	$61.7	$86.5	$81.1	$69.6	$61.1	$76.5	$61.4	$67.7	$79.3

*Does not include monetary benefits obtained through litigation.

Notes: The total of individual percentages may not always sum to 100% due to rounding. Equal Employment Opportunity Commission (EEOC) total workload includes charges carried over from previous fiscal years, new charge receipts and charges transferred to Equal Employment Opportunity Commission (EEOC) from Fair Employment Practice Agencies (FEPAs). Resolution of charges each year may therefore exceed receipts for that year because workload being resolved is drawn from a combination of pending, new receipts and FEPA transfer charges rather than from new charges only.

SOURCE: "Race-Based Charges, FY 1997–FY 2008," in *Enforcement and Litigation Statistics*, U.S. Equal Employment Opportunity Commission, Office of Research, Information, and Planning, 2009, http://www.eeoc.gov/eeoc/statistics/enforcement/race.cfm (accessed December 11, 2009)

FIGURE 4.1

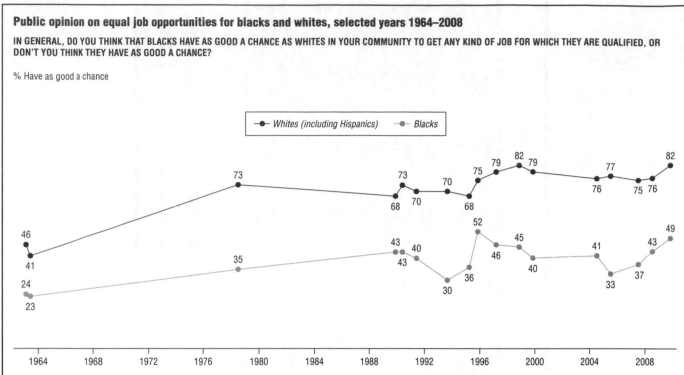

Public opinion on equal job opportunities for blacks and whites, selected years 1964–2008

IN GENERAL, DO YOU THINK THAT BLACKS HAVE AS GOOD A CHANCE AS WHITES IN YOUR COMMUNITY TO GET ANY KIND OF JOB FOR WHICH THEY ARE QUALIFIED, OR DON'T YOU THINK THEY HAVE AS GOOD A CHANCE?

% Have as good a chance

Legend: Whites (including Hispanics) · Blacks

SOURCE: Frank Newport, "In General, Do You Think That Blacks Have As Good a Chance As Whites in Your Community to Get Any Kind of Job for Which They Are Qualified, or Don't You Think They Have As Good a Chance?" in *Little "Obama Effect" on Views about Race Relations*, The Gallup Organization, October 29, 2009, http://www.gallup.com/poll/123944/Little-Obama-Effect-Views-Race-Relations.aspx (accessed December 11, 2009). Copyright © 2009 by The Gallup Organization. Reproduced by Permission of The Gallup Organization.

education and paying the highest salaries—those in management, professional, and related occupations. In 2008, 16 million African-Americans accounted for 11% of the civilian labor force aged 16 years and older. (See Table 4.7.) Only 27.4% of employed African-Americans held management, professional, or related occupations, compared with 37% of white workers. Women of both races were more likely to hold these positions, but only 31.3% of African-American women were managers or professionals, compared with 40.6% of white women. The proportion of African-Americans who held these positions had risen slightly from the previous year.

African-Americans are much more likely than whites to work in the poorly paid service occupations. In 2008, 24.4% of African-Americans worked in service occupations, up from 23.3% the previous year. (See Table 4.7.) By contrast, 15.7% of white Americans worked in service occupations in 2008.

Any growth in professional employment for African-Americans has generally occurred in fields at the lower end of the earnings scale. The BLS notes in *Employment and Earnings* (January 2009, http://www.bls.gov/cps/cpsa2008.pdf) that 22.1% of all licensed practical and vocational nurses were African-American in 2008, but only 10% of registered nurses, 6.6% of physicians and surgeons, and 3.3% of dentists were African-American.

The same pattern holds true for management positions. Even though 10.1% of social service and community service managers and 12.2% of education administrators were African-American in 2008, only 3.9% of chief executives, 3.7% of construction managers, and 1.1% of engineering managers were African-American.

In 2008 most African-Americans were concentrated in the management, professional, and related occupations (27.4%), sales and office occupations (25.5%), and service occupations (24.4%). (See Table 4.7.) However, African-Americans were underrepresented in management, professional, and related occupations (27.4%, compared with 36.3% of workers overall), and overrepresented in service occupations (24.4%, compared with 16.8% of workers overall).

Hispanics and Jobs

Overall, Hispanics are less likely than African-Americans to hold professional and technical positions. In 2008 only 18.3% of employed Hispanics held management, professional, and related occupations, compared with 27.4% of African-Americans. (See Table 4.7.) The largest percentage of Hispanics worked in service occupations (24.2%), where they are seriously overrepresented, compared with 16.8% of workers overall in these low-paying occupations. More than one out of five (21.4%) Hispanic workers worked in sales and office occupations. Like African-Americans, Hispanics, except for Cuban-Americans who came to this

TABLE 4.6

Civilian labor force, by age, sex, race, and ethnicity, 1988, 1998, 2008, and projected 2018

[Numbers in thousands]

Group	Level				Change			Percent change			Percent distribution				Annual growth rate (percent)		
	1988	1998	2008	2018	1988–98	1998–2008	2008–18	1988–98	1998–2008	2008–18	1988	1998	2008	2018	1988–98	1998–2008	2008–18
Total, 16 years and older	121,669	137,673	154,287	166,911	16,004	16,614	12,624	13.2	12.1	8.2	100.0	100.0	100.0	100.0	1.2	1.1	0.8
Age, years																	
16 to 24	22,536	21,894	22,032	21,131	−642	138	−901	−2.8	0.6	−4.1	18.5	15.9	14.3	12.7	−0.3	0.1	−0.4
25 to 54	84,041	98,718	104,396	105,944	14,677	5,678	1,548	17.5	5.8	1.5	69.1	71.7	67.7	63.5	1.6	0.6	0.1
55 and older	15,092	17,061	27,857	39,836	1,969	10,796	11,979	13.0	63.3	43.0	12.4	12.4	18.1	23.9	1.2	5.0	3.6
Sex:																	
Men	66,927	73,959	82,520	88,682	7,032	8,561	6,162	10.5	11.6	7.5	55.0	53.7	53.5	53.1	1.0	1.1	0.7
Women	54,742	63,714	71,767	78,229	8,972	8,053	6,462	16.4	12.6	9.0	45.0	46.3	46.5	46.9	1.5	1.2	0.9
Race:																	
White	104,756	115,415	125,635	132,490	10,659	10,220	6,855	10.2	8.9	5.5	86.1	83.8	81.4	79.4	1.0	0.9	0.5
Black	13,205	15,982	17,740	20,244	2,777	1,758	2,504	21.0	11.0	14.1	10.9	11.6	11.5	12.1	1.9	1.0	1.3
Asian	3,718	6,278	7,202	9,345	2,560	924	2,143	68.9	14.7	29.8	3.1	4.6	4.7	5.6	5.4	1.4	2.6
All other groups*	—	—	3,710	4,832	—	—	1,122	—	—	30.2	—	—	2.4	2.9	—	—	2.7
Ethnicity:																	
Hispanic origin	8,982	14,317	22,024	29,304	5,335	7,707	7,280	59.4	53.8	33.1	7.4	10.4	14.3	17.6	4.8	4.4	2.9
Other than Hispanic origin	112,687	123,356	132,263	137,607	10,669	8,907	5,344	9.5	7.2	4.0	92.6	89.6	85.7	82.4	0.9	0.7	0.4
White non-Hispanic	96,141	101,767	105,210	106,854	5,626	3,443	1,624	5.9	3.4	1.5	79.0	73.9	68.2	64.0	0.6	0.3	0.2
Age of baby boomers	24 to 42	34 to 52	44 to 62	54 to 72	—	—	—	—	—	—	—	—	—	—	—	—	—

*The "all other groups" category includes (1) those classified as being of multiple racial origin and (2) the race categories of (2a) American Indian and Alaska Native and (2b) Native Hawaiian and other Pacific Islanders.

Notes: Dash indicates no data collected for category. Details may not sum to totals because of rounding.

SOURCE: Mitra Toossi, "Table 1. Civilian Labor Force, by Age, Sex, Race, and Ethnicity, 1988, 1998, 2008, and Projected 2018," in "Labor Force Projections to 2018: Older Workers Staying More Active," *Monthly Labor Review*, vol. 132, no. 11, November 2009, http://www.bls.gov/opub/mlr/2009/11/art3full.pdf (accessed December 11, 2009)

TABLE 4.7

Employed persons by occupation, race, Hispanic origin, and sex, 2007–08

[Percent distribution]

Occupation, race, and Hispanic or Latino ethnicity	Total		Men		Women	
	2007	2008	2007	2008	2007	2008
Total						
Total, 16 years and over (thousands)	146,047	145,362	78,254	77,486	67,792	67,876
Percent	100.0	100.0	100.0	100.0	100.0	100.0
Management, professional, and related occupations	35.5	36.3	32.7	33.5	38.6	39.5
Management, business, and financial operations occupations	14.8	15.2	15.8	16.3	13.6	13.9
Professional and related occupations	20.7	21.1	16.9	17.2	25.1	25.6
Service occupations	16.5	16.8	13.2	13.5	20.4	20.6
Sales and office occupations	24.8	24.5	16.9	16.9	33.8	33.1
Sales and related occupations	11.4	11.2	10.8	10.6	12.2	11.9
Office and administrative support occupations	13.4	13.2	6.2	6.3	21.6	21.2
Natural resources, construction, and maintenance occupations	10.8	10.2	19.3	18.3	1.0	.9
Farming, fishing, and forestry occupations	.7	.7	1.0	1.0	.3	.3
Construction and extraction occupations	6.5	6.0	11.9	10.9	.4	.3
Installation, maintenance, and repair occupations	3.6	3.5	6.4	6.4	.3	.3
Production, transportation, and material moving occupations	12.4	12.2	17.9	17.8	6.2	5.9
Production occupations	6.4	6.2	8.4	8.1	4.2	3.9
Transportation and material moving occupations	6.0	6.1	9.5	9.7	2.0	1.9
White						
Total, 16 years and over (thousands)	119,792	119,126	65,289	64,624	54,503	54,501
Percent	100.0	100.0	100.0	100.0	100.0	100.0
Management, professional, and related occupations	36.1	37.0	33.2	34.0	39.5	40.6
Management, business, and financial operations occupations	15.5	15.9	16.7	17.2	13.9	14.3
Professional and related occupations	20.6	21.1	16.5	16.8	25.6	26.3
Service occupations	15.5	15.7	12.4	12.6	19.3	19.3
Sales and office occupations	24.8	24.5	16.7	16.7	34.4	33.7
Sales and related occupations	11.6	11.4	11.0	10.9	12.3	12.0
Office and administrative support occupations	13.2	13.1	5.7	5.8	22.1	21.7
Natural resources, construction, and maintenance occupations	11.6	11.0	20.4	19.4	1.0	.9
Farming, fishing, and forestry occupations	.7	.7	1.1	1.1	.3	.3
Construction and extraction occupations	7.1	6.5	12.7	11.7	.4	.3
Installation, maintenance, and repair occupations	3.8	3.7	6.7	6.6	.3	.3
Production, transportation, and material moving occupations	12.0	11.9	17.3	17.3	5.7	5.4
Production occupations	6.3	6.1	8.4	8.1	3.9	3.6
Transportation and material moving occupations	5.7	5.8	9.0	9.2	1.9	1.8
Black or African American						
Total, 16 years and over (thousands)	16,051	15,953	7,500	7,398	8,551	8,554
Percent	100.0	100.0	100.0	100.0	100.0	100.0
Management, professional, and related occupations	27.1	27.4	22.3	23.0	31.2	31.3
Management, business, and financial operations occupations	10.1	10.0	9.2	9.6	11.0	10.4
Professional and related occupations	16.9	17.4	13.1	13.3	20.3	20.9
Service occupations	23.3	24.4	19.2	20.1	26.8	28.2
Sales and office occupations	26.2	25.5	18.7	18.2	32.7	31.9
Sales and related occupations	10.3	9.9	8.8	8.4	11.7	11.1
Office and administrative support occupations	15.8	15.7	10.0	9.8	21.0	20.7
Natural resources, construction, and maintenance occupations	7.0	6.4	14.0	13.0	.8	.7
Farming, fishing, and forestry occupations	.3	.3	.4	.5	.2	.1
Construction and extraction occupations	4.0	3.4	8.1	7.0	.3	.3
Installation, maintenance, and repair occupations	2.7	2.7	5.5	5.6	.3	.3
Production, transportation, and material moving occupations	16.5	16.2	25.7	25.7	8.5	7.9
Production occupations	7.4	6.9	9.6	9.2	5.4	4.8
Transportation and material moving occupations	9.2	9.3	16.1	16.5	3.1	3.1

country in 1959 following the Cuban revolution, are concentrated primarily in low-paying, low-skilled jobs.

In 2008, 20.3 million Hispanics worked, making up 14% of the workforce. (See Table 4.7.) According to the BLS, in *Employment and Earnings*, Hispanics were concentrated in low-paying jobs and were underrepresented in management, professional, and related occupations, where they held only 7.1% of the available jobs in 2008. Hispanics were overrepresented in service occupations, making up 20.2% of the service workforce, and were concentrated in the lowest-paying occupations in this industry. They made up 28.2% of janitors and building cleaners, 40.5% of maids and housekeepers, and 41% of grounds maintenance workers. They also made up 21% of the food preparation and serving occupations—26.9% of dining room and cafeteria attendants and bartender helpers, 30.2% of cooks, and 35.7% of dishwashers. However, they made up only 14.1% of first-line supervisors of food preparation and serving workers and 9.6% of bartenders.

Significant occupational differences exist among Hispanic subgroups. When it comes to job outlook, Cuban-origin Hispanics have traditionally done better in securing

TABLE 4.7

Employed persons by occupation, race, Hispanic origin, and sex, 2007–08 [CONTINUED]

[Percent distribution]

Occupation, race, and Hispanic or Latino ethnicity	Total		Men		Women	
	2007	2008	2007	2008	2007	2008
Asian						
Total, 16 years and over (thousands)	6,839	6,917	3,677	3,692	3,162	3,225
Percent	100.0	100.0	100.0	100.0	100.0	100.0
Management, professional, and related occupations	48.1	48.2	49.3	50.1	46.8	46.0
Management, business, and financial operations occupations	15.8	16.5	15.8	16.6	15.7	16.4
Professional and related occupations	32.4	31.7	33.5	33.5	31.1	29.7
Service occupations	16.0	16.3	13.5	13.6	18.9	19.4
Sales and office occupations	21.9	21.5	18.4	17.5	26.0	26.1
Sales and related occupations	11.4	11.1	11.5	10.9	11.4	11.4
Office and administrative support occupations	10.5	10.4	6.9	6.6	14.7	14.7
Natural resources, construction, and maintenance occupations	4.4	4.1	7.4	7.2	.9	.6
Farming, fishing, and forestry occupations	.2	.2	.2	.3	.3	.2
Construction and extraction occupations	1.7	1.8	3.1	3.2	.1	.1
Installation, maintenance, and repair occupations	2.4	2.1	4.1	3.7	.5	.3
Production, transportation, and material moving occupations	9.6	9.9	11.4	11.6	7.4	7.8
Production occupations	6.5	6.7	6.7	6.8	6.3	6.6
Transportation and material moving occupations	3.0	3.2	4.7	4.9	1.0	1.2
Hispanic or Latino ethnicity						
Total, 16 years and over (thousands)	20,382	20,346	12,310	12,248	8,072	8,098
Percent	100.0	100.0	100.0	100.0	100.0	100.0
Management, professional, and related occupations	17.8	18.3	14.3	14.8	23.1	23.5
Management, business, and financial operations occupations	7.7	8.1	7.2	7.7	8.6	8.8
Professional and related occupations	10.0	10.2	7.1	7.2	14.5	14.7
Service occupations	24.1	24.2	19.7	19.6	30.7	31.3
Sales and office occupations	21.1	21.4	13.2	13.9	33.1	32.9
Sales and related occupations	9.3	9.3	7.2	7.5	12.4	12.1
Office and administrative support occupations	11.8	12.1	6.0	6.4	20.7	20.7
Natural resources, construction, and maintenance occupations	19.4	18.2	31.0	29.1	1.8	1.7
Farming, fishing, and forestry occupations	1.9	1.9	2.5	2.6	1.0	.9
Construction and extraction occupations	14.0	12.6	22.8	20.7	.6	.4
Installation, maintenance, and repair occupations	3.6	3.7	5.7	5.9	.2	.4
Production, transportation, and material moving occupations	17.6	17.8	21.7	22.6	11.3	10.6
Production occupations	9.4	9.3	10.4	10.6	8.0	7.4
Transportation and material moving occupations	8.2	8.5	11.3	12.0	3.3	3.2

Note: Estimates for the above race groups (white, black or African American, and Asian) do not sum to totals because data are not presented for all races. Persons whose ethnicity is identified as Hispanic or Latino may be of any race. Updated population controls are introduced annually with the release of January data.

SOURCE: "10. Employed Persons by Occupation, Race, Hispanic or Latino Ethnicity, and Sex," in *Employment and Earnings*, U.S. Department of Labor, Bureau of Labor Statistics, 2009, http://www.bls.gov/cps/cpsaat10.pdf (accessed December 11, 2009)

higher-paying jobs, as these immigrants are often well educated. In 2008, 274,000 out of 841,000 (32.6%) Cuban-Americans in the workforce held management, professional, and related occupations. (See Table 4.8.) In contrast, 438,000 out of 1.6 million (26.8%) Puerto Ricans in the workforce and 2 million out of 12.9 million (15.2%) Mexican-Americans in the workforce held management, professional, and related occupations. Mexican-Americans were more likely to work in service occupations (3.2 million, or 24.5%) than in other occupations, especially in food preparation and serving occupations and building and grounds cleaning and maintenance occupations. Puerto Ricans were more likely to work in sales and office occupations (484,000, or 29.6%) than in other occupations.

Asian-Americans and Jobs

The higher educational attainment of many Asian-Americans has resulted in a greater proportion of them working in higher-paying jobs than do other racial and ethnic groups. In 2008 almost half (48.2%) of all Asian-Americans worked in management, professional, and related occupations—16.5% in management, business, and financial operations occupations and 31.7% in professional and related occupations. (See Table 4.7.) In comparison, only 37% of whites worked in these occupations, although the gap narrowed somewhat between 2007 and 2008. Asian-Americans were the next most likely to work in sales and office occupations (21.5%) and service occupations (16.3%), although they were underrepresented in both. In *Employment and Earnings*, the BLS indicates that even though only 4.8% of the workforce was of Asian origin, 6.3% of managers and professionals were Asian-American, and they were especially overrepresented among computer software engineers (29%), medical scientists (24.8%), and chemists and materials scientists (22.3%)—three highly paid occupations.

However, the BLS reports that in 2008 Asian-Americans were underrepresented in natural resources,

TABLE 4.8

Employed Hispanic workers by sex, occupation, class of workers, full- or part-time status, and detailed ethnic group, 2007–08

[In thousands]

| | Hispanic or Latino ethnicity | | | | | | | |
| | Total[a] | | Mexican | | Puerto Rican | | Cuban | |
Category	2007	2008	2007	2008	2007	2008	2007	2008
Sex								
Total, 16 years and over	**20,382**	**20,346**	**12,908**	**12,931**	**1,551**	**1,634**	**862**	**841**
Men	12,310	12,248	8,122	8,106	791	849	490	491
Women	8,072	8,098	4,786	4,825	760	785	372	349
Occupation								
Management, professional, and related occupations	3,621	3,723	1,950	1,966	395	438	253	274
Management, business, and financial operations occupations	1,580	1,652	880	874	136	177	116	135
Management occupations	1,139	1,162	646	621	96	121	88	101
Business and financial operations occupations	441	490	234	252	41	56	28	34
Professional and related occupations	2,041	2,071	1,070	1,093	258	260	137	139
Computer and mathematical occupations	179	188	75	83	26	27	15	15
Architecture and engineering occupations	189	196	102	107	14	19	16	17
Life, physical, and social science occupations	64	62	36	30	5	4	3	4
Community and social services occupations	216	205	119	109	36	27	6	12
Legal occupations	100	110	50	62	16	11	8	9
Education, training, and library occupations	646	641	367	357	88	96	41	37
Arts, design, entertainment, sports, and media occupations	241	234	117	128	23	19	16	12
Healthcare practitioner and technical occupations	407	434	206	218	48	57	33	32
Service occupations	4,904	4,933	3,077	3,170	351	357	141	140
Healthcare support occupations	441	436	225	227	59	52	18	13
Protective service occupations	307	332	151	183	63	54	22	30
Food preparation and serving related occupations	1,633	1,645	1,116	1,163	78	98	33	25
Building and grounds cleaning and maintenance occupations	1,875	1,821	1,222	1,198	86	80	37	51
Personal care and service occupations	648	699	364	399	65	74	31	21
Sales and office occupations	4,306	4,361	2,548	2,580	448	484	222	220
Sales and related occupations	1,891	1,902	1,122	1,142	182	188	94	96
Office and administrative support occupations	2,415	2,459	1,426	1,438	266	296	127	124
Natural resources, construction, and maintenance occupations	3,963	3,701	2,896	2,707	139	137	112	79
Farming, fishing, and forestry occupations	388	389	361	358	4	4	5	3
Construction and extraction occupations	2,851	2,564	2,096	1,875	83	72	63	50
Installation, maintenance, and repair occupations	725	749	439	474	53	61	44	27
Production, transportation, and material moving occupations	3,588	3,628	2,436	2,508	218	220	134	128
Production occupations	1,921	1,892	1,349	1,358	110	107	59	51
Transportation and material moving occupations	1,667	1,736	1,087	1,150	107	113	75	77

TABLE 4.8

Employed Hispanic workers by sex, occupation, class of workers, full- or part-time status, and detailed ethnic group, 2007–08 [CONTINUED]

[In thousands]

	Hispanic or Latino ethnicity							
	Total[a]		Mexican		Puerto Rican		Cuban	
Category	2007	2008	2007	2008	2007	2008	2007	2008
Class of worker								
Agriculture and related industries:								
Wage and salary workers	406	419	382	386	3	2	4	1
Self-employed workers	20	22	15	18	—	—	—	—
Unpaid family workers	—	1	—	1	—	—	—	—
Nonagricultural industries:								
Wage and salary workers	18,728	18,682	11,735	11,728	1,495	1,579	795	801
Government	1,960	2,026	1,213	1,208	237	256	82	107
Private industries	16,767	16,656	10,522	10,519	1,258	1,323	713	694
Private households	283	302	156	166	7	6	9	9
Other industries	16,484	16,354	10,365	10,353	1,251	1,317	709	685
Self-employed workers	1,213	1,203	767	784	53	53	60	38
Unpaid family workers	16	19	11	15	—	—	2	—
Full- or part-time status[b]								
Full-time workers	17,600	17,298	11,181	11,009	1,326	1,365	770	744
Part-time workers	2,782	3,048	1,727	1,923	225	269	92	97

[a]Includes persons of Central or South American origin and of other Hispanic or Latino ethnicity, not shown separately.
[b]Employed persons are classified as full- or part-time workers based on their usual weekly hours at all jobs regardless of the number of hours they are at work during the reference week. Persons absent from work also are classified according to their usual status.
Note: Persons whose ethnicity is identified as Hispanic or Latino may be of any race. Updated population controls are introduced annually with the release of January data. Dash indicates no data or data that do not meet publication criteria.

SOURCE: "13. Employed Hispanic or Latino Workers by Sex, Occupation, Class of Worker, Full- or Part-Time Status, and Detailed Ethnic Group," in *Employment and Earnings*, U.S. Department of Labor, Bureau of Labor Statistics, 2009, http://www.bls.gov/cps/cpsaat13.pdf (accessed December 11, 2009) construction, and maintenance occupations (1.9%) and in installation, maintenance, and repair occupations (2.8%). Even though only 4.6% of service workers were Asian-American, 55% of miscellaneous personal appearance workers were Asian-American—reflecting the large number of Asian-Americans, particularly women, who work in nail salons and other personal care establishments.

Native Americans and Alaskan Natives and Jobs

As stated previously, detailed data on Native American and Alaskan Native workers are difficult to obtain. However, the EEOC keeps some basic data on job patterns for minorities in private industry that includes Native Americans and Alaskan Natives as a separate category. In 2007 Native Americans made up only 0.6% of the total workforce. (See Table 4.9.) They made up only 0.3% of all executives and senior-level managers, 0.4% of all first- and midlevel officials and managers, and only 0.4% of professionals. However, Native Americans and Alaskan Natives were overrepresented among operatives (0.7%), laborers (0.7%), sales workers (0.7%), and craft workers (0.8%).

MINORITIES AND THE FEDERAL GOVERNMENT

Traditionally, non-Hispanic white men have held most of the higher-level positions in the federal government. Along with cabinet members, who are selected by the president, these high-level officials wield the power in the federal government. This holds true for many agencies, including the Federal Bureau of Investigation, the U.S. Immigration and Customs Enforcement, and the U.S. Customs and Border Protection.

In *Federal Equal Opportunity Recruitment Program, FY 2008* (February 2009, http://main.opm.gov/About _OPM/Reports/FEORP/2008/feorp2008.pdf), the U.S. Office of Personnel Management finds that in FY 2008 minorities were overrepresented in the federal workforce with one exception: Hispanics were significantly underrepresented in federal jobs. African-Americans represented 17.9% of the federal workforce in FY 2008, but only 10% of the total civilian labor force. Asians and Pacific Islanders represented 5.4% of the federal workforce, but only 4.3% of the total civilian workforce. Native Americans represented 1.9% of the federal workforce, but only 0.7% of the total civilian labor force. Hispanics represented 7.9% of the federal workforce, but 13.2% of the total civilian workforce in FY 2008.

Even though minorities are generally overrepresented in the federal workforce, they are underrepresented at the senior pay grades. For example, African-Americans made up 17.9% of the federal workforce in FY 2008 but were overrepresented at the lowest pay grades. In FY 2008, 26.6% of employees in the lowest positions—General Schedule and Related (GSR) grades one through four—

were African-American. Another 25.8% of GSR five through eight, 16.8% of GSR nine through 12, 12.7% of GSR 13 through 15, and just 6.1% of the senior pay levels were African-American. Asians and Pacific Islanders were also underrepresented at the senior pay levels, but less so than African-Americans, representing 6.2% of the GSR one-through-four pay levels and 5.8% of the senior pay levels. Hispanics represented 8.5% of the GSR one-through-four pay levels and only 4% of the senior pay levels. Native Americans represented 4.9% of the GSR one-through-four pay levels and only 0.9% of the senior pay levels.

A major contributor to this situation is time. It takes about 20 years to rise to the top of any organization. In the late 1980s few people of color held any management positions in the federal government. Another possible factor is partiality or discrimination. Some lower-level government employees believe they have been deprived of promotions because of their gender or race and have filed bias complaints.

MINORITIES IN BUSINESS

The Census Bureau indicates in *2002 Survey of Business Owners: Advance Report on Characteristics of Employer Business Owners: 2002* (February 2, 2005, http://www .census.gov/econ/census02/sbo/sboadvance.htm) that in 2002—the most recent year for which data were available, as of February 2010—93% of business owners in the United States were non-Hispanic white. All minority groups except Asian-Americans were underrepresented among business owners when compared with their presence in the U.S. residential population aged 25 years and older. Only 3.9% of business owners were of Hispanic origin, even though the U.S. population was 11.1% Hispanic. African-Americans represented only 1.6% of business owners, even though 11.6% of the U.S. population was African-American. Only 0.5% of business owners were Native American and Alaskan Native, even though 1.3% of the U.S. population was Native American and Alaskan Native. Asian-Americans, who represented 5.9% of business owners, were overrepresented in comparison with their presence in the U.S. population, at 4.4%.

Minority Women-Owned Businesses

According to the Census Bureau, in *2002 Survey of Business Owners*, 26.5% of business owners in 2002 were women. The Center for Women's Business Research reports in *Businesses Owned by Women of Color in the United States, 2006* (2007) that between 1997 and 2006 the number of businesses that were majority owned (51% or more) by women of color grew by 119.7%. By 2006 there were nearly 2.1 million firms majority owned by minority women in the United States. In 2006 one out of five (21.4%) of all privately held, women-owned businesses in the United States were owned by minority

TABLE 4.9

Occupational employment in private industry, by race, ethnicity, sex, and industry, 2007

Racial/ethnic group and sex	Total employment	Executive/senior level officials & managers	First/mid level officials & managers	Professionals	Technicians	Sales workers	Office & clerical workers	Craft workers	Operatives	Laborers	Service workers
					Number employed						
					Participation Rate						
All employees	100.00	100.00	100.00	100.00	100.00	100.00	100.00	100.00	100.00	100.00	100.00
Men	52.44	71.40	62.62	46.88	51.63	44.82	21.48	90.47	74.67	67.34	41.14
Women	47.56	28.60	37.38	53.12	48.37	55.18	78.52	9.53	25.33	32.66	58.86
White	65.75	87.42	80.54	76.24	70.69	68.96	66.11	70.61	60.14	45.61	50.51
Men	34.82	63.25	51.19	36.24	37.29	32.32	13.44	64.72	46.28	30.97	19.39
Women	30.93	24.17	29.35	40.00	33.40	36.64	52.66	5.89	13.86	14.65	31.12
Minority	34.25	12.58	19.46	23.76	29.31	31.04	33.89	29.39	39.86	54.39	49.49
Men	17.62	8.14	11.43	10.65	14.34	12.50	8.03	25.75	28.39	36.37	21.75
Women	16.63	4.43	8.03	13.12	14.97	18.54	25.86	3.64	11.47	18.01	27.74
Black	14.10	3.57	7.25	7.59	13.15	13.98	16.85	9.31	17.27	17.55	23.23
Men	6.36	1.89	3.74	2.52	5.04	5.20	3.46	7.81	12.19	11.60	8.95
Women	7.74	1.68	3.51	5.08	8.11	8.78	13.39	1.50	5.09	5.95	14.28
Hispanic	13.63	4.46	5.77	4.97	8.69	11.58	11.50	16.06	17.36	31.81	20.10
Men	7.89	3.03	4.33	2.32	5.11	4.97	3.01	14.58	12.82	21.75	10.05
Women	5.74	1.42	2.44	2.65	3.58	6.61	8.49	1.47	4.54	10.07	10.05
Asian American	5.15	3.70	4.50	10.14	6.12	3.91	4.14	2.66	3.95	3.24	4.33
Men	2.67	2.67	2.81	5.33	3.48	1.71	1.23	2.14	2.46	1.85	1.95
Women	2.48	1.03	1.69	4.81	2.64	2.20	2.91	0.52	1.49	1.39	2.37
American Indian	0.58	0.33	0.42	0.39	0.59	0.70	0.56	0.81	0.68	0.69	0.65
Men	0.31	0.22	0.26	0.18	0.31	0.26	0.12	0.73	0.50	0.46	0.25
Women	0.28	0.12	0.16	0.21	0.29	0.44	0.44	0.08	0.18	0.23	0.39
Hawaiian	0.34	0.23	0.20	0.34	0.37	0.28	0.32	0.26	0.31	0.49	0.45
Men	0.17	0.14	0.11	0.14	0.20	0.11	0.08	0.24	0.21	0.31	0.19
Women	0.17	0.09	0.09	0.20	0.17	0.17	0.24	0.03	0.10	0.18	0.26
Two or more races	0.46	0.29	0.32	0.33	0.39	0.59	0.50	0.29	0.29	0.60	0.73
Men	0.23	0.19	0.18	0.15	0.20	0.24	0.12	0.25	0.21	0.41	0.34
Women	0.23	0.10	0.14	0.18	0.18	0.35	0.38	0.04	0.07	0.19	0.39

SOURCE: Adapted from "2007 EEO-1 National Aggregate Report," in *Job Patterns for Minorities and Women in Private Industry*, U.S. Equal Employment Opportunity Commission, October 2009, http://archive.eeoc.gov/stats/jobpat/2007/us/national.html (accessed January 7, 2010) women. These businesses generated over $161 billion in sales in 2006. Most (80.1%) of the firms were in the service industry.

The Center for Women's Business Research reports that of the nearly 2.1 million businesses owned by minority women in 2006, 770,396 (36.9%) were owned by African-American women, 745,246 (35.7%) were owned by Hispanic women, 436,751 (20.9%) were owned by Asian-American women, 119,198 (5.7%) were owned by Native American or Alaskan Native women, and 15,258 (0.7%) were owned by Native Hawaiian or Pacific Islander women. Firms owned by Native Hawaiian or Pacific Islander women experienced the greatest growth between 1997 and 2006 (190.2%). There was also triple-digit growth in the number of firms owned by African-American women (147%), Native American or Alaskan Native women (122.5%), and Hispanic women (121.3%). Firms owned by Asian-American women achieved a more modest growth of 80.4%.

Minority Set-Aside Programs under Increasing Attack

Many levels of government, including the federal government, have set-aside programs that award a certain percentage of contracts to minority- and women-owned businesses. These programs were developed to remedy the effects of past discrimination and to address the difficulties these firms faced in competing with larger, more established firms for government contracts. Minority businesses are often newer and smaller and have difficulty competing with older, larger businesses that know the process and can afford to make lower bids. Acquiring government contracts can be involved and confusing for businesses unfamiliar with the process. Governments, especially the federal government, are often slow to pay their bills, so businesses frequently have to borrow money to bridge the gap between the delivery of goods and services that must be paid for and the time it takes the government to pay them.

Even though the U.S. Supreme Court has not yet declared the use of racial classifications unconstitutional, it has ruled them suspect and subject to strict judicial scrutiny. As a result, set-aside programs came under increasing attack in the 1990s and at the turn of the 21st century.

In *Richmond v. J. A. Croson Co.* (488 U.S. 469 [1989]), the Supreme Court struck down a Richmond, Virginia, city ordinance that reserved 30% of city-financed construction contracts for minority-owned businesses. The court ruled that the ordinance violated equal protection because there was no "specific" and "identified" evidence of past discrimination, "public or private," against the Richmond Minority Business Enterprise in city contracting. The majority opinion, written by Justice Sandra Day O'Connor (1930–), also noted that the city had failed to "narrowly tailor" the remedy to accomplish any objective "except perhaps outright racial balancing." The opinion further stated that it was a "completely unrealistic" assumption that a 30% assignment to minority business enterprises in a particular trade would be a fair representation of the community.

In a similar case, Adarand Constructors, a white-owned company, sued the federal government, claiming the company failed to receive a government contract because racial preferences had violated the owner's right to equal protection under the Fifth Amendment. In 1989 the U.S. Department of Transportation awarded a contract for a federal highway project to a construction firm, that in turn subcontracted the job to a Disadvantaged Business Enterprise in compliance with the Subcontractor Compensation Clause. In *Adarand Constructors Inc. v. Peña* (515 U.S. 200 [1995]), the Supreme Court expressed doubt in the validity of the affirmative action programs, which were based on the Surface Transportation and Uniform Relocation Assistance Act of 1987 that channeled $10 billion a year in construction contracts to women- and minority-owned businesses. The court, citing the need for stricter and narrower standards in determining racial preferences when awarding contracts, returned the case to the district court for review.

In June 2000 a federal court in *Associated General Contractors of Ohio v. Sandra A. Drabik* (No. 98-4393) decided that the Ohio state program of setting aside 5% of state construction projects for minority-owned businesses was unconstitutional. Even though that court had upheld the state's program in 1983, subsequent U.S. Supreme Court decisions required the federal court to apply a more stringent standard of judicial review and no longer allowed legislatures to use "implicit fact-finding of discrimination" to justify racial preferences and affirmative action programs such as set-aside programs.

In the meantime, the federal government created a new set-aside program in 1993 called the Small and Disadvantaged Business Set-Aside Program. This program supplemented other set-aside programs, allowing agencies to set aside some competitions solely for small and disadvantaged businesses with awards made through the agencies rather than through the government.

TRIBAL CASINOS—A MATTER OF SELF-RULE

The Indian Gaming Regulatory Act of 1988 gives tribes "the exclusive right to regulate gaming on Indian lands if the gaming activity is not specifically prohibited by federal law and is conducted within a State which does not, as a matter of criminal law and public policy, prohibit such gaming activity." The law requires that only tribes, not individuals, run gaming operations. The tribes do not need state approval for class-two casinos, which are supposedly bingo halls but which in many cases have slot machine parlors that skirt the law. Class-three casinos offer slots, roulette, craps, and poker, and they require state approval. Thus, governors make deals with tribes, granting class-three approval in exchange for a share of the profits going to the state treasury. With many states facing severe budget problems, tribal gaming has become an attractive source of revenue. As a result, tribal gaming has gained considerable political influence. The Tribal Law and Policy Institute reports in "Native Gaming Resources" (November 23, 2009, http://www.tribal-institute.org/lists/gaming.htm) that in 2008, 224 out of 562 federally recognized Native American tribes were engaged in gaming. How much has tribal gaming helped the Native American population as a whole?

In "Wheel of Misfortune" (*Time*, December 16, 2002), Donald L. Barlett and James B. Steele provide a scathing and controversial review of tribal gaming. According to Barlett and Steele, when tribal gaming emerged in the late 1980s "in a frenzy of cost cutting and privatization, Washington perceived gaming on reservations as a cheap way to wean tribes from government handouts, encourage economic development and promote tribal self-sufficiency." However, the 1988 Gaming Act "was so riddled with loopholes, so poorly written, so discriminatory and subject to such conflicting interpretations that 14 years later, armies of high-priced lawyers are still debating the definition of a slot machine." Barlett and Steele maintain that only a handful of tribal gaming establishments, those operating close to major population centers, are successful, whereas the overwhelming majority are either too small or too remote in location: "Casinos in California, Connecticut and Florida—states with only 3% of the Indian population—haul in 44% of all revenue, an average of $100,000 per Indian." Barlett and Steele state that in 2002 "290 Indian casinos in 28 states pulled in at least $12.7 billion in revenue. Of that sum, ... the casinos kept more than $5 billion as profit. That would place overall Indian gaming among *Fortune* magazine's 20 most profitable U.S. corporations." However, "just 39 casinos generated $8.4 billion. In short, 13% of the casinos accounted for 66% of the take."

Also controversial was the authenticity of the tribes involved in gaming. According to Barlett and Steele, leaders of tribes involved in gaming "are free to set their own whimsical rules for admission, without regard to Indian heritage. They may exclude rivals, potential whistle-blowers and other legitimate claimants. The fewer tribe members, the larger the cut for the rest. Some tribes are booting out members, while others are limiting membership." Moreover, many "long-defunct tribes and extended families" have attempted to gain congressional certification to become involved in tribal gaming. In New York state some tribes that are not even recognized as New York tribes, including tribes from Oklahoma and Wisconsin, have teamed with area developers to buy land in the Catskills and elsewhere in the state in hopes of building casinos. They are opposed, how-ever, by local communities—as well as by Donald Trump (1946–)—who fear further competition to casinos operating in Atlantic City, New Jersey.

By contrast, many proponents point out the positive effects of tribal gaming, arguing that it spurs economic development and helps tribes solidify tribal sovereignty. The immediate effect of tribal gaming seems to have done just that. In "The Economic Impact of Native American Gaming: Cost-Benefit Analysis of the Mashantucket Pequot Tribal Nation" (2002, http://economics.illinoisstate.edu/uauje/PDF%27s/issue2002/LisaBorromeo.pdf), Lisa Borromeo of George Washington University notes that "Indian gaming appears to be the most successful strategy in turning around 150 years of failed attempts by [the] United States government to aid American Indians, by providing a means to self-sufficiency for Tribal nations." The casinos employ large numbers of Native Americans, and with the profits from casinos, the tribes are building schools and community centers; financing education trust funds, local government, and new businesses; and putting in water and sewer systems on reservation lands. Thaddieus W. Conner and William A. Taggart studied tribal gaming in New Mexico and published their findings in "The Impact of Gaming on the Indian Nations in New Mexico" (*Social Science Quarterly*, vol. 90, no. 1, March 2009). The researchers find that gaming tribes have higher incomes, lower poverty, and improvement in some social areas when compared with nongaming tribes. Stephen Cornell of the University of Arizona points out in "The Political Economy of American Indian Gaming" (*Annual Review of Law and Social Science*, vol. 4, December 2008) that tribal gaming has had positive economic, political, and social effects on both gaming and nongaming Native American reservations.

Proponents of tribal gaming also point to a number of success stories. Marks and Spilde Contreras find that in 2007 tribal gaming reduced poverty and improved employment and income in the communities near the California casinos. The Oneidas of Wisconsin took advantage of a bingo hall to lower the tribe's unemployment rate in the early 1990s and used proceeds to build an elementary school and subsidize a Head Start program. The Suquamish in Washington state used gambling profits to buy back former reservation land. Only a handful of tribal casinos generate large revenues, but even those operations that break even create jobs that benefit many Native Americans. Furthermore, tribes not able to take advantage of gambling can benefit from revenue-sharing programs, such as the one set up in California. The California Nations Indian Gaming Association reports in the press release "California's Gaming Tribes Share More Than $200 Million with Other Tribes" (November 17, 2005, http://www.cniga.com/media/press release_detail.php?id=73) that in 2005, 61 tribes with gaming compacts shared profits with 70 qualifying tribes via the Indian Gaming Special Distribution Fund, which was established in September 1999.

Tribal Casinos and the Global Economic Recession

Interestingly, tribal casinos were much less affected by the global economic recession than were nontribal casinos. According to Howard Stutz, in "Tribal Casinos: Gaming Revenue Tight in 2008" (*Las Vegas Review-Journal*, December 10, 2009), tribal casinos collected $26.8 billion in gaming revenue in 2008, a 1.5% increase over the previous year. Hugo Martín reports in "Recession Is in Play at California's Tribal Casinos" (*Los Angeles Times*, November 20, 2009) that the recession did not decrease the number of visitors to California's tribal casinos—

although Atlantic City and Las Vegas did see drops in visitors—but it did affect how much money those visitors spent. The article "Tribal Casinos No Longer Sure Bet in Washington" (Associated Press, February 3, 2010) notes that even though a few Washington state tribal casinos closed and most casinos saw revenues drop in 2009, a few saw revenues increase. Furthermore, tribal casinos overall were performing more strongly than nontribal casinos.

Regardless, wary that the future might see the curtailment in revenues, some tribes began to diversify by expanding their facilities into full-fledged resorts, whereas others started investing proceeds into nongaming businesses, thereby establishing an economic base independent of gambling.

CHAPTER 5
MONEY, INCOME, AND POVERTY STATUS

Income greatly influences where people live, what they eat, how they dress, what cars they drive or transportation they take, and what schools their children can attend. How much money and income people have is usually determined by their occupation, which is often directly related to their level of education. Racial and ethnic backgrounds can play a big role in all these factors as well.

INCOME DIFFERENCES
All Households

A household consists of a person or people who occupy the same housing unit and may have just one person (the householder who owns or rents the house). It may also consist of related family members (family household) or unrelated people (nonfamily household).

The median income (half of all households earned more and half earned less) of U.S. households in 2008, including money income before taxes but excluding the value of noncash benefits such as food stamps, Medicare (the federally administered system of health insurance for people aged 65 years and older and people with disabilities), Medicaid (the federally funded health care program for low-income people), public housing, and employer-provided benefits, was $50,303, down from $52,163 the year before. (See Table 5.1.) The decrease in median income in 2008 can be attributed to the worldwide economic recession that began in 2007 and resulted in soaring unemployment and underemployment rates. Median income varied substantially between races and ethnic groups. The median income of non-Hispanic white households was $55,530, which was considerably higher than that of Hispanic households ($37,913) and African-American households ($34,218). However, non-Hispanic white income was significantly less than the median household income of Asian-Americans ($65,637). Some of the reasons for these income disparities are discussed in this chapter.

Married-Couple Households

In 2008 there were 59.1 million married-couple households in the United States, representing 51% of all households and 75% of all family households. (See Table 5.1.) Married couples tend to have a higher household income than single householders do, because often both the husband and wife work outside of the home. In 2008 married-couple households had a median income of $73,010. The median income for female-headed households with no husband present was substantially lower, at $33,073—less than half the median income of married-couple households. The median income for male-headed households with no wife present was also lower than the married-couple median but substantially higher than the female-headed households, at $49,186.

Per Capita Income

Per capita income is figured by dividing the total (aggregate or composite) national income by the total population. This means that if all the nation's earnings were divided equally among every man, woman, and child, each person would receive this amount. The per capita figure is often used to compare the wealth of countries. It can also be used to compare the wealth of minority groups within countries. In 2008 the per capita income for non-Hispanic whites in the United States was $31,313, which was only slightly higher than the per capita income of Asian-Americans ($30,292). (See Table 5.1.) Hispanics and African-Americans had significantly lower per capital incomes, at $15,674 and $18,406, respectively. In fact, the per capita income for Asian-Americans and non-Hispanic whites was almost twice that of Hispanics.

Minority Incomes

HISPANIC INCOME. Even though Table 5.1 shows that Hispanic households earned an average median income of $37,913 in 2008, down from $40,165 in 2007, the

TABLE 5.1

Median household and per capita income by selected characteristics, 2007 and 2008

[Income in 2008 dollars. Households and people as of March of the following year.]

| Characteristic | 2007 | | 2008 | | Percentage change in real median income (2008 less 2007) |
	Number (thousands)	Median income (dollars) Estimate	Number (thousands)	Median income (dollars) Estimate	Estimate
Households					
All households	116,783	52,163	117,181	50,303	−3.6
Type of household					
Family households	77,873	64,755	78,850	62,621	−3.3
Married-couple	58,370	75,582	59,118	73,010	−3.4
Female householder, no husband present	14,404	34,652	14,480	33,073	−4.6
Male householder, no wife present	5,100	51,754	5,252	49,186	−5.0
Nonfamily households	38,910	31,335	38,331	30,078	−4.0
Female householder	21,038	25,227	20,637	25,014	−0.8
Male householder	17,872	38,180	17,694	36,006	−5.7
Race[a] and Hispanic origin of householder					
White	95,112	54,117	95,297	52,312	−3.3
White, not Hispanic	82,765	57,030	82,884	55,530	−2.6
Black	14,551	35,219	14,595	34,218	−2.8
Asian	4,494	68,643	4,573	65,637	−4.4
Hispanic (any race)	13,339	40,165	13,425	37,913	−5.6
Nativity of householder					
Native born	101,104	52,904	101,585	51,056	−3.5
Foreign born	15,680	45,929	15,596	43,493	−5.3
Naturalized citizen	7,469	54,094	7,668	51,524	−4.8
Not a citizen	8,211	39,083	7,928	37,951	−2.9
Earnings of full-time, year-round workers					
Men with earnings	62,984	46,846	59,861	46,367	−1.0
Women with earnings	45,613	36,451	44,156	35,745	−1.9
Per capita income[b]					
Total[a]	**299,106**	**27,834**	**301,483**	**26,964**	**−3.1**
White	239,399	29,413	240,852	28,502	−3.1
White, not Hispanic	196,768	32,244	197,159	31,313	−2.9
Black	37,775	19,136	38,076	18,406	−3.8
Asian	13,268	31,050	13,315	30,292	−2.4
Hispanic (any race)	46,026	16,203	47,485	15,674	−3.3

[a]Federal surveys now give respondents the option of reporting more than one race. Therefore, two basic ways of defining a race group are possible. A group such as Asian may be defined as those who reported Asian and no other race (the race-alone or single-race concept) or as those who reported Asian regardless of whether they also reported another race (the race-alone-or-in-combination concept). This table shows data using the first approach (race alone). The use of the single-race population does not imply that it is the preferred method of presenting or analyzing data. The Census Bureau uses a variety of approaches. Information on people who reported more than one race, such as white and American Indian and Alaska Native or Asian and black or African American, is available from Census 2000 through American FactFinder. About 2.6 percent of people reported more than one race in Census 2000. Data for American Indians and Alaska Natives, Native Hawaiians and other Pacific Islanders, and those reporting two or more races are not shown separately in this table.
[b]The data shown in this section are per capita incomes and their respective confidence intervals. Per capita income is the mean income computed for every man, woman, and child in a particular group. It is derived by dividing the total income of a particular group by the total population in that group (excluding patients or inmates in institutional quarters).

SOURCE: Adapted from Carmen DeNavas-Walt, Bernadette D. Proctor, and Jessica C. Smith, "Table 1. Income and Earnings Summary Measures by Selected Characteristics: 2007 and 2008," in *Income, Poverty, and Health Insurance Coverage in the United States: 2008*, U.S. Census Bureau, September 2009, http://www.census.gov/prod/2009pubs/p60–236.pdf (accessed December 11, 2009).

financial situation among Hispanic subgroups tends to vary. The U.S. Census Bureau notes in *The Hispanic Population in the United States: 2008* (September 29, 2009, http://www.census.gov/population/www/socdemo/hispanic/cps2008.html) that in 2007 more than three out of 10 (30.9%) Hispanic households had money income under $25,000 a year, compared with only 21.9% of non-Hispanic white households. Among family households, more than a quarter (26.2%) of Hispanic families earned under $25,000 per year, compared with just 11.6% of non-Hispanic white families.

Among the Hispanic subgroups, however, the Census Bureau indicates that the yearly earnings outlook was best for Hispanic families of Central and South American origin. (See Table 5.2.) About 18.6% of South American family households and 22% of Central American family households earned under $25,000 per year in 2007, compared with 24.8% of Cuban family households, 27.3% of Mexican family households, and 28.9% of Puerto Rican family households. Even though only 22.4% of Hispanic family households earned $75,000 per year or more, 34% of South American and 27.5% of Cuban family households did. In contrast, only 25.3% of Puerto Rican families, 20.2% of Mexican families, and 20.1% of Central American families earned $75,000 per year or more in 2007.

TABLE 5.2

Total money income of households by type and Hispanic origin type of householder, 2007

[Numbers in thousands. Civilian noninstitutionalized population[a]]

Household type and money income[d]	Total Hispanic		Hispanic origin type[b]												
			Mexican		Puerto Rican		Cuban		Central American		South American		Other Hispanic[c]	
	Number	Percent	Number	Percent	Number	Percent	Number	Percent	Number	Percent	Number	Percent	Number	Percent
Total households	**13,339**	**100.0**	**8,150**	**100.0**	**1,395**	**100.0**	**611**	**100.0**	**1,071**	**100.0**	**834**	**100.0**	**1,278**	**100.0**
Under $5,000	469	3.5	285	3.5	68	4.9	14	2.3	31	2.9	26	3.2	44	3.4
$5,000 to $9,999	715	5.4	367	4.5	140	10.0	55	9.0	26	2.4	31	3.7	96	7.5
$10,000 to $14,999	946	7.1	561	6.9	109	7.8	58	9.4	57	5.4	45	5.4	116	9.1
$15,000 to $19,999	956	7.2	628	7.7	87	6.3	34	5.6	85	8.0	40	4.8	81	6.4
$20,000 to $24,999	1,021	7.7	693	8.5	84	6.0	40	6.6	76	7.1	54	6.5	74	5.8
$25,000 to $34,999	1,905	14.3	1,267	15.6	156	11.1	71	11.6	191	17.8	78	9.3	142	11.1
$35,000 to $49,999	2,208	16.6	1,412	17.3	232	16.6	90	14.8	192	17.9	106	12.7	176	13.8
$50,000 to $74,999	2,443	18.3	1,435	17.6	236	16.9	111	18.1	219	20.4	192	23.0	250	19.6
$75,000 to $99,999	1,291	9.7	776	9.5	136	9.8	38	6.2	89	8.3	120	14.4	132	10.4
$100,000 and over	1,385	10.4	727	8.9	147	10.5	99	16.3	104	9.8	141	17.0	167	13.0
Family households[e]	**10,394**	**100.0**	**6,620**	**100.0**	**967**	**100.0**	**427**	**100.0**	**843**	**100.0**	**643**	**100.0**	**892**	**100.0**
Under $5,000	300	2.9	185	2.8	45	4.7	9	2.2	18	2.2	22	3.4	20	2.2
$5,000 to $9,999	336	3.2	198	3.0	58	6.0	10	2.3	13	1.5	12	1.9	45	5.0
$10,000 to $14,999	576	5.5	356	5.4	59	6.1	32	7.4	31	3.7	24	3.7	75	8.5
$15,000 to $19,999	712	6.8	494	7.5	57	5.9	23	5.4	61	7.2	26	4.0	51	5.7
$20,000 to $24,999	806	7.8	569	8.6	60	6.2	32	7.5	63	7.4	36	5.6	45	5.1
$25,000 to $34,999	1,509	14.5	1,048	15.8	100	10.3	51	11.9	154	18.3	56	8.8	100	11.2
$35,000 to $49,999	1,777	17.1	1,181	17.8	165	17.1	69	16.1	152	18.0	81	12.6	129	14.5
$50,000 to $74,999	2,058	19.8	1,254	18.9	179	18.5	84	19.7	183	21.6	168	26.1	190	21.3
$75,000 to $99,999	1,099	10.6	681	10.3	108	11.2	32	7.5	80	9.5	95	14.8	102	11.4
$100,000 and over	1,222	11.8	654	9.9	136	14.1	85	20.0	89	10.6	123	19.2	134	15.1
Nonfamily households	**2,945**	**100.0**	**1,529**	**100.0**	**428**	**100.0**	**183**	**100.0**	**228**	**100.0**	**191**	**100.0**	**386**	**100.0**
Under $5,000	169	5.7	100	6.5	23	5.5	5	2.7	12	5.5	4	2.3	24	6.2
$5,000 to $9,999	379	12.9	169	11.1	82	19.1	45	24.8	13	5.7	18	9.7	51	13.2
$10,000 to $14,999	370	12.5	205	13.4	50	11.6	26	14.3	27	11.7	22	11.4	40	10.5
$15,000 to $19,999	244	8.3	134	8.7	31	7.1	11	6.0	25	10.8	14	7.6	30	7.8
$20,000 to $24,999	216	7.3	124	8.1	24	5.6	8	4.3	13	5.9	18	9.5	28	7.3
$25,000 to $34,999	396	13.5	219	14.3	56	13.0	20	11.0	37	16.2	22	11.3	42	11.0
$35,000 to $49,999	431	14.6	231	15.1	67	15.6	22	11.7	40	17.5	25	13.2	47	12.1
$50,000 to $74,999	384	13.1	180	11.8	57	13.3	27	14.5	36	16.0	24	12.7	60	15.6
$75,000 to $99,999	192	6.5	94	6.2	28	6.6	6	3.0	9	3.9	25	12.9	31	8.0
$100,000 and over	163	5.5	73	4.8	10	2.4	14	7.7	15	6.8	18	9.5	32	8.4

[a]Plus armed forces living off post or with their families on post.

[b]Hispanic refers to people whose origin is Mexican, Puerto Rican, Cuban, Spanish-speaking Central or South American countries, or other Hispanic/Latino, regardless of race. Central American totals exclude Mexican. Household type is shown by the Hispanic origin type of the householder.

[c]This category includes Dominicans and people who responded "Hispanic," "Latino," or provided other general terms.

[d]Total money income is the sum of wages and salaries, net income from self-employment, and income other than earnings.

[e]Households in which at least one member is related to the person who owns or rents the occupied housing unit (householder).

SOURCE: "Table 24. Total Money Income of Households by Type and Hispanic Origin Type of Householder: 2007," in *The Hispanic Population in the United States: 2008*, U.S. Census Bureau, September 2009, http://www.census.gov/population/www/socdemo/hispanic/cps2008.html (accessed December 11, 2009)

Hispanic incomes are relatively low for a variety of reasons, including language barriers and discrimination in the workplace. However, the lack of educational attainment is a major reason for low Hispanic incomes. In *The Hispanic Population in the United States*, the Census Bureau indicates that in 2008, 21.6% of all Hispanics aged 25 years and older had less than a ninth-grade education, another 16.1% did not have a high school diploma, and only 13.4% had a bachelor's degree or higher.

AFRICAN-AMERICAN INCOME. African-American households had the lowest median income in 2008, at $34,218. As shown earlier, households headed by an unmarried adult have a substantially lower income than do married-couple households. This puts African-Americans at a disadvantage. Among those over the age of 15, African-Americans are far more likely than whites, Hispanics, or Asian-Americans to have never married. According to the Census Bureau, in *America's Families and Living Arrangements: 2008* (February 25, 2009, http://www.census.gov/population/www/socdemo/hh-fam/cps2008.html), 45.6% of African-Americans aged 15 years and older had never been married in 2008, compared with 36.8% of Hispanics, 29.2% of Asian-Americans, and 25.8% of non-Hispanic whites.

However, the differences in marriage rates do not explain the entire discrepancy between household incomes of non-Hispanic whites and African-Americans. Married-couple African-American households have lower incomes than married-couple non-Hispanic white households; African-American female- and male-headed households also have lower incomes than comparable non-Hispanic white households. The Census Bureau reports in the Current Population Survey (September 11, 2009, http://www.census.gov/hhes/www/cpstables/032009/faminc/new01_000.htm) that in 2008, African-American married-couple households had a median household income of $61,509, compared with a median household income of $77,356 among non-Hispanic white married-couple households. African-American families headed by a single mother had a median income of only $24,903, whereas non-Hispanic white single-mother families had a median income of $35,883. Lower educational attainment and discrimination in the workforce are two factors that may work together to lower the incomes of African-American households.

ASIAN-AMERICAN INCOME. Conversely, Asian-American households tend to have higher incomes than comparable non-Hispanic white households. The Census Bureau reports in the Current Population Survey that married-couple Asian-American households in 2008 had a median income of $81,310, which was higher than non-Hispanic white married couples' median income. In addition, Asian-American single-mother families were decidedly better off than were their non-Hispanic white counterparts, with a median income of $43,080. This higher median income is probably almost entirely explained by the higher educational attainment of Asian-Americans.

POVERTY STATUS OF MINORITIES

Every year the Census Bureau establishes poverty thresholds that determine the distribution of different welfare benefits. In 2009 the poverty threshold ranged from $10,830 for single people to $37,010 for families of eight. (See Table 5.3.) In 2008, 39.8 million people, or 13.2% of the U.S. population, were in poverty. (See Figure 5.1.) The number of people in poverty and the poverty rate rose sharply after 2007, when the United States entered the worst recession since the Great Depression of the 1930s. It was the first statistically significant rise in the poverty rate since 2004.

In 2008, 24.7% of African-Americans and 23.2% of Hispanics lived in poverty. (See Table 5.4.) Asian-Americans had a relatively low rate of poverty, at

TABLE 5.3

Poverty guidelines, 2009

2009 poverty guidelines for the 48 contiguous states and the District of Columbia

Persons in family	Poverty guideline
1	$10,830
2	14,570
3	18,310
4	22,050
5	25,790
6	29,530
7	33,270
8	37,010

For families with more than 8 persons, add $3,740 for each additional person.

2009 poverty guidelines for Alaska

Persons in family	Poverty guideline
1	$13,530
2	18,210
3	22,890
4	27,570
5	32,250
6	36,930
7	41,610
8	46,290

For families with more than 8 persons, add $4,680 for each additional person.

2009 poverty guidelines for Hawaii

Persons in family	Poverty guideline
1	$12,460
2	16,760
3	21,060
4	25,360
5	29,660
6	33,960
7	38,260
8	42,560

For families with more than 8 persons, add $4,300 for each additional person.

SOURCE: Adapted from "2009 Poverty Guidelines for the 48 Contiguous States and the District of Columbia," "2009 Poverty Guidelines for Alaska," and "2009 Poverty Guidelines for Hawaii," in *Federal Register*, vol. 74, no. 14, January 23, 2009, http://aspe.hhs.gov/ poverty/09fedreg.pdf (accessed December 11, 2009)

FIGURE 5.1

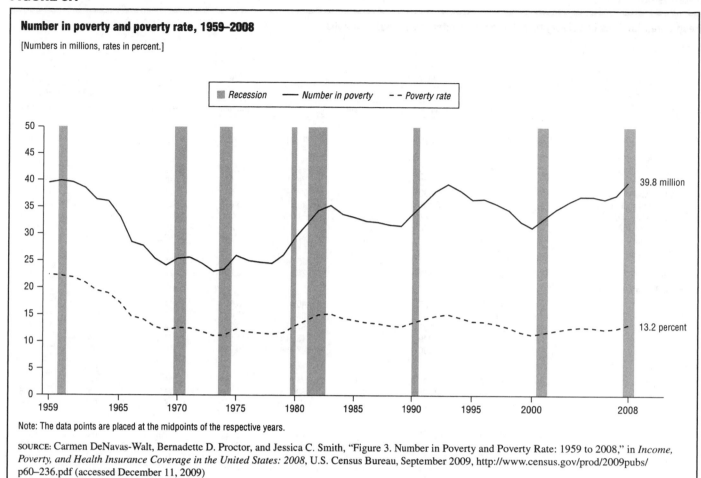

Number in poverty and poverty rate, 1959–2008

[Numbers in millions, rates in percent.]

Note: The data points are placed at the midpoints of the respective years.

SOURCE: Carmen DeNavas-Walt, Bernadette D. Proctor, and Jessica C. Smith, "Figure 3. Number in Poverty and Poverty Rate: 1959 to 2008," in *Income, Poverty, and Health Insurance Coverage in the United States: 2008*, U.S. Census Bureau, September 2009, http://www.census.gov/prod/2009pubs/ p60–236.pdf (accessed December 11, 2009)

11.8%, although it was still higher than the poverty rate of non-Hispanic whites, at 8.6%. According to Carmen DeNavas-Walt, Bernadette D. Proctor, and Jessica C. Smith of the Census Bureau, in *Income, Poverty, and Health Insurance Coverage in the United States: 2008* (September 2009, http://www.census.gov/prod/2009 pubs/p60-236.pdf), the poverty rate for non-Hispanic whites, Hispanics, and Asian-Americans increased between 2007 and 2008, while it remained statistically unchanged for African-Americans.

The poverty rate varies among Hispanic subgroups. The Census Bureau notes in *Hispanic Population in the United States* that in 2007, 24.8% of Puerto Ricans lived below the poverty line, compared with 22.9% of Mexicans and 17.1% of Central Americans. Cubans and South Americans had the lowest poverty rates, at 14.6% and 11.6%, respectively. Cubans and South Americans tend to be better educated than other Hispanic subgroups, which partially explains the income disparities between the groups.

Depth of Poverty

Even though measuring the proportions of people in various groups who are above and below the pov-

erty threshold provides one measure of poverty, it does not account for the levels of poverty. Some people below the poverty level are moderately poor, whereas others are extremely poor. Some households with incomes above the poverty threshold are just above it and barely getting by. The ratio of income to poverty compares a family's income with its poverty threshold, providing one way to measure how poor a family actually is.

Table 5.5 shows income-to-poverty ratios by race and Hispanic origin, with people 0.50 over the poverty threshold (extreme poverty), people between 0.50 and 1.00 of the poverty threshold (below poverty, but above extreme poverty), and people between 1.00 and 1.25 of the poverty threshold (low income). In 2008, 11.4% of African-Americans lived on incomes under 0.50 of the poverty threshold, compared with 9.1% of Hispanics, 5.5% of Asian-Americans, and only 3.7% of non-Hispanic whites. In other words, a far greater proportion of African-Americans live in extreme poverty than people from other racial and ethnic backgrounds. In addition, families with children under the age of six were much more likely than other families to live in extreme poverty in 2008.

TABLE 5.4

People and families in poverty by selected characteristics, 2007 and 2008

[Numbers in thousands.]

Characteristic	2007 Total	Below poverty Number	Below poverty Percentage	2008 Total	Below poverty Number	Below poverty Percentage	Change in poverty (2008 less 2007)[a] Number	Change in poverty (2008 less 2007)[a] Percentage
People								
Total	298,699	37,276	12.5	301,041	39,829	13.2	2,553	0.8
Family status								
In families	245,443	26,509	10.8	248,301	28,564	11.5	2,055	0.7
Householder	77,908	7,623	9.8	78,874	8,147	10.3	525	0.5
Related children under 18	72,792	12,802	17.6	72,980	13,507	18.5	705	0.9
Related children under 6	24,543	5,101	20.8	24,884	5,295	21.3	194	0.5
In unrelated subfamilies	1,516	577	38.1	1,207	555	46.0	−22	7.9
Reference person	609	222	36.5	452	207	45.7	−15	9.2
Children under 18	819	332	40.5	712	341	47.8	9	7.3
Unrelated individuals	51,740	10,189	19.7	51,534	10,710	20.8	521	1.1
Male	25,447	4,348	17.1	25,240	4,759	18.9	411	1.8
Female	26,293	5,841	22.2	26,293	5,951	22.6	110	0.4
Race[b] and Hispanic origin								
White	239,133	25,120	10.5	240,548	26,990	11.2	1,870	0.7
White, not Hispanic	196,583	16,032	8.2	196,940	17,024	8.6	992	0.5
Black	37,665	9,237	24.5	37,966	9,379	24.7	142	0.2
Asian	13,257	1,349	10.2	13,310	1,576	11.8	227	1.7
Hispanic (any race)	45,933	9,890	21.5	47,398	10,987	23.2	1,097	1.6
Age								
Under 18 years	73,996	13,324	18.0	74,068	14,068	19.0	744	1.0
18 to 64 years	187,913	20,396	10.9	189,185	22,105	11.7	1,709	0.8
65 years and older	36,790	3,556	9.7	37,788	3,656	9.7	100	—
Nativity								
Native born	261,456	31,126	11.9	264,314	33,293	12.6	2,167	0.7
Foreign born	37,243	6,150	16.5	36,727	6,536	17.8	386	1.3
Naturalized citizen	15,050	1,426	9.5	15,470	1,577	10.2	151	0.7
Not a citizen	22,193	4,724	21.3	21,257	4,959	23.3	235	2.0
Region								
Northeast	53,952	6,166	11.4	54,123	6,295	11.6	130	0.2
Midwest	65,403	7,237	11.1	65,589	8,120	12.4	883	1.3
South	109,545	15,501	14.2	110,666	15,862	14.3	361	0.2
West	69,799	8,372	12.0	70,663	9,552	13.5	1,180	1.5
Metropolitan status								
Inside metropolitan statistical areas	251,023	29,921	11.9	253,048	32,570	12.9	2,649	1.0
Inside principal cities	96,731	15,983	16.5	97,217	17,222	17.7	1,240	1.2
Outside principal cities	154,292	13,938	9.0	155,831	15,348	9.8	1,410	0.8
Outside metropolitan statistical areas[c]	47,676	7,355	15.4	47,993	7,259	15.1	−96	−0.3
Work experience								
Total, 16 years and older	233,885	25,297	10.8	236,024	27,216	11.5	1,919	0.7
All workers	158,468	9,089	5.7	158,317	10,085	6.4	996	0.6
Worked full-time, year-round	108,617	2,768	2.5	104,023	2,754	2.6	−14	0.1
Not full-time, year-round	49,851	6,320	12.7	54,294	7,331	13.5	1,011	0.8
Did not work at least one week	75,417	16,208	21.5	77,707	17,131	22.0	923	0.6

Children Living in Poverty

In 2007 Hispanic and African-American children were more than three times as likely to live in poverty than non-Hispanic white children. One out of three (34.3%) African-American children and 28.3% of Hispanic children lived in poverty, whereas 9.7% of non-Hispanic white children lived in poverty. (See Table 5.6.) According to the Federal Interagency Forum on Child and Family Statistics, in *America's Children: Key National Indicators of Well-Being, 2009* (July 2009, http://www.childstats.gov/pdf/ac2009/ac_09.pdf), in families headed by married couples, only 4.7% of non-Hispanic white children lived in poverty in 2007. The African-American poverty rate of children living in married-couple families was significantly lower than for all African-American children, at 11%, but more than double the poverty rate of non-Hispanic white children in married-couple families. Hispanic children living in married-couple families did not have as significant a drop in their poverty rates; 19.2% of Hispanic children living with married parents lived in poverty. Children were particularly at risk in households headed by a single female. One out of two Hispanic (51.6%) and African-American (50.4%) children living in female-headed families lived in poverty. One out of three (32.4%) non-Hispanic white children living in female-headed families lived in poverty.

[Numbers in thousands.]

Characteristic	2007			2008			Change in poverty (2008 less 2007)[a]	
	Total	Below poverty		Total	Below poverty			
		Number	Percentage		Number	Percentage	Number	Percentage
Families								
Total	77,908	7,623	9.8	78,874	8,147	10.3	525	0.5
Type of family								
Married-couple	58,395	2,849	4.9	59,137	3,261	5.5	412	0.6
Female householder, no husband present	14,411	4,078	28.3	14,482	4,163	28.7	85	0.4
Male householder, no wife present	5,103	696	13.6	5,255	723	13.8	27	0.1

—Represents or rounds to zero.

[a]Details may not sum to totals because of rounding.

[b]Federal surveys now give respondents the option of reporting more than one race. Therefore, two basic ways of defining a race group are possible. A group such as Asian may be defined as those who reported Asian and no other race (the race-alone or single-race concept) or as those who reported Asian regardless of whether they also reported another race (the race-alone-or-in-combination concept). This table shows data using the first approach (race alone). The use of the single-race population does not imply that it is the preferred method of presenting or analyzing data. The Census Bureau uses a variety of approaches. Information on people who reported more than one race, such as white and American Indian and Alaska Native or Asian and black or African American, is available from Census 2000 through American FactFinder. About 2.6 percent of people reported more than one race in Census 2000. Data for American Indians and Alaska Natives, Native Hawaiians and other Pacific Islanders, and those reporting two or more races are not shown separately.

[c]The "outside metropolitan statistical areas" category includes both micropolitan statistical areas and territory outside of metropolitan and micropolitan statistical areas.

SOURCE: Carmen DeNavas-Walt, Bernadette D. Proctor, and Jessica C. Smith, "Table 4. People and Families in Poverty by Selected Characteristics: 2007 and 2008," in *Income, Poverty, and Health Insurance Coverage in the United States: 2008*, U.S. Census Bureau, September 2009, http://www.census.gov/prod/2009pubs/p60–236.pdf (accessed December 11, 2009)

The Federal Interagency Forum on Child and Family Statistics notes that African-American children were also much more likely to live in extreme poverty than non-Hispanic white children in 2007; 17.3% of African-American children lived in families with incomes below 50% of the poverty threshold, compared with 11% of Hispanic children and only 4.3% of non-Hispanic white children. More than one out of four African-American children (25.9%) and Hispanic children (24.4%) living in female-householder families lived below 50% of the poverty threshold, compared with 15.9% of non-Hispanic white children living in female-householder families.

The National School Lunch Program provides free or reduced-price meals to children from low-income families. Sometimes eligibility for the program is used as a rough guide to determine family income. Angelina KewalRamani et al. note in *Status and Trends in the Education of Racial and Ethnic Minorities* (September 2007, http://nces.ed.gov/pubs2007/2007039.pdf) that nationwide, 41% of all fourth graders were eligible for free or reduced-price lunches in 2005. The percentages of African-American (70%) and Hispanic (73%) fourth graders who were eligible for these lunches were three times the percentage of non-Hispanic white (24%) fourth graders who were eligible. Also, a high proportion (65%) of Native American and Alaskan Native students were eligible. A third (33%) of Asian and Pacific Islander fourth graders were eligible for the reduced-price lunches.

The percent of students eligible for the National School Lunch Program also varied by where they lived. African-American and Hispanic fourth graders who lived in a central city (75% and 79%, respectively) or a rural area (78% and 72%, respectively) were more likely than fourth graders who lived in the suburbs or a large town (60% and 66%, respectively) to be eligible for a free or reduced-price lunch. (See Figure 5.2.) Asian and Pacific Islander fourth graders were the most likely to be eligible if they lived in a central city, where 42% were eligible, rather than in the suburbs or a rural area, where only 25% were eligible. Native American and Alaskan Native fourth graders who lived in rural areas, including reservations, were the most likely to be eligible for the program. Almost three-quarters (73%) of Native American and Alaskan Native fourth graders in rural areas, compared with a little over half of Native American and Alaskan Native fourth graders in central cities (57%) or suburban areas (52%), were eligible.

The Haves and Have-Nots

A 2008 Gallup poll finds that African-Americans are much more likely than non-Hispanic whites to believe that American society is divided into two groups: the haves and have-nots. Two-thirds (72%) of African-Americans answered that society is divided, whereas only 45% of non-Hispanic whites did. (See Figure 5.3.) What is surprising, considering Hispanics' experience of lower income and higher poverty rates than non-Hispanic whites in the United States, Hispanics were only slightly more likely than non-Hispanic whites to answer that society is divided into the haves and have-nots. Only 49% of Hispanics believed society is divided; this was sharply up from a 2006 poll, however, perhaps reflecting the Hispanic experience of the recession that began in late 2007.

Part of the explanation for Hispanics' relative optimism might lie in their recent immigration experience. In

TABLE 5.5

People with income below specified ratios of their poverty thresholds, by selected characteristics, 2008

[Numbers in thousands.]

| Characteristic | Total | Income-to-poverty ratio | | | | | |
| | | Under 0.50 | | Under 1.00 | | Under 1.25 | |
		Number	Percent	Number	Percent	Number	Percent
All people	301,041	17,075	5.7	39,829	13.2	53,805	17.9
Age							
Under 18 years	74,068	6,278	8.5	14,068	19.0	18,553	25.0
18 to 24 years	28,688	2,640	9.2	5,283	18.4	6,790	23.7
25 to 34 years	40,520	2,437	6.0	5,351	13.2	7,130	17.6
35 to 44 years	41,322	1,733	4.2	4,277	10.4	5,760	13.9
45 to 54 years	44,366	1,721	3.9	4,047	9.1	5,351	12.1
55 to 59 years	18,755	692	3.7	1,642	8.8	2,206	11.8
60 to 64 years	15,534	579	3.7	1,504	9.7	1,999	12.9
65 years and older	37,788	995	2.6	3,656	9.7	6,018	15.9
Race* and Hispanic origin							
White	240,548	11,135	4.6	26,990	11.2	37,460	15.6
White, not Hispanic	196,940	7,286	3.7	17,024	8.6	23,903	12.1
Black	37,966	4,327	11.4	9,379	24.7	11,982	31.6
Asian	13,310	738	5.5	1,576	11.8	1,927	14.5
Hispanic (any race)	47,398	4,305	9.1	10,987	23.2	14,861	31.4
Family status							
In families	248,301	11,638	4.7	28,564	11.5	38,995	15.7
Householder	78,874	3,390	4.3	8,147	10.3	11,164	14.2
Related children under 18	72,980	5,894	8.1	13,507	18.5	17,893	24.5
Related children under 6	24,884	2,521	10.1	5,295	21.3	6,932	27.9
Unrelated subfamilies	1,207	308	25.5	555	46.0	675	55.9
Unrelated individuals	51,534	5,129	10.0	10,710	20.8	14,135	27.4
Male	25,240	2,420	9.6	4,759	18.9	6,096	24.2
Female	26,293	2,708	10.3	5,951	22.6	8,039	30.6

*Federal surveys now give respondents the option of reporting more than one race. Therefore, two basic ways of defining a race group are possible. A group such as Asian may be defined as those who reported Asian and no other race (the race-alone or single-race concept) or as those who reported Asian regardless of whether they also reported another race (the race-alone-or-in-combination concept). This table shows data using the first approach (race alone). The use of the single-race population does not imply that it is the preferred method of presenting or analyzing data. The Census Bureau uses a variety of approaches. Information on people who reported more than one race, such as white and American Indian and Alaska Native or Asian and Black or African American, is available from Census 2000 through American FactFinder. About 2.6 percent of people reported more than one race in Census 2000. Data for American Indians and Alaska Natives, Native Hawaiians and other Pacific Islanders, and those reporting two or more races are not shown separately.
Note: Details may not sum to totals because of rounding.

SOURCE: Carmen DeNavas-Walt, Bernadette D. Proctor, and Jessica C. Smith, "Table 5. People with Income below Specified Ratios of Their Poverty Thresholds by Selected Characteristics: 2008," in *Income, Poverty, and Health Insurance Coverage in the United States: 2008*, U.S. Census Bureau, September 2009, http://www.census.gov/prod/2009pubs/p60–236.pdf (accessed December 11, 2009)

"The Optimistic Immigrant: Among Latinos, the Recently Arrived Have the Most Hope for the Future" (May 30, 2006, http://pewresearch.org/pubs/28/the-optimistic-immigrant), Gabriel Escobar of the Pew Research Center points out what has been a historic truism in American society: that first-generation immigrants to the United States expect their children to have better opportunities than they have at present. Escobar notes that "Hispanics in general, and Hispanic immigrants in particular, are more inclined than blacks or whites to take an upbeat view about one of the most enduring tenets of the American dream—the idea that each generation will do better in life than the one that preceded it." Part of the explanation for this positive view lies in the general optimism of immigrants. Immigrants take on the challenge to move to an entirely new country because they strongly believe in their hope for the future.

GOVERNMENT PROGRAMS

Because minorities are disproportionately poor, they have long accounted for a major portion of the welfare rolls across the United States. The U.S. government offers various forms of assistance to people living with economic hardship. Some of these programs are federally run, and others are run at the state level. In many cases states run federally mandated government programs, which can make tracking them complicated.

In 1996 Congress enacted the Personal Responsibility and Work Opportunity Reconciliation Act to reform the welfare system. The primary goal of the legislation was to get as many people as possible into the paid labor force and off welfare rolls. The law set limits on how long people could receive welfare benefits. Aid to Families with Dependent Children, a guaranteed assistance program for low-income families, was eliminated and replaced in 1996 with the Temporary Assistance for Needy Families (TANF) program. The House Ways and Means Committee reports in *The Green Book* (2008, http://waysandmeans.house.gov/media/pdf/110/tanf.pdf) that the number of families receiving welfare had dropped from 5.1 million in 1994 to 1.9 million in 2006, a decrease of 63%.

TABLE 5.6

Percentage of related children under age 18 living below selected poverty levels, by age, family structure, race, and Hispanic origin, selected years, 1980–2007

Characteristic	1980	1985	1990	1995	2000	2003	2004	2005	2006	2007
Below 100% of poverty										
Related children[a]										
Children in all families, total	17.9	20.1	19.9	20.2	15.6	17.2	17.3	17.1	16.9	17.6
Related children ages 0–5	20.3	22.6	23.0	23.7	17.8	19.8	20.0	20.0	20.0	20.8
Related children ages 6–17	16.8	18.8	18.2	18.3	14.5	15.9	16.0	15.7	15.4	16.0
White, non-Hispanic	11.3	12.3	11.6	10.6	8.5	—	—	—	—	—
White-alone, non-Hispanic	—	—	—	—	—	9.3	9.9	9.5	9.5	9.7
Black	42.1	43.1	44.2	41.5	30.9	—	—	—	—	—
Black-alone	—	—	—	—	—	33.6	33.4	34.2	33.0	34.3
Hispanic[b]	33.0	39.6	37.7	39.3	27.6	29.5	28.6	27.7	26.6	28.3
Children in married-couple families, total	—	—	10.2	10.0	8.0	8.6	9.0	8.5	8.1	8.5
Related children ages 0–5	—	—	11.6	11.1	8.7	9.6	10.1	9.9	9.4	9.5
Related children ages 6–17	—	—	9.5	9.4	7.6	8.1	8.4	7.7	7.5	8.0
White, non-Hispanic	—	—	6.8	5.9	4.7	—	—	—	—	—
White-alone, non-Hispanic	—	—	—	—	—	4.8	5.2	4.5	4.3	4.7
Black	—	—	18.1	12.8	8.8	—	—	—	—	—
Black-alone	—	—	—	—	—	11.2	12.6	12.5	12.0	11.0
Hispanic[b]	—	—	26.5	28.4	20.7	21.4	20.6	20.1	18.5	19.2
Children in female-householder families, no husband present, total	50.8	53.6	53.4	50.3	40.1	41.8	41.9	42.8	42.1	43.0
Related children ages 0–5	65.2	65.8	65.5	61.8	50.3	52.9	52.5	52.9	52.7	54.0
Related children ages 6–17	45.5	48.3	47.3	44.6	35.7	37.1	37.3	38.3	37.4	37.8
White, non-Hispanic	—	—	39.6	33.5	28.0	—	—	—	—	—
White-alone, non-Hispanic	—	—	—	—	—	30.7	31.5	33.1	32.9	32.4
Black	64.8	66.9	64.7	61.6	49.3	—	—	—	—	—
Black-alone	—	—	—	—	—	49.7	49.2	50.2	49.7	50.4
Hispanic[b]	65.0	72.4	68.4	65.7	49.8	50.6	51.9	50.2	47.2	51.6
Below 50% of poverty										
Related children[a]										
Children in all families, total	—	—	8.3	7.9	6.3	7.3	7.2	7.2	7.1	7.4
Related children ages 0–5	—	—	10.3	10.4	7.9	9.5	9.1	8.9	9.2	9.6
Related children ages 6–17	—	—	7.2	6.6	5.5	6.2	6.3	6.4	6.0	6.3
White, non-Hispanic	—	—	4.4	3.4	3.3	—	—	—	—	—
White-alone, non-Hispanic	—	—	—	—	—	3.7	4.0	3.6	3.9	3.9
Black	—	—	22.3	20.1	14.8	—	—	—	—	—
Black-alone	—	—	—	—	—	17.4	16.8	16.9	15.7	17.1
Hispanic[d]	—	—	13.5	15.6	9.4	10.6	9.9	10.8	10.0	10.5
Children in married-couple families, total	—	—	2.7	2.6	2.2	2.4	2.5	2.4	2.2	2.6
Related children ages 0–5	—	—	3.1	2.9	2.2	2.8	2.8	2.8	2.8	2.8
Related children ages 6–17	—	—	2.4	2.5	2.2	2.2	2.3	2.1	1.9	2.5
White, non-Hispanic	—	—	1.9	1.4	1.5	—	—	—	—	—
White-alone, non-Hispanic	—	—	—	—	—	1.4	1.8	1.2	1.2	1.4
Black	—	—	3.9	2.9	3.1	—	—	—	—	—
Black-alone	—	—	—	—	—	4.0	3.6	4.5	2.9	4.4
Hispanic[b]	—	—	6.7	8.6	4.4	5.3	3.8	5.2	4.7	5.4
Children in female-householder families, no husband present, total	—	—	27.7	23.8	18.9	21.5	21.7	21.8	21.1	21.2
Related children ages 0–5	—	—	37.0	33.7	27.9	31.4	30.6	29.1	29.5	30.2
Related children ages 6–17	—	—	23.0	18.9	15.2	17.3	17.9	18.5	17.4	17.0
White, non-Hispanic	—	—	19.1	13.1	12.0	—	—	—	—	—
White-alone, non-Hispanic	—	—	—	—	—	14.6	14.6	15.2	16.1	15.9
Black	—	—	36.8	32.2	24.2	—	—	—	—	—
Black-alone	—	—	—	—	—	27.1	27.2	26.1	26.0	25.9
Hispanic[b]	—	—	31.9	32.5	24.8	25.3	27.7	27.7	22.9	24.4

—Not available.

[a]A related child is a person ages 0–17 who is related to the householder by birth, marriage, or adoption, but is not the householder or the householder's spouse.

[b]Persons of Hispanic origin may be of any race.

Note: The 2004 data have been revised to reflect a correction to the weights in the 2005 Annual Social and Economic Supplement. Data for 1999, 2000, and 2001 use Census 2000 population controls. Data for 2000 onward are from the expanded Current Population Survey sample. The poverty level is based on money income and does not include noncash benefits, such as food stamps. Poverty thresholds reflect family size and composition and are adjusted each year using the annual average Consumer Price Index level. The average poverty threshold for a family of four was $21,203 in 2007. The levels shown here are derived from the ratio of the family's income to the family's poverty threshold.

SOURCE: Adapted from "Table ECON1.A. Child Poverty: Percentage of All Children and Related Children Ages 0–17 Living below Selected Poverty Levels by Selected Characteristics, Selected Years 1980–2007," in *America's Children: Key National Indicators of Well-Being, 2009*, Federal Interagency Forum on Child and Family Statistics, July 2009, http://www.childstats.gov/pdf/ac2009/ac_09.pdf (accessed December 11, 2009)

The U.S. Department of Health and Human Services (HHS) indicates that in 2005, 32.9% of all African-Americans received some portion of their total annual family income from means-tested assistance programs, which include TANF, Supplementary Security Income, and food stamps. (See Table 5.7.) One out of four (24%) Hispanics received means-tested

FIGURE 5.2

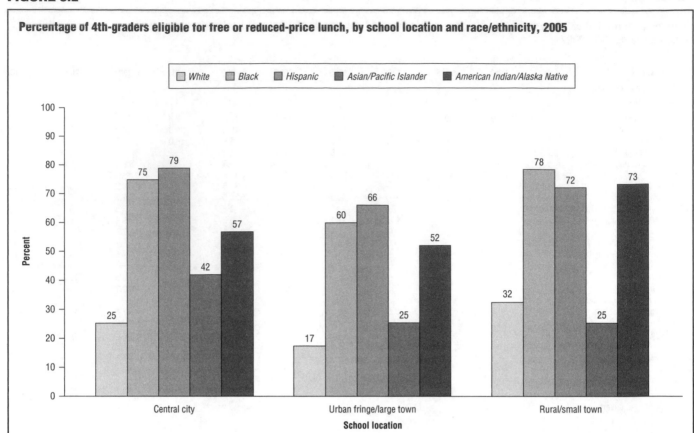

Percentage of 4th-graders eligible for free or reduced-price lunch, by school location and race/ethnicity, 2005

☐ White ☐ Black ☐ Hispanic ■ Asian/Pacific Islander ■ American Indian/Alaska Native

Note: To be eligible for the National School Lunch Program, a student must be from a household with an income at or below 185 percent of the poverty level for reduced-price lunch or at or below 130 percent of the poverty level for free lunch. Race categories exclude persons of Hispanic origin.

SOURCE: Angelina KewalRamani et al., "Figure 7.4. Percentage of 4th-Graders Eligible for Reduced-Price Lunch, by School Location and Race/Ethnicity: 2005," in *Status and Trends in the Education of Racial and Ethnic Minorities*, U.S. Department of Education, National Center for Education Statistics, Institute of Education Sciences, September 2007, http://nces.ed.gov/pubs2007/2007039.pdf (accessed December 11, 2009)

FIGURE 5.3

Percentage perceiving the American population as being divided into "haves" and "have-nots," by race and Hispanic origin, 2008

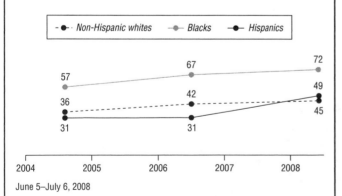

June 5–July 6, 2008

SOURCE: Lydia Saad, "Percentage Perceiving U.S. As Divided into 'Haves' and 'Have-Nots' by Race/Ethnicity," in *More Americans Say U.S. a Nation of Haves and Have-Nots*, The Gallup Organization, July 11, 2008, http://www.gallup.com/poll/108769/More-Americans-Say-US-Nation-Haves-HaveNots.aspx (accessed December 11, 2009). Copyright © 2009 by The Gallup Organization. Reproduced by Permission of The Gallup Organization.

assistance. Only 10.1% of non-Hispanic whites received such assistance. Moreover, 10.2% African-Americans received more than half of their total annual family income from means-tested assistance programs, compared with only 5.7% of Hispanics and only 2.2% of non-Hispanic whites.

Therefore, African-Americans are the most likely to receive means-tested assistance, especially food stamps—15.1% of African-Americans received food stamps in 2005, compared with 8.5% of Hispanics and 4.1% of non-Hispanic whites. (See Table 5.8.) In addition, African-Americans are more likely than non-Hispanic whites or Hispanics to receive assistance from multiple programs. Whereas a quarter (24.9%) of African-Americans received means-tested assistance in 2005, 4.4% of them received both TANF and food stamps, compared with 2.7% of Hispanics and 0.7% of non-Hispanic whites.

The high number of female-headed families in the African-American community may be part of the explanation for the high rate of means-tested assistance receipt. More than four out of 10 (44.5%) individuals in female-headed families received means-tested assistance in 2005, compared with only 8.8% of individuals in married-couple

TABLE 5.7

Percentage of total family income from means-tested assistance programs, by race, Hispanic origin, and age, 2005

	0%	> 0% and ≤ 25%	> 25% and ≤ 50%	> 50% and ≤ 75%	> 75% and ≤ 100%	Total > 50%
All persons	84.7	8.9	2.6	1.1	2.7	3.8
Racial/ethnic categories						
Non-Hispanic white	89.9	6.4	1.4	0.6	1.6	2.2
Non-Hispanic black	67.1	15.9	6.8	3.2	7.0	10.2
Hispanic	76.0	14.1	4.2	1.7	3.9	5.7
Age categories						
Children ages 0–5	74.4	13.0	5.2	2.4	5.0	7.4
Children ages 6–10	77.4	11.9	4.6	1.9	4.2	6.1
Children ages 11–15	79.1	11.4	4.0	1.9	3.7	5.5
Women ages 16–64	84.6	8.9	2.5	1.1	2.9	4.0
Men ages 16–64	88.3	7.7	1.6	0.6	1.8	2.4
Adults ages 65 and over	89.7	6.3	1.8	0.7	1.5	2.2
Family categories						
Persons in married-couple families	91.2	6.4	1.2	0.4	0.7	1.1
Persons in female-headed families	55.5	20.8	9.6	4.6	9.5	14.0
Persons in male-headed families	77.9	13.9	3.9	1.5	2.8	4.3
Unrelated persons	87.8	6.4	1.2	0.6	4.1	4.7

Notes: Means-tested assistance includes Temporary Assistance for Needy Families (TANF), Supplemental Security Income (SSI), and food stamps. Total >50% includes all persons with more than 50 percent of their total annual family income from these means-tested programs. Income includes cash income and the value of food stamps. Spouses are not present in the female-headed and male-headed family categories. Persons of Hispanic ethnicity may be of any race. Beginning in 2002, estimates for whites and blacks are for persons reporting a single race only. Persons who reported more than one race are included in the total of all persons but are not shown under any race category. Due to small sample size, American Indians/Alaska Natives, Asians and Native Hawaiians/other Pacific Islanders are included in the total for all persons but are not shown.

SOURCE: Gil Crouse, Susan Hauan, and Annette Waters Rogers, "Table IND 1a. Percentage of Total Income from Means-Tested Assistance Programs by Selected Characteristics: 2005," in *Indicators of Welfare Dependence, Annual Report to Congress, 2008*, U.S. Department of Health and Human Services, 2007, http://aspe.hhs.gov/hsp/indicators08/ch2.pdf (accessed December 11, 2009)

TABLE 5.8

Percentage of population receiving assistance from Temporary Assistance for Needy Families (TANF), Food Stamps (FS), and/or Supplemental Security Income (SSI), by race, Hispanic origin, and age, 2005

	Any receipt	One program only			Two programs	
		TANF	FS	SSI	TANF & FS	FS & SSI
All persons	10.2	0.2	6.2	1.3	1.5	1.2
Racial/ethnic categories						
Non-Hispanic white	6.7	0.1	4.1	0.9	0.7	0.8
Non-Hispanic black	24.9	0.5	15.1	2.0	4.4	2.9
Hispanic	14.6	0.4	8.5	1.7	2.7	1.3
Age categories						
Children ages 0–5	20.7	0.6	13.4	0.7	5.3	0.7
Children ages 6–10	17.6	0.5	11.6	0.7	4.2	0.6
Children ages 11–15	15.9	0.7	10.2	0.9	3.3	0.8
Women ages 16–64	9.6	0.1	6.1	0.9	1.2	1.3
Men ages 16–64	6.3	0.1	3.8	1.2	0.4	0.9
Adults ages 65 and over	8.0	0.0	2.4	3.1	0.0	2.4
Family categories						
Persons in married-couple families	4.8	0.1	3.0	0.7	0.5	0.4
Persons in female-headed families	33.4	0.7	20.1	2.5	7.4	2.7
Persons in male-headed families	13.9	0.3	8.2	2.2	1.9	1.3
Unrelated persons	9.4	0.0	4.9	1.8	0.0	2.7

Notes: Categories are mutually exclusive. SSI receipt is based on individual receipt; AFDC/TANF and food stamp receipt are based on the full recipient unit. In practice, individuals do not tend to receive both AFDC/TANF and SSI; hence, no individual receives benefits from all three programs. The percentage of individuals receiving assistance from any one program in an average month (shown here) is lower than the percentage residing in families receiving assistance at some point over the course of a year. Spouses are not present in the female-headed and male-headed family categories.
Persons of Hispanic ethnicity may be of any race. Beginning in 2002, estimates for whites and blacks are for persons reporting a single race only. Persons who reported more than one race are included in the total for all persons but are not shown under any race category. Due to small sample size, American Indians/Alaska Natives, Asians and Native Hawaiians/other Pacific Islanders are included in the total for all persons but are not shown separately.

SOURCE: Gil Crouse, Susan Hauan, and Annette Waters Rogers, "Table IND 5a. Percentage of Population Receiving Assistance from Multiple Means-Tested Assistance Programs by Selected Characteristics: 2005," in *Indicators of Welfare Dependence, Annual Report to Congress, 2008*, U.S. Department of Health and Human Services, 2007, http://aspe.hhs.gov/hsp/indicators08/ch2.pdf (accessed December 11, 2009) families. (See Table 5.7.) In addition, individuals in female-headed families were the most likely to receive more than half of the annual family income from these programs—14% did so, compared with only 1.1% of individuals living in married-couple families. These percentages suggest that it is particularly difficult for single women with children to make ends meet without turning to government programs for assistance.

In spite of the work requirements of the welfare law, earnings contributed substantially less to the total family income of African-American families than they did to non-Hispanic white or Hispanic families in 2005. Among families in poverty, earnings contributed only 35.3% of the total family income of African-American families, but 41.9% of the total family income of non-Hispanic white families and 62.4% of the total family income of Hispanic families. (See Table 5.9.) Among families in extreme poverty, earnings contributed only 18.9% of the total family income of African-American families, but 25.5% of the total family income of non-Hispanic white families and 32.7% of the total family income of Hispanic families.

The TANF program has been criticized since its inception in 1996. Critics maintain that the drop in the number of recipients cannot measure success. Caseloads initially decreased simply because the eligibility requirements were stiffened. As a result, many immigrants, especially Hispanics who were working poor, were denied aid, adversely affecting their children, who were U.S. citizens. Moreover, the type of work available to individuals on welfare was generally low paying, offering no health insurance or other benefits, and doing little to lift welfare-to-work participants above the poverty level. So, despite falling numbers of TANF recipients, rising poverty levels perhaps provide a more telling portrayal of the program's progress. (See Figure 5.1 and Table 5.4.)

The American Recovery and Reinvestment Act, which was signed into law by President Barack Obama (1961–) in February 2009, contained a provision for a TANF Emergency Fund of $5 billion for fiscal years 2009 and 2010. The HHS explains in "Questions and Answers on the American Recovery and Reinvestment Act of 2009" (April 30, 2009, http://www.hhs.gov/recovery/programs/tanf/tanf-faq.html) that states could apply for monies from the emergency fund to help meet increased need for TANF funding among their residents. The act also provided some relief for the TANF work requirements.

TABLE 5.9

Percentage of total family income from various sources, by poverty status, race and Hispanic origin, 2005

	<50% poverty	<100% of poverty	<200% of poverty	200%+ of poverty	All persons
All persons					
TANF, SSI and food stamps	58.5	32.5	10.4	0.2	1.1
Earnings	25.3	46.6	68.2	86.6	84.9
Other income	16.2	20.8	21.4	13.2	13.9
Racial/ethnic categories					
Non-Hispanic white					
TANF, SSI and food stamps	53.1	29.9	8.0	0.1	0.6
Earnings	25.5	41.9	62.7	85.6	84.3
Other income	21.4	28.3	29.4	14.3	15.1
Non-Hispanic black					
TANF, SSI and food stamps	66.3	43.5	17.9	0.5	4.0
Earnings	18.9	35.3	60.6	88.1	82.5
Other income	14.7	21.2	21.6	11.5	13.5
Hispanic					
TANF, SSI and food stamps	55.6	26.5	9.4	0.5	2.7
Earnings	32.7	62.4	81.5	91.6	89.1
Other income	11.7	11.1	9.0	7.9	8.2
Age categories					
Children ages 0–5					
TANF, SSI and food stamps	65.5	37.2	13.5	0.2	2.3
Earnings	22.8	52.0	78.0	94.6	92.1
Other income	11.6	10.7	8.5	5.2	5.7
Children ages 6–10					
TANF, SSI and food stamps	65.1	35.5	12.0	0.2	1.9
Earnings	20.7	50.2	77.4	93.7	91.3
Other income	14.2	14.3	10.6	6.2	6.8
Children ages 11–15					
TANF, SSI and food stamps	61.8	36.1	12.5	0.1	1.7
Earnings	22.6	47.3	74.3	92.0	89.8
Other income	15.6	16.6	13.2	7.9	8.5
Women ages 16–64					
TANF, SSI and food stamps	55.6	33.3	11.2	0.2	1.1
Earnings	26.6	46.3	71.4	89.1	87.7
Other income	17.8	20.5	17.5	10.7	11.2
Men ages 16–64					
TANF, SSI and food stamps	48.0	27.4	8.0	0.2	0.7
Earnings	34.4	53.1	76.4	90.2	89.3
Other income	17.6	19.5	15.5	9.6	10.0
Adults ages 65 and over					
TANF, SSI and food stamps	37.2	21.4	6.5	0.3	1.0
Earnings	9.2	6.5	9.9	40.2	36.6
Other income	53.6	72.2	83.5	59.5	62.4
Family categories					
Persons in married-couple families					
TANF, SSI and food stamps	49.7	22.4	5.9	0.1	0.5
Earnings	35.0	62.0	77.0	87.6	86.9
Other income	15.3	15.6	17.1	12.3	12.6
Persons in female-headed families					
TANF, SSI and food stamps	66.9	45.2	21.7	1.0	6.9
Earnings	17.8	36.4	58.6	81.9	75.3
Other income	15.2	18.4	19.7	17.1	17.8
Persons in male-headed families					
TANF, SSI and food stamps	65.8	31.2	11.0	0.5	2.0
Earnings	21.0	50.7	72.1	87.3	85.2
Other income	13.2	18.0	16.9	12.2	12.8

Notes: Total income is total annual family income, including the value of food stamps. Other income is non-means-tested, non-earnings income such as child support, alimony, pensions, Social Security benefits, interest and dividends. Poverty status categories are not mutually exclusive. Spouses are not present in the female-headed and male-headed family categories. Persons of Hispanic ethnicity may be of any race. Beginning in 2002, estimates for whites and blacks are for persons reporting a single race only. Persons who reported more than one race are included in the total for all persons but are not shown under any race category. Due to small sample size, American Indians/Alaska Natives, Asians and Native Hawaiians/other Pacific Islanders are included in the total for all persons but are not shown separately.
TANF = Temporary Assistance for Needy Families
SSI = Supplemental Security Income

SOURCE: Gil Crouse, Susan Hauan, and Annette Waters Rogers, "Table IND 1c. Percentage of Total Income from Various Sources by Poverty Status and Selected Characteristics: 2005," in *Indicators of Welfare Dependence, Annual Report to Congress, 2008*, U.S. Department of Health and Human Services, 2007, http://aspe.hhs.gov/hsp/indicators08/ch2.pdf (accessed December 11, 2009)

CHAPTER 6
HEALTH

The demographic profiles of African-Americans, Hispanics, Asian-Americans, Pacific Islanders, Native Americans, and Alaskan Natives differ considerably from those of the majority population in the United States. Because a high percentage of minorities live in urban areas, they are exposed to a greater number of environmental hazards, including pollution, traffic hazards, substandard and/or overcrowded housing, and crime. Occupational risks are also greater for minorities because a greater percentage of them are employed in potentially dangerous jobs. Poverty, which is experienced disproportionately by African-Americans, Hispanics, and Native Americans and Alaskan Natives, leads to poor nutrition, poor housing conditions, and poor access to health care. In addition, the amount of stress involved in facing daily discrimination and changing cultural environments as well as the lack of resources for solving stressful situations can play a critical role in the mental and physical health of minority groups.

As a whole, Hispanics enjoy better health on a variety of measures than do non-Hispanic whites, despite Hispanics' disadvantaged position, higher poverty rates, lower educational attainment, and the obstacles to health care that they encounter. This is most likely due in part to the fact that Hispanics in the United States are younger than the non-Hispanic white population. According to the U.S. Census Bureau, in *The Hispanic Population in the United States: 2008* (September 2009, http://www.census.gov/population/www/socdemo/hispanic/cps2008.html), 34.2% of the Hispanic population was under the age of 18 in 2008, compared with 21.4% of the non-Hispanic white population. (See Table 6.1.) Conversely, only 5.6% of Hispanics were aged 65 years and older, compared with 15% of non-Hispanic whites.

In *The Hispanic Population in the United States: March 2002* (June 2003, http://www.census.gov/prod/2003pubs/p20-545.pdf), Roberto R. Ramirez and G. Patricia de la Cruz of the Census Bureau explain that this age differential is partly due to the higher fertility rate of Hispanics and partly to their recent immigration status—younger people tend to immigrate. According to the Census Bureau, in *The Hispanic Population in the United States*, in 2008, 38.8% of Hispanics in the United States were foreign born, compared with 12.5% of the larger U.S. population. In addition, first-generation immigrants tend to have more children than do other Americans.

HEALTH CARE
Quality of Care

In *National Healthcare Disparities Report, 2008* (March 2009, http://www.ahrq.gov/qual/nhdr08/nhdr08.pdf), the U.S. Department of Health and Human Services (HHS) defines quality health care as "doing the right thing, at the right time, in the right way, for the right people—and having the best possible results." Quality health care is defined as care that is effective, safe, and timely, as well as equitable—meaning that the care does not vary in quality because of personal characteristics such as race or ethnicity.

The HHS focuses on 22 core measures of quality and six core measures of access to care to compare the health care received across racial and ethnic groups. It finds that minorities consistently receive a poorer quality of care than do non-Hispanic whites. In 2006 (the most recent year that detailed data on race and quality of health care were available, as of February 2010) African-Americans received poorer quality of care than whites for 73% of the quality measures, Native Americans and Alaskan Natives for 41% of quality measures, and Asian-Americans for 32% of the quality measures. (See Figure 6.1.) Hispanics received lower quality of care than non-Hispanic whites for 77% of the quality measures. The health care gap appears to be growing; these disparities were more pronounced in 2006 than HHS had found in 2004.

TABLE 6.1

Population by sex, age, Hispanic origin, and race, 2008

[Numbers in thousands. Civilian noninstitutionalized population[a]]

					Hispanic origin and race[b]						
							Non-Hispanic				
	Total		Hispanic		Total		White alone		All other races		
Sex and age	Number	Percent	Number	Percent	Number	Percent	Number	Percent	Number	Percent
Both sexes	299,106	100.0	46,026	100.0	253,079	100.0	196,768	100.0	56,312	100.0
Under 15 years	60,958	20.4	13,337	29.0	47,622	18.8	34,134	17.3	13,488	24.0
15 years and over	238,148	79.6	32,690	71.0	205,458	81.2	162,634	82.7	42,824	76.0
Under 16 years	65,221	21.8	14,129	30.7	51,092	20.2	36,613	18.6	14,479	25.7
16 years and over	233,885	78.2	31,897	69.3	201,988	79.8	160,155	81.4	41,832	74.3
Under 18 years	74,403	24.9	15,741	34.2	58,662	23.2	42,165	21.4	16,497	29.3
18 years and over	224,703	75.1	30,286	65.8	194,417	76.8	154,603	78.6	39,814	70.7
Under 21 years	86,319	28.9	17,882	38.9	68,436	27.0	49,405	25.1	19,031	33.8
21 years and over	212,787	71.1	28,144	61.1	184,643	73.0	147,363	74.9	37,280	66.2
Under 65 years	262,316	87.7	43,471	94.4	218,844	86.5	167,326	85.0	51,519	91.5
65 years and over	36,790	12.3	2,555	5.6	34,235	13.5	29,442	15.0	4,793	8.5
Male	146,855	100.0	23,652	100.0	123,203	100.0	96,613	100.0	26,591	100.0
Under 15 years	31,178	21.2	6,815	28.8	24,362	19.8	17,513	18.1	6,850	25.8
15 years and over	115,678	78.8	16,837	71.2	98,841	80.2	79,100	81.9	19,741	74.2
Under 16 years	33,354	22.7	7,223	30.5	26,131	21.2	18,786	19.4	7,344	27.6
16 years and over	113,502	77.3	16,429	69.5	97,073	78.8	77,826	80.6	19,247	72.4
Under 18 years	37,994	25.9	8,028	33.9	29,965	24.3	21,626	22.4	8,339	31.4
18 years and over	108,862	74.1	15,624	66.1	93,238	75.7	74,986	77.6	18,252	68.6
Under 21 years	44,100	30.0	9,152	38.7	34,948	28.4	25,348	26.2	9,601	36.1
21 years and over	102,755	70.0	14,500	61.3	88,255	71.6	71,265	73.8	16,990	63.9
Under 65 years	131,093	89.3	22,558	95.4	108,535	88.1	83,899	86.8	24,636	92.7
65 years and over	15,762	10.7	1,094	4.6	14,668	11.9	12,714	13.2	1,954	7.3
Female	152,250	100.0	22,374	100.0	129,876	100.0	100,155	100.0	29,721	100.0
Under 15 years	29,780	19.6	6,521	29.1	23,259	17.9	16,621	16.6	6,638	22.3
15 years and over	122,470	80.4	15,853	70.9	106,617	82.1	83,534	83.4	23,083	77.7
Under 16 years	31,867	20.9	6,906	30.9	24,961	19.2	17,826	17.8	7,135	24.0
16 years and over	120,383	79.1	15,468	69.1	104,915	80.8	82,329	82.2	22,586	76.0
Under 18 years	36,409	23.9	7,712	34.5	28,697	22.1	20,538	20.5	8,158	27.5
18 years and over	115,841	76.1	14,662	65.5	101,179	77.9	79,617	79.5	21,562	72.5
Under 21 years	42,219	27.7	8,731	39.0	33,488	25.8	24,058	24.0	9,431	31.7
21 years and over	110,031	72.3	13,643	61.0	96,388	74.2	76,098	76.0	20,290	68.3
Under 65 years	131,222	86.2	20,914	93.5	110,309	84.9	83,427	83.3	26,882	90.4
65 years and over	21,028	13.8	1,461	6.5	19,567	15.1	16,729	16.7	2,838	9.6

[a]Plus armed forces living off post or with their families on post.
[b]Hispanic refers to people whose origin is Mexican, Puerto Rican, Cuban, Spanish-speaking Central or South American countries, or other Hispanic/Latino, regardless of race.

SOURCE: "Table 1. Population by Sex, Age, Hispanic Origin, and Race: 2008," in *The Hispanic Population in the United States: 2008*, U.S. Census Bureau, September 2009, http://www.census.gov/population/www/socdemo/hispanic/cps2008.html (accessed December 14, 2009)

Access to Care

In *National Healthcare Disparities Report, 2006* (December 2006, http://www.ahrq.gov/qual/nhdr06/nhdr06report.pdf), the HHS measures access to health care, finding that minorities, particularly those of low socioeconomic status, face barriers to accessing health care that make receiving basic health services a struggle. Access is measured in several ways, including ability to get into the health care system, to get care within the health care system, and to find providers to meet their needs.

The HHS finds that in 2006 Native Americans and Alaskan Natives had worse access to care than did whites for 17% of the access measures and African-Americans and Asian-Americans each for 33% of access measures. (See Figure 6.2.) Hispanics had worse access to care than non-Hispanic whites for a staggering 83% of access measures.

Part of these differences in access to care for minority groups had to do with socioeconomics; people below the poverty level had worse access to care than did high-income people (family incomes above 400% of the poverty level) for every one of the access measures.

The HHS notes that the change in disparities in core access measures varied greatly by race and ethnic group in 2006. Even though 80% of disparities in access to care were improving for Native Americans and Alaskan Natives and 60% of disparities in access to care were improving for African-Americans and Asian-Americans, only 20% of disparities in access to care were improving for Hispanics. Likewise, no core access measures were worsening for Native Americans and Alaskan Natives, while 20% were worsening for Asian-Americans, and 40% were worsening for African-Americans. However, fully 80% of core access

FIGURE 6.1

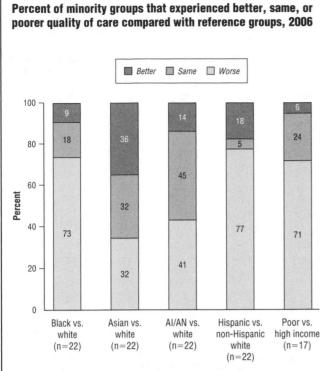

Percent of minority groups that experienced better, same, or poorer quality of care compared with reference groups, 2006

Better ■ Same □ Worse

Better = Population received better quality of care than the reference group.
Same = Population and reference group received about the same quality of care.
Worse = Population received poorer quality of care than reference group.
Key: AI/AN = American Indian or Alaska Native.
Note: "Asian" includes "Asian or Pacific Islander" (API) when information is not collected separately for each group. Data presented are the most recent data available. Totals may not add to 100% due to rounding.
n = Sample size.

SOURCE: "Figure H.1. Core Quality Measures for Which Members of Selected Group Experienced Better, Same, or Poorer Quality of Care Compared with Reference Group," in *National Healthcare Disparities Report, 2006*, U.S. Department of Health and Human Services, Agency for Healthcare Research and Quality, June 2007, http://www .ahrq.gov/qual/nhdr06/nhdr06high.pdf (accessed December 14, 2009)

FIGURE 6.2

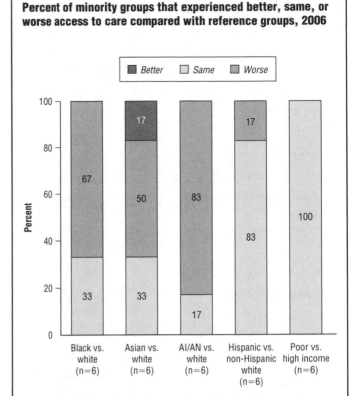

Percent of minority groups that experienced better, same, or worse access to care compared with reference groups, 2006

Better □ Same ■ Worse

Better = Population received better access to care than the reference group.
Same = Population and reference group received about the same access to care.
Worse = Population received poorer access to care than reference group.
Key: AI/AN = American Indian or Alaska Native.
Note: "Asian" includes "Asian or Pacific Islander" (API) when information is not collected separately for each group. Data presented are the most recent data available. Totals may not add to 100% due to rounding.
n = Sample size.

SOURCE: "Figure H.2. Core Access Measures for Which Members of Selected Group Experienced Better, Same, or Worse Access to Care Compared with Reference Group," in *National Healthcare Disparities Report, 2006*, U.S. Department of Health and Human Services, Agency for Healthcare Research and Quality, December 2006, http://www.ahrq.gov/qual/nhdr06/nhdr06high.pdf (accessed December 14, 2009)

measures were worsening for Hispanics. In 2006 African-Americans' access to their primary care provider and their ability to pay for health care were getting worse. Hispanics were increasingly uninsured, had worse access to their primary care provider, and were getting less likely to have access to a source of ongoing health care.

HEALTH INSURANCE. Lack of health insurance is one formidable barrier to receiving health care. Carmen DeNavas-Walt, Bernadette D. Proctor, and Jessica C. Smith of the Census Bureau indicate in *Income, Poverty, and Health Insurance Coverage in the United States: 2008* (September 2009, http://www.census.gov/prod/2009pubs/ p60-236.pdf) that 46.3 million people were uninsured in 2008. The lack of insurance coverage is a significant barrier to getting basic health care services. The HHS emphasizes in *National Healthcare Disparities Report, 2008* that uninsured people are more likely to have a poor health status and to die early because it is more difficult

for the uninsured to get health care and therefore they are diagnosed at later disease stages.

Between 2006 and 2008 members of minority groups were much less likely to carry health insurance coverage than were their non-Hispanic white counterparts. On average during this period, 32.3% of Hispanics, 31.7% of Native Americans and Alaskan Natives, 19.7% of African-Americans, 18.5% of Native Hawaiians and other Pacific Islanders, and 16.6% of Asian-Americans lacked coverage. (See Table 6.2.) In comparison, only 10.7% of non-Hispanic whites lacked health insurance coverage during this period.

Those minorities who do have health insurance are more likely than non-Hispanic whites to be covered by government programs rather than by private health insurance. In 2006 members of all minority groups were more likely to be

TABLE 6.2

People without health insurance coverage, by race and Hispanic origin, 2005–06 and 2007–08

[Numbers in thousands.]

Race[a] and Hispanic origin	3-year average 2006–2008 Estimate	2-year average 2005–2006[b] Estimate	2-year average 2007–2008 Estimate	Change (2007–2008 average less 2005–2006[b] average)[c] Estimate
Number uninsured				
All races	**46,330**	**45,905**	**45,998**	**94**
White	34,892	34,716	34,595	−121
White, not Hispanic	21,010	21,035	20,935	−101
Black	7,436	7,329	7,328	−1
American Indian and Alaska Native	857	773	857	85
Asian	2,208	2,103	2,289	186
Native Hawaiian and other Pacific Islander	142	138	144	5
Hispanic (any race)	14,874	14,625	14,664	39
Percentage uninsured				
All races	**15.5**	**15.5**	**15.3**	**−0.2**
White	14.6	14.7	14.4	−0.2
White, not Hispanic	10.7	10.7	10.6	−0.1
Black	19.7	19.7	19.3	−0.4
American Indian and Alaska Native	31.7	32.1	30.7	−1.5
Asian	16.6	16.3	17.2	0.9
Native Hawaiian and other Pacific Islander	18.5	20.9	18.0	−2.9
Hispanic (any race)	32.3	33.2	31.4	−1.8

[a]Federal surveys now give respondents the option of reporting more than one race. Therefore, two basic ways of defining a race group are possible. A group such as Asian may be defined as those who reported Asian and no other race (the race-alone or single-race concept) or as those who reported Asian regardless of whether they also reported another race (the race-alone-or-in-combination concept). This table shows data using the first approach (race alone). The use of the single-race population does not imply that it is the preferred method of presenting or analyzing data. The Census Bureau uses a variety of approaches. About 2.6 percent of people reported more than one race in Census 2000.
[b]The 2005 data were revised in March 2007.
[c]Details may not sum to totals because of rounding.

SOURCE: Carmen DeNavas-Walt, Bernadette D. Proctor, and Jessica C. Smith, "Table 8. People without Health Insurance Coverage by Race and Hispanic Origin Using 2- and 3-Year Averages: 2005–2006 and 2007–2008," in *Income, Poverty, and Health Insurance Coverage in the United States: 2008*, U.S. Census Bureau, September 2009, http://www.census.gov/prod/2009pubs/p60–236.pdf (accessed December 11, 2009)

covered by Medicaid (the federally funded health care program for low-income people) than were non-Hispanic whites. In that year Medicaid covered 9.5% of non-Hispanic whites and 9.7% of Asian-Americans. (See Table 6.3.) However, Medicaid covered 26.6% of African-Americans, 24.3% of Native Americans or Alaskan Natives, and 23.1% of Hispanics. Among Hispanics, Puerto Ricans were the most likely (35.7%) and Cubans were the least likely (11.3%) to be covered by Medicaid. The large proportion of minorities on Medicaid is in part explained by eligibility requirements; only poor and low-income people qualify, and members of these groups are disproportionately poor. However, Medicaid coverage does not necessarily translate into good or even adequate health care. Benjamin Le Cook of Mathematica Policy Research Inc. in Cambridge, Massachusetts, notes in "Effect of Medicaid Managed Care on Racial Disparities in Health Care Access" (*Health Services Research*, vol. 42, no. 1, February 2007) that because Medicaid reimburses physicians at lower rates than do private insurance plans, fewer doctors accept it, thereby erecting further barriers for those covered by Medicaid to receiving adequate health care.

Nearly all people aged 65 years and older are covered by health insurance largely due to Medicare (the federally administered system of health insurance for people aged 65 years and older and people with disabilities). However, Medicaid additionally covers a much higher proportion of minorities of this age, whereas non-Hispanic whites tend to be covered by private insurance. For example, in 2006 only 5.9% of non-Hispanic whites aged 65 years and older were covered by Medicaid, compared with 21.8% of non-Hispanic African-Americans and 23.4% of Hispanics. (See Table 6.4.) In 2006 non-Hispanic whites aged 65 years and older were more likely to be covered either by an employer-sponsored plan (37.1%) or by a Medigap plan (26.7%), both of which are forms of private health insurance, although in both cases the percentages covered by private plans had been dropping steadily since 1992. Nevertheless, lower proportions of minority groups were covered by private plans. In 2006, 23.7% of non-Hispanic African-Americans and 17.1% of Hispanics were covered by an employer-sponsored plan and 8.8% and 8.9%, respectively, were covered by a Medigap plan.

HEALTH CARE REFORM The availability of insurance coverage may change for many Americans, particularly members of minority groups, due to health care reform passed by Congress and signed into law by President Barack

TABLE 6.3

Medicaid coverage among persons under 65 years of age, by race and Hispanic origin, selected years, 1984–2006

[Data are based on household interviews of a sample of the civilian noninstitutionalized population]

Characteristic	1984[a]	1989[a]	1995[a]	1997	2000	2003	2004 (1)[b]	2004 (2)[b]	2005[b]	2006[b]
					Number in millions					
Total[c]	14.0	15.4	26.6	22.9	23.2	30.9	31.1	31.6	33.2	36.2
					Percent of population					
Total[c]	6.8	7.2	11.5	9.7	9.5	12.3	12.3	12.5	12.9	14.0
Race[d]										
White only	4.6	5.1	8.9	7.4	7.1	10.4	10.2	10.4	11.0	11.8
Black or African American only	20.5	19.0	28.5	22.4	21.2	23.7	24.5	24.9	24.9	26.6
American Indian or Alaska Native only	*28.2	29.7	19.0	19.6	15.1	18.5	18.0	18.4	24.2	24.3
Asian only	*8.7	*8.8	10.5	9.6	7.5	8.0	9.6	9.8	8.2	9.7
Native Hawaiian or other Pacific Islander only	—	—	—	—	*	*	*	*	*	*
2 or more races	—	—	—	—	19.1	23.5	19.0	19.3	22.0	24.0
Hispanic origin and race[d]										
Hispanic or Latino	13.3	13.5	21.9	17.6	15.5	21.8	21.9	22.5	22.9	23.1
Mexican	12.2	12.4	21.6	17.2	14.0	21.7	21.9	22.4	23.0	23.0
Puerto Rican	31.5	27.3	33.4	31.0	29.4	31.0	28.5	29.1	31.9	35.7
Cuban	*4.8	*7.7	13.4	7.3	9.2	13.8	17.9	17.9	17.7	*11.3
Other Hispanic or Latino	7.9	11.1	18.2	15.3	14.5	19.3	19.9	20.8	19.7	20.2
Not Hispanic or Latino	6.2	6.5	10.2	8.7	8.5	10.6	10.5	10.7	11.1	12.3
White only	3.7	4.1	7.1	6.1	6.1	8.0	7.8	7.9	8.5	9.5
Black or African American only	20.7	19.0	28.1	22.1	21.0	23.4	24.1	24.6	24.8	26.2

*Estimates are considered unreliable.

—Data not available.

[a]Data prior to 1997 are not strictly comparable with data for later years due to the 1997 questionnaire redesign.

[b]Beginning in quarter 3 of the 2004 National Health Insurance Survey (NHIS), persons under 65 years with no reported coverage were asked explicitly about Medicaid coverage. Estimates were calculated without and with the additional information from this question in the columns labeled 2004(1) and 2004(2), respectively, and estimates were calculated with the additional information starting with 2005 data.

[c]Includes all other races not shown separately, those with unknown marital status, and, in 1984 and 1989, persons with unknown poverty level.

[d]The race groups, white, black, American Indian or Alaska Native, Asian, Native Hawaiian or other Pacific Islander, and 2 or more races, include persons of Hispanic and non-Hispanic origin. Persons of Hispanic origin may be of any race. Starting with 1999 data, race-specific estimates are tabulated according to the 1997 Revisions to the Standards for the Classification of Federal Data on Race and Ethnicity and are not strictly comparable with estimates for earlier years. The five single-race categories plus multiple-race categories shown in the table conform to the 1997 Standards. Starting with 1999 data, race-specific estimates are for persons who reported only one racial group; the category 2 or more races includes persons who reported more than one racial group. Prior to 1999, data were tabulated according to the 1977 Standards with four racial groups and the Asian only category included Native Hawaiian or other Pacific Islander. Estimates for single-race categories prior to 1999 included persons who reported one race or, if they reported more than one race, identified one race as best representing their race. Starting with 2003 data, race responses of other race and unspecified multiple race were treated as missing, and then race was imputed if these were the only race responses. Almost all persons with a race response of other race were of Hispanic origin.

Notes: Medicaid includes other public assistance through 1996. Starting with 1997 data, state-sponsored health plan coverage is included as Medicaid coverage. Starting with 1999 data, coverage by the State Children's Health Insurance Program (SCHIP) is included as Medicaid coverage. In 2006, 11.3% of persons under 65 years of age were covered by Medicaid, 1.2% by state-sponsored health plans, and 1.6% by SCHIP.

SOURCE: Adapted from "Table 139. Medicaid Coverage among Persons under 65 Years of Age, by Selected Characteristics: United States, Selected Years 1984–2006," in *Health, United States, 2008. With Chartbook*, U.S. Department of Health and Human Services, Centers for Disease Control and Prevention, National Center for Health Statistics, 2009, http://www.cdc.gov/nchs/data/hus/hus08.pdf (accessed December 14, 2009)

Obama (1961–) in March 2010. The Patient Protection and Affordable Care Act (PPACA) and an amendment, titled the Health Care and Education Reconciliation Act of 2010, aim to implement changes over an eight-year period that would offer insurance to an estimated 32 million Americans who were uninsured when the legislation passed, as well as provide better access to health care, including preventative care. Among other reforms, the legislation would expand Medicaid; provide insurance premium subsidies for individuals and incentives to companies to offer employees health care; keep dependent children on their parents' insurance until age 26; prohibit insurance companies from dropping people when they get sick; and end the practice of denying people coverage due to pre-existing conditions. The Obama administration and Congress proposed to offset the costs for the reforms with methods that include taxes on upper income recipients of Medicare, businesses like tanning salons, and

"Cadillac" (high-cost) health care plans; fees on some medical and pharmaceutical companies; and other cost-saving measures.

Yet the act was controversial and was fiercely opposed by Republicans in Congress. Democratic legislators who worked to pass the bill, as well as a few Republicans who opposed it, reported receiving death threats from angry constituents. The controversy and anger stemmed from several factors. Some critics were concerned about the cost to the country as it faced a steadily increasing federal deficit following the recession that began in December of 2007. Despite a Congressional Budget Office report that estimated a $143-billion net reduction in the deficit in the decade following passage of the legislation, some critics asserted that the measures put in place by Congress would not be able to cover the costs of the reform, much less decrease the deficit. Another objection was that the PPACA

TABLE 6.4

Health insurance coverage for persons 65 years of age and over, by type of coverage and race and Hispanic origin, selected years 1992–2006

[Data are based on household interviews of a sample of the civilian noninstitutionalized population]

Characteristic	Medicare Health Maintenance Organization[a]					Medicaid[b]				
	1992	1995	2000	2005	2006	1992	1995	2000	2005	2006
Age					Number in millions					
65 years and over	1.1	2.6	5.9	4.6	6.7	2.7	2.8	2.7	3.2	3.3
					Percent of population					
65 years and over	3.9	8.9	19.3	14.5	19.2	9.4	9.6	9.0	10.1	9.4
65–74 years	4.2	9.5	20.6	13.9	19.1	7.9	8.8	8.5	9.9	9.2
75–84 years	3.7	8.3	18.5	15.3	19.7	10.6	9.6	8.9	9.9	9.1
85 years and over	*	7.3	16.3	13.9	17.7	16.6	13.6	11.2	11.9	10.9
Race and Hispanic origin										
White, not Hispanic or Latino	3.6	8.4	18.4	13.2	17.2	5.6	5.4	5.1	6.1	5.9
Black, not Hispanic or Latino	*	7.9	20.7	17.1	24.1	28.5	30.3	23.6	23.6	21.8
Hispanic	*	15.5	27.5	27.2	37.0	39.0	40.5	28.7	29.2	23.4

Characteristic	Employer-sponsored plan[c]					Medigap[d]				
	1992	1995	2000	2005	2006	1992	1995	2000	2005	2006
Age					Number in millions					
65 years and over	12.5	11.3	10.7	11.6	11.9	9.9	9.5	7.6	8.2	8.2
					Percent of population					
65 years and over	42.8	38.6	35.2	36.4	34.1	33.9	32.5	25.0	25.7	23.5
65–74 years	46.9	41.1	36.6	38.1	35.6	31.4	29.9	21.7	23.2	21.3
75–84 years	38.2	37.1	35.0	35.5	33.3	37.5	35.2	27.8	27.3	24.8
85 years and over	31.6	30.2	29.4	31.8	30.0	38.3	37.6	31.1	30.8	28.9
Race and Hispanic origin										
White, not Hispanic or Latino	45.9	41.3	38.6	39.5	37.1	37.2	36.2	28.3	29.1	26.7
Black, not Hispanic or Latino	25.9	26.7	22.0	27.9	23.7	13.6	10.2	7.5	9.5	8.8
Hispanic	20.7	16.9	15.8	18.6	17.1	15.8	10.1	11.3	11.1	8.9

Characteristic	Medicare fee-for-service only or other[e]				
	1992	1995	2000	2005	2006
Age			Number in millions		
65 years and over	2.9	3.1	3.5	4.3	4.9
			Percent of population		
65 years and over	9.9	10.5	11.5	13.3	13.9
65–74 years	9.7	10.7	12.6	14.9	14.8
75–84 years	10.1	9.9	9.9	11.9	13.1
85 years and over	10.8	11.3	12.1	11.6	12.5
Race and Hispanic origin					
White, not Hispanic or Latino	7.7	8.7	9.6	12.2	13.1
Black, not Hispanic or Latino	26.7	25.0	26.1	21.9	21.6
Hispanic	18.3	17.1	16.7	13.9	13.6

*Estimates are considered unreliable if the sample cell size is 50 or fewer.
[a]Enrollee has Medicare Health Maintenance Organization (HMO) regardless of other insurance.
[b]Enrolled in Medicaid and not enrolled in a Medicare risk HMO.
[c]Private insurance plans purchased through employers (own, current, or former employer, family business, union, or former employer or union of spouse) and not enrolled in a Medicare risk HMO or Medicaid.
[d]Supplemental insurance purchased privately or through organizations such as AARP (Association of American Retired Persons) or professional organizations, and not enrolled in a Medicare risk HMO, Medicaid, or employer-sponsored plan.
[e]Medicare fee-for-service only or other public plans (except Medicaid).
Notes: Insurance categories are mutually exclusive. Persons with more than one type of coverage are categorized according to the order in which the health insurance categories appear.

SOURCE: Adapted from "Table 141. Health Insurance Coverage of Persons 65 Years of Age and over, by Type of Coverage and Selected Characteristics: United States, Selected Years 1992–2006," in *Health, United States, 2008. With Chartbook*, U.S. Department of Health and Human Services, Centers for Disease Control and Prevention, National Center for Health Statistics, 2009, http://www.cdc.gov/nchs/data/hus/hus08.pdf (accessed December 14, 2009)

requires people to obtain health insurance or pay a tax penalty. Some critics are also concerned that the plan could lead to health care rationing due to increased costs and that the country will not have enough health care professionals.

There was also concern that the act undermines the sovereignty of the individual states. As of April 29, 2010, at least 19 states had considered or were planning to sue the federal government over the implementation of the legislation in its entirety or of parts with which they had particular concerns. A spokesperson for the Justice Department stated that the bill was constitutional.

DOCTOR VISITS. Another measure of a group's access to care is the number of doctor visits made annually. Since the 1980s, as more outpatient clinics and other outreach health facilities have opened, Americans have had increased opportunities to seek medical help. However, in 2006 members of most minority groups were more likely than non-Hispanic whites not to have visited a doctor's office or emergency room in the previous 12 months. In that year, 27.1% of Hispanics, 21.9% of Asian-Americans, 15.7% of non-Hispanic African-Americans, and 13.5% of Native Americans or Alaskan Natives had not visited health care providers. (See Table 6.5.) Only Native Americans or Alaskan Natives were less likely than non-Hispanic whites (15%) to have not visited health care providers in that year. This disparity can be explained in part by the disproportionate number of minorities who are poor or low income; these groups were more likely than non-low income people to make no visits to a doctor's office or an emergency room in 2006.

INDIAN HEALTH SERVICE. Federal funding for Native American health care is provided through the Indian Health Service (IHS; February 2010, http://www.ihs.gov/Public Info/PublicAffairs/Welcome_Info/IHSintro.asp), whose mission is "to raise the physical, mental, social, and spiritual health of American Indians and Alaska Natives to the highest level." Delivery of health care to Native Americans is complicated by the lack of services and the long distances that sometimes must be traveled to receive care. Alaskan Natives are often able to get preventive medical care only by flying to a medical facility, and, even though transportation costs are covered for emergency care, they are not provided for routine care. The HHS indicates in *National Healthcare Disparities Report, 2008* that nationwide about 74% of Native Americans sought health care through the IHS in 2004.

Many Native American tribes have invested some of the money earned from casinos to improve health services. For example, Herman Williams Jr. states in "Gambling Expansion Advocates Ignore the Facts about Tribal Gaming" (*Tulalip–Quil Ceda Messenger*, March 2003) that the Tulalip Tribes in Washington state were able to build a new, state-of-the-art health center as well as improve other social services and reduce unemployment with proceeds from tribal gaming. According to Kate Spilde, in "The Rumsey Band of the Wintun Indians: A Return to Self-Sufficiency" (February 2001, http://www.indiangaming.org/library/articles/rumsey-band.shtml), the Rumsey Band of the Wintun Indians in California operate the Rumsey Chapa-De Indian Health Clinic with profits from their casino, which also funds schools and contributes to the cultural life of the area. In

"Tribes Hit the Jackpot" (*New Mexico Resources*, Fall 2003), Kevin Robinson-Avila reports that the Sandia Pueblo in New Mexico built a wellness center that provides free medical care to all tribe members as well as child care, education, and training.

PREGNANCY AND BIRTH
Prenatal Care

The importance of early prenatal care cannot be over-emphasized, as doctors are now better able to detect, and often correct, potential problems early in pregnancy. Every pregnant woman should receive prenatal care, and the National Center for Health Statistics (NCHS) believes the United States is capable of guaranteeing that more than 90% of pregnant women receive prenatal care during the first trimester of pregnancy.

In 2005, 83.9% of all women in the United States received prenatal care during their first trimester of pregnancy, but that percentage was significantly lower among some minority groups. (See Table 6.6.) Almost nine out of 10 non-Hispanic white women (88.7%) and Asian or Pacific Islander women (85.3%) received prenatal care during their first trimester. By contrast, only 77.6% of Hispanic women, 76.5% of non-Hispanic African-American women, and 69.6% of Native American or Alaskan Native women did so. It is worthy of note, however, that despite the low rates of first-trimester prenatal care among Hispanic women in general, Cuban women had among the highest rates of prenatal care of all racial and ethnic groups except for non-Hispanic whites, at 86.2%.

Births and Fertility

Of the 4.3 million births in 2007, 2.3 million were to non-Hispanic white mothers, 1.1 million were to Hispanic mothers, 627,230 were to non-Hispanic African-American mothers, 254,734 were to Asian or Pacific Islander mothers, and 49,284 were to Native American or Alaskan Natives mothers. (See Table 6.7.) However, the birth rate (live births per 1,000 population in a specified group) was highest among Hispanics (23.3), followed by Asians or Pacific Islanders (17.2), non-Hispanic African-Americans (16.4), and Native Americans or Alaskan Natives (15.2). Non-Hispanic whites had the lowest birthrate, at 11.5 per 1,000 population.

The fertility rate refers to the number of live births per 1,000 women aged 15 to 44 in a specified group. In 2007 Hispanic women had the highest fertility rate (102.1), followed by non-Hispanic African-American women (71.6), Asian or Pacific Islander women (71.4), and Native American or Alaskan Native women (64.7). (See Table 6.7.) Non-Hispanic white women had the lowest fertility rate, at 60.1. Even though Hispanic women had the highest fertility rate, it varied among Hispanics from different countries of origin. According to Joyce A. Martin et al. of the Centers for Disease Control and Prevention (CDC), in

TABLE 6.5

Health care visits to doctor offices, emergency departments, and home visits within the past 12 months, by race and Hispanic origin, health insurance, and poverty level, 1997, 2005, and 2006

[Data are based on household interviews of a sample of the civilian noninstitutionalized population]

| | Number of health care visits[a] | | | | | | | | | | | |
| | None | | | 1–3 visits | | | 4–9 visits | | | 10 or more visits | | |
Characteristic	1997	2005	2006	1997	2005	2006	1997	2005	2006	1997	2005	2006
						Percent distribution						
Race[b, c]												
White only	16.0	15.2	17.2	46.1	46.0	46.2	23.9	24.9	23.4	14.0	14.0	13.2
Black or African American only	16.8	16.0	16.0	46.1	47.5	49.2	23.2	23.6	23.3	13.9	12.9	11.5
American Indian or Alaska Native only	17.1	20.5	13.5	38.0	36.6	44.2	24.2	29.4	27.6	20.7	13.4	14.7
Asian only	22.8	21.6	21.9	49.1	49.5	51.3	19.7	20.5	18.1	8.3	8.5	8.7
Native Hawaiian or other Pacific Islander only	—	*	*	—	*	*	—	*	*	—	*	*
2 or more races	—	15.6	16.3	—	37.9	44.8	—	26.7	21.3	—	19.9	17.6
Hispanic origin and race[b, c]												
Hispanic or Latino	24.9	24.0	27.1	42.3	42.4	43.0	20.3	21.7	19.6	12.5	11.9	10.3
Mexican	28.9	26.7	31.1	40.8	41.7	40.8	18.5	20.5	18.3	11.8	11.1	9.8
Not Hispanic or Latino	15.4	13.9	15.4	46.7	46.8	47.6	24.0	25.2	23.7	13.9	14.0	13.2
White only	14.7	13.1	15.0	46.6	46.7	46.9	24.4	25.7	24.2	14.3	14.6	13.9
Black or African American only	16.9	16.0	15.7	46.1	47.5	49.5	23.1	23.6	23.4	13.8	12.9	11.4
Hispanic origin and race and percent of poverty level[b, c, d]												
Hispanic or Latino:												
Below 100%	30.2	28.1	32.8	34.8	37.4	35.3	19.9	19.8	19.2	15.0	14.7	12.7
100%–less than 200%	28.7	27.8	29.9	39.7	39.0	42.0	20.4	22.2	19.3	11.2	11.1	8.8
200% or more	18.9	19.4	22.2	48.8	47.1	47.4	20.4	22.7	20.4	11.9	10.8	10.1
Not Hispanic or Latino:												
White only:												
Below 100%	17.0	16.6	16.3	38.3	36.4	38.7	23.9	27.4	24.2	20.9	19.7	20.8
100%–less than 200%	17.3	17.6	18.8	44.1	42.2	43.7	22.2	23.2	22.2	16.3	17.0	15.4
200% or more	13.8	11.8	14.0	48.2	48.7	48.6	24.9	26.0	24.6	13.1	13.6	12.7
Black or African American only:												
Below 100%	17.4	17.9	18.1	38.5	40.2	45.0	23.4	24.5	21.9	20.7	17.4	15.0
100%–less than 200%	18.8	16.2	17.9	43.7	47.1	45.5	22.9	24.0	24.2	14.5	12.7	12.5
200% or more	15.6	15.2	13.5	51.7	50.4	53.6	22.7	23.4	23.5	10.0	11.0	9.3
Health insurance status prior to interview[e, f]												
Under 65 years:												
Insured continuously all 12 months	14.1	12.4	14.3	49.2	50.1	50.8	23.6	24.5	23.1	13.0	12.9	11.9
Uninsured for any period up to 12 months	18.9	18.9	19.1	46.0	45.1	46.3	20.8	22.1	20.9	14.4	13.8	13.7
Uninsured more than 12 months	39.0	43.6	45.6	41.4	40.1	40.2	13.2	12.1	9.6	6.4	4.2	4.5

*Estimates are considered unreliable.

—Data not available.

[a]This table presents a summary measure of health care visits to doctor offices, emergency departments, and home visits during a 12-month period.

[b]Estimates are age-adjusted to the year 2000 standard population using six age groups: Under 18 years, 18–44 years, 45–54 years, 55–64 years, 65–74 years, and 75 years and over.

[c]The race groups, white, black, American Indian or Alaska Native, Asian, Native Hawaiian or other Pacific Islander, and 2 or more races, include persons of Hispanic and non-Hispanic origin. Persons of Hispanic origin may be of any race. Starting with 1999 data, race-specific estimates are tabulated according to the 1997 Revisions to the Standards for the Classification of Federal Data on Race and Ethnicity and are not strictly comparable with estimates for earlier years. The five single-race categories plus multiple-race categories shown in the table conform to the 1997 Standards. Starting with 1999 data, race-specific estimates are for persons who reported only one racial group; the category 2 or more races includes persons who reported more than one racial group. Prior to 1999, data were tabulated according to the 1977 Standards with four racial groups and the Asian only category included Native Hawaiian or other Pacific Islander. Estimates for single-race categories prior to 1999 included persons who reported one race or, if they reported more than one race, identified one race as best representing their race. Starting with 2003 data, race responses of other race and unspecified multiple race were treated as missing, and then race was imputed if these were the only race responses. Almost all persons with a race response of other race were of Hispanic origin.

[d]Percent of poverty level is based on family income and family size and composition using U.S. Census Bureau poverty thresholds. Missing family income data were imputed for 24%–29% of persons in 1997–1998 and 31%–34% in 1999–2006.

[e]Estimates for persons under 65 years of age are age-adjusted to the year 2000 standard population using four age groups: Under 18 years, 18–44 years, 45–54 years, and 55–64 years of age.

[f]Health insurance categories are mutually exclusive. Persons who reported both Medicaid and private coverage are classified as having private coverage. Starting with 1997 data, state-sponsored health plan coverage is included as Medicaid coverage. Starting with 1999 data, coverage by the State Children's Health Insurance Program (SCHIP) is included as Medicaid coverage. In addition to private and Medicaid, the insured category also includes military plans, other government-sponsored health plans, and Medicare, not shown separately. Persons not covered by private insurance, Medicaid, SCHIP, state-sponsored or other government-sponsored health plans (starting in 1997), Medicare, or military plans are considered to have no health insurance coverage. Persons with only Indian Health Service coverage are considered to have no health insurance coverage.

Note: In 1997, the National Health Interview Survey questionnaire was redesigned.

SOURCE: Adapted from "Table 83. Health Care Visits to Doctor Offices, Emergency Departments, and Home Visits within the Past 12 Months, by Selected Characteristics: United States, 1997, 2005, and 2006," in *Health, United States, 2008. With Chartbook*, U.S. Department of Health and Human Services, Centers for Disease Control and Prevention, National Center for Health Statistics, 2009, http://www.cdc.gov/nchs/data/hus/hus08.pdf (accessed December 14, 2009)

"Births: Final Data for 2006" (*National Vital Statistics Reports*, vol. 57, no. 7, January 7, 2009), in 2006 women of Mexican origin had the highest fertility rate (109) among Hispanics, followed by women of Central and South American origin (98.6), women of Puerto Rican origin (74), and women of Cuban origin (49.3).

TABLE 6.6

Prenatal care for live births, according to detailed race and Hispanic origin of mother, selected years 1970–2000, and selected states, 2004–05

[Data are based on birth certificates]

Prenatal care, race, and Hispanic origin of mother	1970	1980	1990	2000	37 states, DC, and NYC		7 states	
					2004[a]	2005[a]	2004[b]	2005[b]
					Percent of live births[c]			
Prenatal care began during 1st trimester								
All races	68.0	76.3	75.8	83.2	84.2	83.9	72.9	72.8
White	72.3	79.2	79.2	85.0	85.9	85.5	75.9	75.6
Black or African American	44.2	62.4	60.6	74.3	76.2	76.3	57.8	58.1
American Indian or Alaska Native	38.2	55.8	57.9	69.3	69.5	69.6	58.7	59.5
Asian or Pacific Islander[d]	—	73.7	75.1	84.0	85.3	85.3	69.1	70.0
Hispanic or Latina[e]	—	60.2	60.2	74.4	77.7	77.6	56.5	57.0
Mexican	—	59.6	57.8	72.9	77.5	77.6	53.2	53.3
Puerto Rican	—	55.1	63.5	78.5	79.7	80.1	62.6	63.3
Cuban	—	82.7	84.8	91.7	86.4	86.2	71.2	72.5
Central and South American	—	58.8	61.5	77.6	77.5	76.6	56.6	58.2
Other and unknown Hispanic or Latina	—	66.4	66.4	75.8	76.7	76.9	58.8	59.0
Not Hispanic or Latina:[e]								
White	—	81.2	83.3	88.5	89.0	88.7	78.0	77.8
Black or African American	—	60.8	60.7	74.3	76.3	76.5	58.9	59.3
Prenatal care began during 3rd trimester or no prenatal care								
All races	7.9	5.1	6.1	3.9	3.5	3.5	6.2	6.0
White	6.3	4.3	4.9	3.3	3.0	3.0	5.1	5.0
Black or African American	16.6	8.9	11.3	6.7	5.7	5.7	11.9	11.3
American Indian or Alaska Native	28.9	15.2	12.9	8.6	8.1	8.2	11.2	11.8
Asian or Pacific Islander[d]	—	6.5	5.8	3.3	3.0	3.0	6.8	6.8
Hispanic or Latina[e]	—	12.0	12.0	6.3	5.2	5.1	11.0	10.8
Mexican	—	11.8	13.2	6.9	5.3	5.0	12.7	12.4
Puerto Rican	—	16.2	10.6	4.5	4.0	4.1	8.5	7.8
Cuban	—	3.9	2.8	1.4	2.8	2.5	*6.5	*5.2
Central and South American	—	13.1	10.9	5.4	5.1	5.6	9.4	9.7
Other and unknown Hispanic or Latina	—	9.2	8.5	5.9	6.0	5.6	11.4	11.3
Not Hispanic or Latina:[e]								
White	—	3.5	3.4	2.3	2.1	2.2	4.5	4.4
Black or African American	—	9.7	11.2	6.7	5.7	5.6	11.4	10.8

—Data not available.

[a]Data for 2004 and 2005 include the 39 reporting areas (37 states, DC, and NYC) that used the 1989 revision of the U.S. Standard Certificate of Live Birth in 2005. Reporting areas that have adopted the 2003 revision of the U.S. Standard Certificate of Live Birth are excluded because prenatal care data based on the 2003 revision are not comparable with data based on the 1989 and earlier revisions of the U.S. Standard Certificate of Live Birth.

[b]Data for 2004 and 2005 include the 7 reporting areas that adopted the 2003 revision of the U.S. Standard Certificate of Live Birth in 2004. Reporting areas that used the 1989 revision of the U.S. Standard Certificate of Live Birth are excluded because prenatal care data based on the 2003 revision are not comparable with data based on the 1989 or earlier revisions.

[c]Excludes live births where trimester when prenatal care began is unknown.

[d]Starting with 2003 data, estimates are not available for Asian or Pacific Islander subgroups during the transition from single-race to multiple-race reporting.

[e]Prior to 1993, data from states lacking an Hispanic-origin item on the birth certificate were excluded. Data for non-Hispanic white and non-Hispanic black women for years prior to 1989 are not nationally representative and are provided for comparison with Hispanic data.

Notes: Prior to 2003, all data are based on the 1989 and earlier revisions of the U.S. Standard Certificate of Live Birth. Data for 1970 and 1975 exclude births that occurred in states not reporting prenatal care. Starting with 2004 data, data for states adopting the 2003 revision of the U.S. Standard Certificate of Live Birth are shown separately. The race groups, white, black, American Indian or Alaska Native, and Asian or Pacific Islander, include persons of Hispanic and non-Hispanic origin. Persons of Hispanic origin may be of any race. Starting with 2003 data, some states reported multiple-race data. The multiple-race data for these states were bridged to the single-race categories of the 1977 Office of Management and Budget standards for comparability with other states. Interpretation of trend data should take into consideration changes in reporting areas and immigration. Data for additional years are available.

SOURCE: "Table 7. Prenatal Care for Live Births, by Detailed Race and Hispanic Origin of Mother, United States, Selected Years, 1970–2000, and Selected States, 2004–2005," in *Health, United States, 2008. With Chartbook*, U.S. Department of Health and Human Services, Centers for Disease Control and Prevention, National Center for Health Statistics, 2009, http://www.cdc.gov/nchs/data/hus/hus08.pdf (accessed December 14, 2009)

Low Birth Weight and Infant Mortality

In "Explaining the 2001–02 Infant Mortality Increase: Data from the Linked Birth/Infant Death Data Set" (*National Vital Statistics Reports*, vol. 53, no. 12, January 24, 2005), Marian F. MacDorman et al. of the CDC explain that moderately low birth weight is defined as being equal to 1,500 to 2,499 grams (3.3 to 5.5 pounds). Very low birth weight is less than 1,500 grams. Low-birth-weight babies,

as well as premature babies (born before 37 weeks of gestation), often suffer serious health problems and encounter developmental problems later in life.

The percentage of babies born with low birth weights increased between 1985 and 2005. According to the CDC, 6.8% of babies born in 1985 weighed less than 2,500 grams, compared with 8.2% of babies born in 2005. (See Table 6.8.) In 2005 non-Hispanic African-Americans

TABLE 6.7

Total births and percentage of births with selected demographic characteristics, by race and Hispanic origin of mother, 2006–07

[Data for 2007 are based on a continuous file of records received from the states. Figures for 2007 are based on weighted data rounded to the nearest individual. Birthrates are live births per 1,000 population in the specific group. Fertility rates are live births per 1,000 women aged 15–44 years in the specific group. Total fertility rates are sums of birthrates for 5-year age groups in the specified group, multiplied by 5.]

Race and Hispanic origin of mother	Number of births		Birthrate		Fertility rate		Total fertility rate		Percent of births to unmarried women	
	2007	2006	2007	2006	2007	2006	2007	2006	2007	2006
All races and origins[a]	4,317,119	4,265,555	14.3	14.2	69.5	68.5	2,122.5	2,100.5	39.7	38.5
Non-Hispanic white[b]	2,312,473	2,308,640	11.5	11.6	60.1	59.5	1,871.0	1,863.5	27.8	26.6
Non-Hispanic black[b]	627,230	617,247	16.4	16.5	71.6	70.6	2,134.5	2,115.0	71.6	70.7
American Indian or Alaska Native total[b, c]	49,284	47,721	15.2	14.9	64.7	63.1	1,860.5	1,829.0	65.2	64.6
Asian or Pacific Islander total[b, c]	254,734	241,045	17.2	16.6	71.4	67.5	2,043.0	1,919.0	16.9	16.5
Hispanic	1,061,970	1,039,077	23.3	23.4	102.1	101.5	2,992.0	2,959.5	51.3	49.9

[a]Includes origin not stated.
[b]Race and Hispanic origin are reported separately on birth certificates. Persons of Hispanic origin may be of any race. Race categories are consistent with the 1977 Office of Management and Budget (OMB) standards. In 2007, 27 states reported multiple-race data. The multiple-race data for these states were bridged to the single-race categories of the 1977 OMB standards for comparability with other states.
[c]Data for persons of Hispanic origin are included for this race group.
[d]Includes all persons of Hispanic origin of any race.

SOURCE: Brady E. Hamilton, Joyce A. Martin, and Stephanie J. Ventura, "Table 1. Total Births and Percentage of Births with Selected Demographic Characteristics, by Race and Hispanic Origin of Mother: United States, Final 2006 and Preliminary 2007," in "Births: Preliminary Data for 2007," *National Vital Statistics Reports*, vol. 57, no. 12, March 18, 2009, http://www.cdc.gov/nchs/data/nvsr/nvsr57/nvsr57_12.pdf (accessed December 2, 2009)

were twice as likely as Hispanics to have low-birth-weight babies. In that year, 14% of non-Hispanic African-American babies were born with low birth weights, whereas 8% of Asian or Pacific Islander babies, 7.4% of Native American or Alaskan Native babies, 7.3% of non-Hispanic white babies, and 6.9% of Hispanic babies were born with low birth weights. The percentage of very low-birth-weight live births also increased during this period, from 1.2% in 1985 to 1.5% in 2005. Again, non-Hispanic African-American mothers (3.3%) faced more than twice the risk of having a very low-birth-weight baby than did all mothers (1.5%).

Marian F. MacDorman and T. J. Mathews report in "Recent Trends in Infant Mortality in the United States" (October 2008, http://www.cdc.gov/nchs/data/databriefs/db09.pdf) that the infant mortality rate (the rate of deaths before one year of age) increased from 6.9 infant deaths per 1,000 live births in 2000 to 7 infant deaths per 1,000 live births in 2002. This increase was due primarily to an increase in the number of births of very low-birth-weight and preterm babies. The rate then decreased to 6.8 infant deaths per 1,000 live births in both 2003 and 2004, before increasing again to 6.9 infant deaths per 1,000 live births in 2005. Even though the infant mortality rate remained stagnant from 2000 to 2005, MacDorman and Mathews report that preliminary data suggest that the infant mortality rate declined to 6.7 infant deaths per 1,000 live births in 2006.

The infant mortality rate is much higher for some groups than for others. As Table 6.9 shows, in 2005 non-Hispanic African-Americans suffered the highest rate of infant mortality, with 13.6 infant deaths per 1,000 live births. This rate was more than double the rate of 5.8 infant deaths per 1,000 live births for non-Hispanic whites. Native Americans or Alaskan Natives also had a relatively high rate of infant deaths, at 8.1 per 1,000 live births. Hispanic women (5.6 deaths per 1,000 live births) and Asian or Pacific Islander women (4.9 deaths per 1,000 live births) had the lowest infant mortality rates. However, Hispanic subgroups varied considerably. Puerto Rican infant mortality rates were quite high at 8.3 per 1,000 live births, whereas Cuban infant mortality rates were quite low, at 4.4 per 1,000 live births. MacDorman and Mathews note that the relatively low infant mortality rates among most Hispanic subgroups remain unexplained.

According to the Pew Hispanic Center, in the fact sheet "Hispanic Health: Divergent and Changing" (January 2002, http://pewhispanic.org/files/factsheets/1.pdf), the connection between low income and low educational attainment and high infant mortality seems to be more complicated than previously thought. Even though Hispanics have a higher rate of poverty and lower educational attainment than do non-Hispanic whites, they have a consistently lower infant mortality rate. Researchers speculate that greater social support, less high-risk behavior, and dietary factors may explain the differences. However, as Hispanic immigrants begin to adopt the lifestyle of the American mainstream, experts worry that the health of this population will decline and the infant mortality rates will rise.

Furthermore, the view of low birth weight as a result of low income and low educational attainment is complicated by other research that shows even professional, middle-class, educated African-American women have a higher risk than their white counterparts of having low-birth-weight babies. Ziba Kashef indicates in "Persistent Peril: Why African American Babies Have the Highest Infant Mortality

TABLE 6.8

Low-birthweight live births, by detailed race, Hispanic origin, and smoking status of mother, selected years 1970–2005

[Data are based on birth certificates]

Birthweight, race and Hispanic origin of mother, and smoking status of mother	1970	1975	1980	1985	1990	1995	2000	2002	2003	2004	2005
					Percent of live births[a]						
Low birthweight (less than 2,500 grams)											
All races	7.93	7.38	6.84	6.75	6.97	7.32	7.57	7.82	7.93	8.08	8.19
White	6.85	6.27	5.72	5.65	5.70	6.22	6.55	6.80	6.94	7.07	7.16
Black or African American	13.90	13.19	12.69	12.65	13.25	13.13	12.99	13.29	13.37	13.44	13.59
American Indian or Alaska Native	7.97	6.41	6.44	5.86	6.11	6.61	6.76	7.23	7.37	7.45	7.36
Asian or Pacific Islander[b]	—	—	6.68	6.16	6.45	6.90	7.31	7.78	7.78	7.89	7.98
Hispanic or Latina[c]	—	—	6.12	6.16	6.06	6.29	6.41	6.55	6.69	6.79	6.88
Mexican	—	—	5.62	5.77	5.55	5.81	6.01	6.16	6.28	6.44	6.49
Puerto Rican	—	—	8.95	8.69	8.99	9.41	9.30	9.68	10.01	9.82	9.92
Cuban	—	—	5.62	6.02	5.67	6.50	6.49	6.50	7.04	7.72	7.64
Central and South American	—	—	5.76	5.68	5.84	6.20	6.34	6.53	6.70	6.70	6.78
Other and unknown Hispanic or Latina	—	—	6.96	6.83	6.87	7.55	7.84	7.87	8.01	7.78	8.27
Not Hispanic or Latina:[c]											
White	—	—	5.69	5.61	5.61	6.20	6.60	6.91	7.04	7.20	7.29
Black or African American	—	—	12.71	12.62	13.32	13.21	13.13	13.39	13.55	13.74	14.02
										7 states	
Cigarette smoker[d]	—	—	—	—	A	A	A	A	A	11.87	12.19
Nonsmoker[d]	—	—	—	—	A	A	A	A	A	7.20	7.34
Very low birthweight (less than 1,500 grams)											
All races	1.17	1.16	1.15	1.21	1.27	1.35	1.43	1.46	1.45	1.48	1.49
White	0.95	0.92	0.90	0.94	0.95	1.06	1.14	1.17	1.17	1.20	1.20
Black or African American	2.40	2.40	2.48	2.71	2.92	2.97	3.07	3.13	3.07	3.07	3.15
American Indian or Alaska Native	0.98	0.95	0.92	1.01	1.01	1.10	1.16	1.28	1.30	1.28	1.17
Asian or Pacific Islander[b]	—	—	0.92	0.85	0.87	0.91	1.05	1.12	1.09	1.14	1.14
Hispanic or Latina[c]	—	—	0.98	1.01	1.03	1.11	1.14	1.17	1.16	1.20	1.20
Mexican	—	—	0.92	0.97	0.92	1.01	1.03	1.06	1.06	1.13	1.12
Puerto Rican	—	—	1.29	1.30	1.62	1.79	1.93	1.96	2.01	1.96	1.87
Cuban	—	—	1.02	1.18	1.20	1.19	1.21	1.15	1.37	1.30	1.50
Central and South American	—	—	0.99	1.01	1.05	1.13	1.20	1.20	1.17	1.19	1.19
Other and unknown Hispanic or Latina	—	—	1.01	0.96	1.09	1.28	1.42	1.44	1.28	1.27	1.36
Not Hispanic or Latina:[c]											
White	—	—	0.87	0.91	0.93	1.04	1.14	1.17	1.18	1.20	1.21
Black or African American	—	—	2.47	2.67	2.93	2.98	3.10	3.15	3.12	3.15	3.27
										7 states	
Cigarette smoker[d]	—	—	—	—	A	A	A	A	A	1.90	1.88
Nonsmoker[d]	—	—	—	—	A	A	A	A	A	1.34	1.35

—Data not available.

[A]Data not shown. Due to a change in reporting, data are not comparable to other years. See footnote d.

*Percents preceded by an asterisk are based on fewer than 50 births in the numerator.

[a]Excludes live births with unknown birthweight. Percent based on live births with known birthweight.

[b]Starting with 2003 data, estimates are not available for Asian or Pacific Islander subgroups during the transition from single-race to multiple-race reporting.

[c]Prior to 1993, data from states lacking an Hispanic-origin item on the birth certificate were excluded. Data for non-Hispanic white and non-Hispanic black women for years prior to 1989 are not nationally representative and are provided for comparison with Hispanic data.

[d]Percent based on live births with known smoking status of mother and known birthweight. Only reporting areas that have adopted the 2003 revision of the U.S. Standard Certificate of Live Birth are shown because maternal tobacco use data based on the 2003 revision are not comparable with data based on the 1989 or earlier revisions to the U.S. Standard Certificate of Live Birth. In addition, California did not require reporting of tobacco use during pregnancy. Data for 2004 and 2005 include the 7 reporting areas (states) that adopted the 2003 revision of the U.S. Standard Certificate of Live Birth in 2004.

Notes: The race groups, white, black, American Indian or Alaska Native, and Asian or Pacific Islander, include persons of Hispanic and non-Hispanic origin. Persons of Hispanic origin may be of any race. Starting with 2003 data, some states reported multiple-race data. The multiple-race data for these states were bridged to the single-race categories of the 1977 Office of Management and Budget standards for comparability with other states. Interpretation of trend data should take into consideration expansion of reporting areas and immigration. Data for additional years are available.

SOURCE: "Table 12. Low Birthweight Live Births, by Detailed Race, Hispanic Origin, and Smoking Status of Mother: United States, Selected Years 1970–2005," in *Health, United States, 2008. With Chartbook*, U.S. Department of Health and Human Services, Centers for Disease Control and Prevention, National Center for Health Statistics, 2009, http://www.cdc.gov/nchs/data/hus/hus08.pdf (accessed December 14, 2009)

Rate in the Developed World" (*RaceWire*, February 2003) that "researchers have found that even when they control for such varied factors as poverty, housing, employment, medical risk, abuse, social support and so on, 90 percent of the differences in birth weight between black and white moms remains unaccounted for." As a result, some experts, such as Paula Braveman of the University of California, San Francisco, in "Racial Disparities at Birth: The Puzzle Persists" (*Issues in Science and Technology*, vol. 24, no. 2, Winter 2008), have begun to look at factors such as chronic emotional stress resulting from living in a racially-biased society to

TABLE 6.9

Infant, neonatal, and postneonatal mortality rates, by detailed race and Hispanic origin of mother, selected years 1983–2005

[Data are based on linked birth and death certificates for infants]

Race and Hispanic origin of mother	1983[a]	1985[a]	1990[a]	1995[b]	2000[b]	2003[b]	2004[b]	2005[b]
	Infant[c] deaths per 1,000 live births							
All mothers	10.9	10.4	8.9	7.6	6.9	6.8	6.8	6.9
White	9.3	8.9	7.3	6.3	5.7	5.7	5.7	5.7
Black or African American	19.2	18.6	16.9	14.6	13.5	13.5	13.2	13.3
American Indian or Alaska Native	15.2	13.1	13.1	9.0	8.3	8.7	8.4	8.1
Asian or Pacific Islander[d]	8.3	7.8	6.6	5.3	4.9	4.8	4.7	4.9
Hispanic or Latina[e, f]	9.5	8.8	7.5	6.3	5.6	5.6	5.5	5.6
Mexican	9.1	8.5	7.2	6.0	5.4	5.5	5.5	5.5
Puerto Rican	12.9	11.2	9.9	8.9	8.2	8.2	7.8	8.3
Cuban	7.5	8.5	7.2	5.3	4.6	4.6	4.6	4.4
Central and South American	8.5	8.0	6.8	5.5	4.6	5.0	4.6	4.7
Other and unknown Hispanic or Latina	10.6	9.5	8.0	7.4	6.9	6.7	6.7	6.4
Not Hispanic or Latina:								
White[f]	9.2	8.6	7.2	6.3	5.7	5.7	5.7	5.8
Black or African American[f]	19.1	18.3	16.9	14.7	13.6	13.6	13.6	13.6
	Neonatal[c] deaths per 1,000 live births							
All mothers	7.1	6.8	5.7	4.9	4.6	4.6	4.5	4.5
White	6.1	5.8	4.6	4.1	3.8	3.9	3.8	3.8
Black or African American	12.5	12.3	11.1	9.6	9.1	9.2	8.9	8.9
American Indian or Alaska Native	7.5	6.1	6.1	4.0	4.4	4.5	4.3	4.0
Asian or Pacific Islander[d]	5.2	4.8	3.9	3.4	3.4	3.4	3.2	3.4
Hispanic or Latina[e, f]	6.2	5.7	4.8	4.1	3.8	3.9	3.8	3.9
Mexican	5.9	5.4	4.5	3.9	3.6	3.8	3.7	3.8
Puerto Rican	8.7	7.6	6.9	6.1	5.8	5.7	5.3	5.9
Cuban	*5.0	6.2	5.3	*3.6	*3.2	3.4	*2.8	*3.1
Central and South American	5.8	5.6	4.4	3.7	3.3	3.6	3.4	3.2
Other and unknown Hispanic or Latina	6.4	5.6	5.0	4.8	4.6	4.7	4.7	4.3
Not Hispanic or Latina:								
White[f]	5.9	5.6	4.5	4.0	3.8	3.8	3.7	3.7
Black or African American[f]	12.0	11.9	11.0	9.6	9.2	9.3	9.1	9.1
	Postneonatal[c] deaths per 1,000 live births							
All mothers	3.8	3.6	3.2	2.6	2.3	2.2	2.3	2.3
White	3.2	3.1	2.7	2.2	1.9	1.9	1.9	2.0
Black or African American	6.7	6.3	5.9	5.0	4.3	4.3	4.3	4.3
American Indian or Alaska Native	7.7	7.0	7.0	5.1	3.9	4.2	4.2	4.0
Asian or Pacific Islander[d]	3.1	2.9	2.7	1.9	1.4	1.4	1.5	1.5
Hispanic or Latina[e, f]	3.3	3.2	2.7	2.1	1.8	1.7	1.7	1.8
Mexican	3.2	3.2	2.7	2.1	1.8	1.7	1.7	1.7
Puerto Rican	4.2	3.5	3.0	2.8	2.4	2.5	2.5	2.4
Cuban	*2.5	*2.3	*1.9	*1.7	*	*	*1.7	*1.4
Central and South American	2.6	2.4	2.4	1.9	1.4	1.4	1.2	1.5
Other and unknown Hispanic or Latina	4.2	3.9	3.0	2.6	2.3	1.9	2.0	2.1
Not Hispanic or Latina:								
White[f]	3.2	3.0	2.7	2.2	1.9	1.9	2.0	2.1
Black or African American[f]	7.0	6.4	5.9	5.0	4.4	4.3	4.5	4.5

explain the poorer birth outcomes of African-American mothers.

DISEASES AND MINORITY POPULATIONS
Cancer

Cancer is the uncontrolled spread of abnormal cells and can lead to death if left unchecked. Cancer incidence varies according to racial and ethnic background. Risk factors such as occupation, use of tobacco and alcohol, sexual and reproductive behaviors, and nutritional and dietary habits influence the development of cancer. Cancer screening, treatment, and mortality rates also vary by race and ethnicity.

African-Americans have both the highest cancer incidence and the highest cancer mortality rates of all racial and ethnic groups, whereas the cancer incidence and mortality rates of other minority groups are relatively low. The Surveillance, Epidemiology, and End Results (SEER) Program of the National Cancer Institute (NCI) is the most authoritative source of information on cancer incidence, mortality, and survival in the United States. M. J. Horner et al. of the NCI report in *SEER Cancer Statistics Review, 1975–2006* (2009, http://seer.cancer.gov/csr/1975_2006/) that the incidence rates of all cancers between 2002 and 2006 were:

- 493.6 per 100,000 African-Americans, down 1.4% annually between 1997 and 2006

- 470.6 per 100,000 non-Hispanic whites, down 0.9% annually between 1997 and 2006

TABLE 6.9

Infant, neonatal, and postneonatal mortality rates, by detailed race and Hispanic origin of mother, selected years 1983–2005

[CONTINUED]

[Data are based on linked birth and death certificates for infants]

Race and Hispanic origin of mother	1983–1985[a, g]	1986–1988[a, g]	1989–1991[a, g]	1995–1997[b, g]	1999–2001[b, g]	2003–2005[b, g]
	Infant[c] deaths per 1,000 live births					
All mothers	10.6	9.8	9.0	7.4	6.9	6.8
White	9.0	8.2	7.4	6.1	5.7	5.7
Black or African American	18.7	17.9	17.1	14.1	13.6	13.3
American Indian or Alaska Native	13.9	13.2	12.6	9.2	9.1	8.4
Asian or Pacific Islander[d]	8.3	7.3	6.6	5.1	4.8	4.8
Hispanic or Latina[e, f]	9.2	8.3	7.5	6.1	5.6	5.6
Mexican	8.8	7.9	7.2	5.9	5.4	5.5
Puerto Rican	12.3	11.1	10.4	8.5	8.4	8.1
Cuban	8.0	7.3	6.2	5.3	4.5	4.5
Central and South American	8.2	7.5	6.6	5.3	4.8	4.8
Other and unknown Hispanic or Latina	9.8	9.0	8.2	7.1	6.7	6.6
Not Hispanic or Latina:						
White[f]	8.8	8.1	7.3	6.1	5.7	5.7
Black or African American[f]	18.5	17.9	17.2	14.2	13.7	13.6
	Neonatal[c] deaths per 1,000 live births					
All mothers	6.9	6.3	5.7	4.8	4.6	4.6
White	5.9	5.2	4.7	4.0	3.8	3.8
Black or African American	12.2	11.7	11.1	9.4	9.2	9.0
American Indian or Alaska Native	6.7	5.9	5.9	4.4	4.5	4.3
Asian or Pacific Islander[d]	5.2	4.5	3.9	3.3	3.2	3.3
Hispanic or Latina[e, f]	6.0	5.3	4.8	4.0	3.8	3.9
Mexican	5.7	5.0	4.5	3.8	3.6	3.8
Puerto Rican	8.3	7.2	7.0	5.7	5.9	5.7
Cuban	5.9	5.3	4.6	3.7	3.1	3.1
Central and South American	5.7	4.9	4.4	3.7	3.3	3.4
Other and unknown Hispanic or Latina	6.1	5.8	5.2	4.6	4.4	4.6
Not Hispanic or Latina:						
White[f]	5.7	5.1	4.6	4.0	3.8	3.7
Black or African American[f]	11.8	11.4	11.1	9.4	9.2	9.2
	Postneonatal[c] deaths per 1,000 live births					
All mothers	3.7	3.5	3.3	2.5	2.3	2.3
White	3.1	3.0	2.7	2.1	1.9	1.9
Black or African American	6.4	6.2	6.0	4.7	4.4	4.3
American Indian or Alaska Native	7.2	7.3	6.7	4.8	4.5	4.1
Asian or Pacific Islander[d]	3.1	2.8	2.6	1.8	1.6	1.5
Hispanic or Latina[e, f]	3.2	3.0	2.7	2.1	1.8	1.7
Mexican	3.2	2.9	2.7	2.1	1.8	1.7
Puerto Rican	4.0	3.9	3.4	2.8	2.5	2.4
Cuban	2.2	2.0	1.6	1.5	1.4	1.4
Central and South American	2.5	2.6	2.2	1.7	1.5	1.4
Other and unknown Hispanic or Latina	3.7	3.2	3.0	2.5	2.3	2.0
Not Hispanic or Latina:						
White[f]	3.1	3.0	2.7	2.2	1.9	2.0
Black or African American[f]	6.7	6.5	6.1	4.8	4.5	4.4

—Data not available.

*Estimates are considered unreliable. Rates preceded by an asterisk are based on fewer than 50 deaths in the numerator. Rates not shown are based on fewer than 20 deaths in the numerator.

[a]Rates based on unweighted birth cohort data.

[b]Rates based on a period file using weighted data.

[c]Infant (under 1 year of age), neonatal (under 28 days), and postneonatal (28 days–11 months).

[d]Starting with 2003 data, estimates are not available for Asian or Pacific Islander subgroups during the transition from single-race to multiple-race reporting.

[e]Persons of Hispanic origin may be of any race.

[f]Prior to 1995, data shown only for states with an Hispanic-origin item on their birth certificates.

[g]Average annual mortality rate.

Notes: The race groups white, black, American Indian or Alaska Native, and Asian or Pacific Islander include persons of Hispanic and non-Hispanic origin. Starting with 2003 data, some states reported multiple-race data. The multiple-race data for these states were bridged to the single-race categories of the 1977 Office of Management and Budget standards for comparability with other states. National linked files do not exist for 1992–1994. Data for additional years are available.

SOURCE: "Table 18. Infant, Neonatal, and Postneonatal Mortality Rates, by Detailed Race and Hispanic Origin of Mother: United States, Selected Years 1983–2005," in *Health, United States, 2008. With Chartbook*, U.S. Department of Health and Human Services, Centers for Disease Control and Prevention, National Center for Health Statistics, 2009, http://www.cdc.gov/nchs/data/hus/hus08.pdf (accessed December 14, 2009)

- 350.6 per 100,000 Hispanics, down 1% annually between 1997 and 2006

- 313.6 per 100,000 Native Americans and Alaskan Natives, down 0.3% annually between 1997 and 2006

- 311.1 per 100,000 Asians and Pacific Islanders, down 0.9% annually between 1997 and 2006 (see Table 6.10)

The mortality rates of all cancers between 2002 and 2006 were:

- 229 per 100,000 African-Americans, down 2% annually between 1997 and 2006

- 185.4 per 100,000 non-Hispanic whites, down 1.2% annually between 1997 and 2006

TABLE 6.10

Cancer incidence rates and trends for the top 15 cancer sites, by race and Hispanic origin, 2002–06

Both sexes

All races	Rate[a]	APC[b]
	2002–2006	1997–2006
All sites	462.9	−1.0*
Prostate[e]	70.6	−1.2
Breast	67.1	−1.9*
Lung and bronchus	63.1	−1.5*
Colon and rectum	49.1	−2.4*
Urinary bladder	21.0	−0.4
Melanoma of the skin	19.6	1.6*
Non-hodgkin lymphoma	19.5	0.1
Kidney and renal pelvis	13.6	2.3*
Corpus and uterus, NOS[e]	12.5	−1.0*
Leukemia	12.2	−0.9*
Pancreas	11.7	0.5
Oral cavity and pharynx	10.4	−1.5*
Thyroid	9.6	5.9*
Stomach	7.9	−1.7*
Ovary[eg]	7.1	−1.8*

White	Rate[a]	APC[b]
	2002–2006	1997–2006
All sites	470.6	−0.9*
Breast	68.7	−2.1*
Prostate[e]	68.5	−1.1
Lung and bronchus	64.4	−1.5*
Colon and rectum	48.6	−2.6*
Melanoma of the skin	22.9	2.1*
Urinary bladder	22.8	−0.3
Non-hodgkin lymphoma	20.4	0.2
Kidney and renal pelvis	14.1	2.4*
Corpus and uterus, NOS[e]	12.9	−1.3*
Leukemia	12.8	−1.0*
Pancreas	11.5	0.6*
Oral cavity and pharynx	10.5	−1.3*
Thyroid	10.1	6.2*
Ovary[eg]	7.4	−1.9*
Brain and ONS[f]	7.1	−0.6

Black	Rate[a]	APC[b]
	2002–2006	1997–2006
All sites	493.6	−1.4*
Prostate[e]	99.6	−2.7*
Lung and bronchus	74.7	−1.8*
Breast	67.4	−0.7*
Colon and rectum	59.9	−1.5*
Pancreas	15.6	−0.2
Kidney and renal pelvis	15.0	1.5
Non-hodgkin lymphoma	14.8	0.3
Urinary bladder	12.8	−0.1
Stomach	12.1	−3.3*
Myeloma	11.7	−0.2
Corpus and uterus, NOS[e]	11.7	1.2
Oral cavity and pharynx	10.5	−2.7*
Leukemia	9.8	−0.7
Liver & IBD[f]	8.2	3.3*
Ovary[eg]	5.8	−1.2

Asian/Pacific Islander	Rate[a]	APC[b]
	2002–2006	1997–2006
All sites	311.1	−0.9*
Breast	48.9	−0.9*
Colon and rectum	40.0	−1.9*
Prostate[e]	39.4	−0.9
Lung and bronchus	38.9	−0.9*
Liver & IBD[f]	14.2	0.1
Stomach	13.4	−3.2*
Non-hodgkin lymphoma	12.9	−0.9
Thyroid	9.4	3.6*
Urinary bladder	9.3	0.1
Corpus and uterus, NOS[e]	9.1	0.6
Pancreas	9.0	−0.1
Oral cavity and pharynx	7.8	−2.0*
Leukemia	7.3	−1.0
Kidney and renal pelvis	6.9	2.2*
Ovary[eg]	5.4	−0.5

American Indian/Alaska Native[c]	Rate[a]	APC[b]
	2002–2006	1997–2006
All sites	313.6	−0.3
Lung and bronchus	44.9	0.6
Colon and rectum	42.3	−1.7
Breast	40.2	1.4
Prostate[e]	33.6	−1.3
Kidney and renal pelvis	17.5	2.7
Stomach	11.2	−4.0
Non-hodgkin lymphoma	10.8	0.5
Liver & IBD[f]	9.9	4.6
Pancreas	9.7	−0.9
Corpus and uterus, NOS[e]	8.8	1.6
Urinary bladder	7.4	—
Oral cavity and pharynx	7.1	−4.3
Leukemia	7.0	2.1
Ovary[eg]	5.9	−2.3
Thyroid	5.8	0.3

Hispanic[d]	Rate[a]	APC[b]
	2002–2006	1997–2006
All sites	350.6	−1.0*
Prostate[e]	58.2	−1.5*
Breast	47.4	−0.9*
Colon and rectum	38.4	−1.4*
Lung and bronchus	32.5	−2.4*
Non-hodgkin lymphoma	16.7	−0.2
Kidney and renal pelvis	13.2	2.0*
Stomach	11.7	−2.3*
Urinary bladder	11.4	0.0
Pancreas	10.6	−0.1
Liver & IBD[f]	10.2	1.9*
Leukemia	9.7	−0.4
Corpus and uterus, NOS[e]	9.5	0.6
Thyroid	8.2	5.2*
Cervix Uteri[e]	6.5	−4.1*
Ovary[eg]	6.1	−1.1

Both sexes

Note: Top 15 cancer sites selected based on 2002–2006 age-adjusted rates for the race/ethnic group.
[a]Incidence data used in calculating the rates are from the 17 SEER areas (San Francisco, Connecticut, Detroit, Hawaii, Iowa, New Mexico, Seattle, Utah, Atlanta, San Jose—Monterey, Los Angeles, Alaska Native Registry, Rural Georgia, California excluding San Francisco/San Jose—Monterey/Los Angeles, Kentucky, Louisiana and New Jersey). Rates are age-adjusted to the 2000 US Std Population (19 age groups—Census P25–1130).
[b]The APC is the Annual Percent Change over the time interval. Incidence data used in calculating the trends are from the 13 SEER areas (San Francisco, Connecticut, Detroit, Hawaii, Iowa, New Mexico, Seattle, Utah, Atlanta, San Jose—Monterey , Los Angeles, Alaska Native Registry and Rural Georgia).
Trends are based on rates age-adjusted to the 2000 US Std Population (19 age groups—Census P25–1130).
[c]Rates for American Indian/Alaska Native are based on the CHSDA (Contract Health Service Delivery Area) counties.
[d]Hispanic is not mutually exclusive from whites, blacks, Asian/Pacific Islanders, and American Indians/Alaska Natives.
[e]Incidence data for Hispanics are based on National Health Information Awards (NHIA) and exclude cases from the Alaska Native Registry. The rates for sex-specific cancer sites are calculated using the population for both sexes combined.
[f]IBD = Intrahepatic Bile Duct. ONS = Other Nervous System.
[g]Ovary excludes borderline cases or histologies 8442, 8451, 8462, 8472, and 8473.
*The APC is significantly different from zero.
—Statistic not shown. Rate based on less than 16 cases for the time interval. Trend based on less than 10 cases for at least one year within the time interval.

SOURCE: M. J. Horner et al., eds., "Table I-23. Age-Adjusted SEER Incidence Rates and Trends for the Top 15 Cancer Sites by Race/Ethnicity," in *SEER Cancer Statistics Review, 1975–2006*, National Cancer Institute, 2009, http://seer.cancer.gov/csr/1975_2006/results_merged/topic_inc_trends.pdf (accessed December 14, 2009)

- 157.8 per 100,000 Native Americans and Alaskan Natives, down 0.5% annually between 1997 and 2006

- 124.7 per 100,000 Hispanics, down 1.6% annually between 1997 and 2006

- 111.8 per 100,000 Asians and Pacific Islanders, down 1.7% annually between 1997 and 2006 (see Table 6.11)

Horner et al. state that more non-Hispanic whites survived five years after diagnosis of invasive cancer than did African-Americans in the 1999 to 2005 period. Nearly seven out of 10 (69.1%) non-Hispanic whites survived five years, compared with only 59.4% of African-Americans. Much of this difference in survival can be attributed to later diagnosis of cancer in African-Americans because of lower screening rates and less access to health care. Among the most diagnosed cancers for all groups in the United States are breast cancer, prostate cancer, lung and bronchus cancer, and colon and rectum cancer. These cancers are examined in more detail in the following sections.

BREAST CANCER. Even though a smaller proportion of African-American women (119.2 per 100,000 females between 2002 and 2006) were diagnosed with breast cancer than were white women (126.6 per 100,000 females between 2002 and 2006), a higher proportion of African-American women (31.7 per 100,000) died of the disease than did white women (22.9 per 100,000). (See Figure 6.3.) For years experts assumed that the difference in mortality rates was due to poor health care and late treatment for African-American women. However, Sue Rochman of the Dr. Susan Love Research Foundation explains in "African American Women and Breast Cancer" (June 29, 2006, http://www.sus anlovemd.com/pdfs/african_american_bc.pdf) that African-American women may be more susceptible to a more deadly form of the

cancer. Tumors from African-American women have been found to contain more actively dividing cells than tumors from white women. The tumor cells in African-American women also lack hormone receptors, which is another indicator of a poor prognosis. After peaking in the early 1990s, the death rate from breast cancer for African-American women showed some improvement by 2006. (See Figure 6.3.)

Hispanics, Asians and Pacific Islanders, and Native Americans and Alaskan Natives are less likely to be diagnosed with breast cancer or to die from breast cancer than either whites or African-Americans. The incidence rates of breast cancer between 2002 and 2006 were 79.7 per 100,000 female Native Americans and Alaskan Natives, 85.8 per 100,000 female Hispanics, and 90.7 per 100,000 female Asians and Pacific Islanders. (See Figure 6.3.) Between 2002 and 2006 the mortality rates of breast cancer were lowest for Asians and Pacific Islanders, at 12.2 per 100,000, despite their higher incidence rate. The mortality rate for Native Americans and Alaskan Natives was highest of the three groups, at 15.7 per 100,000. Figure 6.3 shows the mortality rates of these three groups compared with those of African-American and white women.

PROSTATE CANCER. African-American men have a particularly high incidence of and mortality rate for prostate cancer. In 2006 the prostate cancer incidence rate among African-American men was 232.8 cases per 100,000 population, compared with a rate of only 157.1 cases per 100,000 population among whites. (See Figure 6.4.) In the same year, African-American men had a mortality rate of 51.1 per 100,000 men from prostate cancer, compared with 21.8 deaths per 100,000 white men. Even though the incidence and mortality rates for prostate cancer decreased for both groups between the early 1990s and 2002, the incidence and mortality rates

TABLE 6.11

Cancer mortality rates and trends for the top 15 cancer sites, by race and Hispanic origin, 2002–06

Both sexes

All races	Rate[a]	APC[b]
	2002–2006	1997–2006
All sites	186.9	−1.3*
Lung and bronchus	53.4	−1.1*
Colon and rectum	18.2	−2.7*
Breast	13.8	−2.1*
Pancreas	10.7	0.3*
Prostate[e]	9.8	−3.4*
Leukemia	7.3	−0.9*
Non-hodgkin lymphoma	7.1	−3.2*
Liver & IBD[f]	5.1	2.0*
Ovary[e]	4.9	−0.5*
Esophagus	4.4	0.3*
Urinary bladder	4.3	−0.1
Brain and ONS[f]	4.3	−1.2*
Kidney and renal pelvis	4.1	−0.5*
Stomach	4.0	−3.2*
Myeloma	3.6	−1.2*

White	Rate[a]	APC[b]
	2002–2006	1997–2006
All sites	185.4	−1.2*
Lung and bronchus	53.8	−0.9*
Colon and rectum	17.7	−2.7*
Breast	13.4	−2.2*
Pancreas	10.5	0.4*
Prostate[e]	9.0	−3.2*
Leukemia	7.5	−0.8*
Non-hodgkin lymphoma	7.4	−3.2*
Ovary[e]	5.1	−0.5*
Liver & IBD[f]	4.7	2.1*
Brain and ONS[f]	4.7	−1.1*
Urinary bladder	4.5	0.1
Esophagus	4.4	1.1*
Kidney and renal pelvis	4.2	−0.4
Stomach	3.5	−3.3*
Myeloma	3.4	−1.0*

Black	Rate[a]	APC[b]
	2002–2006	1997–2006
All sites	229.0	−2.0*
Lung and bronchus	59.9	−1.8*
Colon and rectum	25.4	−2.0*
Prostate[e]	20.0	−3.9*
Breast	19.5	−1.6*
Pancreas	13.7	−0.7*
Stomach	7.6	−3.7*
Liver & IBD[f]	6.8	2.0*
Myeloma	6.8	−1.9*
Leukemia	6.4	−1.2*
Esophagus	5.4	−4.4*
Non-hodgkin lymphoma	5.0	−2.8*
Ovary[e]	4.4	−0.7
Corpus and uterus, NOS[e]	4.3	0.5
Kidney and renal pelvis	4.0	−0.8*
Urinary bladder	3.7	−0.9*

Asian/Pacific Islander	Rate[a]	APC[b]
	2002–2006	1997–2006
All sites	111.8	−1.7*
Lung and bronchus	26.2	−1.3*
Colon and rectum	11.6	−2.3*
Liver & IBD[f]	10.3	−1.0
Pancreas	7.4	0.3
Stomach	7.4	−4.0*
Breast	7.0	−0.1
Non-hodgkin lymphoma	4.4	−3.5*
Prostate[e]	4.3	−4.3*
Leukemia	3.8	−1.5*
Ovary[e]	2.8	1.4
Oral cavity and pharynx	2.1	−1.7
Brain and ONS[f]	2.0	0.6
Esophagus	1.8	−2.4
Kidney and renal pelvis	1.7	−1.9
Urinary bladder	1.7	−1.5

American Indian/Alaska Native[c]	Rate	APC[b]
	2002–2006	1997–2006
All sites	157.8	−0.5
Lung and bronchus	39.7	−0.7
Colon and rectum	16.4	−1.8*
Breast	9.9	1.4
Pancreas	8.4	2.7
Liver & IBD[f]	8.3	1.9
Prostate[e]	7.9	−1.0
Stomach	6.7	−2.7
Kidney and renal pelvis	6.3	−0.5
Non-hodgkin lymphoma	4.8	−1.8
Leukemia	4.7	0.2
Esophagus	3.9	2.2
Ovary[e]	3.8	0.4
Myeloma	3.6	−0.5
Oral cavity and pharynx	2.4	−2.0
Brain and ONS[f]	2.0	−1.5

Hispanic[d]	Rate[a]	APC[b]
	2002–2006	1997–2006
All sites	124.7	−1.6*
Lung and bronchus	22.7	−2.1*
Colon and rectum	13.0	−1.6*
Breast	8.6	−2.4*
Pancreas	8.3	0.4
Liver & IBD[f]	7.9	1.4*
Prostate[e]	7.8	−2.9*
Stomach	6.3	−2.8*
Non-hodgkin lymphoma	5.4	−3.6*
Leukemia	4.9	−1.3*
Kidney and renal pelvis	3.6	0.0
Ovary[e]	3.4	0.4
Myeloma	2.9	−1.7*
Brain and ONS[f]	2.8	−1.1*
Urinary bladder	2.4	−0.5
Esophagus	2.3	−1.8*

for African-American men remained substantially higher than for all other races and ethnic groups.

Hispanics, Asians and Pacific Islanders, and Native Americans and Alaskan Natives have lower rates of prostate cancer incidence and lower rates of prostate cancer mortality than do African-Americans or whites. (See Figure 6.4.) The incidence rates of prostate cancer in 2006 were 119.5 per 100,000 Hispanic men, 90.7 per 100,000 Asian and Pacific Islander men, and 75.2 per 100,000 Native American and Alaskan Native men. The mortality rate of prostate cancer

TABLE 6.11

Cancer mortality rates and trends for the top 15 cancer sites, by race and Hispanic origin, 2002–06 [CONTINUED]

Both sexes

Note: Top 15 cancer sites selected based on 2002–2006 age-adjusted rates for the race/ethnic group.
[a]Mortality data used in calculating the rates are analyzed from US mortality files provided by the National Center for Health Statistics, CDC. Rates are age-adjusted to the 2000 US Std Population (19 age groups—Census P25–1130).
[b]The APC is the Annual Percent Change over the time interval. Mortality data used in calculating the trends are analyzed from US mortality files provided by the National Center for Health Statistics, CDC. Trends are based on rates age-adjusted to the 2000 US Std Population (19 age groups—Census P25–1130).
[c]Rates for American Indian/Alaska Native are based on the CHSDA (Contract Health Service Delivery Area) counties.
[d]Hispanic is not mutually exclusive from whites, blacks, Asian/Pacific Islanders, and American Indians/Alaska Natives.
[e]The 2002–2006 Hispanic death rates do not include deaths from the District of Columbia, Minnesota, New Hampshire and North Dakota. The 1997–2006 Hispanic mortality trends do not include deaths from the District of Columbia, Maine, Minnesota, New Hampshire and North Dakota. The rates for sex-specific cancer sites are calculated using the population for both sexes combined.
[f]IBD = Intrahepatic Bile Duct. ONS = Other Nervous System.
*The APC is significantly different from zero.
—Statistic not shown. Rate based on less than 16 cases for the time interval. Trend based on less than 10 cases for at least one year within the time interval.

SOURCE: M. J. Horner et al., eds., "Table I-26. Age-Adjusted U.S. Death Rates and Trends for the Top 15 Cancer Sites by Race/Ethnicity," in *SEER Cancer Statistics Review, 1975–2006*, National Cancer Institute, 2009, http://seer.cancer.gov/csr/1975_2006/results_merged/topic_mor_trends.pdf (accessed December 14, 2009)

was lowest for Asian and Pacific Islander males, at 9.7 per 100,000 men, despite their higher incidence rate. The mortality rates for Hispanic and Native American and Alaskan Native males were much higher at 18.3 per 100,000 and 16.6 per 100,000, respectively.

LUNG AND BRONCHUS CANCER. According to Horner et al., lung cancer is the deadliest cancer in the United States; the five-year survival rate for all races was only 16.3% of those diagnosed between 1999 and 2005. African-Americans have a particularly high incidence of lung cancer and mortality rate compared with other groups. In 2006 the lung cancer incidence rate among African-Americans was 73 cases per 100,000 population, compared with a rate of 60.4 cases per 100,000 whites, 45 cases per 100,000 Native Americans and Alaskan Natives, 39.6 cases per 100,000 Asians and Pacific Islanders, and 27.1 per 100,000 Hispanics. (See Figure 6.5.) Both the incidence and mortality rates for lung cancer decreased between 1997 and 2006, especially for Hispanics and African-Americans; however, the incidence and mortality rates for African-Americans remained substantially higher than for all other races and ethnic groups.

COLON AND RECTUM CANCER. Colon and rectum cancer is the fourth-most frequently diagnosed cancer in the United States after prostate cancer, breast cancer, and lung and bronchus cancer; it is also the second-most deadly. African-Americans are diagnosed more frequently than other groups. In 2006 African-Americans had an incidence of 55.4 cases per 100,000 population, compared with a rate of 45.8 per 100,000 Native Americans and Alaskan Natives, 44.6 per 100,000 whites, 40.5 per 100,000 Asians and Pacific Islanders, and 35.7 per 100,000 Hispanics. (See Figure 6.6.) African-Americans also had the highest mortality rate from colon and rectum cancer, at 24.3 deaths per 100,000, compared with 16.6 deaths per 100,000 whites, 14.5

deaths per 100,000 Native Americans and Alaskan Natives, 12.7 deaths per 100,000 Hispanics, and 11 deaths per 100,000 Asians and Pacific Islanders. Both the incidence and mortality rates of colon and rectum cancer steadily decreased for whites between the mid-1980s and 2006, while the incidence and mortality rates for African-Americans remained relatively constant until 2002, when they began to drop.

Heart Disease and Stroke

Heart disease includes coronary and hypertensive heart diseases and heart failure. According to the HHS, in *National Healthcare Disparities Report, 2008*, each year approximately 16 million Americans suffer from coronary heart disease. About 8.1 million heart attacks occur each year, and 5.3 million Americans have heart failure.

The rates of heart disease vary considerably by race, with higher rates for African-Americans. Along with age, sex, and race, heredity is one of the risk factors for heart disease that cannot be changed. However, because of their higher rates of incidence of heart disease and stroke, African-Americans are encouraged to control other risk factors, including the use of tobacco and alcohol, blood pressure and cholesterol levels, physical activity, weight, and stress.

HIGH BLOOD PRESSURE. Donald Lloyd-Jones et al. explain in *Heart Disease and Stroke Statistics: 2010 Update* (December 17, 2009, http://circ.ahajournals.org/cgi/reprint/CIRCULATIONAHA.109.192667v1) that the prevalence of high blood pressure (hypertension) in both non-Hispanic African-American men and women is significantly higher than in non-Hispanic white men and women, whereas the prevalence of high blood pressure among Mexican-Americans of both sexes is comparable to that in the non-Hispanic white community. Among adults aged 20 years and older, 34.3% of non-Hispanic white males and

FIGURE 6.3

Incidence and death rates, female breast cancer, by race and Hispanic origin, 1975–2006

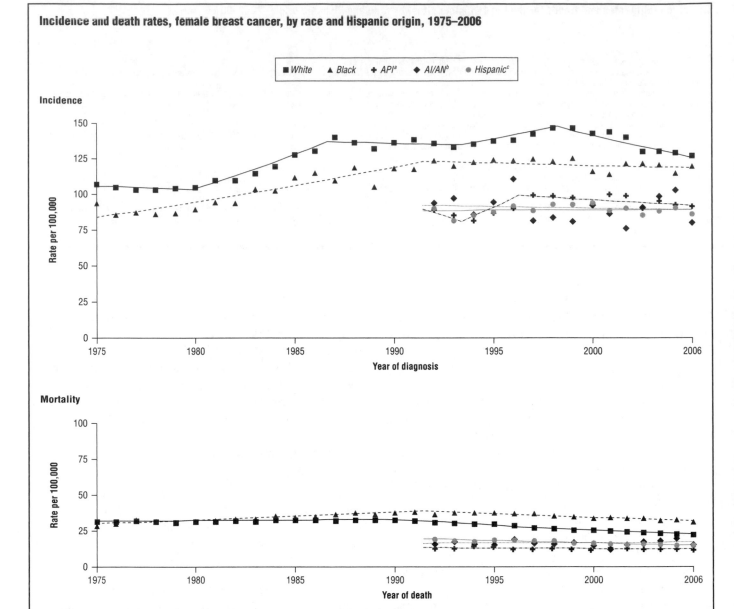

Note: Rates are age-adjusted to the 2000 US Standard Population (19 age groups—Census P25–1103).

[a]Regression lines are calculated using the Joinpoint Regression Program Version 3.3.1, April 2008, National Cancer Institute. Joinpoint analyses for whites and blacks during the 1975–2006 period allow a maximum of 4 joinpoints. Analyses for other ethnic groups during the period 1992–2006 allow a maximum of 2 joinpoints. API = Asian/Pacific Islander.

[b]AI/AN = American Indian/Alaska Native. Rates for American Indian/Alaska Native are based on the CHSDA (Contract Health Service Delivery Area) counties.

[c]Hispanic is not mutually exclusive from whites, blacks, Asian/Pacific Islanders, and American Indians/Alaska Natives. Incidence data for Hispanics are based on National Health Insurance Awards (NHIA) and exclude cases from the Alaska Native Registry. Mortality data for Hispanics exclude cases from Connecticut, the District of Columbia, Maine, Maryland, Minnesota, New Hampshire, New York, North Dakota, Oklahoma, and Vermont.

SOURCE: M. J. Horner et al., eds., "SEER Incidence and U.S. Death Rates: Cancer of the Female Breast," in *SEER Cancer Statistics Review, 1975–2006*, National Cancer Institute, 2009, http://seer.cancer.gov/csr/1975_2006/results_merged/sect_04_breast.pdf (accessed December 14, 2009)

31.1% of non-Hispanic white females had high blood pressure in 2006, and 25.9% of Mexican-American males and 31.6% of Mexican-American females had high blood pressure. However, 43% of non-Hispanic African-American males and 44.8% of non-Hispanic African-American females had high blood pressure in that year. In fact, Lloyd-Jones et al. note that the prevalence of high blood pressure among non-Hispanic African-Americans in the United States is among the highest in the world.

Compared with non-Hispanic whites, non-Hispanic African-Americans develop high blood pressure earlier in life and their average blood pressure is much higher. As a result, non-Hispanic African-Americans had a 1.3 times greater rate of nonfatal stroke, a 1.8 times greater rate of fatal stroke, and a 1.5 times greater rate of death from heart disease than did non-Hispanic whites in 2006. Native American and Alaskan Native adults were slightly less likely than non-Hispanic whites to have high blood

FIGURE 6.4

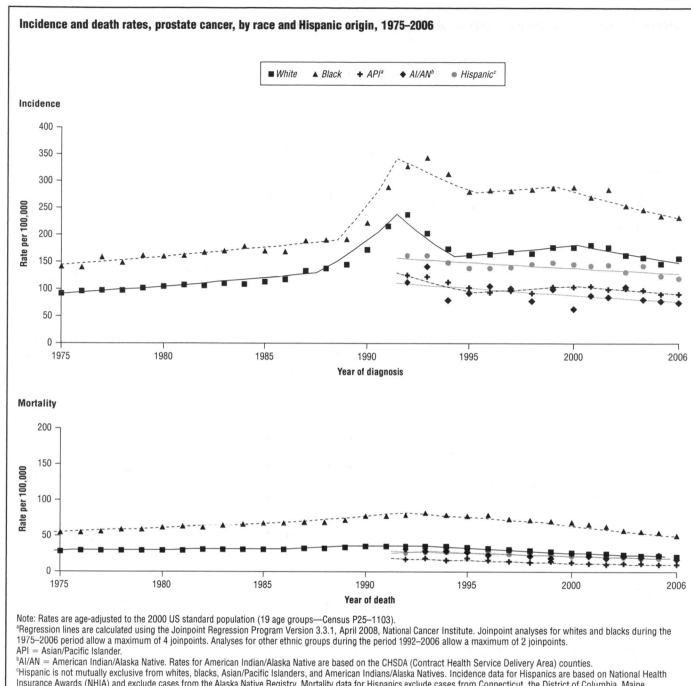

Incidence and death rates, prostate cancer, by race and Hispanic origin, 1975–2006

Legend: ■ White ▲ Black ✛ API[a] ◆ AI/AN[b] ● Hispanic[c]

Note: Rates are age-adjusted to the 2000 US standard population (19 age groups—Census P25–1103).

[a]Regression lines are calculated using the Joinpoint Regression Program Version 3.3.1, April 2008, National Cancer Institute. Joinpoint analyses for whites and blacks during the 1975–2006 period allow a maximum of 4 joinpoints. Analyses for other ethnic groups during the period 1992–2006 allow a maximum of 2 joinpoints. API = Asian/Pacific Islander.

[b]AI/AN = American Indian/Alaska Native. Rates for American Indian/Alaska Native are based on the CHSDA (Contract Health Service Delivery Area) counties.

[c]Hispanic is not mutually exclusive from whites, blacks, Asian/Pacific Islanders, and American Indians/Alaska Natives. Incidence data for Hispanics are based on National Health Insurance Awards (NHIA) and exclude cases from the Alaska Native Registry. Mortality data for Hispanics exclude cases from Connecticut, the District of Columbia, Maine, Maryland, Minnesota, New Hampshire, New York, North Dakota, Oklahoma, and Vermont.

SOURCE: M. J. Horner et al., eds., "SEER Incidence and U.S. Death Rates: Cancer of the Prostate," in *SEER Cancer Statistics Review, 1975–2006*, National Cancer Institute, 2009, http://seer.cancer.gov/csr/1975_2006/results_merged/sect_23_prostate.pdf (accessed December 14, 2009)

pressure (25.3%), whereas Asian-Americans were much less likely to have high blood pressure (21%) than any other race or ethnic group.

DEATHS FROM HEART DISEASE. The NCHS notes in *Health, United States, 2008* (2009, http://www.cdc.gov/nchs/data/hus/hus08.pdf) that the death rate from heart disease was higher for males (when compared with females) among all racial and ethnic groups, but that the rate declined between 1990 and 2005 for all groups.

African-American males had the highest death rate from heart disease in 2005, at 329.8 deaths per 100,000 people, down from 485.4 deaths per 100,000 people in 1990. Hispanic males (192.4), Native American and Alaskan Native males (173.2), and Asian and Pacific Islander males (141.1) all had lower death rates from heart disease than did non-Hispanic white males (262.2).

The NCHS reports that females die of heart disease at high rates as well, although not at the rate that males do.

FIGURE 6.5

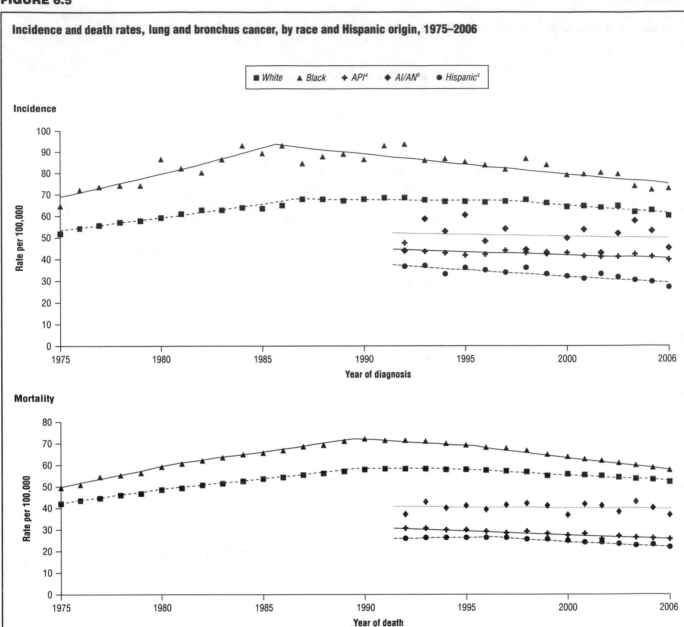

Incidence and death rates, lung and bronchus cancer, by race and Hispanic origin, 1975–2006

■ White ▲ Black + API[a] ◆ AI/AN[b] ● Hispanic[c]

Incidence

Mortality

Note: Rates are age-adjusted to the 2000 US standard population (19 age groups—Census P25–1103).

[a]Regression lines are calculated using the Joinpoint Regression Program Version 3.3.1, April 2008, National Cancer Institute. Joinpoint analyses for whites and blacks during the 1975–2006 period allow a maximum of 4 joinpoints. Analyses for other ethnic groups during the period 1992–2006 allow a maximum of 2 joinpoints. API = Asian/Pacific Islander.

[b]AI/AN = American Indian/Alaska Native. Rates for American Indian/Alaska Native are based on the CHSDA (Contract Health Service Delivery Area) counties.

[c]Hispanic is not mutually exclusive from whites, blacks, Asian/Pacific Islanders, and American Indians/Alaska Natives. Incidence data for Hispanics are based on National Health Insurance Awards (NHIA) and exclude cases from the Alaska Native Registry. Mortality data for Hispanics exclude cases from Connecticut, the District of Columbia, Maine, Maryland, Minnesota, New Hampshire, New York, North Dakota, Oklahoma, and Vermont.

SOURCE: M. J. Horner et al., eds., "SEER Incidence and U.S. Death Rates: Cancer of the Lung and Bronchus, Both Sexes," in *SEER Cancer Statistics Review, 1975–2006*, National Cancer Institute, 2009, http://seer.cancer.gov/csr/1975_2006/results_merged/sect_15_lung_bronchus.pdf (accessed December 14, 2009)

In 2005 African-American females had the highest death rate for heart disease of all racial and ethnic groups, at 228.3 deaths per 100,000 people, down significantly from the 1990 rate of 327.5 deaths per 100,000 people. Non-Hispanic white females had the next highest death rate from heart disease, at 170.3 deaths per 100,000 people. Hispanic females (129.1), Native American and Alaskan Native females (115.9), and Asian and Pacific Islander females (91.9) all had lower death rates from heart disease than did African-American and non-Hispanic white women. The death rates for all females from heart disease had declined since 1990.

Alzheimer's Disease

Alzheimer's disease is a progressive brain disorder that gradually destroys a person's memory and ability to

FIGURE 6.6

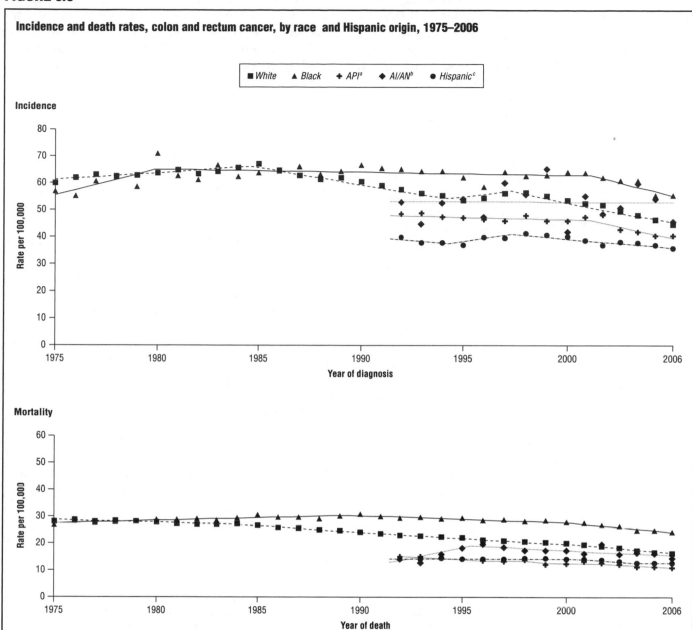

Incidence and death rates, colon and rectum cancer, by race and Hispanic origin, 1975–2006

■ *White*   ▲ *Black*   ✛ *API*[a]   ◆ *AI/AN*[b]   ● *Hispanic*[c]

[a]Regression lines are calculated using the Joinpoint Regression Program Version 3.3.1, April 2008, National Cancer Institute. Joinpoint analyses for whites and blacks during the 1975–2006 period allow a maximum of 4 joinpoints. Analyses for other ethnic groups during the period 1992–2006 allow a maximum of 2 joinpoints. API = Asian/Pacific Islander.
[b]AI/AN = American Indian/Alaska Native. Rates for American Indian/Alaska Native are based on the CHSDA (Contract Health Service Delivery Area) counties.
[c]Hispanic is not mutually exclusive from whites, blacks, Asian/Pacific Islanders, and American Indians/Alaska Natives. Incidence data for Hispanics are based on National Health Insurance Awards (NHIA) and exclude cases from the Alaska Native Registry. Mortality data for Hispanics exclude cases from Connecticut, the District of Columbia, Maine, Maryland, Minnesota, New Hampshire, New York, North Dakota, Oklahoma, and Vermont.

SOURCE: M. J. Horner et al., eds., "SEER Incidence and U.S. Death Rates: Cancer of the Colon and Rectum, Both Sexes," in *SEER Cancer Statistics Review, 1975–2006*, National Cancer Institute, 2009, http:// seer.cancer.gov/csr/1975_2006/results_merged/sect_06_colon_rectum.pdf (accessed December 14, 2009)

reason, communicate, and carry out daily activities. As it progresses, it also tends to affect personality and behavior and may result in anxiety, paranoia, and delusions or hallucinations. The disease can last from three to 20 years, and eventually the loss of brain function will cause death. Even though the underlying causes of Alzheimer's disease remain unclear, some research indicates that minorities, particularly African-Americans, are at a greater risk of developing the disease.

In 1992 scientists first discovered that people with the apolipoprotein E gene (*APOE*-є4; approximately 25% of the total population) have a greater risk for developing the disease. Most early research into the connection between the gene and the development of Alzheimer's concluded that the increased risk associated with the *APOE*-є4 gene applies only to non-Hispanic whites. However, Kathryn Sawyer et al. point out in "Racial Differences in the Influence of the APOE Epsilon 4 Allele on Cognitive

Decline in a Sample of Community-Dwelling Older Adults" (*Gerontology*, vol. 55, no. 1, January 2009) that earlier studies had methodological problems, including racial bias in the assessment of dementia among the elderly, that obscured the link between the gene and the risk factors in minority communities. Contrary to earlier studies, Sawyer et al. find that the allele predicted Alzheimer's in both African-Americans and whites and that those with the gene declined faster than those without the gene.

The Alzheimer's Association emphasizes in *African-Americans and Alzheimer's Disease: The Silent Epidemic* (February 2002, http://www.alz.org/national/documents/report_africanamericanssilentepidemic.pdf) that the prevalence of Alzheimer's disease among African-Americans is estimated to be 14% to 100% higher than among whites. Since the turn of the 21st century, discoveries of risk factors for Alzheimer's disease—high blood pressure and high cholesterol—have begun to provide some explanation for this increased risk, as these risk factors are disproportionately present in the African-American community. The Alzheimer's Association stresses the importance of getting effective medical therapies for vascular disease and its risk factors, as these drugs could potentially protect against Alzheimer's disease as well.

Diabetes

Diabetes is a chronic disease in which the body does not produce or use insulin properly, leading to cells being starved for sugar and often resulting in damage to the heart, kidneys, and eyes. According to the NCHS, in *Health, United States, 2008*, diabetes was the sixth-deadliest disease in the United States in 2005. In fact, the death rate due to diabetes is on the rise at the same time that the death rates due to other diseases such as cancer and heart disease are declining. In "Age-Adjusted Percentage of Civilian, Noninstitutionalized Population with Diagnosed Diabetes, by Race and Sex, United States, 1980–2006" (October 8, 2008, http://www.cdc.gov/diabetes/statistics/prev/national/figraceethsex.htm), the CDC reports that in 2006, 8.4% of African-American males and 9% of African-American females had been diagnosed with diabetes, and 5.4% of white males and 4.9% of white females had diabetes. However, the rates for all groups except for white males had risen since the year before.

Diabetes is a dangerous disease because it can cause many different complications, including heart disease, kidney failure, and loss of circulation in the extremities. The lack of circulation in the lower limbs can lead to infection of small wounds and gangrene, which can eventually require leg amputation. Diabetes requires effective management of hemoglobin A1c and lipids, as well as regular examination of eyes and feet and yearly influenza immunizations. However, the rates of receiving all three diabetic management services vary by race and ethnic group. The HHS explains in *National Healthcare Disparities Report, 2008* that non-Hispanic whites were more likely than either African-Americans or Hispanics to receive the recommended services between 2002 and 2005, although less than a majority of all groups had received the services in the past year. (See Figure 6.7.)

AIDS

The acquired immunodeficiency syndrome (AIDS) is caused by a virus that affects the body's immune system, making it difficult to fight invasions from infection or other foreign substances. As a result, people who have AIDS are subject to a number of opportunistic infections, primarily *Pneumocystis carinii* pneumonia and Kaposi's sarcoma, a form of skin cancer. AIDS, which is caused by the human immunodeficiency virus (HIV), is not transmitted casually, but only through the transfer of bodily fluids, such as blood, semen, and vaginal secretions. The CDC reports in the fact sheet "HIV and Its Transmission" (March 8, 2007, http://www.cdc.gov/hiv/resources/factsheets/transmission.htm) that there are only four methods of transmission: contaminated blood, sexual transmission, contaminated syringes from injection drug use, and perinatal (around the time of birth) transmission from a mother to her child or through breast milk.

Minorities have been especially hard hit by the AIDS epidemic. (See Figure 6.8.) The CDC notes in *HIV/AIDS Surveillance Report, 2007* (February 2009, http://www.cdc.gov/hiv/topics/surveillance/resources/reports/2007report/pdf/2007SurveillanceReport.pdf) that of the estimated 551,932 people living with HIV/AIDS in 34 states and 5 U.S. dependent areas in 2007, 267,116 (48.4%) were African-American, 181,380 (32.9%) were white, and 92,943 (16.8%) were Hispanic. Asians and Native Americans and Alaskan Natives were the least likely groups to be living with HIV/AIDS, at less than 1% (3,160 and 2,281, respectively) each.

In "Pregnancy and Childbirth: HIV/AIDS" (October 10, 2007, http://www.cdc.gov/hiv/topics/perinatal/), the CDC explains that children primarily get HIV in utero from infected mothers. Far more AIDS cases have been diagnosed among African-American children than among children of other racial or ethnic backgrounds. Through 2007, 5,699 cases among African-American children, 1,757 cases among Hispanic children, and 1,602 cases among white children had been diagnosed. (See Table 6.12.) Only 47 cases had been diagnosed among Asian-American children, and only 32 cases had been diagnosed among Native American and Alaskan Native children. The use of antiretroviral drugs has greatly diminished the rate of infection of the children of HIV-positive mothers; the use of these drugs reduces the rate of transmission from 25% to about 2%. The rate of diagnosis among African-American children dropped

FIGURE 6.7

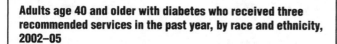

Adults age 40 and older with diabetes who received three recommended services in the past year, by race and ethnicity, 2002–05

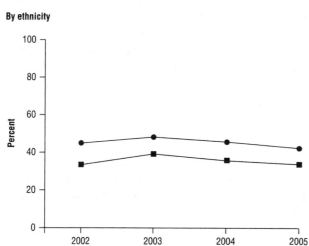

Reference population: Civilian noninstitutionalized population age 40 and over.

Notes: Recommended services for diabetes are: (1) HbA1c (glycated haemoglobin) testing, (2) retinal eye examination, and (3) foot examination. Data include people with both type 1 and type 2 diabetes.

Rate is age adjusted to the 2000 U.S. standard population. Data were insufficient for this analysis for Native Hawaiians and other Pacific Islanders and for American Indians and Alaska Natives.

SOURCE: Adapted from "Figure 2.8. Composite Measure: Adults Age 40 and over with Diagnosed Diabetes Who Received All Three Recommended Services for Diabetes in the Calendar Year, by Race, Ethnicity, Family Income, and Education, 2002–2005," in *National Healthcare Disparities Report, 2008*, U.S. Department of Health and Human Services, Agency for Healthcare Research and Quality, March 2009, http://www.ahrq.gov/qual/nhdr08/nhdr08.pdf (accessed December 14, 2009)

FIGURE 6.8

Percentages of persons aged 13 years and older living with HIV/AIDS and population, by race and Hispanic origin, 2007

[34 States with confidential name-based HIV infection reporting]

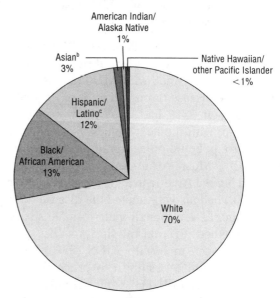

Note: Reported case counts have been adjusted for reporting delays.

[a]Includes 4,770 persons of unknown race or multiple races.

[b]Includes Asian/Pacific Islander legacy cases.

[c]Hispanics/Latinos can be of any race.

SOURCE: "Percentages of Persons Aged 13 Years and Older Living with HIV/AIDS and Population, by Race/Ethnicity, 2007—34 States with Confidential Name-Based HIV Infection Reporting," in *HIV/AIDS Surveillance Report, 2007*, vol. 19, U.S. Department of Health and Human Services, Centers for Disease Control and Prevention, February 2009, http://www.cdc.gov/hiv/topics/surveillance/resources/reports/2007report/pdf/2007SurveillanceReport.pdf (accessed December 14, 2009)

TABLE 6.12

Estimated numbers of AIDS cases in children less than 13 years of age, by year of diagnosis and race and Hispanic origin, 2003–07

	Year of diagnosis					
	2003	2004	2005	2006	2007	Cumulative[a]
Race/ethnicity						
American Indian/Alaska Native	0	1	0	0	0	32
Asian[b]	0	0	1	1	0	47
Black/African American	49	34	39	29	21	5,699
Hispanic/Latino[c]	10	9	9	4	2	1,757
Native Hawaiian/other Pacific Islander	0	1	0	0	0	7
White	12	8	4	3	5	1,602
Total[d]	**73**	**55**	**54**	**38**	**28**	**9,209[e]**

Note: These numbers do not represent reported case counts. Rather, these numbers are point estimates, which result from adjustments of reported case counts. The reported case counts have been adjusted for reporting delays, but not for incomplete reporting.
[a]From the beginning of the epidemic through 2007.
[b]Includes Asian/Pacific Islander legacy cases.
[c]Hispanics/Latinos can be of any race.
[d]Includes children of unknown race or multiple races. Because column totals were calculated independently of the values for the subpopulations, the values in each column may not sum to the column total.
[e]Includes 64 children of unknown race or multiple races.

SOURCE: "Table 5. Estimated Numbers of AIDS Cases in Children <13 Years of Age, by Year of Diagnosis and Race/Ethnicity, 2003–2007 and Cumulative—50 States and the District of Columbia," in *HIV/AIDS Surveillance Report, 2007*, vol. 19, U.S. Department of Health and Human Services,Centers for Disease Control and Prevention, February 2009, http://www.cdc.gov/hiv/topics/surveillance/resources/reports/2007report/pdf/2007SurveillanceReport.pdf (accessed December 14, 2009)

from 49 cases in 2003 to 21 in 2007—a decrease of 57%. Cases among Hispanic children fell from 10 in 2003 to 2 in 2007, and cases among non-Hispanic white children fell from 12 in 2003 to 5 in 2007. The dramatic decrease in the number of AIDS cases in children is shown in Figure 6.9.

The methods of transmission of HIV among the adolescent and adult population differ considerably by race. By 2007 white men with AIDS had overwhelmingly contracted the disease through homosexual (male-to-male sexual) contact; 73% had done so over the course of the epidemic, with the next-highest transmission method for this group being injection drug use, at 9%. (See Table 6.13.) Most Asian-American men with AIDS (67%) and Native American and Alaskan Native men with AIDS (55%) had also contracted the disease through such sexual contact. Even though male-to-male sexual contact was the method of transmission for the plurality of African-American men with AIDS (37%) and Hispanic men with AIDS (44%), a significant proportion of African-American men (29%) and Hispanic men (30%) with AIDS had contracted the disease through injection drug use. In addition, a sizeable portion of African-American men with AIDS had contracted the disease through high-risk heterosexual (male-to-female sexual) contact (11%).

Most women who had contracted AIDS through 2007 had done so through heterosexual contact or injection drug use. White women were about equally likely to have contracted AIDS through heterosexual contact (42%) or injection drug use (40%) as were Native Americans and Alaskan Natives, 42% of whom contracted the disease through heterosexual contact and 40% of whom contracted

the disease through injection drug use. (See Table 6.14.) African-American women were more likely to contract the disease through heterosexual contact (44%) than they were through injection drug use (33%). Hispanic women were also more likely to contract AIDS through heterosexual contact (50%) than through injection drug use (35%). Asian-American women were much more likely to contract AIDS through heterosexual contact (54%) than they were through injection drug use (9%).

African-Americans are extremely overrepresented in new diagnoses of HIV/AIDS each year. However, the disparities in the care that they received earlier in the epidemic seemed to have disappeared by 2003. In *National Healthcare Disparities Report, 2008*, the HHS states that "without adequate treatment, as HIV disease progresses, CD4 cell counts fall and patients become increasingly susceptible to opportunistic infections." The HHS notes that the receipt of antiretroviral therapy (to prevent HIV-infected people from developing AIDS) and drug therapy to prevent *Pneumocystis carinii* pneumonia did not differ significantly by race or ethnicity in 2005.

Sickle-Cell Anemia in African-Americans

In "Facts about Sickle Cell Disease" (February 2010, http://www.cdc.gov/ncbddd/sicklecell/faq_sicklecell.htm), the CDC explains that sickle-cell anemia, a hereditary disease that primarily strikes African-American people in the United States, is a blood disorder in which defective hemoglobin causes red blood cells to become sickle shaped, rather than round. This can create blockages in small arteries and can result in many problems, including chronic anemia, episodes of intense pain, strokes, and

FIGURE 6.9

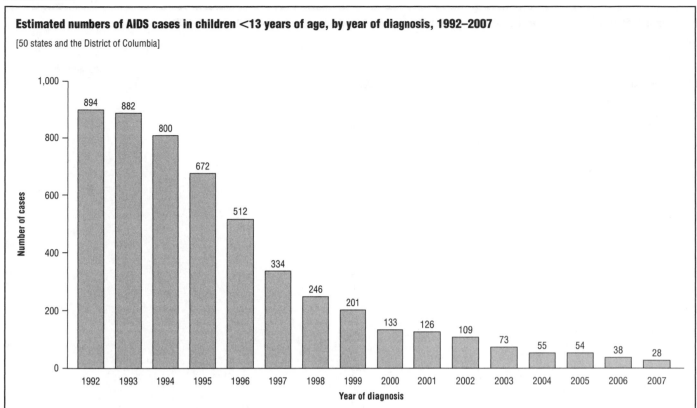

Estimated numbers of AIDS cases in children <13 years of age, by year of diagnosis, 1992–2007

[50 states and the District of Columbia]

Note: These numbers do not represent reported case counts. Rather, these numbers are point estimates, which result from adjustments of reported case counts. The reported case counts have been adjusted for reporting delays, but not for incomplete reporting.

SOURCE: "Figure 1. Estimated Numbers of AIDS Cases in Children <13 Years of Age, by Year of Diagnosis, 1992–2007—50 States and the District of Columbia," in *HIV/AIDS Surveillance Report, 2007*, vol. 19, U.S. Department of Health and Human Services, Centers for Disease Control and Prevention, February 2009, http://www.cdc.gov/hiv/topics/surveillance/resources/reports/2007report/pdf/2007SurveillanceReport.pdf (accessed December 14, 2009)

death. Scientists believe the genetic trait arose randomly in Africa and survived as a defense against malaria. The disease can be inherited only when both parents have the sickle-cell trait and the child inherits the defective gene from both parents. The CDC notes in "Health Care Professionals: Data and Statistics" (February 2010, http://www.cdc.gov/ncbddd/sicklecell/hcp_data.htm) that in 2006 one out of every 12 African-Americans was a carrier for sickle-cell anemia, and about one out of every 500 African-American infants was born with it. Of the more than 70,000 Americans who had sickle-cell anemia in 2006, most were of African descent. More than 1,000 babies are born each year in the United States with the disease.

BEHAVIORS THAT THREATEN HEALTH

Cigarette Smoking

Nicotine is the drug in tobacco that causes addiction; cigarette smoking is the most popular method of taking nicotine in the United States. The National Institutes of Health indicates in the press release "Most Behaviors Preceding Major Causes of Preventable Death Have Begun by Young Adulthood" (January 11, 2006, http://

www.nih.gov/news/pr/jan2006/nichd-11.htm) that tobacco use is the leading cause of preventable death in the United States. According to the CDC, in "Healthy Youth: Tobacco Use" (August 14, 2009, http://www .cdc.gov/HealthyYouth/tobacco/index.htm), each day approximately 3,600 adolescents begin smoking and an estimated 1,100 teens become daily smokers. Smoking during pregnancy causes an increased risk of stillborn, premature birth, low birth weight, and sudden infant death syndrome. The tar in cigarettes increases the user's risk of lung cancer and other bronchial diseases, and the carbon monoxide in the smoke increases the chance of cardiovascular diseases.

In 2008 Native Americans and Alaskan Natives were more likely to smoke than any other group: 48.7% reported smoking in the past month, 55.2% in the past year, and 78.5% had smoked at some point in their lifetime. (See Table 6.15.) Non-Hispanic whites were the next most likely to smoke: 30.4% had smoked within the past month, 36.1% in the past year, and 76.2% in their lifetime. Non-Hispanic African-Americans were slightly more likely to smoke than Hispanics: 28.6% had smoked in the past month, compared with 21.3% of Hispanics; 32.5% had smoked in the past

TABLE 6.13

Male adult/adolescent AIDS cases by exposure category, race and Hispanic origin, reported through 2007

[United States and dependent areas]

Transmission category	2007		Cumulative[a]	
	No.	%	No.	%
American Indian/Alaska Native				
Male-to-male sexual contact	71	54	1,473	55
Injection drug use	18	14	410	15
Male-to-male sexual contact and injection drug use	15	11	477	18
Hemophilia/coagulation disorder	0	0	25	1
High-risk heterosexual contact[b]	6	5	119	4
Sex with injection drug user	1	1	31	1
Sex with person with hemophilia	0	0	0	0
Sex with HIV-infected transfusion recipient	0	0	3	0
Sex with HIV-infected person, risk factor not specified	5	4	85	3
Receipt of blood transfusion, blood components, or tissue	1	1	8	0
Other/risk factor not reported or identified	20	15	171	6
Total	**131**	**100**	**2,683**	**100**
Asian[c]				
Male-to-male sexual contact	216	57	4,154	67
Injection drug use	16	4	299	5
Male-to-male sexual contact and injection drug use	10	3	260	4
Hemophilia/coagulation disorder	1	0	63	1
High-risk heterosexual contact[b]	34	9	378	6
Sex with injection drug user	4	1	49	1
Sex with person with hemophilia	0	0	1	0
Sex with HIV-infected transfusion recipient	2	1	12	0
Sex with HIV-infected person, risk factor not specified	28	7	316	5
Receipt of blood transfusion, blood components, or tissue	4	1	104	2
Other/risk factor not reported or identified	96	25	973	16
Total	**377**	**100**	**6,231**	**100**
Black/African American				
Male-to-male sexual contact	4,497	39	108,134	37
Injection drug use	1,391	12	84,645	29
Male-to-male sexual contact and injection drug use	460	4	22,917	8
Hemophilia/coagulation disorder	9	0	614	0
High-risk heterosexual contact[b]	1,677	15	31,669	11
Sex with injection drug user	149	1	6,949	2
Sex with person with hemophilia	2	0	41	0
Sex with HIV-infected transfusion recipient	11	0	249	0
Sex with HIV-infected person, risk factor not specified	1,515	13	24,430	8
Receipt of blood transfusion, blood components, or tissue	20	0	1,195	0
Other/risk factor not reported or identified	3,497	30	42,527	15
Total	**11,551**	**100**	**291,701**	**100**
Hispanic/Latino[d]				
Male-to-male sexual contact	2,926	48	68,278	44
Injection drug use	903	15	47,344	30
Male-to-male sexual contact and injection drug use	297	5	11,366	7
Hemophilia/coagulation disorder	4	0	468	0
High-risk heterosexual contact[b]	626	10	11,698	8
Sex with injection drug user	67	1	2,489	2
Sex with person with hemophilia	1	0	12	0
Sex with HIV-infected transfusion recipient	8	0	133	0
Sex with HIV-infected person, risk factor not specified	550	9	9,064	6
Receipt of blood transfusion, blood components, or tissue	8	0	663	0
Other/risk factor not reported or identified	1,350	22	15,743	10
Total	**6,114**	**100**	**155,560**	**100**

year, compared with 27.1% of Hispanics; and 58.5% had smoked in their lifetime, compared with 56.4% of Hispanics. Asian-Americans were the least likely to smoke; only 13.9% reported smoking in the past month, 17.6% in the past year, and 38.8% in their lifetime.

The Substance Abuse and Mental Health Services Administration reports in *Results from the 2008 National Survey on Drug Use and Health: Detailed Tables* (September 2009, http://www.drugabusestatistics.samhsa.gov/nsduh/2k8nsduh/2k8Results.pdf) that cigarette smoking is most prevalent among those aged 18 to 25, regardless of race or ethnic group. Among people in this age group, whites are overwhelmingly more likely to smoke than their African-American or Hispanic counterparts. In 2008, 40.6% of 18- to 25-year-old whites smoked, compared with 30% of Hispanics and 26.3% of African-Americans.

Diet and Nutrition

The Healthy Eating Index is computed periodically by the U.S. Department of Agriculture's Center for

TABLE 6.13

[United States and dependent areas]

Transmission category	2007		Cumulative[a]	
	No.	%	No.	%
Native Hawaiian/other Pacific Islander				
Male-to-male sexual contact	39	70	430	76
Injection drug use	2	4	26	5
Male-to-male sexual contact and injection drug use	3	5	29	5
Hemophilia/coagulation disorder	0	0	5	1
High-risk heterosexual contact[b]	1	2	28	5
Sex with injection drug user	0	0	5	1
Sex with person with hemophilia	0	0	0	0
Sex with HIV-infected transfusion recipient	0	0	0	0
Sex with HIV-infected person, risk factor not specified	1	2	23	4
Receipt of blood transfusion, blood components, or tissue	0	0	3	1
Other/risk factor not reported or identified	11	20	42	7
Total	**56**	**100**	**563**	**100**
White				
Male-to-male sexual contact	6,490	66	260,797	73
Injection drug use	737	8	32,425	9
Male-to-male sexual contact and injection drug use	711	7	32,325	9
Hemophilia/coagulation disorder	23	0	4,013	1
High-risk heterosexual contact[b]	417	4	8,260	2
Sex with injection drug user	56	1	2,348	1
Sex with person with hemophilia	1	0	36	0
Sex with HIV-infected transfusion recipient	10	0	183	0
Sex with HIV-infected person, risk factor not specified	350	4	5,693	2
Receipt of blood transfusion, blood components, or tissue	17	0	3,176	1
Other/risk factor not reported or identified	1,410	14	17,302	5
Total	**9,805**	**100**	**358,298**	**100**
Total				
Male-to-male sexual contact	14,383	51	445,645	54
Injection drug use	3,103	11	166,251	20
Male-to-male sexual contact and injection drug use	1,514	5	67,797	8
Hemophilia/coagulation disorder	37	0	5,212	1
High-risk heterosexual contact[b]	2,791	10	52,623	6
Sex with injection drug user	281	1	11,941	1
Sex with person with hemophilia	4	0	90	0
Sex with HIV-infected transfusion recipient	31	0	584	0
Sex with HIV-infected person, risk factor not specified	2,475	9	40,008	5
Receipt of blood transfusion, blood components, or tissue	50	0	5,181	1
Other/risk factor not reported or identified	6,442	23	77,328	9
Total	**28,320**[e]	**100**	**820,037**[f]	**100**

[a]From the beginning of the epidemic through 2007.
[b]Heterosexual contact with a person known to have, or to be at high risk for, HIV infection.
[c]Includes Asian/Pacific Islander legacy cases.
[d]Hispanics/Latinos can be of any race.
[e]Includes 286 males of unknown race or multiple races.
[f]Includes 5,001 males of unknown race or multiple races.

SOURCE: "Table 21. Reported AIDS Cases for Male Adults and Adolescents, by Transmission Category and Race/Ethnicity, 2007 and Cumulative—United States and Dependent Areas," in *HIV/AIDS Surveillance Report, 2007*, vol. 19, U.S. Department of Health and Human Services, Centers for Disease Control and Prevention, February 2009, http://www.cdc.gov/hiv/topics/surveillance/resources/reports/2007report/pdf/2007SurveillanceReport.pdf (accessed December 14, 2009)

Nutrition Policy and Promotion (CNPP). In *Diet Quality of Low-Income and Higher Income Americans in 2003–04 as Measured by the Healthy Eating Index—2005* (December 2008, http://www.cnpp.usda.gov/Publications/NutritionInsights/Insight42.pdf), the CNPP finds that the diet of all Americans is deficient, with the average American scoring a failing grade of 57.5 out of 100. Americans do not eat enough dark green and orange vegetables, legumes, and whole grains, and eat too much sodium and solid fats, alcoholic beverages, and added sugars.

In "Obesity: Halting the Epidemic by Making Health Easier" (2009, http://www.cdc.gov/nccdphp/publications/AAG/pdf/obesity.pdf), the CDC states that "increased food intake, nonhealthful foods, and physical inactivity" by Americans resulted in an "obesity epidemic." Obesity can put people at risk for a variety of obesity-related diseases, including type 2 diabetes, cardiovascular disease, high blood pressure, liver and gallbladder disease, sleep apnea, osteoarthritis, some forms of cancer, and gynecological problems. Even though rates of obesity are high among the entire U.S. population, obesity is more likely among

TABLE 6.14

Female adult/adolescent AIDS cases by exposure category, race and Hispanic origin, reported through 2007

	2007		Cumulative[a]	
Transmission category	No.	%	No.	%
American Indian/Alaska Native				
Injection drug use	8	18	286	40
Hemophilia/coagulation disorder	0	0	3	0
High-risk heterosexual contact[b]	22	50	299	42
Sex with injection drug user	7	16	115	16
Sex with bisexual male	1	2	28	4
Sex with person with hemophilia	0	0	2	0
Sex with HIV-infected transfusion recipient	0	0	6	1
Sex with HIV-infected person, risk factor not specified	14	32	148	21
Receipt of blood transfusion, blood components, or tissue	1	2	18	3
Other/risk factor not reported or identified	13	30	105	15
Total	**44**	**100**	**711**	**100**
Asian[c]				
Injection drug use	2	2	95	9
Hemophilia/coagulation disorder	0	0	7	1
High-risk heterosexual contact[b]	47	53	540	54
Sex with injection drug user	5	6	92	9
Sex with bisexual male	2	2	74	7
Sex with person with hemophilia	0	0	3	0
Sex with HIV-infected transfusion recipient	0	0	18	2
Sex with HIV-infected person, risk factor not specified	40	45	353	35
Receipt of blood transfusion, blood components, or tissue	3	3	87	9
Other/risk factor not reported or identified	36	41	274	27
Total	**88**	**100**	**1,003**	**100**
Black/African American				
Injection drug use	817	13	39,793	33
Hemophilia/coagulation disorder	7	0	149	0
High-risk heterosexual contact[b]	2,928	46	52,928	44
Sex with injection drug user	345	5	13,871	12
Sex with bisexual male	139	2	2,498	2
Sex with person with hemophilia	3	0	122	0
Sex with HIV-infected transfusion recipient	17	0	297	0
Sex with HIV-infected person, risk factor not specified	2,424	38	36,140	30
Receipt of blood transfusion, blood components, or tissue	33	1	1,517	1
Other/risk factor not reported or identified	2,516	40	25,761	21
Total	**6,301**	**100**	**120,148**	**100**
Hispanic/Latino[d]				
Injection drug use	313	18	13,298	35
Hemophilia/coagulation disorder	0	0	68	0
High-risk heterosexual contact[b]	894	52	18,991	50
Sex with injection drug user	152	9	6,705	17
Sex with bisexual male	33	2	857	2
Sex with person with hemophilia	1	0	46	0
Sex with HIV-infected transfusion recipient	3	0	142	0
Sex with HIV-infected person, risk factor not specified	705	41	11,241	29
Receipt of blood transfusion, blood components, or tissue	8	0	613	2
Other/risk factor not reported or identified	490	29	5,370	14
Total	**1,705**	**100**	**38,340**	**100**
Native Hawaiian/other Pacific Islander				
Injection drug use	2	14	22	19
Hemophilia/coagulation disorder	0	0	0	0
High-risk heterosexual contact[b]	8	57	63	54
Sex with injection drug user	1	7	23	20
Sex with bisexual male	1	7	7	6
Sex with person with hemophilia	0	0	1	1
Sex with HIV-infected transfusion recipient	0	0	2	2
Sex with HIV-infected person, risk factor not specified	6	43	30	26
Receipt of blood transfusion, blood components, or tissue	1	7	6	5
Other/risk factor not reported or identified	3	21	25	22
Total	**14**	**100**	**116**	**100**

some groups. The CDC reports in "Differences in Prevalence of Obesity among Black, White, and Hispanic Adults—United States, 2006–2008" (*Morbidity and Mortality Weekly Report*, vol. 58, no. 27, July 17, 2009) that from 2006 to 2008, 35.7% of non-Hispanic African-Americans were obese; non-Hispanic African-American women were particularly likely to be obese (39.2%). Hispanics also had elevated rates of obesity compared with

TABLE 6.14

Female adult/adolescent AIDS cases by exposure category, race and Hispanic origin, reported through 2007 [CONTINUED]

Transmission category	2007 No.	2007 %	Cumulative[a] No.	Cumulative[a] %
White				
Injection drug use	471	28	15,473	40
Hemophilia/coagulation disorder	2	0	125	0
High-risk heterosexual contact[b]	756	45	16,541	42
Sex with injection drug user	188	11	5,839	15
Sex with bisexual male	55	3	1,915	5
Sex with person with hemophilia	6	0	336	1
Sex with HIV-infected transfusion recipient	5	0	344	1
Sex with HIV-infected person, risk factor not specified	502	30	8,107	21
Receipt of blood transfusion, blood components, or tissue	12	1	1,858	5
Other/risk factor not reported or identified	452	27	5,046	13
Total	**1,693**	**100**	**39,043**	**100**
Total				
Injection drug use	1,633	16	69,591	35
Hemophilia/coagulation disorder	9	0	355	0
High-risk heterosexual contact[b]	4,713	47	90,229	45
Sex with injection drug user	704	7	26,825	13
Sex with bisexual male	233	2	5,415	3
Sex with person with hemophilia	10	0	513	0
Sex with HIV-infected transfusion recipient	25	0	819	0
Sex with HIV-infected person, risk factor not specified	3,741	37	56,657	28
Receipt of blood transfusion, blood components, or tissue	59	1	4,134	2
Other/risk factor not reported or identified	3,563	36	36,896	18
Total	**9,977**[e]	**100**	**201,205**[f]	**100**

[a]From the beginning of the epidemic through 2007.
[b]Heterosexual contact with a person known to have, or to be at high risk for, HIV infection.
[c]Includes Asian/Pacific Islander legacy cases.
[d]Hispanics/Latinos can be of any race.
[e]Includes 132 females of unknown race or multiple races.
[f]Includes 1,844 females of unknown race or multiple races.

SOURCE: "Table 23. Reported AIDS Cases for Female Adults and Adolescents, by Transmission Category and Race/Ethnicity, 2007 and Cumulative—United States and Dependent Areas," in *HIV/AIDS Surveillance Report, 2007*, vol. 19, U.S. Department of Health and Human Services, Centers for Disease Control and Prevention, February 2009, http://www.cdc.gov/hiv/topics/surveillance/resources/reports/2007report/pdf/2007SurveillanceReport.pdf (accessed December 14, 2009)

non-Hispanic whites (28.7% and 23.7%, respectively); Hispanic women (29.4%) were more likely than Hispanic men (27.8%) to be obese. Among non-Hispanic whites, men (25.4%) were more likely to be obese than women (21.8%).

One reason that Asians and Pacific Islanders enjoy better health than other racial and ethnic groups is their diet. The typical Asian and Pacific Islander diet is low in fat and cholesterol. The staple food for many Asians and Pacific Islanders is rice. The consumption of vegetables is relatively high, and pork and fish are also commonly eaten. Dairy products are used less frequently in Asian cuisine. The traditional sources of calcium are soybean curd, sardines, and green, leafy vegetables, which are all healthy sources of nutrients. As a result, Patricia M. Barnes, Patricia F. Adams, and Eve Powell-Griner of the CDC note in *Health Characteristics of the Asian Adult Population: United States, 2004–2006* (January 22, 2008, http://www.cdc.gov/nchs/data/ad/ad394.pdf) that from 2004 to 2006, 59.3% of Asian-Americans had a healthy weight, compared with 39.7% of whites, 31.5% of Hispanics, 29.7% of African-Americans, and 28.6% of Native Americans and Alaskan Natives.

Drug Abuse

ALCOHOL. Alcohol depresses the central nervous system. The consumption of small amounts of alcohol can actually have a beneficial effect on the body. However, when consumed in larger amounts, alcohol impairs judgment and increases reaction time, can interfere with prescription and nonprescription medications in adverse ways, and can cause serious damage to developing fetuses. Chronic health consequences of excessive drinking include increased risk of liver cirrhosis, pancreatitis, certain types of cancer, high blood pressure, and psychological disorders. Addiction to alcohol is a chronic disease that is often progressive and sometimes fatal.

In 2008 Asian-Americans, Native Americans and Alaskan Natives, Hispanics, and non-Hispanic African-Americans were all less likely to report having used alcohol in the past month than were non-Hispanic whites. (See Table 6.16.) The rate of binge alcohol use, defined as five or more drinks on one occasion in at least one day in the previous month, was lowest among Asian-Americans (11.9%) and non-Hispanic African-Americans (20.4%). Hispanics (25.6%) and Native Americans and Alaskan

TABLE 6.15

Tobacco product use by age, gender, and race and Hispanic origin, 2007 and 2008

Demographic characteristic	Lifetime (2007)	Lifetime (2008)	Past year (2007)	Past year (2008)	Past month (2007)	Past month (2008)
Total	**69.5**	**69.6**	**34.2**	**33.8**	**28.6**	**28.4**
Age						
12–17	27.8	27.2	19.8	18.9	12.4[a]	11.4
18–25	70.3	70.2	52.3	52.2	41.8	41.4
26 or older	75.0	75.0	33.0	32.5	28.5	28.3
Gender						
Male	77.2	77.0	42.2	41.1	35.2	34.5
Female	62.4	62.6	26.7	26.8	22.4	22.5
Hispanic origin and Race						
Not Hispanic or Latino	71.9	71.8	35.1	34.9	29.6	29.5
White	76.2	76.2	36.5	36.1	30.7	30.4
Black or African American	58.1	58.5	31.2	32.5	26.8	28.6
American Indian or Alaska Native	74.5	78.5	47.9	55.2	41.8	48.7
Native Hawaiian or other Pacific Islander	69.1	*	*	*	*	*
Asian	41.4	38.8	20.2	17.6	15.4	13.9
Two or more races	69.0	75.4	39.6	41.6	35.2	37.3
Hispanic or Latino	55.0	56.4	29.1	27.1	22.7	21.3

*Low precision; no estimate reported.
Notes: Tobacco products include cigarettes, smokeless tobacco (i.e., chewing tobacco or snuff), cigars, or pipe tobacco. Tobacco product use in the past year excludes past year pipe tobacco use, but includes past month pipe tobacco use.
[a]Difference between estimate and 2008 estimate is statistically significant at the 0.05 level.

SOURCE: "Table 2.17B. Tobacco Product Use in Lifetime, Past Year, and Past Month among Persons Aged 12 or Older, by Demographic Characteristics: Percentages, 2007 and 2008," in *Results from the 2008 National Survey on Drug Use and Health: Detailed Tables*, U.S. Department of Health and Human Services, Substance Abuse and Mental Health Services Administration, Office of Applied Studies, September 2009, http://www.oas.samhsa.gov/NSDUH/2K8NSDUH/tabs/Sect2peTabs17to21.pdf (accessed December 14, 2009)

TABLE 6.16

Alcohol use, binge alcohol use, and heavy alcohol use in the past month among persons aged 12 or older, by age, gender, and race and Hispanic origin, 2007 and 2008

Demographic characteristic	Alcohol use (2007)	Alcohol use (2008)	Binge alcohol use (2007)	Binge alcohol use (2008)	Heavy alcohol use (2007)	Heavy alcohol use (2008)
Total	**51.1**	**51.6**	**23.3**	**23.3**	**6.9**	**6.9**
Age						
12–17	15.9[b]	14.6	9.7[b]	8.8	2.3	2.0
18–25	61.2	61.2	41.8	41.0	14.7	14.5
26 or Older	54.1	54.8	21.9	22.1	6.1	6.3
Gender						
Male	56.6	57.7	31.7	31.6	10.6	10.6
Female	46.0	45.9	15.4	15.4	3.3	3.4
Hispanic origin and race						
Not Hispanic or Latino	52.6	53.0	23.3	22.9	7.1	7.1
White	56.1	56.2	24.6	24.0	7.8	7.7
Black or African American	39.3	41.9	19.1	20.4	4.1[a]	5.6
American Indian or Alaska Native	44.7	43.3	28.2	24.4	11.6	5.7
Native Hawaiian or other Pacific Islander	*	*	*	*	*	3.5
Asian	35.2	37.0	12.6	11.9	2.6	2.4
Two or more races	47.5	47.5	23.2	22.0	7.3	7.4
Hispanic or Latino	42.1	43.2	23.4	25.6	5.5	5.7

*Low precision; no estimate reported.
Note: Binge alcohol use is defined as drinking five or more drinks on the same occasion (i.e., at the same time or within a couple of hours of each other) on at least 1 day in the past 30 days. Heavy alcohol use is defined as drinking five or more drinks on the same occasion on each of 5 or more days in the past 30 days; all heavy alcohol users are also binge alcohol users.
[a]Difference between estimate and 2008 estimate is statistically significant at the 0.05 level.
[b]Difference between estimate and 2008 estimate is statistically significant at the 0.01 level.

SOURCE: "Table 2.42B. Alcohol Use, Binge Alcohol Use, and Heavy Alcohol Use in the Past Month among Persons Aged 12 or Older, by Demographic Characteristics: Percentages, 2007 and 2008," in *Results from the 2008 National Survey on Drug Use and Health: Detailed Tables*, U.S. Department of Health and Human Services, Substance Abuse and Mental Health Services Administration, Office of Applied Studies, September 2009, http://www.oas.samhsa.gov/NSDUH/2K8NSDUH/tabs/Sect2peTabs37to46.pdf (accessed December 14, 2009)

Natives (24.4%) had rates comparable to or higher than that of non-Hispanic whites (24%) in 2008. The rates of heavy alcohol use, defined as drinking five or more drinks on each of five or more days in the past 30 days, were highest among non-Hispanic whites (7.7%) and lowest among Asian-Americans (2.4%) in 2008. At the same time, about one out of five non-Hispanic African-Americans (5.6%), Native Americans and Alaskan Natives (5.7%), and Hispanics (5.7%) were heavy alcohol users.

ILLICIT DRUG USE. According to the CDC, illicit drugs include marijuana/hashish, cocaine (including crack), heroin, hallucinogens, inhalants, and any prescription-type psychotherapeutic drug used nonmedically. In 2008 the rate of illicit drug use in the past month was highest for non-Hispanic African-Americans (10.1%) and Native Americans and Alaskan Natives (9.5%), followed closely by non-Hispanic whites (8.2%). (See Table 6.17.) Rates of illicit drug use in the past month were lowest for Asian-Americans (3.6%) and Hispanics (6.2%). Native Americans and Alaskan Natives (19.5%) had the highest rates of illicit drug use in the past year, followed by non-Hispanic African-Americans (16.9%), non-Hispanic whites (14.4%), Hispanics (12.3%), and Asian-Americans (7.4%). Lifetime illicit drug use was also highest among Native Americans and Alaskan Natives (57.6%), followed by non-Hispanic whites (50.7%), non-Hispanic African-Americans (46.1%), Hispanics (36.4%), and Asian-Americans (21.2%).

LIFE EXPECTANCY AND DEATH

Life Expectancy

Women tend to live longer than men, and whites are likely to live longer than African-Americans. When comparing the life expectancies of African-American and white babies, African-American males born in 2006 had the shortest life expectancy of 69.7 years, whereas white females had the longest life expectancy of 80.6 years. (See Figure 6.10.) African-American females had a life expectancy of 76.5 years, and white males had a life expectancy of 75.7 years. The life expectancy of all groups at birth had risen since 1970, especially for African-Americans.

Age-adjusted death rates are measured per 100,000 population in a specified population group. In 2006 African-Americans died at a higher rate than whites (1.3 African-Americans died for every 1 white death). (See Table 6.18.) Native Americans and Alaskan Natives died at a lower rate than did whites (0.8 Native Americans and Alaskan Natives died for every 1 white death), as did Hispanics (0.7 Hispanics died for every 1 non-Hispanic white death) and Asians and Pacific Islanders (0.6 Asians and Pacific Islanders died for every 1 white death.).

Leading Causes of Death

In 2006 heart disease was the leading cause of death among Americans, with 200.2 deaths per 100,000 population. (See Table 6.18.) Cancers (malignant neoplasms) were the second-leading cause of death, with 180.7 deaths

TABLE 6.17

Illicit drug use by age, gender, and race and Hispanic origin, 2007 and 2008

Demographic characteristic	Lifetime (2007)	Lifetime (2008)	Past year (2007)	Past year (2008)	Past month (2007)	Past month (2008)
Total	46.1	47.0	14.4	14.2	8.0	8.0
Age						
12–17	26.2	26.2	18.7	19.0	9.5	9.3
18–25	57.4	56.6	33.2	33.5	19.7	19.6
26 or older	46.8	48.0	10.6	10.3	5.8	5.9
Gender						
Male	50.6	51.3	17.4[b]	16.4	10.4	9.9
Female	41.8	42.9	11.6	12.2	5.8[b]	6.3
Hispanic origin and race						
Not Hispanic or Latino	48.0	48.7	14.8	14.5	8.2	8.3
White	50.3	50.7	14.9	14.4	8.2	8.2
Black or African American	43.1	46.1	16.0	16.9	9.5	10.1
American Indian or Alaska Native	54.6	57.6	18.4	19.5	12.6	9.5
Native Hawaiian or other Pacific Islander	[a]	[a]	13.3	[a]	[a]	7.3
Asian	22.8	21.2	7.2	7.4	4.2	3.6
Two or more races	51.5	56.1	22.1	21.2	11.8	14.7
Hispanic or Latino	34.2	36.4	12.2	12.3	6.6	6.2

[a]Low precision; no estimate reported.
[b]Difference between estimate and 2008 estimate is statistically significant at the 0.05 level.
Note: Illicit drugs include marijuana/hashish, cocaine (including crack), heroin, hallucinogens, inhalants, or prescription-type psychotherapeutics used nonmedically, based on data from original questions not including methamphetamine items added in 2005 and 2006.

SOURCE: "Table 1.19B. Illicit Drug Use in Lifetime, Past Year, and Past Month among Persons Aged 12 or Older, by Demographic Characteristics: Percentages, 2007 and 2008," in *Results from the 2008 National Survey on Drug Use and Health: Detailed Tables,* U.S. Department of Health and Human Services, Substance Abuse and Mental Health Services Administration, Office of Applied Studies, September 2009, http://www.oas.samhsa.gov/NSDUH/2K8NSDUH/tabs/Sect1peTabs19to23.pdf (accessed December 14, 2009)

FIGURE 6.10

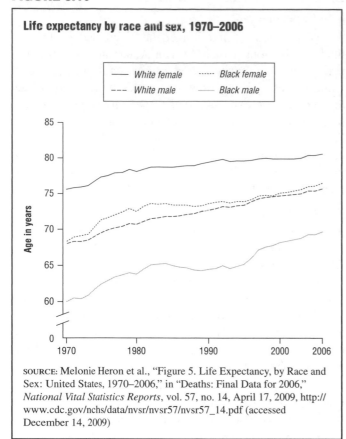

Life expectancy by race and sex, 1970–2006

— White female ······ Black female
--- White male —— Black male

SOURCE: Melonie Heron et al., "Figure 5. Life Expectancy, by Race and Sex: United States, 1970–2006," in "Deaths: Final Data for 2006," *National Vital Statistics Reports*, vol. 57, no. 14, April 17, 2009, http://www.cdc.gov/nchs/data/nvsr/nvsr57/nvsr57_14.pdf (accessed December 14, 2009)

ninth-leading cause of death; and whites, when it was the tenth-leading cause of death. Homicide ranked as the sixth-leading cause of death among African-Americans and the seventh-leading cause of death among Hispanics.

HOMICIDE. The NCHS indicates in *Health, United States, 2008* that homicides are disproportionately high in the African-American population and that the high homicide rate among African-Americans is one of the reasons African-American men in their 20s and 30s have a higher death rate than men this age in other ethnic and racial groups. In 2005, 7,412 African-American males were murdered. The highest rate of death by homicide was among African-American men aged 25 to 34 years (86.2 per 100,000), followed by African-American men aged 15 to 24 (84.1 per 100,000) and African-American men aged 35 to 44 (40.6 per 100,000). In comparison, there were 4.7 homicides per 100,000 non-Hispanic white men aged 15 to 24 and 5.4 deaths per 100,000 non-Hispanic white men aged 25 to 34. After declining to 35.1 deaths per 100,000 in 2004, the death rate by homicide for African-American men rose to 37.3 deaths per 100,000 in 2005.

According to the NCHS, in 2005 Hispanics, like African-Americans, had a higher homicide rate than most other groups, particularly among youth. The homicide rate for Hispanic men aged 15 to 24 was 31 per 100,000 and for Hispanic men aged 25 to 34 it was 22.3 per 100,000. However, between 1990 and 2005 the homicide death rate among all Hispanic men dropped from 27.4 to 12.1 per 100,000, although it rose slightly between 2004 and 2005.

HIV AND AIDS. The difference in the HIV/AIDS death rate among races and ethnic groups is staggering, with a much higher rate among African-Americans than any other group of Americans. In 2007, 7,124 African-Americans died from AIDS, compared with 4,187 whites, 2,312 Hispanics, 84 Asian-Americans, and 70 Native Americans and Alaskan Natives. (See Table 6.19.) In *Health, United States, 2008*, the NCHS reports that the HIV/AIDS death rate for African-American males in 2005 was 28.2 per 100,000, compared with 7.5 per 100,000 Hispanic males, 4 per 100,000 Native American or Alaskan Native males, 3 per 100,000 non-Hispanic white males, and 1 per 100,000 Asian or Pacific Islander males. The death rate for African-American females in 2005 was also extremely high in comparison with other groups, at 12 per 100,000, compared with 1.9 per 100,000 Hispanic females, 1.5 per 100,000 Native American or Alaskan Native females, and 0.6 per 100,000 non-Hispanic white females.

per 100,000 population, followed by cerebrovascular diseases, which caused 43.6 deaths per 100,000 population. Chronic lower respiratory diseases and accidents rounded out the top-five leading causes of death that year, with 40.5 and 39.8 deaths per 100,000 population, respectively.

In *Health, United States, 2008*, the NCHS notes that in 2005 heart disease was the leading cause of death among every racial or ethnic group except for Asians and Pacific Islanders, who died more often from malignant neoplasms. That year, 564,796 whites died of heart disease, accounting for 26.9% of all deaths among whites that year; 74,159 African-Americans (25.3%), 29,555 Hispanics (22.5%), 10,477 Asians or Pacific Islanders (24.2%), and 2,659 Native Americans or Alaskan Natives (19.1%) died of heart disease in 2005. Cancer was the second-leading cause of death among most groups.

Suicide and homicide were responsible for more deaths among some groups than others. The NCHS reports that suicide was particularly high among Native Americans or Alaskan Natives in 2005, when it was the eighth-leading cause of death; Asians or Pacific Islanders, when it was the

TABLE 6.18

Deaths by causes of death, race, Hispanic origin, and sex, 2006

[Crude death rates on an annual basis per 100,00 population age-adjusted rates per 100,00 U.S. standard population. Data for specified races other than white and black should be interpreted with caution because of inconsistencies between reporting race on death certificates and on censuses and surveys.]

Rank[a]	Cause of death	Number	Percent of total deaths	2006 crude death rate	2006	Percent change 2005 to 2006	Male to female	Black[b] to white	AIAN[b, c] to white	API[b, d] to white	Hispanic[e] to non-Hispanic white
									Age-adjusted deathrate — Ratio		
—	All causes	2,426,264	100.0	810.4	776.5	-2.8	1.4	1.3	0.8	0.6	0.7
1	Diseases of heart	631,636	26.0	211.0	200.2	-5.2	1.5	1.3	0.7	0.6	0.7
2	Malignant neoplasms	559,888	23.1	187.0	180.7	-1.7	1.4	1.2	0.7	0.6	0.6
3	Cerebrovascular diseases	137,119	5.7	45.8	43.6	-6.4	1.0	1.5	0.7	0.9	0.8
4	Chronic lower respiratory diseases	124,583	5.1	41.6	40.5	-6.3	1.3	0.7	0.6	0.3	0.4
5	Accidents (unintentional injuries)	121,599	5.0	40.6	39.8	1.8	2.2	0.9	1.4	0.4	0.7
6	Diabetes mellitus	72,449	3.0	24.2	23.3	-5.3	1.4	2.1	1.9	0.7	1.5
7	Alzheimer's disease	72,432	3.0	24.2	22.6	-1.3	0.7	0.8	0.5	0.4	0.6
8	Influenza and pneumonia	56,326	2.3	18.8	17.8	-12.3	1.4	1.1	0.8	0.8	0.8
9	Nephritis nephrotic syndrome and nephrosis	45,344	1.9	15.1	14.5	1.4	1.4	2.3	1.1	0.7	1.0
10	Septicemia	34,234	1.4	11.4	11.0	-1.8	1.2	2.1	1.0	0.5	0.8
11	Intentional self-harm (suicide)	33,300	1.4	11.1	10.9	0.0	4.0	0.4	1.0	0.5	0.4
12	Chronic liver disease and cirrhosis	27,555	1.1	9.2	8.8	-2.2	2.1	0.8	2.4	0.4	1.5
13	Essential hypertension and hypertensive renal disease[a]	23,855	1.0	8.0	7.5	-6.3	1.0	2.7	0.9	0.9	1.0
14	Parkinson's disease	19,566	0.8	6.5	6.3	-1.6	2.2	0.4	0.5	0.5	0.6
15	Assault (homicide)	18,573	0.8	6.2	6.2	1.6	3.9	5.8	2.0	0.8	2.7
—	All other causes (residual)	447,805	18.5	149.6	—	—	—	—	—	—	—

Notes: Race categories are consistent with the 1977 Office of Management and Budget (OMB) standards. Cause-of-death coding changes in 2006 may affect comparability of data between 2006 and previous years for various causes of death.

—Category not applicable.

[a]Based on number of deaths.

[b]Multiple-race data were reported by 25 states and the District of Columbia in 2006. The multiple-race data for these reporting areas were bridged to the single-race categories of the 1977 OMB standards for comparability with other reporting areas.

[c]AIAN is American Indian or Alaska Native, including Aleuts and Eskimos.

[d]Persons of Hispanic origin may be of any race. Data for Hispanic origins should be interpreted with caution because of inconsistencies between reporting Hispanic origin on death certificates and on censuses and surveys.

[e]Cause-of-death title was changed in 2006 to reflect the addition of secondary hypertension.

SOURCE: Melonie Heron et al., "Table B. Percentage of Total Deaths, Death Rates, Age-Adjusted Death Rates for 2006, Percentage Change in Age-Adjusted Death Rates in 2006 from 2005, and Ratio of Age-Adjusted Death Rates by Race and Sex for the 15 Leading Causes of Death for the Total Population in 2006: United States," in "Deaths: Final Data for 2006," *National Vital Statistics Reports*, vol. 57, no. 14, April 17, 2009, http://www.cdc.gov/nchs/data/nvsr/nvsr57/nvsr57_14.pdf (accessed December 14, 2009)

TABLE 6.19

Estimated numbers of deaths of persons with AIDS, by year of death and race and Hispanic origin, 2003–07

Data for 50 states and the District of Columbia	Year of death					
	2003	2004	2005	2006	2007	Cumulative[a]
Race/ethnicity						
American Indian/Alaska Native	75	85	70	79	70	1,792
Asian[b]	73	92	71	99	84	3,114
Black/African American	8,926	8,656	8,546	7,886	7,124	226,879
Hispanic/Latino[c]	2,627	2,601	2,450	2,256	2,312	82,894
Native Hawaiian/other Pacific Islander	5	17	14	4	11	291
White	5,231	4,963	4,933	4,398	4,187	245,127

Note: These numbers do not represent reported death counts. Rather, these numbers are point estimates, which result from adjustments of reported death counts. The reported death counts have been adjusted for reporting delays and missing risk-factor information, but not for incomplete reporting.
[a]From the beginning of the epidemic through 2007.
[b]Includes Asian/Pacific Islander legacy cases.
[c]Hispanics/Latinos can be of any race.

SOURCE: Adapted from "Table 8. Estimated Numbers of Deaths of Persons with AIDS, by Year of Death and Selected Characteristics, 2003–2007 and Cumulative—United States and Dependent Areas," in *HIV/AIDS Surveillance Report, 2007*, vol. 19, U.S. Department of Health and Human Services, Centers for Disease Control and Prevention, February 2009, http://www.cdc.gov/hiv/topics/surveillance/resources/reports/2007report/pdf/2007SurveillanceReport.pdf (accessed December 14, 2009)

CHAPTER 7
CRIME

VICTIMIZATION OF MINORITIES

Certain groups in American society, including the poor, younger people, males, African-Americans, Hispanics, and residents of inner cities, are more likely to be victimized and are more vulnerable to violence than other groups. As discussed in other chapters of this book, African-Americans and Hispanics are more likely to be poor and to be unemployed than are non-Hispanic whites. These factors put minorities at an especially high risk of being victimized.

Violent Crimes

African-Americans are more likely than individuals of other races to be victims of violent crimes. In *Criminal Victimization, 2008* (September 2009, http://bjs.ojp.usdoj .gov/content/pub/pdf/cv08.pdf), Michael R. Rand of the Bureau of Justice Statistics (BJS) reports that in 2008, 25.9 per 1,000 African-Americans were victims of a violent crime, compared with 18.1 per 1,000 whites and 15.2 per 1,000 people of other races. (See Table 7.1.) People who reported they were two or more races had twice the rate of violent victimization as did African-Americans, at 51.6 per 1,000 people. Data on the rate of violent victimization in the Hispanic community were not given in the 2008 report. Interestingly, Rand reports that Hispanics had a lower rate of victimization than non-Hispanics (16.4 per 1,000 people and 19.7 per 1,000 people, respectively), perhaps because African-Americans and people of two or more races were included among the non-Hispanics.

Shannan M. Catalano of the BJS reports in *Criminal Victimization, 2005* (September 2006, http://bjs.ojp.usdoj .gov/content/pub/pdf/cv05.pdf) that even though minorities were particularly likely to be victimized, the rate of violent crimes in each racial and ethnic group declined significantly between 1993 and 2005. The rate of violent crimes committed against Hispanics had dropped 54.7%, the rate of violent crimes committed against African-Americans had dropped 59.9%, and the rate of violent crimes commit-

ted against people of other minority groups had dropped 65.1%. Rand reports that the overall rate of violent crime dropped an additional 8.8% between 2005 and 2008, and this decrease held true for all racial and ethnic groups.

The rates of violent crimes by type of crime show that minorities are more likely than whites to be victims of some types of violent crime and about equally likely to be victims of other types of violent crime. In 2008 African-Americans were about twice as likely as whites to be victims of aggravated assault (5.2 per 1,000 and 3 per 1,000, respectively) and of robbery (5.5 per 1,000 and 1.6 per 1,000, respectively). (See Table 7.1.) The rate of rape and sexual assault was three times higher among African-Americans than among whites (1.9 per 1,000 and 0.6 per 1,000, respectively), although rape and sexual assault data are unreliable because so many of these crimes go unreported. The rates of aggravated assault were also higher among Hispanics than among non-Hispanics (3.5 per 1,000 and 3.3 per 1,000, respectively), as were the rates of robbery (3.4 per 1,000 and 2 per 1,000, respectively). People who reported that they were multiracial were much more likely than any other group to be victims of simple assault (36.1 per 1,000), aggravated assault (6.8 per 1,000), or robbery (6.8 per 1,000).

REPORTING VIOLENT CRIMES. Rand finds that in general African-Americans are more likely to report violent crimes to the police than are Hispanics or whites. In 2008, 50.4% of African-American male victims of violent crimes reported them to police, whereas only 44.1% of white male victims and 44% of Hispanic victims did so. (See Table 7.2.) The contrast is even sharper among females. In 2008, 68.5% of African-American female victims of violent crime reported the crimes to police, compared with 54.1% of Hispanic women and only 47.9% of white women. By contrast, members of minority groups were less likely to report property crimes to the police.

HOMICIDE. African-Americans are also more likely than people of other races to be victims of homicides.

TABLE 7.1

Rates of violent crime, by gender, race, Hispanic origin, and age of victim, 2008

Demographic characteristic of victim	Population	All	Violent victimizations per 1,000 persons age 12 or older				
			Rape/sexual assault	Robbery	All assault	Aggravated assault	Simple assault
Gender							
Male	123,071,020	21.3	0.3^	2.7	18.3	3.9	14.5
Female	129,171,510	17.3	1.3	1.7	14.3	2.8	11.5
Race							
White	204,683,500	18.1	0.6	1.6	15.9	3.0	12.8
Black	30,709,860	25.9	1.9^	5.5	18.5	5.2	13.3
Other race*	13,952,240	15.2	0.9^	3.0^	11.3	2.8	8.5
Two or more races	2,896,930	51.6	1.9^	6.8	42.9	6.8	36.1
Hispanic origin							
Hispanic	34,506,680	16.4	0.6^	3.4	12.4	3.5	8.9
Non-Hispanic	217,351,750	19.7	0.8	2.0	16.9	3.3	13.6
Age							
12–15	16,414,550	42.2	1.6^	5.5	35.2	6.1	29.0
16–19	17,280,270	37.0	2.2	4.8	30.0	5.6	24.5
20–24	20,547,620	37.8	2.1	5.4	30.3	8.7	21.5
25–34	40,649,500	23.4	0.7	2.3	20.5	4.0	16.5
35–49	65,123,030	16.7	0.8	1.9	14.1	2.7	11.4
50–64	55,116,320	10.7	0.2^	0.8	9.7	2.0	7.7
65 or older	37,111,240	3.1	0.2^	0.2^	2.7	0.4^	2.3

Note: Violent crimes measured by the National Crime Victimization Survey (NCVS) include rape, sexual assault, robbery, and aggravated and simple assault. Because the NCVS interviews persons about their victimizations, murder and manslaughter cannot be included.
^Based upon 10 or fewer sample cases.
*Includes American Indians, Alaska Natives, Asians, Native Hawaiians, and other Pacific Islanders.

SOURCE: Michael R. Rand, "Table 4. Rates of Violent Crime, by Gender, Race, Hispanic Origin, and Age of Victim, 2008," in *Criminal Victimization, 2008*, U.S. Department of Justice, Bureau of Justice Statistics, September 2009, http://bjs.ojp.usdoj.gov/content/pub/pdf/cv08.pdf (accessed December 14, 2009)

TABLE 7.2

Crime reported to the police, by gender, race, and Hispanic origin, 2008

Victim gender, race, and Hispanic origin	Percent of crime reported to police, 2008	
	Violent	Property
Total	**47.1%**	**40.3%**
Male	44.2%	41.6%
White	44.1	42.1
Black	50.4	39.4
Other race*	30.7	36.8
Hispanic	44.0%	36.7%
Non-Hispanic	44.3	42.6
Female	50.4%	39.0%
White	47.9	37.1
Black	68.5	48.7
Other race*	46.7	33.7
Hispanic	54.1%	35.4%
Non-Hispanic	50.0	39.7

Note: Total includes estimates for persons identifying with two or more races, not shown separately. Racial categories displayed are for persons who identified with one race.
*Includes American Indians, Alaska Natives, Asians, Native Hawaiians, and other Pacific Islanders.

SOURCE: Michael R. Rand, "Table 8. Crime Reported to the Police, by Gender, Race, and Hispanic Origin, 2008," in *Criminal Victimization, 2008*, U.S. Department of Justice, Bureau of Justice Statistics, September 2009, http://bjs.ojp.usdoj.gov/content/pub/pdf/cv08.pdf (accessed December 14, 2009)

African-American males between the ages of 18 and 24 had the highest homicide victimization rate in the last half of the 20th century and into the 21st century. This proportion rose from 89.8 homicide victims per 100,000 population in 1976 to a high of 183.5 in 1993. (See Table 7.3.) By 2005 the homicide rate for African-American males of that age group had dropped to 102 per 100,000 population. The homicide victimization rate among white men between the ages of 18 and 24 had also risen, from 11.3 homicides per 100,000 population in 1976 to 12.2 homicides per 100,000 in 2005. There was a spike in homicides among young white males in the early 1990s, with the victimization rate topping out at 18.2 in 1991. Among African-American and white women, the homicide victimization rate decreased in all age categories between 1976 and 2005. Nevertheless, African-Americans are overrepresented among homicide victims; in 2008, 47.8% of all homicide victims were African-American, and the majority of them were in their 20s. (See Table 7.4.)

Circumstances surrounding homicides vary from racial group to racial group. African-Americans are overrepresented as both victims and offenders in all types of homicide compared with their presence in the U.S. population as a whole, but they are also overrepresented compared with their already heightened representation among homicide victims in homicides involving drugs. Even though 46.9% of all

TABLE 7.3

Homicide victimization rates per 100,000 population by age, race, and gender, 1976–2005

	White male			Black male			White female			Black female		
	14–17	18–24	25+	14–17	18–24	25+	14–17	18–24	25+	14–17	18–24	25+
1976	3.7	11.3	9.8	24.2	89.8	97.2	2.1	4.2	3.0	6.3	25.1	19.3
1977	4.1	12.5	9.9	22.4	86.9	94.1	2.4	4.4	3.1	8.7	24.5	17.2
1978	4.7	13.3	10.4	21.9	86.4	90.3	2.5	4.4	3.1	7.6	23.7	16.5
1979	4.9	16.0	11.0	23.2	90.9	95.7	2.3	5.2	3.2	7.8	24.0	18.2
1980	5.1	16.2	11.4	26.3	96.7	94.8	2.6	5.3	3.3	6.8	23.5	17.1
1981	4.3	14.9	11.3	23.0	89.7	93.2	2.4	4.9	3.3	6.0	20.4	16.0
1982	4.0	13.9	10.4	22.3	82.6	79.5	1.9	5.2	3.3	7.5	17.7	14.4
1983	3.8	12.7	9.4	21.4	75.0	70.7	2.0	4.2	3.1	5.2	19.4	13.0
1984	3.5	11.9	9.1	18.4	68.0	64.6	2.1	5.1	3.0	6.4	18.2	12.4
1985	3.9	12.1	8.9	23.7	73.3	62.4	1.9	4.2	3.2	7.3	16.5	13.2
1986	4.1	13.3	9.0	26.8	87.9	70.2	2.3	4.7	3.1	6.5	19.7	14.1
1987	3.7	12.3	8.5	36.2	96.4	64.0	2.2	4.6	3.3	7.1	19.6	14.4
1988	3.9	12.3	8.1	43.3	109.5	69.2	2.2	4.5	3.0	7.2	20.8	14.8
1989	5.3	13.4	8.2	54.3	128.3	70.5	2.1	4.4	2.8	8.6	20.0	14.7
1990	7.5	16.7	8.7	59.0	151.0	74.4	2.5	4.0	2.9	10.3	20.5	14.3
1991	8.5	18.2	8.8	71.9	173.7	72.7	2.5	4.6	2.8	9.4	23.4	15.0
1992	9.0	17.4	8.4	67.3	171.8	67.6	2.4	4.4	2.8	12.8	20.8	14.4
1993	9.1	17.2	8.1	76.4	183.5	68.3	2.7	4.3	3.0	12.7	24.1	14.5
1994	8.7	17.8	7.7	71.6	176.2	64.3	2.0	3.8	2.6	10.0	20.7	13.7
1995	8.6	17.3	6.9	63.2	148.9	56.4	2.7	4.2	2.7	11.9	17.1	12.2
1996	7.9	15.4	6.5	52.2	138.2	50.0	2.0	3.3	2.4	8.9	15.4	11.3
1997	5.7	14.5	5.9	42.0	136.5	45.5	1.7	3.5	2.1	7.2	15.4	9.9
1998	5.7	14.5	5.3	32.8	117.4	40.6	1.9	3.4	2.2	5.9	14.3	9.3
1999	5.1	12.5	5.0	31.0	102.4	36.5	1.7	3.4	2.0	5.9	12.9	7.9
2000	4.1	12.1	4.7	25.8	100.6	38.1	1.4	2.9	2.0	4.5	13.5	7.6
2001	3.8	12.9	4.8	26.3	104.0	37.5	1.4	3.2	2.0	3.9	10.1	7.6
2002	3.6	12.7	4.8	22.6	102.5	39.0	1.5	2.9	1.9	6.1	11.8	7.4
2003	3.5	13.0	4.8	24.7	104.8	39.8	1.1	3.2	1.9	3.8	11.9	6.9
2004	4.0	12.0	4.9	25.8	95.6	38.3	1.1	2.9	1.9	3.7	9.7	6.6
2005	4.4	12.2	4.9	26.4	102.0	39.9	1.1	2.5	1.9	4.0	11.3	6.2

SOURCE: James Alan Fox and Marianne W. Zawitz, "Homicide Victimization Rates per 100,000 Population by Age, Race, and Gender," in *Homicide Trends in the United States*, U.S. Department of Justice, Bureau of Justice Statistics, July 2007, http://bjs.ojp.usdoj.gov/content/homicide/homtrnd.cfm (accessed December 29, 2009)

homicide victims between 1976 and 2005 were African-American, they represented 61.6% of all victims of drug-related homicides. (See Table 7.5.) Also, African-Americans are overrepresented as victims among gang-related homicides (39%), sex-related homicides (30.5%), and workplace killings (12.2%). Approximately 50.9% of all victims killed by guns were African-American, whereas only 16.9% of all victims were killed by poison.

Most murders are intraracial (of the same race). In 2008, 3,036 of 3,643 white murder victims, or 83.3%, were murdered by whites. (See Table 7.6.) That same year, 2,722 of 3,024 African-American murder victims, or 90%, were murdered by other African-Americans. A low proportion of African-American perpetrators kill white victims, whereas an even smaller percentage of white perpetrators kill African-Americans.

Property Crimes

According to Rand, people with lower incomes are more likely to be victims of property crime than are people with higher incomes. Because members of most minority groups are disproportionately poor, they are more likely to be victims of property crime. In 2008 the rate of victimization of property crime was 204.2 per 1,000 households with incomes less than $7,500; 175 per 1,000 households with incomes from $7,500 to $14,999; 161.7 per 1,000 households with incomes from $15,000 to $24,999; 150.5 per 1,000 households with incomes from $25,000 to $34,999; 142.7 per 1,000 households with incomes from $35,000 to $49,999; and 125.8 per 1,000 households with incomes of $50,000 to $74,999. Only in the highest income group, households earning $75,000 or more, does the property crime rate go up again, to 133.4 per 1,000 households. This rate was still substantially lower than among the lowest-income households. Those with the lowest incomes are often forced to live in the least safe areas and have the fewest resources with which to protect themselves from crime.

Hate Crimes

The Hate Crime Statistics Act of 1990 required the U.S. attorney general to provide the "acquisition and publication of data about crimes that manifest prejudice based on race, religion, homosexuality or heterosexuality, or ethnicity." The Violent Crime and Law Enforcement Act of 1994 amended the Hate Crime Statistics Act to include crimes motivated by discrimination against people with physical and/or mental disabilities. For an offense to be

TABLE 7.4

Homicide victims by age, sex, and race, 2008

Age	Total	Sex			Race			
		Male	Female	Unknown	White	Black	Other	Unknown
Total	14,180	11,059	3,078	43	6,838	6,782	321	239
Percent distribution[a]	100.0	78.0	21.7	0.3	48.2	47.8	2.3	1.7
Under 18[b]	1,494	1,035	452	7	729	699	40	26
Under 22[b]	3,466	2,750	708	8	1,511	1,842	71	42
18 and over[b]	12,454	9,874	2,573	7	6,015	6,012	276	151
Infant (under 1)	221	113	104	4	145	64	7	5
1 to 4	338	190	146	2	171	143	15	9
5 to 8	70	36	33	1	41	19	5	5
9 to 12	73	40	33	0	39	30	3	1
13 to 16	452	361	91	0	194	248	8	2
17 to 19	1,336	1,158	178	0	539	769	16	12
20 to 24	2,428	2,085	342	1	948	1,420	42	18
25 to 29	2,136	1,797	339	0	859	1,207	44	26
30 to 34	1,610	1,322	288	0	680	863	39	28
35 to 39	1,204	937	267	0	588	568	31	17
40 to 44	1,019	750	263	6	551	427	24	17
45 to 49	971	708	263	0	576	366	17	12
50 to 54	687	509	178	0	415	249	16	7
55 to 59	488	346	142	0	310	153	20	5
60 to 64	288	208	80	0	217	59	8	4
65 to 69	203	130	73	0	141	45	12	5
70 to 74	144	74	70	0	110	25	7	2
75 and over	280	145	135	0	220	56	2	2
Unknown	232	150	53	29	94	71	5	62

[a]Because of rounding, the percentages may not add to 100.0.
[b]Does not include unknown ages.

SOURCE: "Expanded Homicide Data Table 2. Murder Victims by Age, Sex, and Race, 2008," in *Crime in the United States, 2008*, U.S. Department of Justice, Federal Bureau of Investigation, September 2009, http://www.fbi.gov/ucr/cius2008/offenses/expanded_information/data/shrtable_02.html (accessed December 15, 2009)

TABLE 7.5

Homicide type by race, 1976–2005

	Victims			Offenders		
	White	Black	Other	White	Black	Other
All homicides	50.9%	46.9%	2.1%	45.8%	52.2%	2.0%
Victim/offender relationship						
Intimate	56.6%	41.2%	2.2%	54.4%	43.4%	2.2%
Family	60.7%	36.9%	2.4%	59.2%	38.5%	2.3%
Infanticide	55.9%	41.6%	2.5%	55.4%	42.1%	2.5%
Eldercide	69.2%	29.1%	1.6%	54.5%	43.8%	1.6%
Circumstances						
Felony murder	54.7%	42.7%	2.6%	39.1%	59.3%	1.6%
Sex related	66.9%	30.5%	2.5%	54.7%	43.4%	1.9%
Drug related	37.4%	61.6%	.9%	33.9%	65.0%	1.1%
Gang related	57.5%	39.0%	3.5%	54.3%	41.2%	4.4%
Argument	48.6%	49.3%	2.1%	46.8%	51.1%	2.2%
Workplace	84.6%	12.2%	3.2%	70.5%	26.7%	2.8%
Weapon						
Gun homicide	47.2%	50.9%	1.9%	41.9%	56.4%	1.7%
Arson	58.9%	38.1%	2.9%	55.7%	42.0%	2.3%
Poison	80.6%	16.9%	2.5%	79.8%	18.4%	1.8%
Multiple victims or offenders						
Multiple victims	63.4%	33.2%	3.3%	55.7%	40.8%	3.5%
Multiple offenders	54.8%	42.5%	2.7%	44.6%	53.0%	2.4%

SOURCE: James Alan Fox and Marianne W. Zawitz, "Homicide Type by Race, 1976–2005," in *Homicide Trends in the United States*, U.S. Department of Justice, Bureau of Justice Statistics, July 2007, http://bjs.ojp.usdoj.gov/content/homicide/race.cfm (accessed December 29, 2009)

considered a hate crime, the law enforcement investigation must reveal sufficient evidence to lead to the conclusion that the offender's actions were motivated by his or her bias against a certain group. Therefore, data on hate crimes must be considered underreported, as many incidents and offenses motivated by bias go uncounted without sufficient

TABLE 7.6

Race and sex of homicide victims by race and sex of offender, 2008

[Single victim/single offender]

	Total	Race of offender				Sex of offender		
		White	Black	Other	Unknown	Male	Female	Unknown
Race of victim								
White victims	3,643	3,036	504	44	59	3,229	355	59
Black victims	3,024	230	2,722	9	63	2,678	283	63
Other race victims	173	52	29	90	2	154	17	2
Unknown race	100	37	29	3	31	62	7	31
Sex of victim								
Male victims	4,909	2,150	2,563	93	103	4,351	455	103
Female victims	1,931	1,168	692	50	21	1,710	200	21
Unknown sex	100	37	29	3	31	62	7	31

Note: This table is based on incidents where some information about the offender is known by law enforcement; therefore, when the offender age, sex, and race are all reported as unknown, these data are excluded from the table.

SOURCE: "Expanded Homicide Data Table 6. Murder: Race and Sex of Victim by Race and Sex of Offender, 2008," in *Crime in the United States, 2008*, U.S. Department of Justice, Federal Bureau of Investigation, September 2009, http://www.fbi.gov/ucr/cius2008/offenses/expanded_information/data/shrtable_06.html (accessed December 15, 2009)

evidence concerning this motivation. Even though hate crimes can be perpetrated against members of majority groups, most hate crimes are directed at minorities: racial minorities, religious minorities, ethnic minorities, gay and lesbian people, or people with disabilities.

The hate crime data collection program counts one offense for each victim of crimes against people, but only one offense for each distinct crime against property, regardless of the number of victims; therefore, the number of victims is higher than the number of offenses. Of the 9,168 hate-bias offenses reported in 2008, 4,704 were racially motivated and 1,148 were motivated by ethnicity or national origin. (See Table 7.7.) Of the racially motivated offenses, 3,413 were committed against African-Americans and 812 were committed against whites. Another 162 were committed against Asians and Pacific Islanders and 59 were committed against Native Americans and Alaskan Natives. Of the offenses motivated by ethnicity or national origin, 735 were anti-Hispanic and 413 were directed against people of another ethnic minority.

The Intelligence Project (2010, http://www.splcenter.org/intel/map/hate.jsp) of the Southern Poverty Law Center in Montgomery, Alabama, a private organization that monitors hate groups and paramilitary organizations nationwide, reports that there were 926 active hate group chapters in 2008, up from 888 in 2007. These groups included racist groups such as chapters of the Ku Klux Klan, racist skinhead groups (a particularly violent element of the white supremacist movement), neo-Confederate groups (an alliance of southern heritage organizations that claims allegiance to the antebellum South), and others. The project also tracks black separatist groups that typically oppose integration and want separate institutions for African-Americans. Even though the project recognizes that this black racism is in part a response to centuries of white racism, it believes that a criterion for considering a group racist should be applied to all groups regardless of color. In *Terror from the Right: 75 Plots, Conspiracies, and Racist Rampages since Oklahoma City* (August 2009, http://www.splcenter.org/sites/default/files/downloads/publication/terror_from_the_right_0.pdf), the Intelligence Project states that there were 196 neo-Nazi groups, 186 Ku Klux Klan chapters, 113 black separatist groups, 111 white nationalist groups, 93 neo-Confederate groups, 98 racist skinhead groups, 39 Christian identity groups, and 90 other types of hate groups operating nationwide in 2008.

Crime at School

Even though students are less likely to be victimized at school than they are away from school, any crime at school, especially violent crimes, justifiably horrifies students and the community at large. In *Indicators of School Crime and Safety: 2009* (December 2009, http://nces.ed.gov/pubs2010/2010012.pdf), Rachel Dinkes, Jana Kemp, and Katrina Baum state that "any instance of crime or violence at school not only affects the individuals involved but also may disrupt the educational process and affect bystanders, the school itself, and the surrounding community."

Racial and ethnic minorities are disproportionately affected by crimes at school. Rachel Dinkes, Emily Forrest Cataldi, and Wendy Lin-Kelly indicate in *Indicators of School Crime and Safety: 2007* (December 2007, http://nces.ed.gov/pubs2008/2008021.pdf) that all types of crimes (theft, violent, and serious violent) are the most likely to occur in urban, rather than in suburban or rural, schools. In 2005, the most recent year that data on school location were available as of February 2010, the rate of school crime in urban schools was 64 per 1,000 students, whereas the rate in suburban schools was 55 per 1,000 students and the rate in rural schools was 50 per 1,000 students. The rate of

TABLE 7.7

Hate-bias incidents, 2008

Bias motivation	Incidents	Offenses	Victims[a]	Known offenders[b]
Total	7,783	9,168	9,691	6,927
Single-bias Incidents	7,780	9,160	9,683	6,921
Race:	**3,992**	**4,704**	**4,934**	**3,723**
Anti-white	716	812	829	811
Anti-black	2,876	3,413	3,596	2,596
Anti-American Indian/Alaskan Native	54	59	63	61
Anti-Asian/Pacific Islander	137	162	170	140
Anti-multiple races, group	209	258	276	115
Religion:	**1,519**	**1,606**	**1,732**	**632**
Anti-Jewish	1,013	1,055	1,145	353
Anti-Catholic	75	75	89	35
Anti-Protestant	56	60	62	34
Anti-Islamic	105	123	130	85
Anti-other religion	191	212	222	90
Anti-multiple religions, group	65	67	70	33
Anti-atheism/agnosticism/etc.	14	14	14	2
Sexual orientation:	**1,297**	**1,617**	**1,706**	**1,460**
Anti-male homosexual	776	948	981	921
Anti-female homosexual	154	194	198	156
Anti-homosexual	307	415	466	336
Anti-heterosexual	33	33	34	25
Anti-bisexual	27	27	27	22
Ethnicity/National origin:	**894**	**1,148**	**1,226**	**1,034**
Anti-Hispanic	561	735	792	711
Anti-other ethnicity/national origin	333	413	434	323
Disability:	**78**	**85**	**85**	**72**
Anti-physical	22	28	28	26
Anti-mental	56	57	57	46
Multiple-bias incidents[c]	3	8	8	6

[a]The term *victim* may refer to a person, business, institution, or society as a whole.

[b]The term *known offender* does not imply that the identity of the suspect is known, but only that an attribute of the suspect has been identified, which distinguishes him/her from an unknown offender.

[c]In a *multiple-bias incident*, two conditions must be met: (a) more than one offense type must occur in the incident and (b) at least two offense types must be motivated by different biases.

SOURCE: "Table 1. Incidents, Offenses, Victims, and Known Offenders by Bias Motivation, 2008," in *Hate Crime Statistics, 2008*, U.S. Department of Justice, Federal Bureau of Investigation, November 2009, http://www.fbi.gov/ucr/hc2008/data/table_01.html (accessed December 15, 2009)

violent crime was particularly high in urban schools, at 34 per 1,000 students, compared with 19 and 21 per 1,000 students in suburban and rural schools, respectively.

Dinkes, Kemp, and Baum find that the rate of crimes per 1,000 students in 2007 was higher among whites (62) than among Hispanics (52) or African-Americans (42). (See Table 7.8.) However, African-American and Hispanic students were much more likely than other groups to report that gangs were present at school in 2007. (See Figure 7.1.) More than a third of African-Americans (38%) and Hispanics (36%) reported that gangs were present at school, whereas only 17% of Asian-American students and 16% of white students did.

Drugs are another serious problem at school. Dinkes, Kemp, and Baum note that "the availability of drugs on school property has a disruptive and corrupting influence on the school environment." In 2007, 22% of students reported that drugs had been made available to them on school property during the previous 12 months. (See Figure 7.2.)

However, this percentage varied by race and ethnicity. Pacific Islanders and Native Hawaiians (38%) were the most likely to have had drugs made available to them on school property during the previous 12 months, followed by Hispanics (29%), Native Americans and Alaskan Natives (25%), whites (21%), Asian-Americans (21%), and African-Americans (19%).

Students are also the target of hate-related words and see hate-related graffiti at school all too often. In 2007 students were asked if someone at school had called them a derogatory word having to do with their race, ethnicity, religion, gender, sexual orientation, or disability and if they had seen any hate-inspired graffiti in the past six months at school. Ten percent of all students had been the target of hate-related words in the past six months—11% each of African-American, Hispanic, and Asian-American students and 9% of white students. (See Figure 7.3.) More than a third (35%) of all students had seen hate-related graffiti at school; this varied little by race or ethnic group. Dinkes,

TABLE 7.8

Number of student-reported nonfatal crimes against students ages 12–18 and rate of crimes per 1,000 students at school, by type of crime and selected characteristics, 2007

Student or school characteristic	Number of crimes				Rate of crimes per 1,000 students			
	Total	Theft	Violent	Serious violent[a]	Total	Theft	Violent	Serious violent[a]
At school								
Total	1,510,900	826,800	684,100	118,300	57	31	26	4
Sex								
Male	798,000	402,700	395,300	94,500	58	30	29	7
Female	712,900	424,100	288,800	23,800!	56	33	22	2!
Age								
12–14	819,300	387,500	431,800	64,800	67	32	35	5
15–18	691,600	439,300	252,300	53,500	49	31	18	4
Race/ethnicity[b]								
White	969,300	523,600	445,700	55,000	62	33	28	4
Black	159,300	102,100	57,200	‡	42	27	15	‡
Hispanic	269,500	135,500	133,900	38,300!	52	26	26	7!
Other	112,800	65,500	47,300	‡	62	36	26	‡
Household income								
Less than $15,000	99,600	32,900!	66,700	‡	65	21!	43	‡
$15,000–29,999	159,900	83,000	77,000	23,300!	60	31	29	9!
$30,000–49,999	313,800	116,300	197,600	34,100!	75	28	47	8!
$50,000–74,999	285,100	156,300	128,800	16,200!	74	41	33	4!
$75,000 or more	372,800	269,300	103,600	‡	52	37	14	‡

!Interpret data with caution. Estimate based on 10 or fewer sample cases.
‡Reporting standards not met.
[a]Serious violent crimes are also included in violent crimes.
[b]Other includes Asians, Pacific Islanders, and American Indians (including Alaska Natives). Respondents who identified themselves as being of Hispanic origin are classified as Hispanic, regardless of their race.
Notes: Serious violent crimes include rape, sexual assault, robbery, and aggravated assault. Violent crimes include serious violent crimes and simple assault. Theft includes purse snatching, pick pocketing, all burglaries, attempted forcible entry, and all attempted and completed thefts except motor vehicle thefts. Theft does not include robbery in which threat or use of force is involved. Total crimes include violent crimes and theft. "At school" includes inside the school building, on school property, or on the way to or from school. Detail may not sum to totals because of rounding and missing data on student characteristics. Estimates of number of crimes are rounded to the nearest 100. Due to changes in survey methodology in 2006 that mainly affected rural areas, national-level estimates were not comparable to estimates based on National Crime Victimization Survey (NCVS) data from previous years.

SOURCE: Rachel Dinkes, Jana Kemp, and Katrina Baum, "Table 2.2. Number of Student-Reported Nonfatal Crimes against Students Ages 12–18 and Rate of Crimes per 1,000 Students at School, by Type of Crime and Selected Student and School Characteristics: 2007," in *Indicators of School Crime and Safety: 2009*, National Center for Education Statistics and Bureau of Justice Statistics, December 2009, http://nces.ed.gov/pubs2010/2010012.pdf (accessed December 29, 2009)

Kemp, and Baum indicate that of all African-American students surveyed, 7.1% reported being the target of hate-related words related to their race; among Hispanic students, 6.2% reported being the target of hate-related words related to their race and 6.7% reported being the target of hate-related words related to their ethnicity. Students were more likely to report being targeted for their race (4.6%) and ethnicity (2.9%) than for any other reason, including religion, disability, gender, or sexual orientation.

MINORITIES AS OFFENDERS

African-Americans (particularly males) commit a higher number of offenses as a proportion of the population than do other groups. According to the Federal Bureau of Investigation, in *Crime in the United States, 2008* (September 2009, http://www.fbi.gov/ucr/cius2008/index.html), 5,943 (51.5%) of 11,550 known murderers that year were African-American. African-American males between the ages of 14 and 24 made up a growing proportion of homicide offenders between 1976 and 2005. (See Figure 7.4.) In 1994 African-

American males between the ages of 14 and 24 made up over 30% of homicide offenders, but that number dropped somewhat by 2002 before rising again in 2005.

The circumstances under which African-American and white homicide offenders commit their crimes vary by race. African-American offenders are the most likely to commit homicides related to illegal drug activity. Between 1976 and 2005, 65% of homicide offenders who had committed their crimes under drug-related circumstances were African-American. (See Table 7.5.) A high proportion of felony murders (deaths that occur during violent crimes such as burglary, sexual assault, or robbery) between these years were committed by African-Americans (59.3%) as well. By contrast, whites committed a disproportionate number of workplace murders (70.5%), sex-related murders (54.7%), and gang-related murders (54.3%). African-American offenders committed the majority of homicides using guns (56.4%), and whites committed the majority of murders using arson (55.7%) and poison (79.8%).

FIGURE 7.1

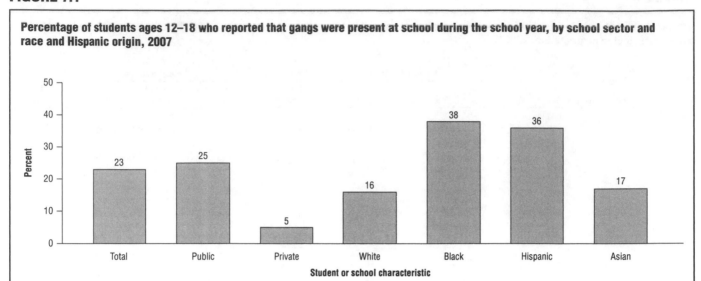

Percentage of students ages 12–18 who reported that gangs were present at school during the school year, by school sector and race and Hispanic origin, 2007

Notes: Race categories exclude persons of Hispanic ethnicity. All gangs, whether or not they are involved in violent or illegal activity, are included. "At school" includes the school building, on school property, on a school bus, or going to and from school.

SOURCE: Rachel Dinkes, Jana Kemp, and Katrina Baum, "Figure 8.1. Percentage of Students Ages 12–18 Who Reported That Gangs Were Present at School during the School Year, by School Sector and Race/Ethnicity: 2007," in *Indicators of School Crime and Safety: 2009*, National Center for Education Statistics and Bureau of Justice Statistics, December 2009, http://nces.ed.gov/pubs2010/2010012.pdf (accessed December 29, 2009)

FIGURE 7.2

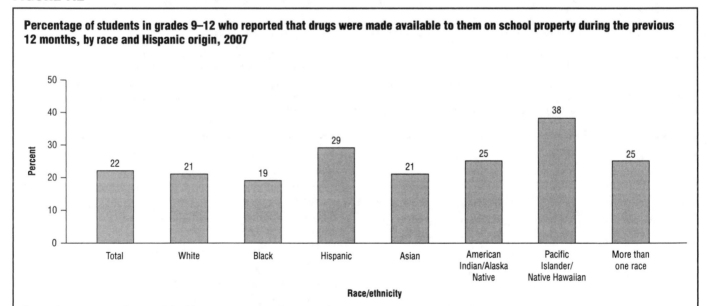

Percentage of students in grades 9–12 who reported that drugs were made available to them on school property during the previous 12 months, by race and Hispanic origin, 2007

Notes: "On school property" was not defined for survey respondents. Race categories exclude persons of Hispanic ethnicity.

SOURCE: Rachel Dinkes, Jana Kemp, and Katrina Baum, "Figure 9.2. Percentage of Students in Grades 9–12 Who Reported That Drugs Were Made Available to Them on School Property during the Previous 12 Months, by Race/Ethnicity: 2007," in *Indicators of School Crime and Safety: 2009*, National Center for Education Statistics and Bureau of Justice Statistics, December 2009, http://nces.ed.gov/pubs2010/2010012.pdf (accessed December 29, 2009)

Whites are more likely than African-Americans to commit homicide in the context of an intimate victim-offender relationship or family relationship. Between 1976 and 2005 whites committed 54.4% of homicides of intimate partners, whereas African-Americans committed 43.4%. (See Table 7.5.) During this same period, whites committed 59.2% of homicides of family members, whereas African-

Americans committed 38.5% of these murders. Most of the perpetrators who killed infants (55.4%) or elder family members (54.5%) were white.

MINORITIES IN PRISONS AND JAILS

In June 2008 there were more African-American males in state and federal prisons and local jails than there were

FIGURE 7.3

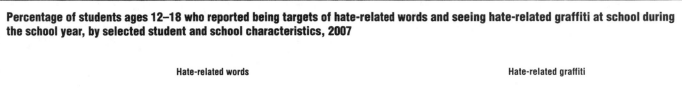

Percentage of students ages 12–18 who reported being targets of hate-related words and seeing hate-related graffiti at school during the school year, by selected student and school characteristics, 2007

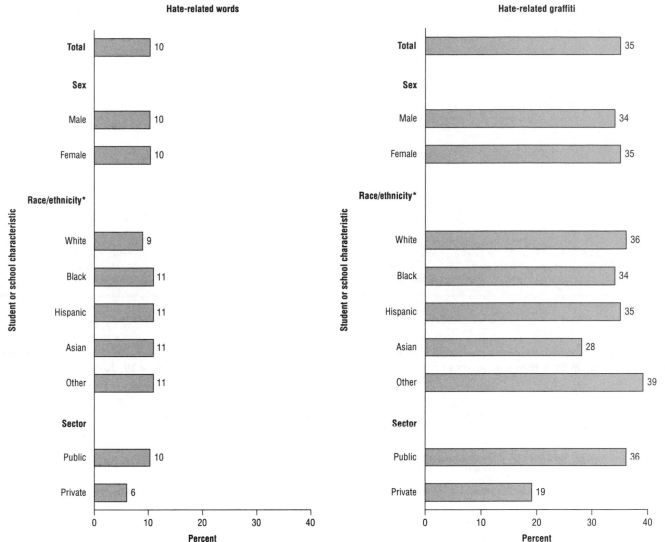

*Race categories exclude persons of Hispanic ethnicity. Other includes American Indian, Alaska Native, Pacific Islander, and more than one race.

Notes: "At school" includes the school building, on school property, on a school bus, and going to and from school. "Hate-related" refers to derogatory terms used by others in reference to students' personal characteristics.

SOURCE: Rachel Dinkes, Jana Kemp, and Katrina Baum, "Figure 10.1. Percentage of Students Ages 12–18 Who Reported Being Targets of Hate-Related Words and Seeing Hate-Related Graffiti at School during the School Year, by Selected Student and School Characteristics: 2007," in *Indicators of School Crime and Safety: 2009*, National Center for Education Statistics and Bureau of Justice Statistics, December 2009, http://nces.ed.gov/pubs2010/2010012 .pdf (accessed December 29, 2009)

non-Hispanic white or Hispanic males. Out of a total of 2.1 million incarcerated males, 846,000 were African-American, 712,500 were non-Hispanic white, and 427,000 were Hispanic. (See Table 7.9.) Men between the ages of 20 and 29 made up the largest proportion of African-American males in the prison population.

The rate of incarceration for African-American males greatly exceeds the rates for non-Hispanic white and Hispanic males. In June 2008 the rate for African-American males was 4,777 inmates for every 100,000 residents. (See Table 7.10.)

This proportion was much higher than that among non-Hispanic whites, with 727 inmates for every 100,000 residents imprisoned during the same period. Among Hispanic men there were 1,760 inmates for every 100,000 residents, more than double the rate for non-Hispanic whites but much lower than the rate of imprisonment of African-Americans.

Even though non-Hispanic white women (94,500) outnumbered African-American women (67,800) in federal and state prisons and local jails at midyear 2008, African-American women were incarcerated at nearly four times

FIGURE 7.4

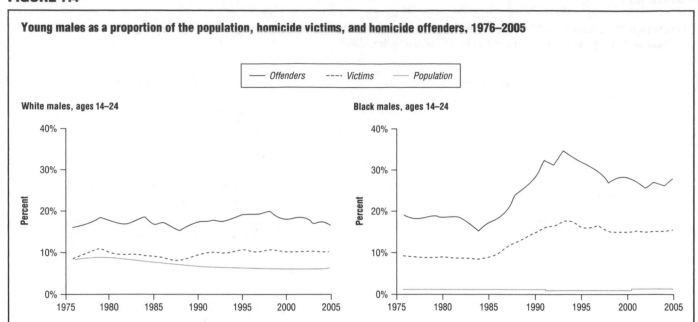

Young males as a proportion of the population, homicide victims, and homicide offenders, 1976–2005

SOURCE: James Alan Fox and Marianne W. Zawitz, "Young Males As a Proportion of the Population, Homicide Victims, and Homicide Offenders, 1976–2005," in *Homicide Trends in the United States*, U.S. Department of Justice, Bureau of Justice Statistics, July 2007, http://bjsdata.ojp.usdoj.gov/content/homicide/ageracesex.cfm#proportion (accessed December 29, 2009)

TABLE 7.9

Number of inmates in state or federal prisons or local jails, by gender, race, Hispanic origin, and age, June 30, 2008

	Male				Female			
	Total[a]	White[b]	Black[b]	Hispanic	Total[a]	White[b]	Black[b]	Hispanic
Total[c]	2,103,500	712,500	846,000	427,000	207,700	94,500	67,800	33,400
18–19	86,300	26,500	37,100	18,400	5,500	2,200	1,500	1,300
20–24	353,100	104,000	148,500	83,300	30,800	13,900	9,000	6,300
25–29	354,600	99,900	148,400	87,100	32,000	14,200	10,100	6,000
30–34	331,400	103,400	132,100	76,400	35,400	16,000	11,600	6,000
35–39	308,500	107,200	124,500	57,300	38,800	18,000	13,200	5,400
40–44	277,200	107,700	107,400	43,500	32,600	14,600	11,700	4,000
45–49	185,600	72,400	73,900	29,000	18,200	8,100	6,600	2,200
50–54	96,900	40,200	37,100	14,500	8,000	4,100	2,300	1,000
55–59	50,200	24,300	15,800	7,900	3,300	1,800	700	600
60–64	21,700	12,100	5,500	3,500	1,300	700	400	100
65 or older	17,500	9,900	4,800	2,200	800	600	100	100

Note: Based on the U.S. resident population estimates for July 1, 2008, by gender, race, Hispanic origin, and age. Detailed categories exclude persons who reported two or more races.
[a]Includes American Indians, Alaska Natives, Asians, Native Hawaiians, other Pacific Islanders, and persons identifying two or more races.
[b]Excludes persons of Hispanic or Latino origin.
[c]Includes persons under age 18.

SOURCE: Heather C. West and William J. Sabol, "Table 17. Estimated Number of Inmates Held in State or Federal Prisons, or in Local Jails, by Gender, Race, Hispanic Origin, and Age, June 30, 2008," in *Prison and Jail Inmates at Midyear 2008—Statistical Tables*, U.S. Department of Justice, Bureau of Justice Statistics, March 2009, http://bjs.ojp.usdoj.gov/content/pub/pdf/pim08st.pdf (accessed December 29, 2009)

the rate of non-Hispanic white women (349 per 100,000 residents and 93 per 100,000 residents, respectively). (See Table 7.9 and Table 7.10.) Hispanic women were incarcerated at a rate of 147 per 100,000 residents.

The National Criminal Justice Association (NCJA) discusses in "Minorities in the Criminal Justice System" (July 22, 2003, http://www.ncja.org/Content/Navigation Menu/PoliciesPractices/PolicyStatements/ArchivedPolicy

Statements/default.htm) the overrepresentation of minorities among the ranks of offenders in the criminal justice system. It notes that social factors play a role in this overrepresentation, including the lack of employment and educational opportunities, poor economic conditions, the lack of minority role models, and the negative portrayal of minorities in the media. Observing that an estimated 4.4% of white males will enter prison during their lifetime, compared with 16% of Hispanic males and 28%

TABLE 7.10

Number of inmates in state or federal prisons or local jails per 100,000 residents, by gender, race, Hispanic origin, and age, June 30, 2008

	Male				Female			
	Total[a]	White[b]	Black[b]	Hispanic	Total[a]	White[b]	Black[b]	Hispanic
Total[c]	1,403	727	4,777	1,760	135	93	349	147
18–19	1,934	976	5,543	2,376	129	86	236	185
20–24	3,256	1,564	9,776	4,281	302	221	608	367
25–29	3,241	1,550	10,408	3,792	308	225	691	326
30–34	3,328	1,793	11,137	3,446	367	281	892	328
35–39	2,919	1,643	10,120	2,868	373	279	961	313
40–44	2,580	1,529	8,622	2,510	303	208	827	262
45–49	1,641	912	5,854	2,011	157	101	451	166
50–54	920	520	3,330	1,320	73	52	178	93
55–59	556	356	1,790	976	34	25	61	74
60–64	299	213	899	607	16	11	50	22
65 or older	106	75	383	191	4	3	7	4

Note: Based on the U.S. resident population estimates for January 1, 2008, by gender, race, Hispanic origin, and age. Detailed categories exclude persons who reported two or more races.
[a]Includes American Indians, Alaska Natives, Asians, Native Hawaiians, other Pacific Islanders, and persons identifying two or more races.
[b]Excludes persons of Hispanic or Latino origin.
[c]Includes persons under age 18.

SOURCE: Heather C. West and William J. Sabol, "Table 19. Estimated Number of Inmates Held in State or Federal Prisons, or in Local Jails per 100,000 U.S. Residents, by Gender, Race, Hispanic Origin, and Age, June 30, 2008," in *Prison and Jail Inmates at Midyear 2008—Statistical Tables*, U.S. Department of Justice, Bureau of Justice Statistics, March 2009, http://bjs.ojp.usdoj.gov/content/pub/pdf/pim08st.pdf (accessed December 29, 2009)

of African-American males, the NCJA indicates that state and local criminal justice policy makers must continually address minority-related criminal justice issues. Among these issues are the overrepresentation of minorities in both the juvenile and adult criminal justice populations and the underrepresentation of minorities in law enforcement, corrections, and legal professions; conscious and unconscious tensions between members of minority groups and law enforcement personnel; accurate reporting of hate crimes; racial profiling by law enforcement and its effects on community relations and prison crowding; racially biased effects of drug laws and enforcement strategies; minorities' equal access to the court system; racially biased sentencing patterns; and unequal socioeconomic conditions.

In "Schools and Prisons: Fifty Years after *Brown v. Board of Education*" (April 20, 2004, http://www.sentencingproject.org/Admin/Documents/publications/rd_brownvboard.pdf), Marc Mauer and Ryan S. King of the Sentencing Project call attention to the dramatic rise in imprisonment in the African-American community after 1954. According to Mauer and King, this rise resulted from a punitive crime policy that disproportionately affects African-Americans. They note that the causes for the rising imprisonment rate of African-Americans include higher crime and imprisonment rates, the War on Drugs, disparities in crack-cocaine and powder-cocaine sentencing policies, school-zone drug laws, three-strikes policies, inadequate defense resources for poor people, and zero-tolerance policies in schools. Mauer and King state that "at current rates of incarceration, one of every three black males born today can expect to be imprisoned at some point in his lifetime. Whether or not one

believes that current crime control policies are 'working' to reduce crime, such an outcome should be shocking to all Americans. Imposing a crime policy with such profound racial dynamics calls into question the nation's commitment to a free and democratic society."

The Sentencing Project identifies in *Reducing Racial Disparity in the Criminal Justice System: A Manual for Practitioners and Policymakers* (August 2008, http://www.sentencingproject.org/doc/publications/rd_reducingracialdisparity.pdf) several causes for this racial disparity. It finds that there is little support for the belief that members of minority groups commit more crimes; instead, they are more likely to be involved in crimes that police observe themselves, are more likely to be arrested, and are more likely to receive longer sentences than non-Hispanic whites. In addition, members of minority communities do not have the same access to health care, employment opportunities, and treatment programs. Some laws, such as the War on Drugs, have a disproportionate impact on minority communities. Finally, the Sentencing Project cites overt racial bias, stating, "So long as racism exists within society at large, it will be found within the criminal justice system."

Native Americans in Jail

Todd D. Minton of the BJS notes in *Jails in Indian Country, 2008* (December 2009, http://bjs.ojp.usdoj.gov/content/pub/pdf/jic08.pdf) that at midyear 2008, 82 jails, detention centers, and other correctional facilities confined 2,135 inmates. This represented a 1.3% decrease from the year before, reversing a previous three-year trend of an increasing jail population. These 2,135 inmates were only a small proportion of the total number of Native Americans held in prisons and jails; 28,388 were held nationwide. At midyear 2008 Native Americans had an incarceration rate of 921 per 100,000 residents. Even though the number of people held in jails run by tribes declined, the number of Native Americans confined in jails and prisons nationwide increased by 2.5% between midyear 2007 and midyear 2008.

Minton reports that most inmates of tribal jails were male; at midyear 2008, 21% of those held were female and 79% were male. About 12% of those held were juveniles. Among the 63% of inmates who had been convicted of a crime (37% were being held before trial), 15% had been convicted of domestic violence, 15% of assault, 9% of driving while intoxicated, 5% of drug offenses, 9% of other violent crimes, and 46% of other crimes.

Parole and Probation

Because African-Americans account for the largest proportion of prison and jail inmates, it is no surprise that African-Americans also outnumber other racial and ethnic groups in the nation's parole system. The parole system grants inmates early release from prison with fewer rights than the general population and under monitored conditions.

Minorities are slightly underrepresented in the parole population compared with their presence in the prisons and jails as a whole. Of the 2.1 million prison and jail inmates at midyear 2008, 913,800 (43.4%) were African-American. (See Table 7.9.) However, only 38% of inmates paroled from prisons and jails at yearend 2008 were African-American. (See Table 7.11.) In the same year, 460,400 (21.9%) were Hispanic, and 19% of those on parole were Hispanic. By contrast, 807,000 (38.4%) were non-Hispanic white, and 41% of those on parole were non-Hispanic white.

The proportion of non-Hispanic whites on probation, a system where people convicted of a crime are under supervision by a probation officer rather than incarcerated, is even more disproportionate to their representation in the criminal justice system. At yearend 2008, 56% of probationers were non-Hispanic white, compared with the 38.4% of non-Hispanic whites who were in prisons and jails. (See Table 7.12 and Table 7.9.) Conversely, only 29% of probationers were African-American, whereas 43.4% of inmates were African-American, and 13% of probationers were Hispanic, whereas 21.9% of inmates were Hispanic. These numbers show that non-Hispanic white offenders are more likely than minority offenders to receive the more lenient sentence of probation.

Hispanics also face harsher treatment in the federal court system. The Sentencing Project points out in "Hispanic Prisoners in the United States" (August 2003, http://www.sentencingproject.org/doc/publications/inc_hispanic_prisoners.pdf) that Hispanic defendants are about one-third

TABLE 7.11

Characteristics of adults on parole, 2000, 2004, and 2008

Characteristics	Percent of adults on parole		
	2000	2004	2008
Total	100%	100%	100%
Gender			
Male	88%	88%	88%
Female	12	12	12
Race and Hispanic origin			
White[a]	38%	40%	41%
Black[a]	40	40	38
Hispanic or Latino	21	18	19
American Indian/Alaska Native[a]	1	1	1
Asian/Native Hawaiian/other Pacific Islander[a]	—	1	1
Two or more races[a]	. . .	. . .	—
Status of supervision			
Active	83%	84%	85%
Inactive	4	3	4
Absconder	7	7	6
Supervised out of state	5	4	4
Financial conditions remaining	. . .	. . .	—
Other	1	1	1
Maximum sentence to incarceration			
Less than 1 year	3%	5%	6%
1 year or more	97	95	94
Most serious offense			
Violent	. . .	25%	26%
Property	. . .	26	23
Drug	. . .	38	37
Weapon	. . .	. . .	3
Other[b]	. . .	12	11

Note: Each characteristic includes persons of unknown type. Detail may not sum to total because of rounding.
—Less than 0.5%.
. . .Not available.
[a]Excludes persons of Hispanic origin.
[b]Includes public-order offenses.

SOURCE: Lauren E. Glaze and Thomas P. Bonczar, "Appendix Table 15. Characteristics of Adults on Parole, 2000, 2004, and 2008," in *Probation and Parole in the United States, 2008*, U.S. Department of Justice, Bureau of Justice Statistics, December 2009, http://bjs.ojp.usdoj.gov/content/pub/pdf/ppus08.pdf (accessed December 29, 2009)

as likely as non-Hispanic defendants (22.7% versus 63.1%) to be released before their cases come to trial. In *Uneven Justice: State Rates of Incarceration by Race and Ethnicity* (July 2007, http://www.sentencingproject.org/doc/publications/rd_stateratesofincbyraceandethnicity.pdf), Mauer and King indicate that between 1990 and 2005 the proportion of prisoners who were Hispanic had risen 43%. By 2007 one out of every six Hispanic males born could expect to be incarcerated in their lifetime if current trends continued.

Minorities on Death Row

Tracy L. Snell of the BJS reports in *Capital Punishment, 2008* (December 2009, http://bjs.ojp.usdoj.gov/content/pub/pdf/cp08st.pdf) that at yearend 2008, 3,207 state and federal prisoners were incarcerated under the sentence of death. (See Table 7.13.) Whites made up 56.1% and African-Americans made up 41.7% of all death-row prisoners. Only 2.2% were

TABLE 7.12

Characteristics of adults on probation, 2000, 2004, and 2008

Characteristics	Percent of adults on probation		
	2000	2004	2008
Total	100%	100%	100%
Gender			
Male	78%	77%	76%
Female	22	23	24
Race and Hispanic origin			
White[a]	54%	56%	56%
Black[a]	31	30	29
Hispanic or Latino	13	12	13
American Indian/Alaska Native[a]	1	1	1
Asian/Native Hawaiian/other Pacific Islander[a]	1	1	1
Two or more races[a]	...	...	1
Status of supervision			
Active	76%	74%	71%
Residential/other treatment program		1	1
Financial conditions remaining			1
Inactive	9	9	8
Absconder	9	9	8
Supervised out of jurisdiction	3	2	3
Warrant status	...	5	6
Other	3	—	2
Type of offense			
Felony	52%	49%	49%
Misdemeanor	46	50	48
Other infractions	2	1	2
Most serious offense			
Violent	...	19%	19%
Property	...	23	25
Drug	24	26	29
Public-order[b]	24	22	17
Other[c]	52	10	10

Note: Each characteristic includes persons of unknown type. Detail may not sum to total because of rounding.
—Less than 0.5%.
...Not available.
[a]Excludes persons of Hispanic origin.
[b]Includes driving while intoxicated and minor traffic offenses only.
[c]Includes violent and property offenses in 2000 because those data were not collected separately.

SOURCE: Lauren E. Glaze and Thomas P. Bonczar, "Appendix Table 5. Characteristics of Adults on Probation, 2000, 2004, and 2008," in *Probation and Parole in the United States, 2008*, U.S. Department of Justice, Bureau of Justice Statistics, December 2009, http://bjs.ojp.usdoj.gov/content/pub/pdf/ppus08.pdf (accessed December 29, 2009)

TABLE 7.13

Demographic characteristics of prisoners under sentence of death, 2008

Characteristic	Prisoners under sentence of death, 2008		
	Yearend	Admissions	Removals
Total inmates	3,207	111	119
Gender			
Male	98.2%	97.3%	99.2%
Female	1.8	2.7	0.8
Race[a]			
White	56.1%	58.6 %	61.3%
Black	41.7	39.6	37.0
All other races[b]	2.2	1.8	1.7
Hispanic origin			
Hispanic	13.2%	19.8%	8.1%
Non-Hispanic	86.8	80.2	91.9
Number unknown	384	5	8
Education			
8th grade or less	13.5%	17.1%	19.2%
9th–11th grade	36.5	31.7	36.4
High school graduate/GED[c]	40.8	41.5	35.4
Any college	9.2	9.8	9.1
Median	12th	12th	11th
Number unknown	528	29	20
Marital status			
Married	22.2%	18.3%	20.2%
Divorced/separated	20.1	19.5	27.9
Widowed	2.9	4.9	1.9
Never married	54.7	57.3	50.0
Number unknown	371	29	15

Note: Calculations are based on those cases for which data were reported. Detail may not add to total due to rounding.
[a]Includes persons of Hispanic/Latino origin.
[b]At yearend 2008, inmates in "all other races" consisted of 27 American Indians, 35 Asians, and 9 self-identified Hispanics. During 2008, 1 American Indian and 1 Asian were admitted; and 1 Asian and 1 self-identified Hispanic were removed.
[c]GED = General Equivalency Diploma

SOURCE: Tracy L. Snell, "Table 5. Demographic Characteristics of Prisoners under Sentence of Death, 2008," in *Capital Punishment, 2008—Statistical Tables*, U.S. Department of Justice, Bureau of Justice Statistics, December 2009, http://bjs.ojp.usdoj.gov/content/pub/pdf/cp08st.pdf (accessed December 29, 2009)

---

of other races. Of those whose ethnicity was known, 13.2% were Hispanic.

Of those sentenced to death row in 2008, 58.6% were white and 39.6% were African-American. (See Table 7.13.) Hispanics made up 19.8% of those sentenced to death row in that year.

Racial Disparities in Sentencing

In 1984 the U.S. Sentencing Commission (USSC) set forth sentencing guidelines in the Sentencing Reform Act of 1984, which was designed to implement uniform sentencing practices that would eliminate disparities based on race. In November 2004 the USSC released *Fifteen Years of Guidelines Sentencing: An Assessment of How Well the Federal Criminal Justice System Is Achieving the Goals of Sentencing Reform* (http://www.ussc.gov/15_year/15_year_study_full.pdf), which evaluated the effectiveness of these practices. The USSC concludes that remaining disparity in sentencing is the result of sentencing rules and charging practices that have "institutionalized" disparity. In fact, variables such as mandatory minimums and plea bargaining have had "a greater adverse impact on Black offenders than did the factors taken into account by judges in the discretionary system ... prior to guidelines implementation."

Tushar Kansal of the Sentencing Project examines in *Racial Disparity in Sentencing: A Review of the Literature* (January 2005, http://www.sentencingproject.org/doc/publications/rd_sentencing_review.pdf) the literature about the nature of this ongoing racial disparity. Kansal finds that in noncapital cases racially discriminatory sentencing outcomes do exist, but that they are not uniform or extensive. Kansal notes that the following groups suffer harsher sentencing: young African-American and Hispanic males, especially if unemployed; African-Americans convicted of harming white victims; and African-American and Hispanic defendants convicted of less serious (nonviolent) crimes. An examination of death-penalty cases finds that in most cases, if the murder victim was white, the defendant was more likely to receive the death sentence, and in the federal system minority defendants, especially African-Americans, were more likely to receive a death sentence than were white defendants.

In "Criminal Sentencing Policies Disproportionately Hurt Black Americans, Mauer Says" (November 6, 2007, http://www.law.virginia.edu/html/news/2007_fall/mauer .htm), Shea Connelly reports on a talk that Marc Mauer of the Sentencing Project gave at Virginia Law School in 2007. Mauer identified the War on Drugs as a prime causal agent in the disproportionate number of African-Americans who are incarcerated. He pointed out that communities with monetary resources do not deal with kids with drug problems through the criminal justice system, but through treatment programs. By contrast, poor communities often call on the police to deal with drug-abuse problems. Because minorities are disproportionately poor, the strict sentencing laws arising from the War on Drugs have fallen heavily on them. Harsher penalties for the possession of crack cocaine, which is more common in low-income communities, as opposed to powder cocaine, which is more common in white and affluent communities, have also contributed heavily to the problem of racial disparities in the criminal justice system.

Ashley Nellis and Ryan S. King examine in *No Exit: The Expanding Use of Life Sentences in America* (July 2009, http://sentencingproject.org/doc/publications/publi cations/inc_noexitseptember2009.pdf) racial disparities in life sentences. The researchers note that this type of sentence has grown dramatically not in response to higher crime rates but in response to a policy of imposing harsher punishments. In 2008, 140,610 prisoners nationwide were serving life sentences, up from 34,000 in 1984. Of these, 41,095 were serving sentences with no possibility of parole, an increase of 22% since 2003. Nellis and King find that minority prisoners served a disproportionate share of life sentences. In 2008 two out of three (66.4%) prisoners serving life sentences were people of color—48.3% were African-American and 14.4% were Hispanic, whereas 33.4% were white. Among the 6,807 juveniles serving life sentences nationwide, 43.7% were African-American and 23.7% were Hispanic.

GANGS

Testifying before the U.S. Senate, Steven R. Wiley (April 23, 1997, http://www.hi-ho.ne.jp/taku77/refer/gang .htm) of the Federal Bureau of Investigation explained that law enforcement agencies define a street gang as a "group of people that form an allegiance based on various social needs and engage in acts injurious to public health and safety."

Law enforcement officers surveyed for the National Youth Gang Survey Analysis (2009, http://www.nationalgangcenter .gov/Survey-Analysis) by the National Youth Gang Center emphasize that gang members generally use tattoos, colors, or other symbols to identify themselves as part of a gang and that important definitional characteristics of gangs include claiming "turf," committing crimes together, and having a leader. Even though gangs have been involved with the drug trade for many years, gang-related deadly violence is more likely to come from territorial conflicts.

Gangs are often (but not always) racially or ethnically based. As a rule, ethnic gangs require that all members belong to a particular race or ethnic group. Erika Harrell of the BJS indicates in "Violence by Gang Members, 1993–2003" (June 2005, http://bjs.ojp.usdoj.gov/content/pub/pdf/ vgm03.pdf) that between 1998 and 2003, 6% of all violent crimes were perpetrated by gang members.

The most frightening crime committed by gangs is murder. More than half of all gang-related homicides between 1976 and 2005 involved whites. (See Table 7.5.) Approximately 57.5% of gang-related homicide victims during this period were white, and 54.3% of offenders were also white. African-Americans were the victims of gang-related homicides 39% of the time, and 41.2% of offenders were African-American.

The National Youth Gang Center notes in the National Youth Gang Survey Analysis the following trends:

- Even though the gang problem declined between 1995 and the turn of the 21st century, it then experienced a resurgence; by 2007, 34.8% of jurisdictions experienced active gangs.

- Gang problems are highly prevalent in larger cities; specifically, 99% of law enforcement agencies serving cities with populations of 100,000 or more reported multiple years of gang problems.

- Between 2002 and 2007 the number of jurisdictions experiencing gang problems increased 12.1% in large cities, 33.2% in suburban counties, 27.4% in smaller cities, and 24.1% in rural areas.

Furthermore, violence by perceived gang members declined between 1993 and 2003. Harrell states that in 1994 violent victimizations by gang members peaked at about 1.1 million, then fell to 341,000 in 2003. During this 11-year period, Hispanic victims were more likely than non-Hispanic white or African-American victims to perceive their attackers as gang members. The rate of violence by victim-perceived gang members was 5.7 per 1,000 Hispanics, 4.1 per 1,000 African-Americans, and 2.4 per 1,000 non-Hispanic whites over the entire period. However, homicides by gang members have not declined. In 1993, 5.6% of all homicides were gang related; in 2003, 6.5% of all homicides were gang related.

CHAPTER 8
POLITICAL PARTICIPATION

A truly postethnic America would be one in which the ethno-racial component in identity would loom less large than it now does in politics.

—David A. Hollinger, *Postethnic America: Beyond Multiculturalism* (1995)

David A. Hollinger's words point out the large divide between minority groups and the majority in the political life of the nation. Not only are there racial and ethnic divides in voter registration and voter turnout but there are also differences in voting by minorities when compared with the majority group. Specifically, minority groups largely cast their support behind Democratic candidates. In addition, only in the last 20 years of the 20th century did minority candidates running for office achieve much success. By November 2008, however, an African-American candidate had done the unthinkable: Barack Obama (1961–), a U.S. senator from Illinois, had been elected the 44th president of the United States.

Perry Bacon Jr. states in "Can Obama Count on the Black Vote?" (*Time*, January 23, 2007) that "much of Obama's overall appeal stems from his image as practically a post-racial politician. Not only does he have a mixed-race background, with a white mother from Kansas and a black father from Kenya, but his rhetoric, most notably his 2004 Democratic National Convention speech, emphasizes the importance of Americans moving beyond political, religious and racial differences." Obama did not rely on racial appeals in the same way that previous African-American candidates—notably Jesse Jackson (1941–) in his runs for the Democratic nomination—had done. According to Dan Balz and Jon Cohen, in "Blacks Shift to Obama, Poll Finds" (*Washington Post*, February 28, 2007), this emphasis allowed him to appeal to a large portion of the white electorate, and early in the primary season African-Americans shifted their support from Hillary Rodham Clinton (1947–), the front-runner, to Obama. Minority voters turned out in record numbers to support Obama's candidacy,

leading to his Democratic primary victory and his election in November 2008.

VOTER REGISTRATION

Minority groups have traditionally trailed behind whites when it comes to registering to vote and actually voting. In 1993 Congress enacted the National Voter Registration Act, which became popularly known as the Motor Voter Act, because it included provisions to enable driver's license applicants to simultaneously register to vote. In "Big Increase in New Voters" (October 15, 1997, http://www-cgi.cnn.com/ALLPOLITICS/1996/news/9610/15/motor.voter/), CNN reports that in the two years after the law went into effect (in January 1995) 9 million people had registered to vote.

To be eligible to vote, a person must be a U.S. citizen and at least 18 years of age. The U.S. Election Assistance Commission states in *The Impact of the National Voter Registration Act of 1993 on the Administration of Elections for Federal Office, 2005–2006* (June 30, 2007, http://www.eac.gov/) that in 2006 the voting-age population numbered 225.7 million. Of that number, 172.8 million (76.6%) were registered to vote, a 7.5% increase over the number of registrants in the 2002 midterm elections. However, since the presidential elections in 2004, the number of registered voters had decreased from 176.2 million voters, reflecting a normal drop in registration after a presidential election, when states remove some nonvoters from the registration rolls. Each state determines for itself how long an individual may remain on the list of registered voters without voting.

In 2008 (a presidential election year) there were 151.3 non-Hispanic white U.S. citizens eligible to vote. (See Table 8.1.) Of this number, 111.2 million (73.5%) were registered to vote, which was a slight decrease from the presidential election in 2004. The U.S. Census Bureau notes in *Voting and Registration in the Election of November 2004* (December 11, 2007, http://www.census.gov/population/www/socdemo/voting/cps2004.html) that in November 2004, 111.3 million (75.1%) non-Hispanic whites were registered to vote. Of the

TABLE 8.1

Reported rates of voting and registration among native and naturalized citizens, by race and Hispanic origin and region of birth, November 2008

[In thousands]

Nativity status, race and Hispanic origin, and region of birth	Total citizen population	US citizen							
		Reported registered		Not registered		Reported voted		Did not vote	
		Number	Percent	Number	Percent	Number	Percent	Number	Percent
United States									
All races	206,072	146,311	71.0	59,761	29.0	131,144	63.6	74,928	36.4
White alone	169,438	122,020	72.0	47,418	28.0	109,100	64.4	60,338	35.6
White non-Hispanic alone	151,321	111,215	73.5	40,106	26.5	100,042	66.1	51,279	33.9
Black alone	24,930	17,375	69.7	7,555	30.3	16,133	64.7	8,797	35.3
Asian alone	7,059	3,901	55.3	3,159	44.7	3,357	47.6	3,702	52.4
Hispanic (of any race)	19,537	11,608	59.4	7,930	40.6	9,745	49.9	9,792	50.1
White alone or in combination	171,798	123,628	72.0	48,170	28.0	110,500	64.3	61,298	35.7
Black alone or in combination	25,768	17,960	69.7	7,808	30.3	16,674	64.7	9,094	35.3
Asian alone or in combination	7,562	4,225	55.9	3,337	44.1	3,627	48.0	3,935	52.0
Native citizen									
All races	190,683	137,001	71.8	53,682	28.2	122,839	64.4	67,844	35.6
White alone	160,266	116,375	72.6	43,891	27.4	104,005	64.9	56,262	35.1
White non-Hispanic alone	146,906	108,438	73.8	38,467	26.2	97,538	66.4	49,367	33.6
Black alone	23,442	16,431	70.1	7,011	29.9	15,249	65.0	8,193	35.0
Asian alone	2,654	1,353	51.0	1,301	49.0	1,194	45.0	1,460	55.0
Hispanic (of any race)	14,461	8,574	59.3	5,886	40.7	6,995	48.4	7,466	51.6
White alone or in combination	162,511	117,910	72.6	44,601	27.4	105,341	64.8	57,170	35.2
Black alone or in combination	24,211	16,965	70.1	7,246	29.9	15,738	65.0	8,472	35.0
Asian alone or in combination	3,114	1,641	52.7	1,473	47.3	1,433	46.0	1,681	54.0
Naturalized citizen									
All races	15,390	9,310	60.5	6,080	39.5	8,305	54.0	7,085	46.0
White alone	9,171	5,645	61.6	3,526	38.4	5,095	55.6	4,076	44.4
White non-Hispanic alone	4,415	2,776	62.9	1,639	37.1	2,504	56.7	1,912	43.3
Black alone	1,488	943	63.4	544	36.6	884	59.4	604	40.6
Asian alone	4,405	2,548	57.8	1,857	42.2	2,163	49.1	2,242	50.9
Hispanic (of any race)	5,077	3,033	59.8	2,043	40.2	2,751	54.2	2,326	45.8
White alone or in combination	9,287	5,718	61.6	3,569	38.4	5,159	55.6	4,128	44.4
Black alone or in combination	1,557	995	63.9	562	36.1	936	60.1	621	39.9
Asian alone or in combination	4,448	2,584	58.1	1,864	41.9	2,194	49.3	2,254	50.7
Region of birth									
Total	15,390	9,310	60.5	6,080	39.5	8,305	54.0	7,085	46.0
Europe	2,725	1,712	62.8	1,013	37.2	1,562	57.3	1,163	42.7
Asia	5,340	3,021	56.6	2,319	43.4	2,555	47.8	2,785	52.2
Northern America	255	207	81.2	48	18.8	194	76.2	61	23.9
Latin America	6,304	3,889	61.7	2,415	38.3	3,558	56.4	2,746	43.6
Africa	637	430	67.5	207	32.5	389	61.1	248	38.9
Other	129	50	38.8	79	61.2	47	36.3	82	63.6

Note: Federal surveys now give respondents the option of reporting more than one race. Therefore, two basic ways of defining a race group are possible. A group such as Asian may be defined as those who reported Asian and no other race (the race-alone or single-race concept) or as those who reported Asian regardless of whether they also reported another race (the race-alone-or-in-combination concept). This table shows data for people who reported they were the single race white and not Hispanic, people who reported the single race black, and people who reported the single race Asian. Use of the single-race populations does not imply that it is the preferred method of presenting or analyzing data.

SOURCE: Table 13. Reported Voting and Registration among Native and Naturalized Citizens, by Race and Hispanic Origin, and Region of Birth: November 2008, in *Voting and Registration in the Election of November 2008—Detailed Tables*, U.S. Census Bureau, July 2009, http://www.census.gov/hhes/www/socdemo/voting/publications/p20/2008/tables.html (accessed December 31, 2009)

24.9 million African-American citizens of the United States in 2008, 17.4 million (69.7%) were registered to vote, up from the 2004 figure of 16 million (68.7%). Of the 7.1 million Asian-American citizens, 3.9 million (55.3%) were registered to vote, up substantially from the 3.2 million (51.8%) who were registered to vote in 2004. Of the 19.5 million Hispanic citizens in 2008, 11.6 million (59.4%) were registered to vote, up from 9.3 million (57.9%) in 2004. In other words, registration among non-Hispanic white citizens was down slightly as the election of Barack Obama approached, whereas registration among minority citizens was up.

Minority voter registration habits tend to vary by region. For example, Obama's candidacy increased African-American voter registration in some regions of the country more than in others. African-American voter registration was particularly increased in the Northeast, where 62.1% of African-American citizens were registered to vote in 2008, compared with 54.9% in 2004; and in the South, where 71.9% of the African-American population was registered to vote in 2008, up from 65.3% in 2004. (See Table 8.2.) Rates of voter registration among African-Americans increased only slightly in the West (66.2% in 2008 compared with 64.3% in

TABLE 8.2

Voting and registration rates by race and Hispanic origin by region, November 2008

[In thousands]

Race, Hispanic origin, age, and geography	Total population	Total citizen population	US citizen								Total population	
			Reported registered		Not registered		Reported voted		Did not vote		Reported registered	Reported voted
			Number	Percent	Number	Percent	Number	Percent	Number	Percent	Percent	Percent
All races	225,499	206,072	146,311	71.0	59,761	29.0	131,144	63.6	74,928	36.4	64.9	58.2
Northeast	41,543	37,886	26,455	69.8	11,431	30.2	23,837	62.9	14,049	37.1	63.7	57.4
Midwest	49,396	47,209	34,897	73.9	12,311	26.1	31,306	66.3	15,903	33.7	70.6	63.4
South	82,402	75,984	53,988	71.1	21,996	28.9	47,536	62.6	28,448	37.4	65.5	57.7
West	52,158	44,994	30,971	68.8	14,023	31.2	28,465	63.3	16,529	36.7	59.4	54.6
White non-Hispanic alone	154,472	151,321	111,215	73.5	43,106	26.5	100,042	66.1	51,279	33.9	72.0	64.8
Northeast	30,403	29,436	21,449	72.9	7,987	27.1	19,310	65.6	10,126	34.4	70.5	63.5
Midwest	40,418	39,891	29,995	75.2	9,896	24.8	26,864	67.3	13,027	32.7	74.2	66.5
South	53,122	52,284	38,117	72.9	14,168	27.1	33,690	64.4	18,594	35.6	71.8	63.4
West	30,529	29,710	21,654	72.9	8,056	27.1	20,177	67.9	9,532	32.1	70.9	66.1
Black alone	26,528	24,930	17,375	69.7	7,555	30.3	16,133	64.7	8,797	35.3	65.5	60.8
Northeast	4,710	4,081	2,533	62.1	1,548	37.9	2,389	58.6	1,691	41.4	53.8	50.7
Midwest	4,630	4,467	3,194	71.5	1,273	28.5	3,006	67.3	1,462	32.7	69.0	64.9
South	14,698	14,001	10,071	71.9	3,930	28.1	9,238	66.0	4,762	34.0	68.5	62.9
West	2,490	2,381	1,577	66.2	805	33.8	1,500	63.0	882	37.0	63.3	60.2
Asian	10,455	7,059	3,901	55.3	3,159	44.7	3,357	47.6	3,702	52.4	37.3	32.1
Northeast	2,346	1,524	697	45.7	827	54.3	608	39.9	916	60.1	29.7	25.9
Midwest	1,175	676	392	57.9	284	42.1	326	48.2	351	51.8	33.4	27.7
South	2,146	1,276	669	52.4	607	47.6	545	42.7	731	57.3	31.2	25.4
West	4,788	3,583	2,143	59.8	1,440	40.2	1,879	52.5	1,704	47.5	44.8	39.3
Hispanic (of any race)	30,852	19,537	11,608	59.4	7,930	40.6	9,745	49.9	9,792	50.1	37.6	31.6
Northeast	4,059	2,786	1,663	59.7	1,123	40.3	1,445	51.9	1,341	48.1	41.0	35.6
Midwest	2,490	1,496	840	56.2	656	43.8	703	47.0	792	53.0	33.7	28.2
South	11,571	7,475	4,424	59.2	3,051	40.8	3,466	46.4	4,010	53.6	38.2	30.0
West	12,731	7,780	4,680	60.2	3,100	39.8	4,131	53.1	3,649	46.9	36.8	32.4

SOURCE: Adapted from "Table 3. Reported Voting and Registration, by Race, Hispanic Origin, and Age, for the United States, Regions, and Divisions, November 2008," in *Voting and Registration in the Election of November 2008—Detailed Tables*, U.S. Census Bureau, July 2009, http://www.census.gov/hhes/www/socdemo/voting/publications/p20/2008/tables.html (accessed December 31, 2009)

2004) and stayed the same in the Midwest (71.5% in 2008 compared with 71.6% in 2004.)

Since the 1960s the number of minority registered voters in the South has increased. This increase is due in large part to the passage of the Civil Rights Act of 1964 and the Voting Rights Act of 1965. These laws removed voting restrictions and led to often volatile and dangerous voter registration campaigns conducted during the 1960s and 1970s. Before these changes many southern states enforced poll taxes, charging citizens for the right to vote and knowing that many poor African-Americans could not afford to pay. Some southern states had so-called grandfather clauses that permitted voting rights only to those whose grandfathers had been able to vote. Many elderly African-Americans were the grandchildren of slaves who had not been able to vote, so these clauses restricted their rights. Furthermore, because they did not have the right to vote, their own children and grandchildren were also prevented from voting under the grandfather clauses. It took more than laws to open voting booths to southern African-Americans—it took marches, demonstrations, and the loss of a number of lives.

The Census Bureau notes that Asian-American citizens living in the West were the most likely to be registered to vote in 2008—59.8% of them were registered to vote. (See Table 8.2.) In the Midwest 57.9% of Asian-American citizens were registered to vote, in the South 52.4% were registered to vote, and in the Northeast 45.7% were registered to vote. Hispanic citizens were also the most likely to be registered to vote if they lived in the West, where 60.2% were registered to vote in 2008, followed closely by the Northeast, where 59.7% of Hispanic citizens were registered to vote, and the South, where 59.2% of Hispanic citizens were registered to vote. Hispanic citizens living in the Midwest had the lowest rate of voter registration at 56.2%.

VOTER TURNOUT

Registering to vote is one thing, but actually going out to the polls on election day is another. Often, people will register to vote but fail to exercise their right to vote when the time comes. However, Sam Roberts reports in "No Racial Gap Seen in '08 Vote Turnout" (*New York Times*, April 30, 2009) that according to a Pew Research Center analysis the rates of minority turnout on election day in November 2008 were historically high. Turnout among non-Hispanic whites declined 1.1%, but turnout among minorities rose. Among African-Americans, the turnout rose by 4.9%, making it the most diverse voter turnout in U.S. history.

Even though African-Americans are somewhat less likely to vote than whites, both groups are much more likely to vote than Hispanics and Asian-Americans. In 2008, 66.1% of non-Hispanic white citizens voted, down from 67.2% in the previous presidential election. (See Table 8.1.) Among African-Americans, 64.7% of eligible citizens voted, compared with 60% in 2004. Among Hispanic citizens, 49.9%

voted, up from 47.2% in 2004. Results were similar among Asian-American citizens; in 2008, 47.6% voted, up from 44.2% in 2004.

African-Americans living in the Midwest were more likely to vote in 2008 than were African-Americans living in other parts of the country. Two-thirds (67.3%) of African-American citizens in the Midwest voted that year, and nearly the same proportion (66%) voted in the South. (See Table 8.2.) The lowest turnout of African-American citizens was in the Northeast, where only 58.6% voted. Hispanic turnout was best in the West, where 53.1% of Hispanic citizens voted in 2008, whereas the lowest turnout of Hispanics was in the South, where only 46.4% voted. Asian-Americans living in the West were also the most likely to vote—52.5% of them did so—whereas the lowest turnout of Asian-Americans was in the Northeast, at 39.9%.

A General Decline in Voting Participation

Since 1964 there has been a decline in the percentage of Americans who vote in presidential elections. The Census Bureau (November 1964, http://www.census.gov/population/socdemo/voting/p20-143/tab01.pdf; February 27, 2002, http://www.census.gov/population/socdemo/voting/p20-542/tab02.pdf) reports that in 1964, 69.3% of the voting-age population voted, compared with 54.7% in 2000. In 2004 this rate increased to 58.3%, and in 2008 the rate stayed about the same, at 58.2%. (See Table 8.2.) These figures include the resident voting-age population that is not eligible to vote, such as noncitizens.

A general decline in the proportion of Americans who vote was also seen across racial and ethnic groups, although voting was sharply up in 2008 among these populations. In *Historical Voting and Registration Reports* (August 26, 2008, http://www.census.gov/population/www/socdemo/voting/past-voting.html), the Census Bureau reports that only among non-Hispanic whites (who were counted separately from Hispanic whites starting in 1980) did the percentage of the voting-age population that votes rise; after dropping from 62.8% in 1980 to 60.4% in 2000, it rose to 65.8% in 2004. However, voting among this group dropped in 2008 to 64.8%. (See Table 8.2.) In 1968, the first year African-Americans were counted separately from other races, 57.6% of the African-American voting-age population voted. This percentage dropped to 53.5% in 2000, but rose again to 56.3% in 2004 and then skyrocketed in 2008 to 60.8%, the highest rate since recording began. Among Hispanics, 37.5% of the voting-age population voted in 1972, whereas in 2000 only 27.5% voted—and this percentage rose only slightly, to 28%, in 2004. However, voting among this population was up sharply in 2008 as well, to 31.6%. The number of Asian-Americans who vote has been tracked only since the 1992 presidential election. In 1992, 27.3% of the Asian-American voting-age population voted, down to 25.4% in 2000 but up to 29.8% in 2004 and to 32.1% in 2008.

Reasons for Not Voting

Age seems to affect one's likelihood to vote. Traditionally, the demographic group between the ages of 18 and 24 has the lowest percentage of voters. This may partially explain the low voter turnout of Hispanics, because they are on average younger than other segments of the U.S. population. According to the Census Bureau, in *Voting and Registration in the Election of November 2008* (July 20, 2009, http://www.census.gov/population/www/socdemo/voting/cps2008.html), only 44.3% of young adults between the ages of 18 and 24 voted in 2008. Obama had mobilized young voters in ways that previous candidates had been unable to do; 41.9% of this population had voted in 2004, and only 32.3% had voted in 2000. Scott Keeter, Juliana Horowitz, and Alec Tyson of the Pew Research Center for the People and the Press report in "Young Voters in the 2008 Election" (November 12, 2008, http://pewresearch.org/pubs/1031/young-voters-in-the-2008-election) that the young vote made the difference: 66% of voters under the age of 30 voted for Obama. As citizens age, however, they are more likely to vote. The Census Bureau indicates that in 2008, 51.9% of the voting-age population between the ages of 25 and 44 voted, 65% of those between the ages of 45 and 64 voted, and 70.1% of those between the ages of 65 and 74 voted.

According to the Census Bureau, the number-one reason people gave for not voting in the 2008 presidential election was that they were too busy, an excuse given by 17.5% of registered nonvoters. (See Table 8.3.) Other leading reasons were illness or disability (14.9%), no interest (13.4%), dislike of candidates or campaign issues (12.9%), and out of town (8.8%). Asian-Americans and Hispanics were especially likely to state they were too busy to vote (26.9% and 24.8%, respectively), and African-Americans were especially likely to say they were ill or out of town (20.3% each).

AFRICAN-AMERICAN POLITICAL PARTICIPATION

Elected Officials

The number of African-Americans elected to public offices at all levels of the U.S. government has increased significantly since the 1980s. The largest gain has been in city and county offices, which include county commissioners, city council members, mayors, vice mayors, and aldermen/alderwomen. Obama became only the fifth African-American to serve in the U.S. Senate and only the third since the period of Reconstruction (1865–1877), when he was sworn in as a senator from Illinois on January 4, 2005. He had received international media coverage after delivering a stirring keynote address at the 2004 Democratic National Convention. In 2008 he won the presidency and became the first African-American president in U.S. history.

African-Americans and Political Parties

According to the Pew Research Center for the People and the Press, in *Evenly Divided and Increasingly Polarized: The 2004 Political Landscape* (November 5, 2003, http://people-press.org/reports/pdf/196.pdf), African-Americans are the strongest supporters of the Democratic Party. In 2003, 64% of African-Americans described themselves as Democrats, another 21% said they leaned toward the Democratic Party, and only 7% identified themselves as Republicans. Even though many Americans shifted toward the Republican Party after the terrorist attacks against the United States on September 11, 2001 (9/11), African-Americans did not. The Pew Research Center notes that across regions, socioeconomic groups, and ages, the preference for the Democratic Party among African-Americans is uniform; the most affluent African-Americans' party affiliation is almost identical to the least affluent, and the Democratic advantage is only slightly smaller among younger people.

By 2008 disillusionment with the administration of George W. Bush (1946–) and excitement over the candidates in the Democratic primary had drawn more Democratic voters to the polls. The Pew Research Center notes in "Inside Obama's Sweeping Victory" (November 5, 2008, http://pewresearch.org/pubs/1023/exit-poll-analysis-2008) that even though equal numbers of Democrats and Republicans had voted in 2004, in 2008 Democrats had the advantage, 39% to 32%. Obama won 60% of those with low or moderate incomes of less than $50,000 per year. He also won 66% of the Hispanic vote, which was 13 percentage points higher than the Democratic candidate had won in 2004, and 95% of African-American votes, seven percentage points higher than the Democratic candidate won in 2004.

The traditional African-American political goals, as presented by the 13 original members of the Congressional Black Caucus (CBC; February 2010, http://www.cbcfinc.org/cbc.html), are to "promote the public welfare through legislation designed to meet the needs of millions of neglected citizens." In February 2010 there were 42 members of the CBC. The CBC encourages and seeks out African-American participation in government, especially as elected officials, to correct the ills of the disadvantaged, many of whom are minorities.

As the African-American middle class continues to grow, party loyalties may change. Some younger professional African-Americans who may not have experienced poverty or the deprivation of the inner cities may be attracted to the Republican Party platform of less government and lower taxes. A vast majority of African-Americans embraced the programs of President Lyndon B. Johnson's (1908–1973) Great Society and his War on Poverty in the 1960s. In the 21st century a small minority believe that reliance on government has actually disempowered many African-Americans

TABLE 8.3

Reasons for not voting by selected characteristics, November 2008

[In thousands]

Characteristic	Total	Percent distribution of reasons for not voting											
		Illness or disability	Out of town	Forgot to vote	Not interested	Too busy, conflicting schedule	Transportation problems	Did not like candidates or campaign issues	Registration problems	Bad weather conditions	Inconvenient polling place	Other reason	Don't know or refused
Total	**15,167**	**14.9**	**8.8**	**2.6**	**13.4**	**17.5**	**2.6**	**12.9**	**6.0**	**0.2**	**2.7**	**11.3**	**7.0**
Age													
18 to 24 years	2,567	3.2	14.2	4.5	12.1	21.0	2.4	8.0	9.0	0.2	2.6	11.6	1.2
25 to 44 years	5,819	6.8	8.4	2.8	14.2	24.3	1.4	12.7	7.3	0.1	3.0	11.7	7.2
45 to 64 years	4,201	14.8	8.3	1.8	15.2	14.9	3.4	16.5	4.3	0.1	2.6	12.5	5.8
65 years and over	2,581	45.3	5.1	1.3	9.9	3.0	4.5	12.5	2.6	0.8	2.3	8.0	4.6
Sex													
Male	7,512	10.5	10.5	2.8	14.9	18.4	2.0	13.1	5.3	0.2	2.9	11.4	7.9
Female	7,655	19.3	7.1	2.3	11.9	16.6	3.2	12.7	6.6	0.2	2.4	11.2	6.2
Race and Hispanic origin													
White alone	12,920	15.0	8.9	2.4	14.1	17.3	2.4	14.2	5.7	0.2	2.5	11.0	6.3
White non-Hispanic alone	11,172	15.6	9.1	2.4	14.1	16.2	2.4	15.2	5.6	0.2	2.3	10.9	6.1
Black alone	1,242	20.3	20.3	6.4	3.1	8.5	16.9	4.8	4.3	5.6	1.2	3.3	12.7
Asian alone	543	6.8	12.0	2.6	9.4	26.9	1.7	4.5	7.9	—	5.5	11.8	11.0
Hispanic (of any race)	1,862	10.8	7.8	2.4	14.0	24.8	2.5	7.6	7.0	—	4.1	11.7	7.3
White alone or in combination	13,128	15.0	15.0	9.0	2.5	14.0	17.2	2.5	14.1	5.8	0.2	2.5	11.1
Black alone or in combination	1,286	19.8	19.8	6.2	3.2	8.5	16.4	4.6	4.4	6.0	1.1	3.5	13.3
Asian alone or in combination	598	7.2	7.2	12.8	2.4	8.8	26.3	2.4	4.1	8.1	—	5.2	11.4
Educational attainment													
Less than high school graduate	2,556	25.6	4.0	3.0	13.8	12.2	4.7	13.6	3.2	0.7	3.1	10.8	5.3
High school graduate	6,015	14.3	6.8	2.5	15.6	18.0	2.8	14.0	5.8	0.2	2.6	10.9	6.6
Some college	4,427	10.9	11.1	2.7	11.4	20.2	1.9	11.9	7.2	0.0	2.5	11.6	8.7
Bachelors degree or more	2,169	12.5	15.3	1.9	10.8	16.9	1.4	11.4	7.4	0.3	3.0	12.4	6.8
Nativity													
Native-born citizen	14,162	15.0	8.6	2.7	13.5	17.0	2.6	13.4	6.0	0.3	2.6	11.3	7.0
Naturalized citizen	1,005	14.2	11.0	1.1	11.1	24.9	2.9	5.8	6.3	—	3.5	11.2	8.0
Tenure													
Less than 1 year	2,917	8.2	9.1	2.7	10.8	21.4	4.3	9.8	14.9	0.2	2.5	12.8	3.5
1 to 2 years	2,351	10.9	10.2	3.6	11.3	20.3	1.9	11.7	6.6	0.1	3.0	14.1	6.3
3 years or longer	9,719	18.0	8.5	2.3	14.8	15.7	2.4	14.2	3.3	0.3	2.7	10.2	7.8
Don't know, refused	180	12.1	4.8	—	7.8	19.5	1.4	8.5	0.8	—	1.1	10.7	33.3
Region													
Northeast	2,618	15.7	8.7	2.6	13.4	14.5	2.4	14.2	5.4	—	4.2	10.6	8.4
Midwest	3,591	14.4	8.3	2.3	13.0	18.2	2.9	15.5	4.7	0.0	2.2	11.0	7.4
South	6,452	16.7	8.2	2.3	13.3	17.5	2.9	12.0	6.4	0.5	2.2	11.6	6.4
West	2,506	10.5	11.1	3.7	14.3	20.0	1.8	10.2	7.2	—	3.1	11.5	6.6
Annual family income													
Total family members	10,665	13.6	8.9	2.5	14.4	18.5	2.0	12.3	5.8	0.3	2.5	11.5	7.8
Less than $10,000	563	19.9	4.5	4.1	7.6	16.7	7.0	11.5	9.4	0.4	3.1	10.2	5.5
$10,000 to $14,999	522	22.4	5.5	2.9	12.1	14.7	3.6	8.7	6.5	0.5	2.1	12.7	8.2
$15,000 to $19,999	422	20.5	4.1	0.8	10.8	21.9	4.0	13.6	4.0	—	2.1	11.3	6.8
$20,000 to $29,999	1,263	17.5	6.0	0.7	11.4	14.6	3.9	15.6	7.6	0.0	2.2	11.5	9.0
$30,000 to $39,999	1,258	14.1	4.9	2.2	16.9	18.5	1.8	15.1	5.3	0.2	2.4	11.4	7.1

TABLE 8.3

Reasons for not voting by selected characteristics, November 2008 [CONTINUED]

[In thousands]

		Percent distribution of reasons for not voting											
Characteristic	Total	Illness or disability	Out of town	Forgot to vote	Not interested	Too busy, conflicting schedule	Transportation problems	Did not like candidates or campaign issues	Registration problems	Bad weather conditions	Inconvenient polling place	Other reason	Don't know or refused
$40,000 to $49,999	896	13.6	6.8	2.3	14.7	18.8	3.2	15.0	3.9	—	3.4	11.4	7.0
$50,000 to $74,999	2,022	10.9	10.5	3.3	17.2	21.1	0.5	12.7	4.7	0.0	2.1	11.4	5.7
$75,000 to $99,999	998	6.6	13.3	3.1	17.1	22.0	0.7	7.1	7.5	0.0	3.6	12.4	6.7
$100,000 to $149,999	976	9.6	10.8	1.9	11.7	19.4	0.6	12.0	8.5	—	3.3	13.2	9.0
$150,000 and over	550	5.3	20.9	4.5	12.5	19.1	0.8	10.0	4.1	—	0.4	10.2	12.1
Income not reported	1,195	17.1	10.0	1.8	16.2	15.5	0.4	9.9	3.7	1.6	2.8	10.2	10.7

"—" Represents zero or rounds to zero.

Note: Federal surveys now give respondents the option of reporting more than one race. Therefore, two basic ways of defining a race group are possible. A group such as Asian may be defined as those who reported Asian and no other race (the race-alone or single-race concept) or as those who reported Asian regardless of whether they also reported another race (the race-alone-or-in-combination concept). This table shows data for people who reported they were the single race white and not Hispanic, people who reported the single race black, and people who reported the single race Asian. Use of the single-race populations does not imply that it is the preferred method of presenting or analyzing data. Total figure is the number of registered citizens who reported not voting, excluding those who were counted as "not voting" based on non-response to the initial question on voting. Separate estimates for the race group "white non-Hispanic alone or in combination," which were included in 2004, have been removed from this table.

SOURCE: Table 12. Reasons for Not Voting, by Selected Characteristics: November 2008, in *Voting and Registration in the Election of November 2008—Detailed Tables*, U.S. Census Bureau, July 2009, http://www.census.gov/hhes/www/socdemo/voting/publications/p20/2008/tables.html (accessed December 31, 2009) and other underprivileged people. For example, the African American Republican Leadership Council (February 2010, http://www.aarlc.org/issues/index.shtml) argues in favor of limited government. It states that African-Americans "suffer the greatest losses under today's Social Security system," and charges that civil liberties groups who "represent entire groups or category of people" actually "strip away individual civil liberties and maintain power over those purportedly protected by these organization's leaders."

However, any movement toward the Republican Party before the 2008 election was slowed by Obama's election in 2008. A January 2009 Pew Research Center poll found that nearly four out of five (79%) African-Americans believed that "people like themselves" would gain influence under the Obama administration. (See Table 8.4.) This was more than the African-Americans who believed they would gain influence under the Bush administration, which took office in January 2001, or even under the Democratic Clinton administration, which took office in January 1993. Only 30% of African-Americans believed they would gain influence under Bush, and only 67% believed they would gain influence under Bill Clinton (1946–).

TABLE 8.4

Percent of people who believe they will gain influence under incoming presidents by selected characteristics, 1993, 2001, and 2009

Influence of "People Like Yourself"

	Clinton Jan 1993 %	Bush Jan 2001 %	Obama Jan 2009 %
People like yourself will . . .			
Gain influence	43	35	47
Lose influence	22	26	18
Not affected	27	33	29
Don't know	8	6	6
	100	100	100
Percent saying people like themselves will 'gain influence' among . . .			
White	41	35	41
Black	67	30	79
18–29	49	40	62
30–49	45	35	50
50–64	44	34	41
65+	29	33	32
*Household income**			
$75k+	37	37	39
$30k–74,999	45	36	53
Less than $30,000	47	31	53
Republican	22	60	24
Democrat	62	18	66
Independent	40	32	45

*1993 income categories are $50k+, $20–49,999 and less than $20,000 for comparison.

SOURCE: "Influence of 'People Like Yourself," in *Strong Confidence in Obama—Country Seen As Less Politically Divided*, Pew Research Center for People and the Press, a project of the Pew Research Center, January 15, 2009, http://people-press.org/report/?pageid=1456 (accessed December 31, 2009)

HISPANIC POLITICAL PARTICIPATION
Factors Contributing to Low Political Participation

There was a tremendous increase in the Hispanic population in the United States during the late 20th century. According to the Census Bureau (December 22, 2009, http://www.census.gov/popest/national/asrh/NC-EST2008-srh.html), by 2008, 46.9 million Hispanics lived in the United States. However, the Hispanic community has not attained political power equal to its proportion of the population. Two characteristics of Hispanic demography help account for this. First, even though the Hispanic voting-age population grew during the 1970s and 1980s, Hispanics have a young population, with many in the 18- to 24-year-old category—the age group that is the least likely to vote. In addition, a smaller proportion of Hispanics than of society as a whole are in the 55 and older category—the age group that is the most likely to vote. The second and perhaps more important characteristic is the issue of U.S. citizenship. In 2008, 36.7% Hispanics living in the United States were not U.S. citizens, thus eliminating over 11.3 million potential Hispanic voters. (See Table 8.2.)

Political Participation

Civil rights gains of the 1960s, such as the 24th Amendment eliminating the poll tax, the extension of the Voting Rights Act of 1965 to the Southwest, and the elimination of the English literacy requirement, helped a number of Hispanics attain political office. During the 1970s both major political parties started wooing Hispanic voters and drafting Hispanic candidates. Advocacy groups, such as the Mexican American Legal Defense and Education Fund, the Southwest Voter Registration Education Project, and the Puerto Rican Legal Defense and Education Fund, were formed. All these groups helped develop the political influence of the Hispanic community.

The National Association of Latino Elected and Appointed Officials (NALEO; 2009, http://www.naleo.org/aboutnalco.html) is a research, policy, and education organization that is made up by over 6,000 Latino elected and appointed officials. The organization's mission is to facilitate the integration of Latino immigrants into U.S. society, to develop leadership abilities among Latino youth, and to support the nation's Latino elected and appointed officials. In 2004 the NALEO Educational Fund announced that it was collaborating with Univision Communications Inc. in a program aimed at mobilizing Hispanic voters throughout the United States. The "Voces del Pueblo" campaign included nonpartisan public service announcements on radio and television as well as voter education forums, phone contact, and targeted mailings. According to Univision Communications, in the press release "The NALEO Educational Fund and Univision Launch Effort to Mobilize Latino Electorate" (March 5, 2004, http://www.univision.net/corp/en/pr/Los_Angeles_05032004-2.html), Ivelisse Estrada of Univision Communications is quoted as saying that "with the significant growth of the Latino population in the U.S. and the increasing number of Latinos registering to vote, the U.S. Hispanic community's ability to influence the course of our nation can no longer be ignored. Now more than ever, Latinos are demonstrating that they are key players on the political stage. With this campaign, we have the opportunity to listen to Latino voters and identify their concerns." The program was an attempt to mobilize Hispanic voters, in part by encouraging immigrants to become U.S. citizens, and to develop the political influence of the Hispanic community. In "Univision Gives Citizenship Drive an Unusual Life" (*Wall Street Journal*, May 10, 2007), Miriam Jordan reported that according to some observers, this citizenship drive could influence the outcome of the 2008 presidential race. In fact, NALEO noted in *2008 Latino Election Handbook* (2008, http://www.naleo.org/downloads/NALEO_LEH_2008_final.pdf) that the significant rise in naturalized Latinos in 2006 and 2007 would translate into an increased political influence at the polls. It argued that Latinos played a crucial role in Senator John McCain's (1936–) Republican primary victory in Florida and in keeping the primary campaign of Democrat Hillary Rodham Clinton alive in California, Texas, and Puerto Rico.

Hispanics and Political Parties

As a group, Hispanics have been important supporters of the Democratic Party. Like many other Americans in the aftermath of 9/11, many Hispanics shifted their party affiliation to the Republican Party, although by 2007 that trend had reversed itself. Paul Taylor and Richard Fry of the Pew Research Center reported in *Hispanics and the 2008 Election: A Swing Vote?* (December 6, 2007, http://pewhispanic.org/files/reports/83.pdf) that even though Democrats outnumbered Republicans among Hispanics by more than two to one in the 1990s, after 9/11 Democrats led by a smaller margin. In fact, Bush received an estimated 40% of the Hispanic vote in 2004, a record for a Republican presidential candidate.

However, between 2006 and 2007 the shift of Hispanic voters to the Republican Party reversed course. Taylor and Fry found that in 2006, 28% of Hispanics said they supported Republicans and 49% said they supported Democrats. Within a year, only 23% of Hispanics identified as Republicans and 57% identified as Democrats. According to Taylor and Fry, more Hispanics believed the Democratic Party showed greater concern for Latinos and thought the Democrats were doing a better job on the issue of illegal immigration. In addition, 41% of Hispanics surveyed believed the Bush administration's policies had been harmful to Latinos, whereas only 16% believed these policies had been helpful.

Taylor and Fry suggested that Hispanics had the potential to be a swing vote in helping decide the 2008 presidential election. Latino voters represented a sizeable share of the electorate in four of the six states that Bush carried by margins of five percentage points or fewer in the 2004 election: New Mexico, Florida, Nevada, and Colorado. The Pew Research Center predicted that the Hispanic vote in Florida, in particular, would play a strong part in the 2008 elections. Even though Cuban-Americans in southern Florida had been traditionally Republican, the Latino vote in central Florida had grown. Much of this population was from Puerto Rico. In addition, the state had a growing population of Latinos from South America, Central America, and Mexico. The Pew Hispanic Center notes in the fact sheet "Among Hispanics in Florida, 2008 Voter Registration Rolls Swing Democrat" (October 29, 2008, http://pewhispanic.org/files/factsheets/44.pdf) that by mid-2008 more Hispanics in the state were Democrats (35.3%) than Republicans (33.5%), and that a third had chosen to remain independent. The Pew Research Center also reports in "How Hispanics Voted in the 2008 Election" (November 7, 2008, http://pewresearch.org/pubs/1024/exit-poll-analysis-hispanics) that Obama won 57% of the Hispanic vote in Florida, a significant shift from 2004, when Bush carried 56% of the Hispanic vote in that state.

RACE, ETHNICITY, AND ELECTORAL DISTRICTS

The design of electoral districts can have a tremendous impact on the political power of minorities. Depending on how the lines are drawn, an electoral district might have a large concentration of minorities, enhancing their political power, or minority populations may be split up between many electoral districts, weakening their political influence.

Designing electoral districts to favor one group over another is known as gerrymandering, named after the Massachusetts governor Elbridge Gerry (1744–1814), who became notorious for the salamander-shaped district he approved in 1812. In the first half of the 20th century gerrymandering was widely used as an attempt to prevent African-Americans and other minorities from gaining true political representation. Another practice was creating at-large districts, in which the entire population of a large area elected several representatives. The alternative, having several smaller districts each elect only one representative, allowed concentrated populations of minorities to elect their own representatives.

Under the requirements of the Voting Rights Act of 1965, jurisdictions with a history of systematic discrimination (such as a poll tax or literacy test) must create districts with majorities of African-Americans or Hispanics wherever the demographics warrant it. At the same time, they must avoid weakening existing "minority-majority" districts (i.e., districts "in which a majority of the population is a member of a specific minority group"). This law helped eliminate some districts that had been designed to favor whites. At the same time, however, it superseded the traditional criterion of compact districts and made for some oddly defined districts in the name of creating Hispanic- or African-American–majority districts.

Computerized Redistricting

Douglas J. Amy notes in *Real Choices/New Voices: How Proportional Representation Elections Could Revitalize American Democracy* (2002) that with computer software, gerrymandering in the 21st century has become highly sophisticated. Redistricters can now incorporate a variety of information—party registration, voting patterns, and ethnic makeup—from a variety of sources, including census data, property tax records, and old district lines. This information allows them to produce a number of potential scenarios in an instant. Contemporary gerrymandering techniques are called "packing" (concentrating a group of voters in the fewest number of districts), "cracking" (spreading a group of voters across districts), and "kidnapping" (remapping so that two incumbents from the same party are now located in the same district and vying for the same seat). Gerrymandering in the past was essentially self-correcting; by attempting to control as many districts as possible, parties risked losing, should a small percentage of voters shift allegiances. However, contemporary software has become so sophisticated, and politics have become so partisan that the idea of self-correction is no longer applicable. As a result, few seats in the U.S. House of Representatives are now competitive, with incumbents enjoying a locked-in advantage that is almost impossible to overcome.

The article "Political Gerrymandering 2000–2008: 'A Self-Limiting Enterprise'?" (*Harvard Law Review*, vol. 122, March 2009) also argues against the idea that gerrymandering will always be "self-limited." By looking at seven cases of redistricting schemes after the 2000 census, the article finds that the most damaging gerrymandering occurs in areas where a very strong party is in control and attempts to push its advantage to the limit, and in places where the two political parties collude in a gerrymander in an attempt to keep their own incumbents in office. In particular, "big party gerrymanders at least leave open the possibility of self-correction, but bipartisan gerrymanders make the idea fanciful." Whether voters want a change or not, the bipartisan gerrymanders fix incumbent parties in place for 10 years.

Challenges to Electoral Districting

Redistricting has become a major source of contention between Republicans and Democrats since the 2000 census. One notorious case took place in Texas. The Texas lawmakers were unable to agree on new congressional districts because Republicans controlled the state senate and Democrats controlled the state house of representatives. A compromise plan was forced on the parties by a panel of federal judges, essentially leaving the current partisan balance in place. However, after Republicans took control of the state house in 2002, they sought to reopen the redistricting question, breaking an unwritten rule that remapping was to be a matter dealt with once every 10 years to avoid incessant wrangling on the subject. To resist, Democrats in both the state house and senate fled to Oklahoma and New Mexico to prevent the creation of a quorum (the minimum number of representatives present to conduct business) and thwart the ability of the Republicans to push through their redistricting plan.

Eventually, the Democrats gave in and the congressional districts were redrawn, with the potential that the Republicans would pick up seven seats in the 2004 elections. Staff lawyers in the U.S. Department of Justice approved the plan, even though lawyers for the department had concluded that the redistricting plan undercut minority voting rights. In fact, Republicans won 21 of Texas's 32 seats in the U.S. House of Representatives in 2004, up from 15. The U.S. Supreme Court announced in December 2005 that it would consider the constitutionality of the redistricted congressional map. In June 2006 the court ruled that the redistricting violated the rights of some Hispanics, but did not violate the rights of African-American voters in the state. Furthermore, it ruled that nothing in the U.S. Constitution barred states from redrawing political lines at any time, and it established no timetable for reviewing the redistricting that had violated the rights of Hispanics. As of February 2010, the court had not reviewed this redistricting issue.

A redistricting effort in Pennsylvania also drew a great deal of attention. After losing two seats in Congress due to a drop in population, Pennsylvania redrew its districts, a process that the Republican majority in the General Assembly openly sought to benefit the party through the latest techniques in gerrymandering. Some of the unusually shaped districts that resulted were called the "supine seahorse" and the "upside-down Chinese dragon." Even though a Democrat won the governor's race in Pennsylvania in 2002, Republicans took 12 of the 19 U.S. House of Representatives seats.

Vieth v. Jubelirer (541 U.S. 267 [2004]) contended that the Republicans went too far in their efforts to favor their own party in redrawing congressional lines. However, in May 2004 the Supreme Court upheld the Pennsylvania map in a 5–4 decision. Justice Antonin Scalia (1936–) and others of the majority opinion maintained that it was the responsibility of Congress and not the court to define fair districting practices. Justice John Paul Stevens (1920–), a minority opinion holder, characterized the decision as "a failure of judicial will to condemn even the most blatant violations of a state legislature's fundamental duty to govern impartially."

IMPORTANT NAMES
AND ADDRESSES

Bureau of Justice Statistics
U.S. Department of Justice
810 Seventh St. NW
Washington, DC 20531
(202) 307-0765
E-mail: askbjs@usdoj.gov
URL: http://bjs.ojp.usdoj.gov/

Center for Women's Business Research
1760 Old Meadow Rd., Ste. 500
McLean, VA 22102
(703) 556-7162
FAX: (703) 506-3266
URL: http://www.cfwbr.org/

Centers for Disease Control
and Prevention
1600 Clifton Rd.
Atlanta, GA 30333
1-800-232-4636
E-mail: cdcinfo@cdc.gov
URL: http://www.cdc.gov/

Children's Defense Fund
25 E St. NW
Washington, DC 20001
1-800-233-1200
E-mail: cdfinfo@childrensdefense.org
URL: http://www.childrensdefense.org/

Civil Rights Project
8370 Math Sciences, Box 951521
Los Angeles, CA 90095-1521
(310) 267-5562
FAX: (310) 206-6293
E-mail: crp@ucla.edu
URL: http://www.civilrightsproject.ucla.edu/

Congressional Black Caucus Foundation
1720 Massachusetts Ave. NW
Washington, DC 20036
(202) 263-2800
FAX: (202) 775-0773
E-mail: info@cbcfinc.org
URL: http://www.cbcfinc.org/

Congressional Hispanic Caucus Institute
911 Second St. NE
Washington, DC 20002
(202) 543-1771
1-800-EXCEL-DC
FAX: (202) 546-2143
URL: http://www.chci.org/

Lawyers' Committee for Civil Rights
under Law
1401 New York Ave. NW, Ste. 400
Washington, DC 20005
(202) 662-8600
1-888-299-5227
FAX: (202) 783-0857
URL: http://www.lawyerscommittee.org/

League of United Latin American
Citizens
2000 L St. NW, Ste. 610
Washington, DC 20036
(202) 833-6130
FAX: (202) 833-6135
URL: http://www.lulac.org/

National Association for the Advancement
of Colored People
4805 Mt. Hope Dr.
Baltimore, MD 21215
(410) 580-5777
1-877-NAACP-98
URL: http://www.naacp.org/

National Association of Latino Elected
and Appointed Officials Educational
Fund
1122 W. Washington Blvd., Third Floor
Los Angeles, CA 90015
(213) 747-7606
FAX: (213) 747-7664
URL: http://www.naleo.org/

National Black Child Development
Institute
1313 L St. NW, Ste. 110
Washington, DC 20005-4110

(202) 883-2220
FAX: (202) 833-8222
E-mail: moreinfo@nbcdi.org
URL: http://www.nbcdi.org/

National Caucus and Center on
Black Aged
1220 L St. NW, Ste. 800
Washington, DC 20005
(202) 637-8400
FAX: (202) 347-0895
URL: http://www.ncba-aged.org/

National Center for Education Statistics
U.S. Department of Education
1990 K St. NW
Washington, DC 20006
(202) 502-7300
URL: http://nces.ed.gov/

National Hispanic Council on Aging
734 Fifteenth St. NW, Ste. 1050
Washington, DC 20005
(202) 347-9733
FAX: (202) 347-9735
E-mail: nhcoa@nhcoa.org
URL: http://www.nhcoa.org/

National Urban League
120 Wall St.
New York, NY 10005
(212) 558-5300
FAX: (212) 344-5332
URL: http://www.nul.org/

Organization of Chinese Americans
1322 18th St. NW
Washington, DC 20036-1803
(202) 223-5500
FAX: (202) 296-0540
E-mail: oca@ocanational.org
URL: http://www.ocanational.org/

Pew Hispanic Center
1615 L St. NW, Ste. 700
Washington, DC 20036-5610

(202) 419-3600
FAX: (202) 419-3608
E-mail: info@pewhispanic.org
URL: http://pewhispanic.org/

Poverty and Race Research Action Council
1015 15th St. NW, Ste. 400
Washington, DC 20005
(202) 906-8023
FAX: (202) 842-2885
E-mail: info@prrac.org
URL: http://www.prrac.org/

Sentencing Project
514 10th St. NW, Ste. 1000
Washington, DC 20004
(202) 628-0871
FAX: (202) 628-1091
E-mail: staff@sentencingproject.org
URL: http://www.sentencingproject.org/

Southern Poverty Law Center
400 Washington Ave.
Montgomery, AL 36104
(334) 956-8200
URL: http://www.splcenter.org/

U.S. Bureau of Labor Statistics
U.S. Department of Labor
2 Massachusetts Ave. NE
Washington, DC 20212-0001
(202) 691-5200
URL: http://www.bls.gov/

U.S. Census Bureau
4600 Silver Hill Rd.
Washington, DC 20233
(301) 763-4636
1-800-923-8282
URL: http://www.census.gov/

U.S. Department of Education
400 Maryland Ave. SW
Washington, DC 20202

1-800-872-5327
URL: http://www.ed.gov/

U.S. Department of Health and Human Services
200 Independence Ave. SW
Washington, DC 20201
1-877-696-6775
URL: http://www.hhs.gov/

U.S. Department of Labor
200 Constitution Ave. NW
Washington, DC 20210
1-866-4-USA-DOL
URL: http://www.dol.gov/

U.S. Equal Employment Opportunity Commission
131 M St. NE
Washington, DC 20507
(202) 663-4900
E-mail: info@eeoc.gov
URL: http://www.eeoc.gov/

RESOURCES

The U.S. Census Bureau collects and distributes the nation's statistics. Demographic data from the bureau include *Profiles of General Demographic Characteristics*, *Population Projections Program* (projections released periodically), and *American Community Survey* (released annually). The Census Bureau also produces studies on racial and ethnic groups, including *The Asian Alone Population in the United States: March 2004* (August 2008), *The American Community—Blacks: 2004* (February 2007), and *U.S. Hispanic Population: 2008* (September 2009).

The Census Bureau releases the *Statistical Abstract* each year; the latest edition is *Statistical Abstract of the United States: 2009* (2008). It releases financial and family statistics in *America's Families and Living Arrangements: 2008* (February 2009) and *Income, Poverty, and Health Insurance Coverage in the United States: 2008* (Carmen DeNavas-Walt, Bernadette D. Proctor, and Jessica C. Smith, September 2009). It also compiles statistics on homeownership rates, business data, state and metropolitan population data, and voting data. Publications include *Voting and Registration in the Election of November 2008* (July 2009), *Housing Vacancies and Homeownership Annual Statistics: 2008* (March 2009), and *State and Metropolitan Area Data Book: 2006* (July 2006). The Census Bureau periodically publishes the *Survey of Minority-Owned Business Enterprises*.

The U.S. Bureau of Labor Statistics (BLS) provides labor force data. The BLS publishes *Employment and Earnings*, *Household Data Annual Averages*, and the monthly *Employment Situation Summary*. The *Monthly Labor Review* provides detailed analysis of labor force statistics on a periodic basis. Other job-related sources published by the U.S. Equal Employment Opportunity Commission are *Job Patterns for Minorities and Women in Private Industry* (October 2009) and *Enforcement Statistics and Litigation* (2009). The Center for Women's Business Statistics provided information on businesses owned by minority women in *Businesses Owned by Women of Color in the United States, 2006* (2007).

A variety of government resources on minority health proved invaluable. The National Center for Health Statistics produces *Health, United States, 2008* (2009) and the monthly *National Vital Statistics Reports*, which provide birth and mortality statistics. The Centers for Disease Control and Prevention publishes the annual *HIV/AIDS Surveillance Report*. Another helpful source, *America's Children: Key National Indicators of Well-Being, 2009* (July 2009), is published by the Federal Interagency Forum on Child and Family Statistics. The *SEER Cancer Statistics Review, 1975–2006* (M. J. Horner et al., 2009), published by the National Cancer Institute, provides invaluable data on cancer.

A number of U.S. Department of Health and Human Services publications were used in this book. The *National Healthcare Disparities Report, 2008* (March 2009) is helpful in examining differences in health care access and utilization among minority populations. *Indicators of Welfare Dependence, Annual Report to Congress, 2008* (2007) examines rates of utilization of a variety of social programs. *Results from the 2008 National Survey on Drug Use and Health: Detailed Tables* (September 2009) provides information on tobacco, alcohol, and illicit drug use.

The U.S. Department of Education's National Center for Education Statistics (NCES) publishes *The Condition of Education 2009* (Michael Planty et al., June 2009). Other NCES reports that proved helpful were *Indicators of School Crime and Safety: 2009* (Rachel Dinkes, Jana Kemp, and Katrina Baum, December 2009), *The Children Born in 2001 at Kindergarten Entry: First Findings from the Kindergarten Data Collections of the Early Childhood Longitudinal Study, Birth Cohort* (Kristin Denton Flanagan and Cameron McPhee, October 2009), *Digest of Education Statistics, 2008* (Thomas D. Snyder, Sally A. Dillow, and Charlene M. Hoffman, March 2009), *Preschool: First Findings from the Preschool Follow-up of the Early Childhood Longitudinal Study, Birth Cohort* (Jodi Jacobson Chernoff et al., October 2007), *Status and Trends in the Education of Racial and Ethnic Minorities*

(Angelina KewalRamani et al., September 2007), *American Indian and Alaska Native Children: Findings from the Base Year of the Early Childhood Longitudinal Study, Birth Cohort* (Kristin Denton Flanagan and Jen Park, August 2005), and *Status and Trends in the Education of American Indians and Alaska Natives* (Catherine Freeman and Mary Ann Fox, August 2005). The College Board provides useful data in *College-Bound Seniors 2009* (July 2009).

The BJS produces *Homicide Trends in the United States* (James Alan Fox and Marianne W. Zawitz, July 2007) as well as numerous other reports. Other BJS reports used in this publication include *Capital Punishment, 2008* (Tracy L. Snell, December 2009), *Probation and Parole in the United States, 2008* (Lauren E. Glaze and Thomas P. Bonczar, December 2009), *Criminal Victimization, 2008* (Michael R. Rand, September 2009), and *Prison and Jail Inmates at Midyear 2008* (Heather C. West and William J. Sabol, March 2009). *Hate Crime Statistics, 2008* (November 2009) and *Crime in the United States, 2008* (September 2009) were published by the Federal Bureau of Investigation.

Finally, the Gallup Organization provides valuable polling information. Gallup publications used in this book include *U.S. Waiting for Race Relations to Improve under Obama* (Lydia Saad, November 9, 2009), *Little "Obama Effect" on Views about Race Relations* (Frank Newport, October 29, 2009), *Whites May Exaggerate Black-Hispanic Tensions* (Lydia Saad, July 17, 2008), *More Americans Say U.S. a Nation of Haves and Have-Nots* (Lydia Saad, July 11, 2008), *Blacks Convinced Discrimination Still Exists in College Admission Process* (Frank Newport, August 24, 2007), *Most Americans Approve of Interracial Marriages* (Joseph Carroll, August 16, 2007), and *Whites, Minorities Differ in Views of Economic Opportunities in U.S.* (Joseph Carroll, July 10, 2006).

INDEX